A
MICHIGAN
READER

A MICHIGAN READER

1865
to
the Present

Edited by

Robert M. Warner
C. Warren Vander Hill

William B. Eerdmans
Publishing Company   Grand Rapids, Michigan

Library of Congress Cataloging in Publication Data

Warner, Robert Mark, 1927-   comp.
  A Michigan reader: 1865 to the present.

  Companion vol. to A Michigan reader: 11,000 B. C.
to A. D. 1865, edited by G. S. May and H. J. Brinks.
    1. Michigan—History—Addresses, essays, lectures.
I. Vander Hill, C. Warren, 1937-   joint comp.
II. Title.
F566.W28   917.74'03'4   73-23054
ISBN 0-8028-7030-9

For the memory of
Willis F. Dunbar, 1902-1970
Teacher, Scholar, and Friend

Contents

Preface

Teachers of United States history have the problem of selecting supplemental readings for their classes from large numbers of monographs and articles of potential usefulness to their students and to the structure of their classes. Teachers of state and local history have a contrary problem. The reading materials useful as supplements to their classes are not nearly so plentiful, so varied, or so skillfully written. What exists is frequently not easily available, and inexpensive paperbacks are virtually nonexistent. This reader has been assembled with no pretenses of solving this problem for students of Michigan history, but it does provide in convenient form a modest selection of articles from a wide variety of sources on the history of Michigan from the Civil War to the present. A companion volume, edited by Herbert J. Brinks and George S. May, provides readings in the state's history from prehistory to the Civil War.

The reader does not present material on all major themes or events in the history of the state during the period covered. The selection of articles was frankly subjective, reflecting as much the interests and approaches to history of its individual compilers as it does the importance of the events and periods covered. The editors of both volumes agreed that each would have a large amount of freedom in the selection process. This wise decision saved much time and probably disputes among the writers. We all reviewed each contributor's selection, however. As a result, all of us made modifications of our original choices.

The general editor and prime mover of the reader is C. Warren Vander Hill, professor of history at Ball State University, who has published substantially in the field of Michigan history. Vander Hill also compiled the section of the reader on Michigan from 1920 to the present. His selections reflect a growing awareness of the importance of black history as well as significant facets of labor and industrial history of a society undergoing rapid change.

My section covers the transformation years in Michigan when the state changed from rural to urban. It was a period that saw the rapid rise and decline of the lumbering and mining frontiers, the coming of the automobile, and the appearance of reform and reformers attempting to meet the challenge of change in Michigan and the nation.

In sum, we have given you a potpourri of writings that will, we hope, add a useful, interesting, and stimulating dimension to classes in Michigan history.

Robert M. Warner
Director, Michigan Historical Collections
Professor of History, University of Michigan

Part I

THE REAL
MICHIGAN

Introduction

The state of Michigan has meant many things to many people during the past four centuries. Indeed, a fair number of people, particularly native sons, travelers, immigrants, and foreign observers, have written accounts of how they viewed the state and what it meant to them. Among the most noteworthy of these reflections is that of Bruce Catton, the noted historian of the Civil War, and a native of Benzonia. In the following article Catton, while not pretending to be an authority on the history of Michigan, captures the unique flavor of life in the state as only a native son with his extraordinary literary skills could do. It is also a view of the Wolverine State that is "pre-expressway," of a time not so long ago when automobile travel was a journey from town to town at a much more leisurely pace than most of us are accustomed to today. Those interested in learning more about Catton's views of his early years in Michigan should read his autobiographical work, *Waiting for the Morning Train* (Garden City, N.Y., 1972).

The Real Michigan

BRUCE CATTON

Michigan is perhaps the strangest state in the Union, a place where the past, the present and the future are all tied up together in a hard knot. It is the 20th Century incarnate, and if you look closely you can also see the twenty-first coming in; but it is also the 19th Century, the backward glance and the authentic feel and taste of a day that is gone forever. It killed the past and it is the past; it is the skyscraper, the mass-production line and the frantic rush into what the machine will some day make of all of us, and at the same time it is golden sand, blue water, green pine trees on empty hills, and a wind that comes down from the cold spaces, scented with the forests that were butchered by hard-handed men in checked flannel shirts and floppy pants. It is the North Country wedded to the force that destroyed it.

You enter Michigan, mostly, by way of Detroit, which is something special. It is a profound weight on the land; an enormous city, with great skyscrapers taking the light from Canada, automobile factories and used-car lots scattered across the flat prairies, enough business strewn along the Detroit River to make a Russian's eyes pop; and in the old days, which lasted until World War II, you came into Detroit, usually, by steamboat, which was an experience in itself.

The boats came up from the Lake Erie ports, Cleveland and Buffalo and Sandusky, and they gave a theatrical touch to the whole business. Lake Erie is beautiful and shallow and treacherous, with a capacity for whipping up unexpected storms that would bother any mariner who ever lived, although mostly it is pleasant enough; and the old side-wheelers came paddling down its length, usually in the middle of the night—it was nice sleeping, in a snug stateroom on one of those boats, with an air-conditioned wind coming in at the open porthole, and the wash of the paddle wheels

Reprinted from *Holiday* (August, 1957), pp. 26-39, by permission of the author.

beating a quiet rhythm in the darkness—and in the morning the boat came up the Detroit River, and the factories and pumping stations on the bank suddenly made you realize that man had taken over Nature and was trying to make something out of it. Then, a little after breakfast time, the boat docked along the Detroit water front, and no city in America offered a more thrilling or exciting entrance.

The boats are mostly gone, and this is really Detroit's fault. Detroit did not exactly invent the automobile, but it picked the thing up when it was nothing better than a costly and unreliable toy for the rich and made it a necessity for everybody in America, and the automobile—getting slightly out of hand—killed the Great Lakes passenger boats, except for a few cruise ships. You come into Detroit nowadays in your own car, or perhaps by train, and the old impact is gone. The place dawns on you gradually now; it used to hit you between the eyes, with the early light slanting in from beyond Ontario. But even now Detroit clamors at you, arrogantly, with all the confidence that comes to men who know they are really in charge of things and who don't mind enjoying the feeling, and there is something overwhelming about it all.

For here is a foretaste of what the machine is doing to us. Here men picked up the Industrial Revolution and swung it; this place, with its infinite genius for making any sort of contrivance men have ever dreamed of, and making it more cheaply and better than anyone else, is the doorway to the future. Everything goes in a rush, everybody is busy—and the place is big and sprawling and grimy and pulsing with life. Here is where we are going, make no mistake about it, and the big financial centers down East can say what they like and be hanged. Detroit sets the pace because this is where the muscle and the knowledge are; and if you don't think the future belongs to America, you should come here and breathe the air for a while.

Detroit makes its bow to the past, of course. It has such a place as Greenfield Village, in Dearborn, and here the past that Detroit killed forever—the past of wayside inns, one-man machine shops, quiet country villages snuggling by the route of stagecoaches, and rural dancers moving to the wheezy tunes scraped out by self-taught fiddlers—is preserved like a fly in amber, and it is very much worth visiting. But this, after all, is only a gesture. Detroit has been taking us away from that for half a century, and if it shows you Greenfield Village it also shows you the machine-age pace which turned everything Dearborn has on exhibit into museum pieces. Dearborn houses both this fragment of the past and also the Ford Motor

Company, which did as much as any one organism could do to put the past in its place.

Detroit's streets come in like the spokes of a wheel, the other half of the wheel having been cut off by the Detroit River. Because the pace has been uneven there are vast skyscrapers standing beside parking lots, with rummy old brick buildings from the Civil War era snuggling up against twenty-story hotels and elongated office buildings; burlesque theaters and sleazy secondhand-book stores rub elbows with the most up-to-date, chromium-and-cutstone buildings that America can build, and the river drifts by, down in front, bearing the iron ore and coal and petroleum on which modern America is built; and whether you like it or not you can feel the hard pulse of America beating up and down these automobile-clogged streets.

Some years ago a civic-minded booster dreamed up the phrase, "dynamic Detroit," to express the essence of this city. He hit it off perfectly. Detroit *is* dynamic. Here is where they call the tune, and it is not a tune the Greenfield Village fiddlers ever quite managed to express.

But Detroit, after all, is not really Michigan. Its industrial empire spraddles over a good part of the state, to be sure—with Flint, and Pontiac, and Jackson and Lansing and Grand Rapids and all the rest—but the tremendous industrial nexus centered here is only half of the story. The other half is something very different—old times, the breath of bygone days and memories that went out of date before the men who remembered them were old—and as a man born out of his proper time I love this other Michigan a good deal more than I love Detroit.

The map of the Lower Peninsula is shaped like a fat old-fashioned mitten—a left-hand mitten, placed palm down, with a bulky thumb sticking out into the cold blue of Lake Huron. Detroit is down in the lower right-hand margin, below where the thumb begins, and the great industrial network lies across the lower part of the state: across the upper part of the wrist. But if you will take the map, and draw a line from Bay City—at the bottom of the gap between the bulbous thumb and the rest of the hand—straight west across the state, you will have cut Michigan into its two distinctive parts. Everything below the line is 20th Century; everything above it is North Country—old, half empty, touched by the cold winds that drift down from the Arctic, with trees and sand and crystal-clear water and drowsy small towns as its distinguishing marks. It is a country that will put its seal on you if you are not careful, because it offers a lonely beauty and an escape from almost everything Detroit stands for.

The present falls away, when you go up into this part of the state. Suppose you drive up from Detroit, along U. S. Route 10; it goes through places like Flint and Saginaw and Midland, any one of which would be world-famous if it were in some other country—and then, suddenly, it takes you into the empty cut-over land, where ghost towns cluster by the road, where the rivers flow cold and clear past hills that furnished lumber for half the world a generation or two ago, where cabins nestle down by quiet lakes and where the air drifts straight through you as if nobody had ever soiled it with smoke or grime or gas fumes. From here on north there are not so many farms, the soil is very sandy, excellent for growing pine trees, not often so good for growing anything else, and if it amuses you to count abandoned farms (unpainted shacks going peacefully to ruin amid fields nobody has tilled for a quarter century or more) you can make quite a list in an afternoon's drive. The road leads you out of ambition into peace and contentment; the deceptive light of an eternal summer afternoon lies on the rolling country; the innumerable lakes glitter brightly blue in the fading light, and when you stop your car and listen you hear a blessed quiet.

This part of the state must have been quite a sight, a hundred years ago. Over an area of better than 25,000 square miles there was a magnificent forest—great pines, mostly, with a healthy sprinkling of hardwoods like maples and beeches—like nothing you can find in America today. From lake to lake and for 250 miles from north to south there was an eternal green twilight, with open spaces where the lakes and rivers were; twilight, with the wind forever making an unobtrusive noise in the branches overhead, brown matted needles and leaves underfoot—everything just about as it was shortly after the last ice age.

There is one tiny fragment of it left. If you will go to the little town of Kalkaska, in the northwest part of the state's Lower Peninsula, and drive thirty miles or so to the east, you will reach Hartwick Pines State Park; and here, running down to the bank of the Au Sable River, is an eighty-five-acre tract of virgin timber, the last that remains, preserved for tourists. You leave your car by the park-administration building and suddenly you are in the middle of it, with trees rising 150 feet overhead, and a shaded coolness all about that is proof against the summer's worst heat wave. Walking through it is not unlike walking through a cathedral. It has that effect on people. It is even more moving in the dead of winter, with the big trees coming up out of a white silence that is all but absolute; the trouble is that then you have to use skis or snowshoes to get there.

Anyway, Michigan a century ago was one magnificent forest, and even as recently as the Civil War it had hardly been touched. But then the lumberjacks went to work, and they shaved the country-side the way a razor shaves a man's chin. Where there had been wilderness, boom lumber towns sprang up, with rickety railroad lines threading their way back into the hills. In the springtime, every stream was clogged with logs, with lumberjacks scampering across the treacherous shifting carpet with peavy and cant hook, mounds of sawdust rising beside the busy mills, and a mill town with 1200 inhabitants normally supported from twelve to twenty saloons. Michigan voted for prohibition before the Federal prohibition amendment went into effect in 1920, and anyone who remembers what those saloons did to small-town life can easily understand why. For a time Saginaw was the greatest lumber city in the world, then Muskegon had the title, and then some other place; fresh-cut boards were stacked in endless piles by the railroad sidings or the lakeside wharves . . . and then, all of a sudden, it was all over. The lumber was gone, the mills were dismantled, the booming cities and towns lapsed into drowsiness, store-fronts were boarded up—and the razor which had done all of this shaving had left a stubble of stumps like a frowsy three-day beard across thousands of square miles. Some towns died entirely, some almost died, and the endless whine of the gang saws became quiet forever.

All of which put its mark on a whole generation of people. Here was a region half the size of Ireland which, after only fifty years of history, suddenly found itself at a dead end. A society began to decay before it had matured. Towns dwindled and died before the eyes of the very men who had founded them. Boys who grew to manhood in these dying towns moved off to the city, leaving behind the old folks and the girls—half a century ago it was not so simple for an untrained girl to make a place for herself in a far-off city, and thousands upon thousands of these girls were condemned to lives of unwanted loneliness. They were strong and healthy and they had dreams and high hopes, and these came to very little because life had shoved them off into a side alley, since marriage was just about the only career a girl could hope for in those days. The human cost of a dying boom can be pretty high.

So they killed the infinite forest, once and for all. But there was still the land itself, rolling in vast gentle waves under a clear blue sky; there were the hundreds and hundreds of lakes, blue and cold and sparkling with imitation whitecaps; there was the great stretch of sand, putting a golden border on the water; there were the rivers, so clear you could count bits of gravel ten feet deep, so cold they turned your feet numb if you tried to wade; and there was the air, filtered by its eternal drift down from the ultimate edge of icy nowhere, fresh enough to revive a Peruvian mummy, odorous with the scent of jack pines.

All of this adds up to an earthly paradise for people from the hot cities who want to get away from asphalt and noise and muggy heat when they have a chance and touch base with Mother Nature; and today the tourist trade is the second industry in the entire state, topped only by the exalted automobile industry itself. This place where the wilderness used to be may indeed be the North Country, but it is only a hop-skip-and-jump from enormous centers of population. From Detroit or Chicago, it is a handy one-day drive to any spot in the Lower Peninsula, but at the end of the drive you feel that you have left the city and all of its works in another world.

So the old lumber area has had a rebirth, and the air of defeat and decline has vanished. This change has gone hand in hand with others. For one thing, the trees are coming back; huge state and national forests lie across vast stretches of empty land. In addition, there is a belt of cherry and peach orchards twenty miles wide and 200 miles long down the western side of the state. In spring, when the blossoms are out, the rolling hillsides near Lake Michigan offer a spectacle of breath-taking beauty, and many a town that used to live on its sawmills now lives on its cannery-and-packing plant. Every July they have a big "cherry festival" at Traverse City—a bright, bustling little city which has made full recovery from the death of the lumber boom—and a pretty girl is named Cherry Queen; her function, usually in addition to posing for photographs, is to take a cherry pie to Washington and present it to the President. This makes a nice trip for the girl, nets the President a first-rate pie, and presumably makes everybody happy.

But under everything there is this strange, beautiful, lonely land itself, this land of blue sky and clear water, where puff-ball clouds drift lazily overhead, trailing pleasant shadows over water and forest and bright little towns as if nobody ever had to be in a hurry about anything and time had come to a standstill just because what is here and now is too pleasant to leave. This is good country to come from and it is even better to go back to. It is a land of memories and also a land of escape: a place where you can be utterly idle in more pleasant ways than any other place I know.

I was born in Michigan and I grew up there, and not long ago I went back to see what it is like today. I came in through the industrial network in the lower right-hand corner of the state, and after a while I was driving northwest on U.S. Route 10—a fine road which goes for many miles at a stretch without touching a town, and which cannot in any case touch a real, full-dress city because in all of Michigan, north of that east-west line from Bay City, there is not a single place with as many as 20,000 permanent residents.

Beyond Clare, which calls itself the gateway to the northland, I turned right on M 115, which goes on past pleasant little lakes dotted with summer cottages, past a sprinkling of drowsy farms, and past uncounted miles of unused land. Yet a road, after all, takes you where you yourself are going, and not where the road goes, and what you see depends mostly on what's inside of you; and when you go back to re-explore your own country you are likely to find memories and dreams all mixed up with solid reality. I was heading for my own particular corner of the state, where I spent my boyhood, because I wanted to see what the years had done to it; and if in the end I learned more about what the years had done to me—well, that is what usually happens when you go on a pilgrimage.

My own land is mostly Benzie County, which has fewer inhabitants now than it had half a century ago but which has lost its old backwoods isolation and is a homey, friendly sort of country. There is a tiny town with the improbable name of Benzonia, which was founded by some eager folk from Oberlin College just before the Civil War when all of this land was new. The air was so clear and good that they wanted a name that would tell about it, so they dipped into their erudition and came up with a Latin-Greek hybrid which means, roughly, fragrant air. They built a little college, and for fifty years it struggled along, graduating eight or ten people a year; then it was turned into a preparatory school, and my father was principal of it when I was a boy, and just after World War I there was no longer any need for this school because the state's high schools had improved, and it quietly died. Nothing is left of it now except a brick building which has been turned into a village community house, but the little town drowses under the long sunlight, with a special flavor that other little towns don't have, touched by the memory of the old-timers who wanted to bring education to the lumber country.

Every man makes his own state—or maybe his state makes him; it is hard to be certain about such things. But you grow up with something on your mind, and it comes out of the place where you were born and reared, and you never can get away from it no matter where you go. And if you go back, long afterward, to the place you knew when you were young, you see it through eyes that were specially conditioned; you cannot be objective about it; you try to write about your background and find that you are really writing about yourself.

I remember, forty years ago, a January night when the thermometer registered five below and there was a brilliant full moon, and I went to the front door, late at night, to lock up. I stood in the doorway for a moment, looking out at the moonlit landscape, the little grove of trees across the street and the three feet of snow that covered everything. There is not in all America today anything quite as still and quiet as a Michigan small town could be, late on a moon-swept night, in January, in the days before World War I. Nobody in all the earth was making a sound, nothing was moving, there was only the white snow, the black trees, the blue shadows lying on the whiteness, and the big moon in a cloudless sky; and to stand there and look out at it was, inexplicably, to be in touch with the Infinite—and, somehow, the Infinite was good, it was lonely but friendly, it meant something you did not have to be afraid of if you understood it. So Michigan means that to me—along with much else—and coldness and loneliness and shattering loveliness go hand in hand, so that while you will always be awed and abashed when you come up against the Infinite you do not really need to be afraid. And maybe that is a fairly good idea to get and take with you.

I can remember another night, in summer time, much earlier, when as a rather small boy my family took me across Lake Michigan on a steamboat from Milwaukee. It was dark and cool and windy, and we came out of the river and out past the breakwater, and the steamer began to rise and fall on the waves of the big lake. For a small child it was quite scary—nothing but water and the dark, with big waves coming in from nowhere and making foaming noises under the bow, and the Michigan shore seemed an unimaginable distance away and the dark sea ahead was what all adventurers have always seen when they pitted themselves against the great emptiness and its wonder and peril, and life itself is an enormous gamble played by people who are eager and frightened at the same time, with nothingness before and above and the chance of a dawn-swept landfall in the morning lying there, insubstantial and improbable beyond the night, as the possible reward. That is really the truth of it, and that too is good to know.

I am well aware, of course, that, as the world's seas go, Lake Michigan is not really a very large body of water. To cross it by steamer is to spend no more than half a dozen hours afloat, and when the trip is over you have reached only the state of Michigan, which actually is as prosaic a bit of land as you can find. Yet the thoughts of a small boy can be lonely, frightening and touched with unfathomable wonder, and the borders of an unattainable land can glimmer, insubstantial but genuine, over the most matter-of-fact horizon. What you owe the land where you were born and reared is something you can never quite pin down; but if that land can stir dreams and fears and the hints of a completely illogical but convincing promise, you are that much ahead of the game. For what you think and feel when you are very small never quite leaves you, and if it always lures you on to something that the visible landscape does not quite make explicit you are immeasurably the gainer.

All of this means very little, probably, by any rational scheme of things. Yet somehow it is part of the color and the flavor which this strange, light-struck, improbable country gave to me when I was too young to know any better, and it has had its own queer effect on everything I have thought or done ever since. So I bring it in here, along with the pine trees and the cold winds and the everlasting golden sands, to try to explain why I like to go back to Michigan. I am probably trying to recapture something unattainable, but that does not matter; so long as the feel and the gleam of it still lie on the edge of my subconscious it is real, for me, and the only value in any dream consists in the fact that you have to keep pursuing it even though you know that you can never quite reach it. If the real Michigan keeps getting overlaid with the Michigan I thought I saw in the old days, I can only say that I am that much better off—for what I thought I saw then was worth a lifetime's quest.

There is plenty to see up here. Half a mile from this hilltop village is one of America's loveliest lakes—Crystal Lake, named with an utter literalness; it is so clear you can see the bottom where it is twenty feet deep—nine miles long by three miles wide, with wooded hills all around and a fringe of pleasant summer cottages along its sandy shores.

Crystal Lake itself will always be something special for me, because it symbolizes an emotion that goes beyond time and space. When I was very small the minister of the one church in my town of Benzonia took some months off, and—by dint of what patient frugality I do not know: the pastor of a country church at that time earned precious little money—made a trip to the Holy Land. When he returned he made his report, and of it I remember just one thing. The magical Sea of Galilee, he said, the sea where our Lord walked and taught and performed miracles, was just about the size and shape of our Crystal Lake. To be sure, the hills which bordered Galilee were dun-colored, barren of trees, a bleak and impoverished landscape; while our hills, green as the heart of a maple leaf, were ringed with clear water, set about with pleasant little towns, cool and pleasant, inviting people to linger on their long journey from one mystery to another. But the resemblance was there, and the lake in which I caught diminutive perch was very like the lake on which Peter tried to walk dry-shod; and for some reason my life is richer because a saintlike little pastor, half a century ago, saw Galilee through innocent eyes which could interpret any lake in terms of Michigan's pine trees and green open valleys. I have never been to Palestine, but somehow I have seen the Sea of Galilee and the Word that was preached by that Near-Eastern sea has a special sound for me.

. . . .

From Frankfort you swing up toward Traverse City on route M 22, which cuts up across what is known as the Leelenau Peninsula. Once this was lumber country and now it is cherry country, but mostly it is a region for summer vacationers. Every little town has its lake (Glen Lake, which lies back of Sleeping Bear Point, is a show place) and there are other lakes with no towns at all, locked in by ice and snow for four or five months of the year.

Sleeping Bear Point is an enormous sand dune, five miles long by 500 feet high, jutting out into Lake Michigan. A road of sorts leads to the top, but your car would stall in the deep, fine sand, so you go to the town of Glen Haven and take passage in one of the special low-gear cars with oversized, half-inflated tires, which waddle through the sand as if they were made for it. On the crest there is nothing at all to see but this golden empty ridge and the great blue plain of Lake Michigan far below, with white surf curling on the beach at the foot of the bluff, yet it is one of the finest sights in the Middle West. There is no noise except the lake wind ruffling the spare trees: there is just nothing except a feeling of infinite space and brightness, and utter freedom from the smoke and the rush and the racket of ordinary 20th Century life.

The country north of Traverse City is high and open, with Lake Michigan nearly always in view off to the left, and the little towns and villages along the way reflect the past in a curious manner. First there was the lumber era, in which today's sleepy hamlet was a rip-roaring little city with a solid mile of sawmills along the water front. Then, when the lumber was gone, there was the early summer-resort trade: passenger boats coming up from Chicago or around from Detroit; imposing but flimsy frame hotels, all veranda and white pillars, overlooking every beach; Pullman cars unloading a new consignment of vacationers at the railroad depot every morning . . . and after a while the automobiles came and killed boat lines, passenger trains and most of the hotels, so that these towns which had made one readjustment had to make another. The result is odd.

Every town contains echoes of those two vanished eras, and seems to be looking back regretfully to the past; and yet most of them are brighter and more hopeful than they ever were before, the old feeling of backwoods isolation is gone, the people who live here are having a better time of it than ever before and the general level of prosperity is higher and more stable. Yet the feeling of the past does linger, so that in this area which has hardly been settled more than a century there are haunting echoes of antiquity.

Your memory can play queer tricks on you. At Charlevoix I drove east, skirting the south shore of beautiful Lake Charlevoix to reach Boyne City. Boyne City was perhaps the last lumber boom town in the Lower Peninsula. We lived there, for a year or so, when I was about six years old, and it was a lively place then. There were four immense sawmills along the lake front, and a big "chemical plant"—I suppose it was a place where they extracted turpentine and other by-products from the pines—and there was even a blast furnace, although what it may have been doing there I have never been able to understand. Anyway, Boyne City was bustling and exciting, and our back yard ran down to the Boyne River, where the log drives came down in the spring. To my six-year-old eyes that river was immense; it was, I realized, probably smaller than the Mississippi, but it was fascinating, wide, turbulent, somehow menacing—a dangerous river which easily could (and, two or three times, very nearly did) drown a small boy who incautiously tried to play on its treacherous carpet of moving logs. So I returned to the old back yard and took another look at the river—and realized that either the river had shrunk or I had stretched considerably. The river is charming—gentle, crystal-clear, friendly, no more hostile than a brook. Along the lake front there is an uncommonly pleasant park, where the sawmills used to be. A rusted remnant of the old blast furnace still survives, but everything else seems to be gone; and this is not the exciting town where I used to live, it is just a bright, friendly little community where old memories are held in suspension in the sunlight.

Another of my favorite towns in this part of the state is Petoskey, where I was born. No man ever breaks completely away from his birthplace; you carry the mark of your home town with you. I remember it as a sleepy sort of place, built on a spectacular side hill that slants up steeply from the cold blue of Little Traverse Bay, with funny little tourist-bait shops at the bottom where Indian wares and other trinkets were offered for sale to the "summer people." These shops always smelled pleasantly of birch bark—there were baskets, and toy canoes, and other contrivances—and to this day the odor of birch bark takes me back to tiny stores which must have gone out of existence a whole generation ago.

Petoskey has grown up to date and prosperous. It is no longer a lumber center, and the great trains of flatcars piled high with pine logs no longer go rumbling past what used to be the Grand Rapids & Indiana depot, and the sprawling summer hotels I remember so well are not there any more; but because the hill is so high and because so much of the big lake lies open at the foot of the hill Petoskey gives you what so much of this part of Michigan always gives—the strange feeling that you are at an immense altitude, on some sort of ridge where you can look down on half of the Middle West and where the wind that never quite dies down has come to you without touching anything at all along the way from wherever it is that winds are born.

Even though it always speaks of the past, and seems to look back toward it in a dreamy sort of way, most of this part of Michigan has no particular history. But when you go north from Petoskey you step far back into legend and the distant past. Things were going on here when the eastern seaboard colonies were still young. La Salle, Jolliet and Marquette were here nearly three centuries ago. At Mackinaw City, at the very tip of Michigan's Lower Peninsula, and an hour's easy drive from Petoskey, there is a lake-front park with a rebuilt stockade which marks the site of one of early America's most significant strong points—Fort Michilimackinac. Here, around 1681, missionaries and fur traders and French soldiers and a scattering of just plain adventurers built an outpost of French civilization in a spot which was more remote and isolated than any spot on earth can be today.

After the French left Canada the British took over, and in 1763 Pontiac's painted warriors broke in, seized stockade and fort, and massacred the British garrison. Then the fort was abandoned, to be rebuilt on Mackinac Island, which lies in the center of the straits. The Americans took it over after the Revolution, and the British recaptured it in the War of 1812, and then it was returned to American possession again. Now it stands empty, a tourists' show place, looking out at the unending procession of freighters that cruise slowly past on their way to and from the lower lakes.

Mackinac Island is a delightful spot, and it is unusual in two ways. In the first place, although it is spelled Mackinac it is, for some incomprehensible reason, pronounced Mackinaw; and in the second place it is the one spot in the whole state of Michigan—one of the very few spots in all the United States—where you never see an automobile. Automobiles are not allowed on the island, and to come to this place, with its hotels and boardinghouses and curio shops lining the quiet streets, and the old-fashioned horse-drawn surreys leisurely wheeling their way in and out, is to step straight back into the Victorian era. To get about the island you walk, or ride behind a horse, or get on a bicycle. More so than any other place in the state, this is a refuge from the present.

Big changes are coming to Upper Michigan and the symbol of their approach is the stupendous five-mile-long bridge being built across the straits to connect the Lower and Upper Peninsula. The bridge will cost around $100,000,000; it is expected to be completed this fall, and it will at last tie the two halves of the state firmly together. At present, you cross the straits by one of a fleet of state-owned ferry boats.

Michigan's Upper Peninsula is an immense finger of land running 300 miles from west to east, with cold, steely-blue Lake Superior, the largest lake in the world, lying all along its northern flank. Eighty-five per cent of this area is forested and lumbering is still going on, the Marquette iron range still turns out iron ore, and some copper is still being mined; but comparatively speaking the Upper Peninsula is almost empty, with fewer than 300,000 inhabitants. If the northern half of the Lower Peninsula is North Country the Upper Peninsula is the same thing at treble strength. It is traversed by excellent concrete roads, and you can drive for two hours without seeing a town, or anything that looks like permanent human habitation. For mile after mile there is nothing except clear blue lakes, vast areas of cut-over timber, forests which look as if nobody had ever taken an ax into them, and outcroppings of bleak rock. With Lake Superior so close this country has its own built-in air-conditioning; there is a sharp edge to the air, a feeling of unlimited space and quiet and peace, and that strange quality of half-ominous, half-friendly loneliness is with you all of the time. Once the bridge is finished, all of this will probably be watered down, but it can never be wholly destroyed. After all, up in this country there is nothing between you and the North Pole except a few thousand miles of totally empty land and water.

One of the interesting things to see up here is the canal at Sault Ste. Marie, whose big locks connect Lake Superior with the lower lakes. The Soo, as everybody calls it, is a lively little city during the eight months of the navigation season; it boasts that its canal handles more traffic than Panama and Suez combined. All day and all night the ships—enormous things, 500 and 600 feet in length—come majestically in from the upper lake, floating high above your head, sinking slowly as the water burbles out of the locks, and then gliding off for the great industrial region hundreds of miles to the south. In an average day, eighty or ninety of them will go through. Day and night, you are forever hearing the deep, haunting bass of their whistles—the inescapable, wholly characteristic and somehow deeply romantic noise of the Soo region. (Progress is taking a hand here, these immense boats are being equipped with air horns, which emit a blatting which carries a great deal farther than the traditional steam whistle but which is pure discord and nothing more.)

Driving west from the Soo, on the broad highway that leads to Marquette and the iron-range country, you pass Seney, a drowsy little country town so unobtrusive that you can go all the way through it before you realize you have reached it. It's quiet and orderly today, but half a century ago Seney was a hell-roaring lumber town, with a reputation for unrestrained misconduct that did not need to take second place to any Western cattle town or mining camp. There is a myth, formerly given wide circulation in the Sunday supplements, about a log stockade that once adorned the town. In it, according to one version, dance-hall girls were kept when not dancing; according to another, captive lumberjacks were immured here between spells in the backwoods. There is one odd thing about these fancy yarns of the high-wide-and-handsome days of the lumber towns; the sins which were committed in these places were never really attractive. It is very hard to glamorize a village rowdy, and the lumberjack tough mugs were at bottom village rowdies and nothing better. Seney's most notorious character, for instance, was a loafer who used to win free drinks in bars by biting the heads off frogs, mice and other vermin. He finally came to a well-merited end, according to the story, when he bit the head off a small owl which was the particular pet of a burly lumberjack, who promptly brought this unattractive character's career to a close by smiting him vigorously over the head with the handle of a peavy.

Marquette is the metropolis of the Upper Peninsula. It is a solid industrial town, with red ore from the great ridges behind it coming down to the docks in red hopper cars, and if it is not the most lovely city in the United States it occupies one of the nation's most beautiful sites. The south shore of Lake Superior curves in and out, along here, with deep bays and jutting, pine-crowned headlands; the old primeval rock breaks through the crust of the land to remind you that this is the backbone of the continent, where rocks so ancient they even lack fossils lie bare under the long summer sunlight, grim and lonely and desolate. Just at sunset, from east of Marquette, you can see the city with the opaque blue panel of Lake Superior silent in front of it and a flaming red sky behind it, lying in the evening stillness like a dream of the city that never was; it is transfigured, a strange light lies on its towers and parapets, and this place that for so long was a Mecca for Cornish miners (the roadside stands still peddle Cornish pasties instead of hot dogs, and very good they are too) becomes an unattainable no-place out of fable, dropping long dark shadows on a silent cold sea.

If you are well advised, you will head west from Marquette for the copper country. Do it, if possible, early in October when the lonely road will take you through forests aflame with scarlet and gold and bronze, and a wild, doomed beauty that belongs beyond the farthest edge of the world lies on all the landscape; the touch of everlasting winter is in the air and yet for an hour or so the sunlight is still warm, and nothing you will ever see will move you more or linger with you longer. You come out, at last, onto the long spine of the Keweenaw Peninsula—an outcrop of rock and wild trees, reaching far up into Lake Superior, perhaps the oldest land in the new world. The copper mines which caused men to come here in the first place go deep under the lake—some of the shafts go down for more than a mile. You get the feeling of a land that has been passed by, a hard, forbidding and strangely charming bit of country that had a short hectic history and does not especially want any more; and all about is the cold steely blue of the greatest of lakes, and the picturesque little settlements that manage to be both friendly and forsaken at the same moment.

It would be possible, of course, to drive on, noting the points of interest in the Upper Peninsula, mentioning the more unusual towns—like Eagle Harbor, one of the most completely beautiful villages I ever expect to see, with two long headlands enclosing a quiet strip of water and the great angry lake piling destructive surging waves against the rocks outside—but my state is half reality and half the dim, enchanted memories of a long-lost boyhood, and anyway I did not live in the entire state of Michigan. I knew only selected parts of it, and these parts stay in my memory and call back unforgettable things which were born of the cold emptiness and the inviting, menacing beauty of this North Country.

They are Upper Michigan, the part that lies north of the automobile belt, the doomed, bewitched country which presently will surrender to the Mackinac bridge and to the superhighway and which, ultimately, will undoubtedly become just another part of the sprawling, industrialized Middle West. But while today's light lasts it is still a land apart, there is a pleasantly melancholy flavor of a lost past to it, and although men murdered the forests with a passionate ferocity the forests somehow still live and put their strange touch on the countryside. There are cool shadows under the trees and a timeless peace lies on the cutover tracts and the fields where the young second growth is hiding the stumps.

It is a strange country: lonely enough, even in summer, and cold as the far side of the moon when winter comes, with the far-off hills rising pale blue from the frozen white landscape. It offers a chance to draw a deep breath, to turn around and look back at the traveled path, to stand on a high hill and be alone with the fresh air and the sunlight. It is wood and water, golden sand and blue lakes, emptiness and memories and the sort of isolation which it is hard for a city man to come by, these days. All in all, it is quite a state.

Part II

1865-1920

Introduction

Michigan emerged from the Civil War still an underdeveloped state, primarily agricultural, but with the foundation of a well-developed copper and iron mining industry. The last three decades of the nineteenth century and the first two of the twentieth century were a period of accelerated industrialization, rising population, and growing cities, coupled with the beginning of agricultural decline.

Early in the post-Civil War years came the full development of the lumbering industry, which made Michigan the richest lumber state in the United States by the 1880s. Based on giant stands of white pine and facilitated by an unusually favorable geography, the industry flourished, bringing population growth, expansion of railroads, and the founding of towns and cities on the Lake Huron and Lake Michigan shores. The entrepreneurs who developed lumbering in Michigan exemplified nineteenth-century American laissez-faire business practices—bringing capital but ignoring the future, providing jobs but fighting unionization. Some became rich and built great Victorian mansions. Many more managed only marginal enterprises or failed completely.

Fostered by numerous grievances, the first major labor disputes in Michigan occurred in these nineteenth-century years. Labor met with little success, however, as popular views of these disputes generally supported the alliance of leaders of management and government.

These years saw the population increase steadily despite minor setbacks occasioned by "panics" in 1885 and particularly 1893. The people came to Michigan from other states and countries. During prosperous times, state government encouraged new settlers. But when hard times hit, anti-immigration sentiments appeared, often tinged with nativism and occasionally outright hostility.

As the nineteenth century closed, Michigan was no longer a frontier state. Lumbering, mining, agriculture and manufacturing were all well developed. Especially important in the maturing of the state was the expansion of the railroad. Though the first railroad in Michigan preceded statehood, it was not until the post-Civil War years that the railroad expanded into almost every community of any size in the upper and lower peninsulas, expanding transportation and bringing the outside world much closer to the small towns and villages scattered throughout the two peninsulas. Still, however, rural isolation was never eliminated. The nineteenth-century farmer's life, though perhaps better than that of his equivalent on the prairies to the west, was still a hard one.

The farmer in Michigan sought to do something about his lot in life through such organizations as the Grange. Through the Grange he hoped to find a social outlet for himself and his wife and also to solve some of the economic problems that beset him. Most basic in his eyes was the fact that he was not getting what he regarded to be his fair share of the economy. He tried other organizations too, like the People's Party, although this group, which was strong in other parts of the nation, never really manifested significant strength in Michigan.

The 1880s and 1890s also saw the growth of professional groups that sought both to serve the public more effectively by weeding out charlatans and quacks and to benefit themselves both economically and socially by forming organizations and holding meetings. Educators, medical doctors, and dentists all joined in this march to professionalism, which was also not without its social side, often taking most elaborate form as basically middle-class doctors and dentists sought to emulate the manners and life styles of the well-to-do when they held their annual conventions.

These were the years of Michigan's maturing. The cities expanded, lines of communication vastly improved; society in all of its aspects became much more conventionalized and institutionalized.

During the last quarter of the nineteenth century in Michigan, varying moods and strains of discontent loosely crystallized into the general reform movement historians for want of a better term have called progressivism. The origin and total impact of progressivism are still a matter of debate; nevertheless, it is clear that the period from the end of the nineteenth century up to World War I was one of considerable ferment in society. How much and how profound the change is still a matter of debate among historians today.

Manifestations of progressivism came in the political area in Michigan. The period had leaders who espoused change. In looking back, the rhetoric sometimes sounds much more imposing than the actual accomplishment. Nevertheless, progressive politicians articulated feelings held by large numbers of citizens who abandoned traditional patterns of politics to elect them to office.

Progressivism achieved reform measures such as direct election of United States senators, direct primaries, regulation of business and workmen's compensation, but from that pinnacle of moderate success, it seemed to lose its energy and become more and more a single issue cause—the movement for total prohibition, which was to triumph at the end of World War I.

Of more lasting and fundamental importance to Michigan than either the political reforms of progressivism or the disruption brought about by World War I was the rapid development in these same years of a vast new industry that was to determine the future of the state. In 1896 Ransom E. Olds founded the state's first automobile company and ran the first car down the streets of Lansing. During the closing years of the nineteenth century and the early years of the twentieth, car manufacturing establishments sprang up throughout the state. Most of them were doomed to failure, but some succeeded beyond the greatest dreams of those who pioneered them and have become the industrial giants of today. Besides drawing new population to the state, a different kind of population that changed the character of Michigan, the automobile industry also brought about an enormously rapid urbanization, particularly of the cities of Detroit, which grew from 285,704 in 1900 to 993,678 in 1920, and Flint, which in the same twenty-year period saw its size increase from 13,103 to 91,599.

The first two decades of the twentieth century thus saw the rapid expansion of the automobile industry, the beginnings of a successful good roads movement, and rapid industrialization and urbanization. As yet, unionization was still a minor factor. By 1920 the nature of the state had basically changed. The 1910 census was the last to show more Michigan people living on the farm than in the city. Henceforth, Michigan would be a highly industrialized, urbanized state much beholden to the automobile.

1: Lumbering, Labor Unions and Strikes

Henry Crapo was the personification of the successful lumber baron who became a major force in the state. But the story, as his biographer Martin D. Lewis points out, was much more complicated than that. Crapo was a marginal entrepreneur rather than an immediate success, but ended as the state's leading citizen, governor for two terms at the end of the Civil War. This selection, which briefly summarizes and evaluates his role, captures his basic optimism and his enthusiasm for his adopted state and demonstrates the role of the entrepreneur in the developing of the state.

Lewis' book was his doctoral dissertation done at the University of Chicago and primarily based on the Henry Howland Crapo manuscripts at the Michigan Historical Collections of the University of Michigan. An overall study of Michigan lumbering is George W. Hotchkis' *History of the Lumber and Forest Industry of the Northwest* (Chicago, 1898); though outdated and not interpretive it is still the best. Rolland H. Maybee's *Michigan's White Pine Era 1840-1900* (Lansing, 1960) gives a brief modern summary.

Lumberman from Flint

MARTIN D. LEWIS

Henry Crapo's fourteen-year career in Michigan was dominated by his struggle to bring a new economic enterprise into life and to make it successful. The demands which this effort made on his time and energy shaped his entire existence, forcing him to subordinate all else to the needs of his business. In a very real sense, the man became the business, the business a reflection of the man. No one can read Crapo's letters in the early years of the enterprise without marveling at how completely he had immersed himself in the task

From *Lumberman from Flint, The Michigan Career of Henry H. Crapo, 1855-1869*, pp. 242-253. Copyright © 1958 by Wayne State University Press. Reprinted by permission. Footnotes in the original have been omitted.

of making his lumber business pay. Later he allowed himself the luxury of broadened interests, but even then his ventures into other fields were colored by the dominating fact of his lumber business.

His ill-fated experiment at boring for salt was an attempt to escape the burdensome realities of lumbering and find an easier way to make money. His successful railroad promotion was conceived as an important aid to the prosecution of the lumber enterprise, and was important as much for this reason as for the fact that it proved a sound and profitable investment. His speculative land interests, which in other circumstances might have received a major share of his attention, were permitted to lie neglected except insofar as holdings could be sold off to provide working capital for lumbering.

At least in the beginning, Crapo even sought to justify his excursions into politics by their potential utility to his lumber concern (if we may take at face value his statements in letters to his son). His sense of civic responsibility came to outweigh personal considerations, but we should not forget that in even his most active years in public office he continued to devote much of his time to his business.

His one hobby, if it may be called that, was agriculture and stockbreeding. From the time he moved permanently to Flint, he had carried on some small-scale farming as a sideline to the lumber business, raising crops which could be used to supply his loggers and sawmill gangs. In the early sixties, he undertook drainage operations on two large farms which had formerly been considered worthless swamp, and was soon raising fine crops on both. In addition to his practical farming, he engaged in much experimentation with both crops and livestock breeding, reflecting his deep interest in scientific agriculture. He served a term as president of the Genesee County Agricultural Society, and when he gave the annual address he wrote that "the farmers were highly delighted with it and say it is by far the best address they have ever had since the formation of the society." As always keeping an eye to the business advantages which might be gained, he noted that "I shall . . . be amply paid for it."

> These farmers are a curious set; they are all for you or all against you; and perhaps it was rather hazardous for me to undertake so important a task as a failure would have been a defeat; but I wanted to give the finishing stroke to McFarlin [his competitor in the Flint retail lumber trade], by getting on the side of the farmers, and I have fully succeeded. They call me a great farmer here now, which answers every purpose of really being such.

Since he took three first prizes and one second prize for his livestock exhibits, his appraisal of his own efforts seems unduly modest.

During his tenure as governor, he gave unstinting support to the struggling Agricultural College (now Michigan State University), which was under attack as a waste of public funds. Suggesting in his inaugural address that it be given time to prove its value, he wrote that

> agriculture is no longer what it was once regarded by the majority of other professions of men, and partially admitted by the farmer himself to be—a low, menial employment, a mere drudgery . . . in which no thought, or mind, or study, was necessary, but is becoming recognized as a noble science.

In 1866 he addressed the Sheep-Shearing Exhibition of the Central Michigan Agricultural Society, praising the work of the agricultural societies and giving a practical discussion of wool growing both in terms of breeds and of commercial practices. Only a few months before his death, he had an article published in *The Cultivator and Country Gentleman* on "Wheat Culture in Michigan," detailing methods by which he was raising from eighteen to twenty-five bushels of wheat per acre while the average crop in the state was rarely more than twelve bushels, and often less.

From the standpoint of business history, the significance of Crapo's business career lies not in any spectacular exploits or unusual achievements. There were many men who amassed greater wealth, who brought into being economic enterprises of vastly wider import. His story is of interest precisely because he was representative of the rising business class of mid-nineteenth century America. To say that he was representative of this new group does not, of course, mean that he was typical. But granting all the unique elements in his experience, the fact remains that the pattern of his life falls within a framework common to hundreds or thousands of other men in every state.

The place of Crapo's enterprise in the overall picture of the lumber industry in Michigan merits some comment. His was one of the largest firms in the field, perhaps the largest under individual ownership, though the great number of small operators meant that his annual output of lumber was somewhat less than 1 per cent of the total sawed in the state. Apart from mere size, his enterprise was noteworthy for the way he combined in one concern all of the steps of the lumbering process, from the purchase of pine lands and the cutting of logs to the wholesale and retail marketing of lumber. Such vertical integration was not unknown in this early period of Michigan lumbering, but the general pattern was for each of the several steps to be in the hands of distinct and separate groups of men. The scope of Crapo's enterprise committed him to expenses and involved him in problems which at times he undoubtedly wished he could avoid, yet the fact remains that it gave him a measure of control over his operations which he would not otherwise have had.

He also pioneered in his approach to marketing, taking pains to provide finished lumber in such forms as would best meet the needs of various classes of customers and making strong efforts to reach directly to the ultimate consumer, or at least to the retail yard dealer, without the intervention of middlemen. By way of contrast, marketing at Saginaw consisted largely of piling up green lumber on the docks where it could be purchased in cargo lots by traveling buyers from such large lumber centers as Chicago and Albany. Many of the mill owners there were dependent for operating funds on advances from such brokers, and both for this reason and because they lacked a home market of any importance, Saginaw lumbermen were generally much more at the mercy of prevailing economic conditions than was Crapo. As late as 1874 it was commented that one of Saginaw's most urgent needs was to pay more attention to the buyer of a few carloads of lumber and to spend more time in preparing their product for the ultimate consumer by seasoning and planing it.

When Crapo came to Michigan, the lumber industry in the state had only recently risen to major commercial significance. It had never undergone any serious setbacks in its growth, and the result was a prevailing air of boundless optimism. On all sides he received assurances that the current prosperity was bound to continue. Considering these circumstances, it is easy to understand his original expectations of a large and rapid profit from the purchase of the Driggs tract, even though in practice these expectations proved to be little short of ridiculous. What led him astray in his calculations were, on the one hand, his illusions as to the speed with which the lands could be exploited, and on the other, the radical change in the economic picture caused by the Panic of 1857, which brought an abrupt fall in prices and a drastic curtailment of the market for lumber just when he was beginning to get his operations fully under way.

Had it not been for this turn of events, his story might well have been just another example of an eastern businessman reaping a quick harvest from the resources of the West. As it was, his struggle for survival in the face of a prolonged period of depression forced him to adopt a long-range perspective, keeping his mills running steadily but holding over his lumber for the day when he could secure better prices. Here again he struck out on his own, pursuing a course directly opposite to that of most lumbermen in the region, who were shutting down their mills and selling lumber at any price they could get.

Among the consequences of this enforced change in the outlook of the concern was Crapo's realization that he would have to move permanently to Flint so that he could devote his entire energies to the management of the concern. Although he came to this conclusion reluctantly, once the decision was made he accepted it wholeheartedly, and his personal identification with his adopted state was so complete that only six years after making Michigan his home he could be elected as its chief executive despite his brief period of residence.

His determination to avoid selling at sacrifice prices made it necessary for him to find other means of financing his continued manufacturing operations. Even in the most difficult times he received some revenue from lumber sales, but it was far from sufficient to enable him to meet his mill payroll and loggers' bills as they came due. "I have got over another Saturday night with my men," he wrote on one occasion in 1858, "but it is an ordeal to pass through." In order to keep going, he could not avoid making further calls on his New Bedford partners, who had already provided almost the entire initial investment for lands, mills, and working capital. In addition, he was forced to sink in the business nearly every cent he himself could raise from sales of his speculative landholdings. Since most of these lands had been bought in company with various eastern investors, only a part of the money he was receiving belonged to him, and by using it in the lumber business he was of course gambling that he would be able to pay it back when the day should come for a settlement with his co-owners. By the time of the 1860 reorganization which took Arnold out of the picture, income from lumber sales was generally sufficient to cover the annual round of operating expenses, but what little was left had to be applied towards meeting payments on the mills. Indeed, it was not until 1863 that Crapo felt safe in making any distribution of profits, and this was after the value of his large and well-seasoned stock of lumber, manufactured at low cost during the depression years, had appreciated sharply with the general rise in lumber prices. Nevertheless, his ability to hold over lumber from season to season during the hard times from 1858 to 1862 testified to the fact that his enterprise was more adequately capitalized than most in the field.

The absence of facilities for short-term credit complicated his financing problems by compelling him to keep sizable amounts of cash on hand. Discounts on commercial paper were available only at ruinous rates of 2 or 3 per cent a month, causing him to adopt a strict rule of holding all notes until maturity. As late as the spring of 1862, he commented to his son that "having no bank accommodations to fall back on, nor any friends of whom to borrow money . . . it sometimes will happen that my cash runs almost out."

In view of these difficulties it is hardly surprising that his initial enthusiasm for the lumber business dimmed rapidly. In the early years it was his running complaint that "prices have continued to keep down to a point that is death to the very hope of a profit. Everything goes for labor, taxes, repairs, etc." Long after lumber prices had improved, however, he continued to feel that the rate of profit was far too low in view of the risks involved and the amount of capital employed.

Somewhat wistfully, he wrote his son in 1865 that "I very often feel that if I had the capital in a bank here which I now have in lumbering it would be the most desirable business that could be pursued, and infinitely more profitable than lumbering." Largely because of state legislation severely restricting the establishment and operation of banks, Flint prior to that time had had only, as Crapo put it, "three Broker's offices . . . that let their money at from 10 to 25%, or who rather *buy* paper to run on very short time at their own figures." A new situation had arisen, however, with the National Banking Act of 1863, and Crapo wrote that "Eastern people" had been taking charters under the Act at many "desirable points" in Michigan. In his letter to William he wondered whether the opening for a bank at Flint might not "be secured to ourselves or some of our friends East."

> The National banks in this state are declaring dividends from 15 to 20%. The stock being in government securities upon which we should receive interest, in addition to interest received on our issues, and for Exchange, etc., a bank would pay in Flint a large dividend. . . . I have not had in my business here on an average for years less than $120,000 including real estate, mills, etc. subject to all the hazards and wear and tear connected with such business. This, under our present National Banking System, would have, at one-tenth the care and labor, afforded abundantly greater profits than I have ever been able to reach; and at infinitely less risk.

Even as he wrote he knew that the idea was wishful thinking. Nevertheless it was with some regret that he announced, a month and a half later, the chartering of a bank with $100,000 capital by a group of Flint businessmen.

Quite apart from his zeal in advancing his own enterprise, he was active both as governor and as a private citizen in promoting the development of his adopted state. The *Detroit Free Press* wrote in its obituary that as chief executive of Michigan, he had

> fostered and encouraged any scheme that seemed likely to prove bene-ficial to the growth and welfare of the commonwealth, or to portions of it, being particularly zealous in the movements for opening up to market the great pine interest of Northern Michigan, the protection of our mining industries, the encouragement of immigration, and such acts as might the better develop and increase the salt wealth of the Great Saginaw Valley.

He had been the means of securing the investment of nearly a million dollars of eastern capital in Michigan railroads, in addition to promoting his own Flint and Holly line. His choice of Flint as the site for his sawmill operations had an important influence on the growth of that city, and shortly before his death one of its citizens, though opposed to him in politics, is said to have remarked that "for three years of life to Governor Crapo, Flint could well afford to burn one-third of the city to ashes."

Despite the incessant labor, the anxiety, the many disappoint-ments that Crapo had had to endure from the very beginning of his lumber venture, he had soon become an enthusiast for the West in general and for Michigan in particular. In the midst of the depres-sion in 1858, he wrote William that

> this country has decided advantages to the real working, business man over New England. . . . Whilst New England, or perhaps I should say some of its older cities—New Bedford for instance—may at the present very justly be likened to an infirm old man, who during a life of toil has enriched himself and is now under the decrepitude of old age, sitting quietly—almost helplessly—down with his pockets and coffers full of gold, Michigan, or "the West," may be as justly compared to a young, robust man, the owner of almost unnumbered acres of the richest and unreclaimed lands, with a physical organization perfectly developed and whose thews and sinews give evidence of almost unlimited powers of endurance, but who for the time being, in consequence of a too rapid growth as well as of a sudden and violent derangement of the physical system, induced by the mere surfeiting of food . . . is equally as helpless as the "old man" with his money bags,.

"When I say 'the west,' " Crapo had written on another occasion, "I do not mean fast men nor railroad speculators in Chicago and other cities of the west, but I mean the farmers who are the muscle—the bone and sinew—'the west' in fact."

> Although a great many of them are in debt to their neighbors, still these debts have been made to enable them to hurry forward the clearing

of their land and they have their farms to show for it; and although the East says a great deal about the debts of the west, yet at the same time there are single firms in the East who perhaps owe enough to pay all the debts of every farmer in Michigan. . . . The difference is here a farmer will not make a new debt to pay an old one for he is independent in one sense, whereas East it is necessary for the debtor to do this to keep his credit good, at any sacrifice of means.

Capitalist though he was himself, he was not overly impressed with the power of money alone. "Thirty years since," he wrote in 1860, Michigan "was a wilderness, and almost exclusively the home of the savage; now she has every improvement of the most flourishing and prosperous state in the union, with as many thriving and populous villages as the same extent of purely agricultural country can exhibit anywhere."

> I may venture the assertion with safety that the monied wealth of all the hardy adventurers and settlers who have made her what she is in that short space, and who have reclaimed and subdued . . . wild and uncultivated lands, would not in the outset average $400 each, and I presume it would almost be safe to say $200. Look at what she has done with her limited means, and what she is even now doing without money or capital of any sort, and I say her business men will compare favorably with even New England. . . .
>
> All that Michigan wants is a little time to pay all her debts, and the use of a little capital, a small amount compared with what Massachusetts requires, to set in motion a thousand branches of industry and enterprise, that would at once not only free her from debt, but make her prosperous and rich.

Crapo spent little time declaiming the virtues of "progress," but he was himself an active agent in bringing it about. As a participant in the building of the great Middle West, he decried the failure of eastern men to appreciate or even see what was going on in the rest of the nation. "How very few men there are East," he protested in 1862, "who do or can understand the gigantic power and strength, the unlimited wealth and resources and the extent of the political power which the 'West' is destined to possess in a very few years."

> If its future history could be now written, it would be regarded as the wildest, the most improbable fiction. Its resources are immense, and although it has already reached a point of no small importance, these resources have hardly yet begun to be developed. . . . The time will very soon come when the whole South, whether with us, or opposed to us, will be a matter of very little consequence; and even New England must soon learn that her glory can only be reflected from the "West."

When Crapo penned these words he had barely reached the midpoint of his Michigan career, but they provide a most fitting conclusion to this story of his life in the West.

Ruth Bordin, formerly Curator of Manuscripts at the Michigan Historical Collections, presents a different type of nineteenth-century entrepreneur when she discusses the role of Gideon O. Whittemore, who also
tried his hand in the lumbering operation in Michigan. He, too, was a
pioneer and town founder, but unlike Crapo, his operation was modest.
In fact, Whittemore had to struggle long and hard barely to exist. In this
respect, he was more typical of the lumbermen of his era. Whittemore
left a town that is still in existence and played his role in the development of mid-nineteenth-century Michigan. Like Crapo, he also had a
public side to his career. Although he was never a governor, he did have a
major political role, particularly in educational affairs, and served a term
as Michigan's Secretary of State. Ms. Bordin's article presents another
dimension to the entrepreneurial history of Michigan and the lumbering
era, an important corrective to those who view the story as one of the
unqualified successes of a few wealthy men.

A Michigan Lumbering Family

RUTH B. BORDIN

This is a study of Michigan lumbering in microcosm. In 1853 a man named Gideon Olin Whittemore, together with two associates, bought a tract of pine lands at what was then known as Ottawas Bay on Lake Huron. In the process of lumbering those lands and milling and marketing the white pine timber they produced, Whitte-more incidentally founded a town now known as Tawas City, Michigan. The whole business was a small operation. Whittemore was no rival of lumbermen Peter White, Isaac Staples, or Henry Howland Crapo. He dealt in small quantities in terms of capital, acreage, thousands of board feet and all the rest. But his problems

From *Business History Review*, XXXIV (Spring, 1960), 64-76, by permission of the
author and the *Review*. Footnotes in the original have been omitted.

were much the same as those of the lumber titans of mid-nineteenth-century America. The immediate purpose of this study is to illustrate the nature of those problems as they manifested themselves in a particular situation. But the Whittemore case study can have broader implications in that it probably points to behavior patterns typical of small business generally at that time.

Whittemore, like his better known contemporary, Crapo, was successful, middle-aged, and probably restless when he embarked on the venture that made the earlier part of his life look like a Sunday School picnic. He had been a prominent lawyer, judge, farmer. He had been a member of the Board of Regents of the University of Michigan, the State Board of Education, and Secretary of State in the Felch administration. His children were grown, if not all well-established. There was no good reason why he could not live out his comfortable, relatively uneventful life in the comparative peace and quiet of Pontiac where he had made his home for almost thirty years. Perhaps the current fever of making a fortune in pine lands tempted him; perhaps he was looking for a challenging outlet for sons who had not yet settled down; perhaps he was weary of an ailing, somewhat nagging wife and wanted to have a valid excuse for prolonged absences from home. Whatever the reason, he left peace and stability behind him, and involved himself body, soul, and entire family fortune in that fascinating speculative nineteenth-century game of lumbering, where one set out to make a fortune, usually lost one's shirt and, sometimes, made the whole thing work.

Whittemore made an exploratory visit to the bay area in the summer of 1853, landing at the lighthouse completed on Ottawas Point the previous year. Captain Colin Graham and his family who tended the light were the only inhabitants of the area except for two trappers who lived nearby. Nonetheless, this isolated uninhabited wilderness, for there was no real settlement on the whole Lake Huron shore between Bay City and Mackinac, must have looked promising, for Whittemore proceeded to execute his plans for a lumber operation on Ottawas Bay, purchasing 5,300 acres of land at $1.25 per acre with a mile of frontage on the bay and including the mouth of the Tawas River. Additional purchases of smaller tracts in the area were made from time to time during the next decade.

The financing of Whittemore's entrepreneurial schemes was complicated almost from the very first and became increasingly tortuous as the years went on. The initial capitalization of the Whittemore enterprise was $18,000, of which equal shares were held by three partners. James Covert of Albany, and Whittemore's daughter, Harriet, were his original partners. Harriet was married to A. B.

Mathews, well-established miller and produce broker of Pontiac, Michigan. Mathews was heavily involved in the Tawas operation from the beginning, despite his oft-repeated complaint that his only promise had been to provide in his wife Harriet's name a share of the original capital investment. Actually for ten long and difficult years he acted as the company's agent for the purchase of supplies and equipment and the hiring of hands. From 1855 on, he struggled and sweated to find a profitable market for the lumber, corresponded with jobbers and brokers, arranged transportation, and made an occasional trip to Chicago or Albany in quest of buyers or more favorable terms. Although his original investment was made in his wife's name, he personally carried the firm, year after year, to the extent of thousands of dollars, neglecting his own business, borrowing money at usurious rates of interest on his own signature, mortgaging and, on one occasion, almost losing his entire Pontiac property in the process.

Mathews did not perform these services without complaint. Although he went rarely to Tawas, and not at all in the first years, he carried on a voluminous correspondence with members of the family, particularly James Whittemore, who usually supervised operations at the bay during his father's frequent absences. In his letters to James, Mathews complained, cajoled, and threatened. He painted the direst pictures of his own and the firm's financial predicaments. He accused the Whittemore brothers of mismanagement. He threatened to withdraw his support. But always each fall, as he complained about the losses of the season just passed, he borrowed, begged or mortgaged to find the money to supply Tawas once more, hoping anew for that highly profitable season that would make the sacrifice worthwhile.

The journal of work for 1854, which was kept in a most methodical fashion by G. O. Whittemore, shows in detail the large expenditure of labor and capital necessary before a single dollar could be realized on a lumbering investment. The situation in which the Whittemores found themselves was, of course, far from unique. The problem was the same for all lumbering operations. There was always a full year in the lumbering cycle before any cash could be realized even in established businesses, and the element of risk was always high. Camps had to be built anew for almost every season, marsh hay cut for the horses, a full winter's logging undertaken, and the lumber gotten out of the woods to the mills in the spring. All this had to be done with only a guess as to what the next summer's prices would be on a commodity with highly fluctuating prices and before a single dollar was returned from the sale of logs or lumber.

The Whittemores' problem was even more complicated. Transportation costs always loomed large in computing profit or loss in lumbering ventures. Lumber was a cheap but very bulky product for which the sources of supply were far from the primary consuming markets. However, in the 1850's in the Flint and Saginaw area in lower Michigan, for example, there was at least a growing local market. Settlers were moving in and railroads were beginning to penetrate the area. There were no roads and no settlers in the Tawas region where the Whittemores set up their mill, nor were there to be any for several years. Hence there was absolutely no local market for their lumber. At the same time all their supplies had to be brought in by steamer, except for brief periods during the winter freeze when teams could be sent overland from Pontiac.

Nothing was obtainable locally. For the buildings erected that first summer before the mill was in operation, lumber itself had to be shipped in, and it was many years before Tawas became completely independent of lower Michigan for hay and feed for its draft animals. At the same time, the Whittemores either had to find a buyer willing to take their lumber on the dock at Tawas—usually sight unseen and at an unsatisfactory price—or arrange to send it to brokers in Chicago or Buffalo for sale, where again they were at the mercy of others in a much better position to take advantage of the market, and where they had to pay transportation costs that typically absorbed almost a third of their gross. For example, in 1859 they sold a cargo in Albany for $3,221, of which $904 were freight charges alone.

At the beginning, however, all was hope and optimism. Mathews was as yet unaware of the demanding role he was to play, and Whittemore was blissfully ignorant of many of his future problems and full of enthusiasm for the new venture that lay before him. On July 1, 1854, the steamer Huron approached the point on Ottawas Bay that was later to become Tawas City and discharged its cargo of 15 men, 2 yoke of oxen, and the first summer's supplies. Preliminary operations were under way.

The men began to build a shanty, get stone, dig a well, and cut timber for the mill supports, as well as harvest marsh hay for the draft animals. They began to clear the lower stretches of the river of the accumulated debris of decades, so that logs could eventually be floated down it, an operation that was to continue over several years as logging activities moved inland. Men were set to work making shingles for the buildings and digging a coal pit for the future boiler's fuel. In September they erected a boardinghouse to replace the shanty as housing for their hands, and in October they got stone for the enginehouse and storehouse, and provided a few comforts as they made tables, bedsteads, doors, and windows.

In November their attention was largely focused on the mill and its equipment. The Whittemore company had contracted with the Detroit Locomotive Works in July for a steam engine, boiler, and mill irons, to be built to their specifications at a cost of $5,328 and delivered in 90 days. From the journal of work it would seem that delivery was made in November. There was still no dock on the bay and the boilers had to be plugged, tossed overboard, and poled to shore. How the engine was landed is not indicated in the papers, but probably it was brought in on either a raft or a good-sized dinghy. The workmen were occupied with setting up the engine and boilers and finishing work on the buildings throughout December, when they also began to cut a road to Sand Point. Six months of hard work had gone by and, of course, no logging had been undertaken as yet.

From October 1 to January 1, $7,367.81 had been expended. As Mrs. Whittemore complained, "'Tis money out. But *out* all the time, and of necessity must be so." Total costs for the earlier months are not available, but they included a substantial downpayment on the engine, payment for lands, and large quantities of supplies. In a letter to James Whittemore dated June 28, 1854, G. O. Whittemore stated that the original capital investment totaled $18,000. Presumably by October most of this had been spent because the company already was badly in need of additional funds; the manipulations which somehow staved off bankruptcy during the next 12 years had already begun.

James Covert withdrew from the partnership at this time, for reasons unknown. Perhaps he felt the risk was too great and that the involvement would become too heavy. However, no cash settlement was made with him. Rather, he was given a mortgage on part of the firm's lands. Robert Higham became the new partner and brought an additional $2,500 of working capital into the firm. Higham remained a partner until April, 1856, when he sold his interest to Whittemore and Harriet Mathews for $7,000, payable in three years. Since the firm defaulted on this obligation, like many others, Higham found severing his connection with Whittemore and Company not quite so simple in the end. The Michigan Insurance Company Bank of Detroit through its cashier, Henry K. Sanger, also entered the financial picture, in October of 1854, as holder of a mortgage on 2,600 acres of Whittemore's pine lands. The bank's mortgage was to be a factor for many years, and clear title to the property passed to the Whittemores only after Gideon's death, following many and complicated manipulations and crises. October of 1854 was just the beginning. Nonetheless, even with new sources of capital and new mortgages, the partners were able to pay only

$176 on the second installment of the engine when it fell due in October and had to sign a promissory note for the remaining $1,776. When this fell due a year later, payment was refused.

By January of 1855 logging operations were finally under way. That first season it was possible to cut close to the settlement where logs were relatively easy to get to the mill. Gideon Whittemore returned to his Pontiac home during the coldest winter months, leaving his son James, aided by his younger brother, Charles Whittemore, in charge at the Bay. James wrote to his father that by the end of January they would have hauled enough logs to make 500,000 feet of lumber when sawed. An experiment with starting the engine, in the hope they could at least saw enough lumber to enclose the mill, only resulted in a cracked cylinder, and all attempts to run the mill until the weather moderated were abandoned.

Spring found them with a substantial supply of logs on hand, the mill operating well, and an agreement with Benjamin Brewster and Company, Chicago lumber merchants, to take all the lumber they could ship, 2,000,000 board feet including lath and pickets. During the early summer their most important project was the building of a dock, badly needed to expedite the loading of lumber and unloading of supplies. Whittemore's dock, with its later additions and improvements, remained the principal dock of Tawas City for many years. Another major improvement begun that summer was the building of the so-called railroad, used for hauling logs. Its tracks were made of hard maple ribbands sawed at Tawas, and by June it had been completed as far as Dead Creek. Additions were made to the track from time to time as logging operations moved farther into the interior.

Essentially the plant was now complete. Mill and enginehouse, bunkhouse, store, dock and the first logging roads into the interior had all been built in the course of the first year. Although county organization was not completed until 1857, the village of Tawas was surveyed and platted that summer of 1855. The Whittemores were beginning to see the development of Ottawas Bay as more than a pinery. They were looking ahead to a permanent settlement with a broader economic base resting on agriculture, although over ten years were to pass before this became a reality.

From the beginning, the Whittemores ran what is known in lumbering terminology as an integrated operation. They owned the land, hired the crews, and did their own logging (except for the first winter when they had two men operating teams on commission), hauled the timber to the mill, cut the lumber, shingles, and lath, and arranged for its sale to jobbers in Chicago or in the East. They also owned the only store in Tawas and managed to pay a good deal of their men's wages in goods on which they made a profit. They almost completely controlled local government as soon as Iosco County was organized in 1857, holding most of the county and township offices. When a postoffice was opened in 1856, the first between Bay City and Mackinac, James became the first postmaster and the office remained in his house until 1874. The whole community was under the Whittemores' control. Nonetheless, theirs is a story of unrelenting struggle and almost constant near-bankruptcy.

The first financial crisis came in October of 1854 and has already been described. For the next two years logging, milling, and marketing all went along fairly well, although the company showed no profit. It was in 1857 that the Whittemores' troubles really began. The panic of that year made itself felt in late summer and fall in the form of general hard times and rapidly falling lumber prices. But matters did not come to a head until late 1858 and early 1859, when Sanger began to press the Insurance Company Bank claim. Mathews' business had suffered greatly and he personally was very short of money. Lumber prices were extremely depressed. Fluctuation was normal, but the price range from 1854 to 1857 had been $11 to $18 per thousand. In the summer of 1859, one Whittemore cargo brought only $6.75 delivered in Chicago.

The mild winter of 1858-1859, when there was no snow at Tawas even in January, did not help the situation, and the crisis deepened. The mortgage on the Whittemore homestead in Pontiac was about to be foreclosed. The firm was seriously in default in meeting payments on the mortgage held by Covert, but foreclosure did not seem as likely there for they believed that Covert probably did not really want the property. The defaulting on the Insurance Company Bank mortgage held on their other lands and on the mill property itself was a much more dangerous problem, and the bank was pressing its claims. Suits were also being started on other outstanding notes.

Mathews himself was in serious trouble. He had used (to stock Tawas during the fall and winter) over $1,700 given him to buy wheat for them by Bridge and Lewis, Detroit produce brokers. He now had to buy wheat to cover this misuse of their funds, or face the utter ruin of his business reputation, and he had no money with which to do it. Only another less-than-legal maneuver saved him. He used the receipts from wool he sold, which really belonged to his farmer customers, to cover the wheat. Mathews did not run these risks lightly. He was fully aware of the moral and business implications of making free with money which did not belong to him. His mental anguish was considerable, but the overriding consideration was, as always, Tawas must be kept going.

Meanwhile the depression was mitigating, lumber prices were advancing, and if the Whittemores could hold out through the milling and shipping season of 1859, there was hope the company could stay afloat. By March higher grades of lumber were bringing from $32 to $35 in Albany, and in May the Whittemores were offered $23 for clear on the dock at Tawas, a really good price.

However, misfortune still dogged them; misfortune or mismanagement, it is difficult to tell which. There was for some reason a serious delay in getting sawyers and putting the mill in operation in the spring of 1859 and sawing did not begin until May 21. This was no year for delay in marketing cargoes, for the market became dull in June and the Whittemores' first cargo was not ready to ship until mid-July. By August the market glut and downward trend of prices was serious, and Hill, Thomas and Company of Albany refused to take the Whittemores' second cargo of the season, which meant that Mathews had to make a trip to Albany to dispose of it. One bright spot in their affairs was that the partners were able to re-finance once more, obtaining a new mortgage from the Insurance Bank, which relieved them of immediate jeopardy. However, the lands covered by the Covert mortgage were sold for debts on October 5, 1859, to a Mr. Winne for the exact amount unpaid. There were still other suits and injunctions out against them, and Mathews began counseling the sale of the firm to Charles or James to provide more time for maneuver. Sawing ceased on October 15 that year, and as usual the volume of lumber had proved far short of earlier estimates and would not realize enough to pay advances for the season, to say nothing of past debts. Four cargoes were shipped in the summer of 1859, two to Albany and two to Chicago, representing approximately 800,000 board feet. For these the company received about $8,500. Although the proceeds of the last two cargoes had gone to Bridge and Lewis, Mathews was still in serious trouble, and the Detroit brokers were threatening to sell his Pontiac flour mill, to which they held title, if he could not pay his debts to them.

Nonetheless, the Whittemores stayed in business and did not lose control over their property. There is neither the space nor the necessity for continuing the story in any great detail. Times were again difficult in 1860 and 1861. Heavy snows made cutting and hauling timber easier but also resulted in a glutted market. Charles took title to the mill property and land covered by the bank mortgage in 1860 to avoid losing it, and chattel mortgages were frequently placed on newly cut logs to avoid injunctions by the firm's creditors. The Whittemores were finally saved only by the general boom that followed the first financial uncertainties of the Civil War period. While Whittemore and Company made no spectacular successes, the firm began to hold its own, and Mathews' Pontiac business prospered and grew. As Mathews' solvency increased, Whittemore and Company's insolvency proved less of a threat. The firm was still far from prosperous when Gideon Whittemore died suddenly at Tawas City in July of 1863; old debts were still outstanding and every piece of the family's property was heavily mortgaged, but the firm had weathered the first ten years. Perhaps a sign of permanence, at least of Tawas as a settlement, was to be seen in the fact that the first school, taught by the light-house-keeper's daughter, held its session in the upper story of the Whittemore store that year.

With Gideon's death, the first generation completed its task, leaving all control in the hands of the sons and brother-in-law, and a new third generation, native to Tawas, was arriving on the scene. Charles had married in 1855 and James in 1856; both deserted Pontiac completely and made their homes in Tawas City where their children were born and grew up. After Gideon's death they were joined by their younger brother, William, who remained in business with Charles until the old mill was sold in 1878.

The year 1866 really marked the dividing point. In the winter of that year lumbermen began operating in force on the Au Sable, and other mills were soon erected in Tawas to join the Whittemores in serving the growing industry. While the whole bay area boasted a population of only 53 in 1866, by 1868 there were over 1,000 people living in Tawas City alone. The Whittemores were in a position to reap the benefits of this expansion, for in January of 1866 a final settlement had been arranged with the Insurance Company Bank, in which the bank agreed to give up its large accumulations of interest in return for a settlement of $12,000, payable at the rate of $2,000 per year. The bank gave the Whittemores a deed and took a mortgage, freeing them of their worst encumbrance and making it possible for the Whittemores to sell land, logging rights, and house lots. Tawas City was on its way at last.

This story has been concentrated on two years, 1854 and 1859, partly because of the fullness of the Whittemore papers for those years, but also because those two years illustrate so vividly the enormous difficulties that could attend a lumbering venture. No doubt the Whittemores' greatest disadvantage was lack of capital. Had they had three times $18,000 in 1854, their story might have had a different tone. They would then have been in a position to absorb the inevitable losses of the first years. They could hardly make money when their mill ran at perhaps one third of capacity because they lacked working capital to finance the logging operations that would have given it sufficient fodder. Transportation problems also contributed more than a normal share to their difficulties. In addition to their mill's isolation from markets, there were problems in getting the logs to the mill. The Tawas River was never really satisfactory for floating out logs, even after the enormous effort spent on clearing it. It was short on water and prone to sand bars. The wooden railroad and other logging roads proved more reliable for bringing in the logs, but were of course much more expensive forms of transportation. Without doubt the costs of production for Whittemore and Company were too high.

In mid-century America the courts were full of loggers and lumbermen pleading bankruptcy. That the Whittemores avoided swelling this total is due only to technicalities and Mathews' heroic efforts. As he wrote to his brother-in-law, James, in December of 1866, shortly after his wife Harriet's death:

> I hope the day is coming when Tawas will be and do something! Oh what a crushing burthen it has been—to all no doubt—certainly to me. My dear Harriet was always my confidant in business matters, as I felt it a duty to let her know how matters were going so that she would not be in the dark . . . and she used to sympathize with me over the dreadful Tawas misfortune—over the straits I was frequently in & the means I was forced to resort to, to bear up against it. . . . I did *absolutely expect* that Tawas would do something considerable for me in this way instead of drawing on me! But perhaps that time may yet come when I shall get something from this source. I hope so. But if it had only come in my dear Harriet's time how gratifying it would have been.

The Whittemores' problems—high interest, expensive transportation and marketing costs, and relative inexperience with lumbering—were typical of the difficulties of small operators in the formative years of the Michigan lumbering industry. And in a broader sense, like most small businessmen of the day, the Whittemores' basic problem was their consistent inability to foresee the need for or to command sufficient capital to make their enterprise go. The Whittemores' inexperience, managerial inadequacies, and personal difficulties were perhaps typical of thousands of contemporaries in other small enterprises.

Tawas had extracted a heavy price from its founders. But of such unwilling and unexpected sacrifice was much of America built.

H. W. Sage was one of the most successful of all the lumber entrepreneurs in Michigan. He fits the stereotype of the big businessman—coming into an area, developing it, reaping substantial profits, and not being particularly concerned with the consequences of his enterprise. He also represents the outside capitalist who never settled in Michigan and was never really concerned with the state except as it affected his business.

Sage's empire stretched from New York to the Pacific, but his Michigan activities centered in the Saginaw area in the 1870s and '80s. This selection from Sage's biography discusses his Saginaw lumber interests and the strikes of 1872 and 1875. The 1875 strike involved the Knights of Labor, a nineteenth-century union that flourished for a time but ultimately failed. Ms. Goodstein gives additional details of the strike and labor problem in the region in her article, "Labor Relations in the Saginaw Valley Lumber Industry, 1865-1885," *Bulletin of the Business Historical Society*, 28 (December, 1953), 193-221.

Typical too of the era described in this article was the failure of the strikes to accomplish anything of significance. Their efforts show, however, the beginnings of a labor movement and an awareness in a labor community of its potential.

A New York Capitalist in Michigan's Forests

ANITA SHAFER GOODSTEIN

The mill boss was in charge of construction and operation. He hired the mill hands, but wages, hours, and the number of workers were subject to Sage's approval. Sage demanded accurate and detailed information concerning mill costs and production. He ordered "a tabular statement . . . showing each month . . . the cost of sawing—the no. of men employed—the average cost pr day of each man—the average production pr day of each man." With regular weekly and monthly reports, this type of statement enabled Sage to discover immediately any disadvantageous fluctuation and to set standards of production and cost.

In the camps, the stocker was responsible for determining with the aid of a surveyor the boundaries of the areas purchased by Sage for exploitation by his camps. This was a particularly delicate job, for errors frequently meant long and expensive lawsuits. The stocker was general supervisor of camp operations and of the

From *Biography of a Businessman, Henry W. Sage, 1814-1897*, pp. 72-74, 77-92. Copyright © 1962 by Cornell University Press. Reprinted by permission. Footnotes in the original have been omitted.

company farm. Potatoes, turnips, wheat, and oats were raised at East Tawas to supply the loggers through the winter season. The farm was expanded in the early seventies from year to year; the logging crew did the clearing and planting. Horses needed for hauling were kept at the farm and fed with homegrown hay, and cattle were kept to supply the camps with meat.

The camp foremen were expected to see to cutting timber, hauling it to the rivers or booms, constructing booms, and driving the logs to the mill. Camp labor earned between $25 and $30 a month—more nearly the former—plus board.

In selecting his mill staff, Sage was concerned to discover whether they had "industry enough—capacity enough—convictions of moral character enough" to be trusted with responsibility. When he discovered that the mill office was not open and prepared for work at 6 A.M., he labeled the tardiness of his mill manager a "lazy—poor house habit." Plummer, the mill boss, was taken to task for his interest in horse racing. Sage wrote indignantly: "It should be your duty to *prevent and forbid* any notice of Horse racing or similar entertainment being posted upon our premises—No matter whose the horse—He cant run Race course & Mill too—Must choose which." Plummer was asked to choose also between his position in the mill and his position as Mayor of Wenona. Perhaps the fact that Plummer was a Democrat may have influenced Sage. Plummer resigned his position as Mayor. However, he left Sage's employ shortly thereafter, not without Sage's acknowledgment of his "real staunch nobility of character." Sage also asked that Hiram Emery, his stock jobber, be warned "that using fast horses on a race course will *hurt him*—The time & thought it costs, the expense, the associations & habits—are not in line with principles which control success in business or elevation of character."

. . . .

By his own test, the test of profit, Sage was a successful administrator. The "eleven fat years from 1862 on" which Sage contended that lumber producers had enjoyed had been relatively undisturbed by price declines. A short depression in the fall of 1869 had driven prices down temporarily, but by fall of the following year they were back to the $6—$12—$35 level, which represented the good prices of the fat years in the Saginaw Valley market. The Chicago fire and a short crop of logs in 1871 drove prices up still higher, and in 1872 the great strike and a short crop again maintained the rise. The drop that came after the panic seems the more dramatic because of the unusually high prices that obtained in the two previous years. Perhaps this explains why Sage included 1873 in the fat years, and why as late as July 1874 he regarded the situation with relative complacency, "Two or three sober years, if they don't utterly destroy, wont hurt them [the lumber producers] ." In the fall of 1873 prices dropped to $4—$8—$28 and $30. From 1874 to 1878 they fluctuated between this low figure and one that approached the 1868 price level. In September of 1878 prices dropped again and did not recover until June of 1879, when they were quoted at $6.50—$13—$28 and soon rose to $7—$14—$30, a figure close to that of the exceptionally good prices of 1871. Average prices remained at a high level until the crash of 1884.

In 1880, after seven years of depression prices, Sage estimated "the profit on lumber production will *average $150 M* or more # for the past 10 years—(# much more, as you know, only two years of the past 10 *less*)." That is, in only two years from 1870 to 1880 did the firm's profits average less than $150,000. This represents a 37½ per cent or a 30 per cent return on the entire mill property investment, which was estimated at different times as $400,000 and $500,000. Moreover it does not take into account the profits on salt and lath production and the proceeds of rents which Sage estimated as amounting to $33,276 or more than 6 per cent on $500,000. This profit had been made despite a depressed price level.

Sage felt the pressure of fluctuating and declining prices. Yet complaints seem to be directed at relative rather than absolute losses. Thus in 1874 Sage wrote his son: "We can make a little on Lumber this year if we take from it (in sorting up) all there is in it—But it wont be much at best—*Not* 7 pr ¢ in our capital." In 1878 he repeated that profits were possible but would be small. "It will be a close business to make *anything* & sell at present rates but we can by close management make small profits—say 1 to 1.50 pr M at best—We have reached a time when accumulations must inevitably be slow." A similar comment was made in 1885. Sage wrote W. J. Young: "I think the worst of our depression in trade is over & that we are to have increased production in all things, and a period of reasonable prosperity in business that is *well managed*—but without very large profits—We must learn to be content with moderate gains—There is nothing better or safer than the Lumber trade."

In the last ten years of the mill's life an actual loss was recorded in only one year, 1890. After the crisis of 1884-1885, however, the profit level never fully recovered at the mill or the Albany yard. (See Table 1.)

The unusually high profits of the sixties and early seventies were based not only on the demands of an expanding economy but also

Table I. Annual Profit or Loss

	Mill			Albany yard	
Year	Profit	Loss		Profit	Loss
1882	$148,662			$114,181	
1883	138,032			121,554	
1884	83,740			68,656	
1885	36,330			18,784	
1886	40,937			37,553	
1887	121,211			59,194	
1888	129,154			65,137	
1889	134,829			90,505	
1890		$62,898		68,101	
1891	83,157				$133,133†
1892	22,966			115,565	

†This loss reflects a major embezzlement by an employee in the Albany office.

on the cheap price of stumpage. In the sixties stumpage had cost Sage ten to twenty cents per thousand feet. But in the eighties the supply of cheap timber easily accessible to the mill which Sage had provided in the sixties was being exhausted. By 1885 Sage was evidently beginning to cut the poorer quality timber remaining on his lands. In 1889 Sage predicted, accurately: "Our lumber manufacturing business is very nearly at end in Michigan—Three years will use up all the Timber we have." To continue manufacturing by purchasing pine stumpage now with the price of stumpage at $6 and $10 per thousand feet did not seem "worth doing." The rise in stumpage prices and the foreseeable exhaustion of their own supply in the eighties lent force to the Sage sons' desire to sell the mill. In 1882 the mill was actually advertised for sale, and again in 1885 Sage offered to sell the mill property and three hundred million feet of timber, but he was not willing to sell at a price which did not compensate for the high value he placed upon it even then. The mill property and the returns it represented must not be "wasted or frittered away." In 1890 the valuation of the mill on the books of the firm was reduced to $200,000.

To offset any decline in the profit level Sage relied on "close management," which invariably meant pressure upon the wage level. Sage agreed with the reflection published in the *Lumberman's Gazette* "that the compensations of labor must be regulated by the conditions of trade, and the ratios of profit." The worker's services were factors in production, whose cost was adjusted in terms of the maintenance of production and profit. The adjustment process, Sage believed, was to be controlled by the employer, for "employers know what they can afford to pay for the products of Labor and *will* pay all they can afford to." Worried by the wave of strikes in New York City and by the possibility of a strike at the mill in 1872, Sage wrote, "We cant afford yet, to submit to the charge of an ignorant rabble—the conduct of enterprises upon which the nation's wealth and prosperity depends." Sage justified the unilateral control of the wage level by the employer on the grounds that he produced the goods and provided the capital upon which the community's prosperity was based. His obligation to his workers was defined by supplying them with work.

Over the whole period of lumber production in the Saginaw Valley the money wage of labor did apparently increase. About 1850, when a mill employed seven men for each twelve-hour shift, the average wage for all workers amounted to one dollar a day. By 1860 the average wage paid in the valley for common labor had risen to $1.12½. The post-Civil War period brought even higher wages. A Lumberman's Proclamation published during the 1872 strike listed the average daily wage paid from 1865 to 1872 to demonstrate the rise in money wages. The last figure— $2.30—compared favorably with the first—$1.52. The average wage at Sage's mill in July of 1872 was as high as $2.33. However, higher money wages in this period ran parallel with high prices.

In 1873 began a downward swing of both money and real wages. Sage's mill had reduced its average wage to $2.14 by July of 1873, before the panic struck. Sage contended that manufacturers could not long continue "to be deaf and blind to the fact that we must reduce cost, and restrict production—*both*—if we make lumber trade produce anything save *loss and disaster.*" Sage proposed a "concert of action" among the millowners of the valley to postpone sending men to the woods until they were prepared to accept $20.00 a month as wages. The postponement would serve not only to gain lower wages but also to limit production. It is true that Sage did not cut much timber in 1873, but due to the strike of 1872 and unusually dry weather that year, which kept the stock in the woods, he had a plentiful supply in 1873. His own production figure went from the unusually low 12,940,519 feet in 1872 to 20,370,670 in 1873 and 25,111,595 feet in 1874.

In September of 1873 a 12½ per cent wage reduction was agreed on by manufacturers. In April of 1874 Sage considered $1.50 enough for common labor. The *Lumberman's Gazette* quoted $1.75 as the average daily price of common labor in the valley in 1874; by 1877 this had dropped to $1.25. Evidently the price level was not sufficiently low to compensate for wage reductions. Thus, the editor of the Saginaw *Daily Courier* sought in vain to discover "what is to become of the laborers who get only $1.00 a day and are obliged to pay $13.00 a barrel for flour and $1.50 a bushel for potatoes."

There was no significant improvement in the wage level until 1880. Wages then began to advance, only to drop again in 1884. By 1885 the wage level of the industry was seriously affected. Of the 4,232 men employed by 77 mills in the valley, 54 per cent earned $1.62½ or less.

Thus the substantial rise in money wages from 1860 through 1872 was sharply curtailed in 1873. Though wages tended to rise again in the early eighties, they did not do so in the same proportion as they had in the first period, and again the rise was curtailed by depression. The wage level, then, was highly responsive to a decline in the price of lumber, less responsive to a rise in price.

Strikes occurred in the Saginaw Valley with some regularity. For the most part they were limited in scope, involving only a fraction of the working crew. One lasted only fifteen minutes. Organization of the workers was usually attempted after, not before, the outbreak of a strike, and none of the strikes could be said to be successful. In 1867 talk of a strike for higher wages reached Sage, who warned:

> Lumber is declining in value and slow of sale at *any price*—and wages *should be,* and *will be*—permanently lower before they are permanently higher. . . . We are willing to pay for labor all our business will warrant— but we can't at the same time increase wages of labor—and sell its products *below cost.*—and lumber could not be sold *freely* today in any market I know—East or West—*to pay a* reasonable business profit over the cost of production.

This stock argument was to be heard even more often after 1873.

If a strike was not justified in a poor year it was considered equally unjustified in 1872 after two comparatively prosperous years. Sage wrote:

> *Never* was there so little good reason for discontent—Never was labor so well paid [this was the year when his average wage at the mill was $2.33] —so fully occupied—If we can keep it well occupied and well paid as now our nations wealth will rapidly increase and every interest will prosper—but destroy the foundation or decrease its flow—and we shall very soon go back to poverty—We cant stand the drain of extravagant expenses and partial idleness.

He referred by this last statement to the demand for a ten-hour day in the mills and/or an increase in wages to meet higher prices.

About the fifteenth of June, 1872, the "murmurings" for a ten-hour strike throughout the Saginaw Valley were brought to the attention of the millowners. Strikes on varying scales began to break out in the first days of July. There was perhaps a deliberate slowing down of production in the mills. Thus Sage complained that his mill, which should have been cutting 100,000 to 120,000 feet a day, had averaged only between 60,000 and 70,000. Nevertheless Sage was anxious to keep his mill going as long as possible "on regular time." On July 3 he joined with the millmen of fifty-seven other firms in Bay City, Saginaw City, and East Saginaw in issuing a proclamation to the effect that they would "not submit to any reduction of the hours of labor nor any increase of wages." By July 5 most of the mills had been shut down.

The millowners agreed on a uniform show of resistance toward the strikers' demands. The resolve of the Lumberman's Proclamation was adhered to fairly consistently. A shutdown at this time did not seem disastrous, since the lack of heavy rains that season had resulted in a shortage of logs. Nevertheless, millmen were anxious to cut what they had in expectation of the large returns a scarcity on the market would realize. Sage directed his mill manager as early as July 8 not to "wait to know the real purposes of your men—Get them together and learn how many and *who* want to work on our terms—Then prepare to protect them and our property."

There was real fear of mob violence and destruction of mill property. No effective organization existed among the workers. It was a restless, milling body of men with no apparent leadership which the millmen faced. Sage was prepared to arm his mill staff with six-shooters and Spencer rifles, and gave orders to notify the mob that Company officials were armed and would protect the mill property should the town government prove unwilling or unable to do so. Threats to burn down the mills were received, but never carried out. The mills after all represented the only source of income to the workers.

On July 9, four days after the strike had "officially" begun, the laborers organized a union based on a one-dollar initiation fee and a twenty-five-cent monthly assessment. The Striker's Union contributed little toward the organization of the strike movement. Its main function seems to have been to keep the workers' families provisioned. The establishment of the union did not imply success in treating with the mill operators as a group or in organizing the workers of any one mill to treat as a unit with their employer. The concept of collective bargaining was perhaps as alien to the workers in this period as it most certainly was to employers.

The Sage mill was prepared to start up again several times during the strike period with a partial crew who agreed to Sage's terms. However, the resumption and immediate shutdown of his mill led Sage to feel:

> The only remedy for this case is to let the whole laboring community feel the burden of the strike till there grows up in their own midst a sense of their folly. . . . Collect your rents promptly—especially from strikers— They must not live on us while their conduct destroys us.

And finally, exasperated, he ordered that the workers remaining at the mill be fired if the hands refused to come back at the old wages and hours. This group, he contended, were probably in secret sympathy with the strikers but holding on to their jobs so that they would not lose anything whether the movement succeeded or failed.

By July 17 the Bay City *Daily Journal* claimed that the strike was about broken. Sage's mill had started up with thirty-five men, and he expected to hire seventy or eighty more that day. By July 19 all the mill except the circular saw was running the full twelve-hour day. The greater ability of the millowners to wait out the strike, particularly in the face of a scarcity of logs, was probably the most overwhelming factor in their success.

Sage contended that the strikers "have against them not alone the employers—but the whole interests of society—*and quite as much their own!*" His attempt to discover any within his organization who were "doubtful" with regard to the labor movement, to "learn where they are—who they are—and exactly how to count them—they are either for or against and we should know which—" was in line with the position taken by the *Journal,* which declared that "the entire blame" for the strike "can be laid at the doors of a few discontented demagogues."

> These men are marked, and will have considerable difficulty in procuring situations in the Valley, and it is perfectly right that all such discontented uncongenial spirits should be debarred from work where an insinuating word does as much harm as it has within the last four weeks in this section.

The vocal element, the "respectable" element in the community, did not concede the right of workers to disrupt the processes of production.

The twelve-hour work day was resumed. Perhaps most significant of the results of the strike was the notice: "Before the strike lumber was selling freely at $7.00, $14.00, and $35.00. . . . Since the strike has ended $7.50, $15.00 and $36.00 are the figures at which holders stand firm."

After the panic of 1873 the chances for an effective labor protest were weakened still more. Riots were reported in May of 1876. A few months later Sage directed his manager to "hire your men *low* and pay them from the store—We *cannot raise* cash and there must be no reliance on it."

In the late fall of 1879, when the depression began to ease, a fifteen-minute strike for higher wages among Sage's workers occurred. In May of 1882 fourteen men at work at the salt block of H. W. Sage and Co. struck for a 12½ cents advance which would bring their pay to $1.75 a day. Their places were soon filled by others "quite willing to accept the company's terms, which are the same as all other blocks along the river are paying." Again there were more than enough workers for the places available, and no opportunity for a better-paid job in the mills of the valley.

During the spring of this year the coopers of Sage's mill commenced a series of strikes for a raise in wages. The most interesting notice connected with these strikes was of the existence of a union organization. In 1874 during a workingman's meeting a Mr. Allen, who may have been a local merchant, had risen to express his thought that "the workingmen had all the privileges they wanted already and that we should be careful in organizing to consider the rights of capitalists as well as that of the workingman." Subsequently the meeting carried the motion to convert this "society for the benefit of workingmen" into "a benevolent protective literary society." From this time almost no notice seems to have been given in the newspapers and trade journals to labor organization in the valley.

Nevertheless, the Knights of Labor had been active. Out of an estimated 4,232 men employed by the Saginaw mills in 1885 the Knights claimed to represent 3,000. This did not make it the focal point of militant labor protest, however. The Knights' membership roll was a heterogeneous sort; it included on its lists tradesmen and city officials. Indeed during the Great Strike of 1885 "the official aid rendered by the Knights complicated matters, because nearly all of the city officials in Saginaw, East Saginaw, and Bay City were members of the order." Perhaps because of its motley membership, the Knights tended to be a conservative agency, cautioning the strikers to moderate their demands. While the Great Strike of 1885 was neither organized nor led by the Knights of Labor, individual Knights played a prominent role.

This strike seems to have originated in a misconception of when the ten-hour law, whose passage had been promoted by Thomas Barry—a laborer, Knight, and Democratic-Greenback member of the Michigan legislature—was to take effect. The workers of the valley were convinced that the law was to go into operation on July 1, although it is clear that the law was not to be effective until September 15. About the fifth and sixth of July the Rust mills in Bay City were shut down by the strikers. Soon the whole valley was affected by the agitation.

The years 1884 and 1885 were severe depression years. Sage contended in 1885 that "this year and last year the wages we have paid have been more than our profits." He wished that "all the mills in the Valley would close for 60 days—that would do great good"; that limitation of production which the millmen could not achieve among themselves, the labor force was carrying out for them. "We should welcome with joy an absolute shut down of the mills for the whole of this season—it would enable consumption to overtake production and in that way restore values of property already produced."

With this the prevailing attitude among employers, the workers could hope to achieve little for themselves by striking. Nevertheless, the strike continued. On July 11 the mill hands of Bay City and West Bay City made their dramatic trip to the Saginaws by foot and barge to rout out their fellows with the slogan "Ten hours or no sawdust." Some of the millowners, although by no means all, had no objection to a ten-hour day. The crucial issue was the workers' demand that the reduction in hours be accompanied by no reduction in pay. This the millmen were universally unwilling to concede.

Although the mill operators were indifferent to or even welcomed the closing of the mills, they resented bitterly the "mob action" which precipitated the shutdown. Sage was convinced that his own employees were willing to work but "forced to quit by mobs."

> We clearly recognize the right of men to fix for themselves the price of their labor, and the hours they will work—and also the right of employers to agree or disagree with their terms—the rights of mobs, or illegal combinations of men to enforce their views upon men willing to work, and satisfied with their wages we wholly deny.

Sage himself was sure that "the strike did not originate with the laboring men," that it was the "influence of Labor Knights and Politicians" which had kept it going so long. Nevertheless, a meeting of the employees of the Sage mill resulted in a refusal by the workers to return at the old terms.

The lack of a comprehensive organization among the men was illustrated again and again during the course of the strike by just such meetings of the crews of an individual mill. While indecision and successive proposals marked the stand of the strikers, Sage maintained a fixed policy: The old terms or a ten-hour day and a one-eleventh reduction in pay. By August 23, fifty of his workers were willing to accept the latter proposal. But when the mill started up again on September 1, it was upon the old terms, eleven hours and no increase in wages.

During the course of the strike, Sage noted that valley officials appeared too sympathetic to the laborers' cause. Sage wrote angrily, "Bay City authorities' concessions to mob rule *wrong*—this to be avoided at *all cost.*" And again, "If the Bay City authorities had not been so weak-kneed the strike would never have assumed its present proportions." Undoubtedly the unwillingness of officials to clamp down harshly upon the strikers was due to the fact that many of them were themselves Labor Knights. Also, despite the protests of mob rule made by the employers, there was surprisingly little evidence of violence over this long period. Governor Alger addressed the strikers as freely as did Blinn and Barry, strike advocates, although he spoke as a lumber manufacturer and warned that "to hinder others from working is illegal." On one occasion when a strikers' meeting, complete with band, was ordered to disperse, a Negro jumped to the platform to shout: "In this free country a white man can't speak but a wooly-headed nigger can. I advise you to join your hands like an eagle's claw and a lion's paw and hang together and stay away from the mills till they send for you!" And with such colorful advice he bade the strikers goodnight as they "gradually dispersed." The lack of violence and the affiliation with the Knights may have influenced many in "respectable" places to sympathize with the strikers. Rumor had it that even Sage's chief engineer, Roundsville, who had been with Sage about twenty-five years and was a personage in West Bay City, many times an alderman in fact, sympathized with the strikers and was perhaps himself "a member of the 'skilled laborers association.'"

There may have been yet another reason for sympathy for the workers among the middle class of the valley, and that was the knowledge that the mills could not continue to operate many years longer in the valley because the lumber supply of their hinterland was nearing exhaustion. The closing down of the mills would necessarily affect adversely the basis of the entire community's economy. Such knowledge could not but influence the attitude of the community toward the mill operators, particularly toward the absentee millowners. Though certainly not actively expressed, some feeling of hostility may well have existed. Sage thought it wise to have "the authorities . . . and the People" informed that if nothing were done to curb "rule of mobs" "we propose to close our mill and all business there and not resume it."

By the last days of August the strike had been broken. In general the mill operators' terms were accepted in full: either the old eleven-hour day or a ten-hour day with a one-eleventh or 10 per cent decrease in wages. Sage disagreed with the millowners who insisted upon holding out categorically for the old system. He pointed out that to do so would mean a renewal of the contest when the ten-hour day went into effect by law. He noted that the laborers "certainly have gained nothing except the questionable privilege of an extra hour's rest per day, which they ought to be welcome to enjoy so long as they are willing to pay for it themselves." Nevertheless, a millowners' association was formed in the Bay City area and Sage was influenced by his neighbors to insist on the eleven-hour day. Perhaps the personal tragedy he had experienced in these weeks as a result of his wife's death made him less able and less inclined to press his own point of view. He expressed objections to the methods by which others were attempting to break up the "Labor Organization combination," although he held no brief for the combination itself. Earlier he had advised his mill manager that "we had better avoid saying anything to irritate—such as that we will discharge all 'Knights' etc." The sixty-day shutdown he had welcomed had done its work, and Sage was eager to get back into production. The labor struggle had resulted in substantial gain and outright victory for the employer; future problems could be met as they arose and with less show of aggression on the part of the employer.

On September 3, Sage reported to his son that the mill was running "full crew—old hours and price—cut first day 153 M with considerable not piled." But as he predicted, September 15 meant renewed difficulties. Brief, sporadic strikes occurred in the valley during the next few weeks until a formula was accepted at each mill. Sage acceded to the ten-hour demand and settled for a 5 per cent rather than a 10 per cent reduction. Ten hours were accepted as the general work day in the valley. Wage reductions from 10 per cent down were general, although an occasional mill did not enforce a reduction at all.

The slightly higher wage was won only by a minority of workers in the valley. It was the employer who gained most directly in money terms because of the higher price his limited output could and did obtain on the market. Far more important in long-range terms was the fact that this last significant protest on labor's part came when the industry had reached peak production. H. W. Sage and Co. closed its mill in 1892. Many had done so earlier; many others were to follow shortly. The industry died and with it died the possibility for growth in many Saginaw communities.

The great strikes of 1872 and 1885, one undertaken during a period of relative prosperity, one in the midst of a depression, were both met by the superior resources of the mill operators to wait out the strike and the determination of the operators that labor be reduced once more to its position as a factor in production. By the time the community expressed even a passive sympathy for the workers, it was too late for that sympathy to change the established pattern. The millowners were already investing in new lumber frontiers in expectation of the exhaustion of the valley's timber. Without effective labor organization, the final arbiter of the reasonableness of profit remained the employer with the sanction of a community which depended upon him for industrial and civic development. And the employer was most absorbed by the effort to reduce costs.

Though the entrepreneur might have espoused the cause of laissez-faire, he really did not believe in it. What he wanted was active intervention of government, both federal and state, to strengthen his position whether it be in imposing tariffs or breaking up labor disputes. An excellent example is contained in the report of Governor Charles M. Croswell to the legislature concerning his action in the middle of 1877 when the nation was beset by a wave of railroad strikes, some of which were marked by violence. He called out the national guard even before there had been any disturbances in the state. The mobilization had the desired effect of causing the strikers to abandon their cause. Croswell made clear in his message that the state would not hesitate to utilize military forces, recently armed by the acquisition of "the superior Gatling gun," to put down future unrest.

The Railroad Strike of 1877

CHARLES M. CROSWELL

In July, 1877, a spirit of violence and disorder was manifested in some sections of the country which resulted in serious disturbance, with the destruction of many lives and millions of dollars' worth of property. Combinations were formed, railroad depots, warehouses and shops seized, freight and passenger trains compelled to stop running, and a large part of the carrying business of the country for the time being suspended.

Having reliable information that a similar danger was threatening the peace and good order of this State, I deemed it my duty to take prompt and energetic measures to meet such emergency should it arise. I accordingly ordered out the whole military force of the State to be encamped where they might rapidly be made available in case of need. To this call the troops promptly responded and the three regiments were quickly in the field ready for active duty. On the 26th day of July a portion of hands in the employ of the Michigan Central Railway Company at the city of Jackson struck, and compelling others to abandon work and join with them, proceeded to stop all trains running over such railway to or from said city. On being advised of this action the officers of the railway immediately appealed to me demanding the protection of the State against this unlawful and violent interference with the company's property. Deeming it my duty to use the military power only as a last resort in aid of the civil authorities when their efforts to restore order had proved powerless, I at once placed myself in communication with Hon. James O'Donnell, mayor of the city, requesting him to keep me advised of the situation, and assuring him that I would direct the military to promptly and firmly support the local authorities in maintaining peace and the supremacy of the laws. I further issued a proclamation enjoining all persons to refrain from improperly or violently molesting or interfering with the property of others, and requiring local executive officers to be active and vigilant in their respective localities for the maintenance of the public peace.

I was gratified in a short time to be assured by the mayor of Jackson that the civil authorities, aided by the citizens of the place, were doing all in their power to quiet the disturbance and provide for the passage of trains, with a fair prospect that such result would be speedily attained without resort to the use of military force. I was subsequently advised that the parties engaged in the unlawful proceedings had wholly relinquished their designs, and would no longer hinder the corporation from the regular use of its railway. The trouble was ended fortunately without the destruction of a dollar's worth of property or the loss of life. In view of the excited state of feeling that then prevailed among railroad operatives all

From Governor Croswell's message to the Legislature, January 2, 1879, in George N. Fuller (ed.), *Messages of the Governors* (Lansing: Michigan Historical Commission, 1927), III, 329-333.

over the country consequent upon a reduction of wages, and of the
fearful outbreaks that had taken place elsewhere, the situation was
one of unusual gravity, and the danger imminent. A single ill-judged
move might have resulted in most fearful consequences. That we
escaped a great disaster is in my judgment largely due to the
excellent course pursued by the authorities and citizens of Jackson,
to the prudent measures taken by the railroad officials to prevent a
collision with the strikers, as well as to the near presence of the
military giving assurance that the full power of the State would be
employed if necessary to prevent violence and maintain order. It is
also creditable to the workingmen who engaged in the strike that
they speedily took counsel of wisdom and abandoned their incon-
siderate and unlawful proceedings. The military merit my thanks
for their alacrity with which they responded to my call as well as
for their excellent bearing and good conduct while on duty. Experience in this emergency demonstrates that we must rely chiefly upon
our State military to suppress riots or tumults arising in our midst.

The policy of the general government seems to be to discourage
the employment of federal troops in such cases until it is apparent
that the State alone is unable to overcome the disturbance.

In the outbreak referred to if we had been without a State force,
and had been obliged to wait until a formal application could have
been made on the President and responded to with federal troops,
the strike would undoubtedly have assumed much greater proportions. The U.S. mail, of which there was a large quantity on the
delayed trains, would have been longer detained; while the criminal
and vicious, who seem to have made such disturbances an occasion
for pillage and plunder, would have had greater opportunities to
enable them to do damage.

While not prepared to advise an increase of the military force, I
do recommend the adoption of measures to add to its efficiency. A
step in this direction has already been taken by the military board
in exchanging the firearms heretofore used for the latest pattern of
Sharp's breech-loading rifles, with which all of the regiments are
now equipped.

This should be supplemented by the purchase of haversacks,
blankets and overcoats to be stored with the Quarter Master General, and furnished to the troops, from time to time, for use when
required by the demands of the service.

Companies should be obliged to have enrolled the maximum
number of able-bodied men, as there are always some who cannot
do duty at call; they should have officers of experience, hold
regular meetings for drill, and be subject to frequent and careful
inspection.

With well-organized regiments of this character, supported by the superior Gatling gun recently procured of the General Government . . . we may utilize our State military so that we shall have an efficient force always at command to assist the civil authorities in suppressing outbreaks and maintaining order.

As the century came to an end, government began to take a more sympathetic view of labor. Expressing this new view was Governor John T. Rich in his outgoing message to the legislature in 1896. Though Rich was generally regarded as a conservative, his message strikes a more modern note looking ahead to a liberalized policy of handling labor disputes in the future. For further information on labor see Doris B. McLaughlin, *Michigan Labor, A Brief History from 1818 to the Present* (Ann Arbor, 1970), which gives a useful summary of labor-management-government relations and the rise of organized labor in the state.

A New View of Labor's Rights

JOHN T. RICH

The strikes mentioned above [in Calhoun and Gogebic counties], and others in this and adjoining states, causing incalculable damage to many interests, and some damage to all interests, raises the pertinent question, what can be done to prevent them in the future? Is there not some way in which the differences between capital and labor can be adjusted without the disastrous resort to strikes? Capital is sensitive, and it may be questioned whether the very means used by labor organizations to increase wages and get other concessions to better their conditions does not in the end have the opposite effect in causing capital to seek investment in some other line which does not require the employment of labor. Labor organizations have done much in educating and aiding each

From Governor Rich's message to the Legislature, January 3, 1895, in George N. Fuller (ed.), *Messages of the Governors* (Lansing: Michigan Historical Commission, 1927), III, 716-718.

other in times of need. By their organization they have wielded a power which has compelled concessions from employers which individually they could not have obtained. No matter how orderly the managers of a strike start in, or how strong the resolutions passed to preserve order and refrain from violence or damage to property, it almost invariably happens that before a settlement is effected there is more or less violence used. In any event it is a place where the lawless element congregate ready for the first opportunity for violence and plunder. Among all the numerous sufferers from strikes none suffer so severely, and in the end so disastrously as those engaged in the strike. They also find it much more difficult to recover from its effect than any others. Arbitration, compulsory and voluntary, are proposed as a remedy for the existing evils, but neither of these seems to meet the requirements. Voluntary arbitration involves a mutual agreement to submit matters of difference to arbitrators to be agreed upon, and a further agreement to abide by the decision when rendered. There is ample legal machinery for this now. Compulsory arbitration will be only establishing another court or courts, in which these difficulties can be settled. In case one party to the disagreement should invoke the aid of this new court he must show a violation of contract and an infringement of personal or property rights, or the court would have no jurisdiction. If any of these things have been done, then the courts now existing have jurisdiction and can furnish the remedy. It will be found impossible under our form of government to compel any corporation or individual to employ men, or to pay them any particular wages. Men of means will suspend or abandon business if its management is taken from their control. It will be found equally useless to try and compel men to work unless it is for their interest to do so. In the end there must be mutual agreement between employer and employee, such as will be mutually beneficial; or such relation cannot long exist. Any agreement of this character must also be based on principles of equity and justice. The demands of civilization have made the creation of artificial persons a necessity, and much as corporations are condemned, modern civilization cannot get along without them. Laws have been enacted providing for the association of capital to carry on large operations which would be impossible for an individual to do, and many times the investment is of such a character that no prudent man would be willing to invest his all in it, but is willing to venture a fixed amount which if lost will not ruin him. Thus corporations are given certain powers and privileges and upon them is imposed certain limited liabilities and responsibilities. On the other hand labor has been left to fight on single handed so far as law is concerned.

The necessities of labor have, however, caused them to organize among themselves, but in order to accomplish their object they have been led to do many things not authorized by law and in some instances in direct violation of law. Under the existing circumstances it would seem to be the part of wisdom and justice to provide for the organization of corporations of labor, with as much power and no greater liability than is imposed on corporations of capital. Create them as a body corporate, which may make contracts and enforce them, and be empowered in turn to sue and be sued, and in short to do anything they may be authorized to do in the articles of incorporation. This would place them on an equality, and difficulties between capital and labor would be settled as other difficulties and disagreements are settled, through the courts. It is hardly consistent to condemn labor organizations for taking the law into their own hands unless some lawful and practicable method is provided for the protection of their interests. There is little doubt that there are difficulties in the way of carrying out this plan, and it is hardly probable that any law enacted would at first be satisfactory, but with the object kept steadily in view of providing for equitable contracts and an equitable and practical method for their enforcement, in the end success is certain.

2: Immigration

Immigrants to Michigan were of two kinds. There were immigrants from other countries and those who came into Michigan from other states. The reasons for immigration were many. Probably the most important were those factors in the homeland encouraging the immigrants to leave. However, another side of the story was the role of the states in encouraging immigration. Michigan, for example, at one time had a resident commissioner recruiting immigrants from abroad and official immigration commissioners to direct immigrants to Michigan. Private companies, such as railroads and land developers, sought out immigrants in order to dispose of their land or to add traffic to their lines.

Michigan was inconsistent in its attitude toward immigration. At times, the immigrants were looked upon as an asset and their influx was encouraged. At other times, they were seen as a threat to the people already there, depriving native citizens of jobs. Also, different status was accorded different immigration groups. Certain ethnic groups were looked upon more favorably than others. Governor Jerome, for example, in his 1881 message saw immigrants as a great boon in building up the state, while his successor, Governor Josiah Begole, opposed immigration in his message of 1883, reflecting declining economic conditions. Governor Alger, who at first favored immigration, ultimately opposed official state encouragement and interjected a new element in the argument. He saw the immigrants not so much as builders of American society but as potential paupers, law-breakers, or usurpers of the established government, and he was positively appalled by the thought that Chinese, whom he viewed as disreputable pagans, might somehow find their way to Michigan.

The literature on immigration as a major concern of American history is extensive and has received attention from some of our major historians such as John Higham and Oscar Handlin. The best overall summary of ethnic history in Michigan is C. Warren Vander Hill's *Settling the Great Lakes Frontier* (Lansing, 1970). For statistics on Michigan's population, see Amos H. Hawley, *The Population of Michigan 1840-1960 . . .* (Ann Arbor, 1969).

The following selections from the official messages of the governors of the period demonstrate the schizophrenic nature of official state policy toward immigration.

Immigration: Three Views

DAVID H. JEROME, JOSIAH W. BEGOLE, RUSSELL A. ALGER

Governor Jerome

There are millions of acres of good farming lands in this State unoccupied. The building of the lines of railroad traversing the entire length of the lower peninsula north and south, together with the east and west roads lately completed, and the prospective completion at an early day of the Detroit, Mackinac and Marquette Railroad, has opened and will open to easy access a vast extent of unoccupied farming lands. The influx of settlers upon these lands would add largely to the productive wealth and taxable resources of the State. Through the potent influences of the proper agencies, emigrants have been taken beyond Michigan, and great States have been built up west of us, and this largely by judicious systems of making known their advantages. No State or Territory east or west has advantages superior to those of Michigan. To secure our share of the emigrants now landing upon the shores of the United States, and of the surplus population of the Eastern States, we should make known our resources so rich, numerous and varied. Our fertile lands now in market at moderate prices, our admirable school system, and the many attractions offered to the emigrant who desires not only good soil and a healthy climate, but good markets, good government, and pleasant social relations which are assured by the general character and traditions of Michigan society. The unrest and wide-spread dissatisfaction among the people of Europe will continue to send emigrants to this country in unprecedented numbers. This seems to be a propitious time for us to at least do what other States west of us are doing to secure occupants for our idle lands. The State has a more direct interest in inducing immigration because of the vast tracts of unsold land belonging to our State educational institutions. The true policy is to induce actual settlers to purchase the unoccupied lands held either by private parties or by the State.

. . . .

From Governor Jerome's message to the Legislature, January 7, 1881, Begole's message to the Legislature, January 8, 1885, and Alger's message to the Legislature, January 6, 1887, in George N. Fuller (ed.), *Messages of the Governors* (Lansing: Michigan Historical Commission, 1927), III, 372-373, 504-505, 559-560.

Governor Begole

The act establishing a bureau of immigration places it under the supervision of the Governor. He draws the necessary funds from the State treasury, audits its bills, and pays them from the funds so drawn. He is, therefore, in a position where he becomes intimately acquainted with its operations and uses. After two years careful observation of its working I am of the opinion that the Immigration Bureau should be abolished. As I found it organized there was a Commissioner at a yearly salary of $2,000, and an assistant Commissioner at a salary of $1,500. The expenses for office rent, postage, stationery, incidental expenses, and bills for advertising amount to nearly $5,000 per annum. During the past two years it has distributed over 50,000 copies of the book "Michigan and its Resources" in English, besides small amounts of the German and French editions. The yearly cost for books which are furnished by the State printer is over $3,000, making the entire annual cost of the Bureau about $11,500.

Nearly a year ago I dispensed with the services of the Commissioner. Since that time the efficient Assistant Commissioner has attended to all the duties previously performed by both except drawing the Commissioner's salary. I did not feel at liberty to interfere any farther, but have permitted the Bureau to run as I found it, leaving it to the legislature to determine its future.

The operations of the Bureau have, I think, been disastrous to our workingmen. In numerous newspapers of this and other countries, it has been advertised that Michigan is a desirable place to emigrate to, and that her official commissioner at Detroit is prepared to give all necessary information, and will forward to any person who applies for it, free of expense, an interesting book giving valuable information on the subject. Persons out of employment, or dissatisfied with their condition, might fairly take it for granted that they were very much wanted in Michigan, or else the State authorities would not go to all this trouble and expense in the matter. The result has been that our labor market has been overcrowded from abroad, and this, too, at a time when our laboring men were suffering for want of remunerative employment.

It is possible that the operations of the Bureau may have aided railroad and other corporations to dispose of some of their lands. Indeed, some uncharitable persons claim that it was originally organized to afford free advertising for these corporations.

I recommend that the Immigration Bureau be immediately abolished and its effects transferred to the State Land Office, where all inquiries in regard to lands owned by the State, and all legitimate demands for the book, "Michigan and its Resources," can be met with but slight expense to the State.

. . . .

Governor Alger

Another great problem that must be solved in the near future is the one of immigration. Two years ago I recommended the continuance of the Commissionership of Immigration, but the Legislature saw fit to abolish the office, and I am now satisfied that they were much wiser than I. An examination of the records of our asylums, prisons, poorhouses and jails, will startle you when you find the great per cent of inmates that are foreign born. Bad people of all classes and conditions, criminals, paupers, partially insane, cripples, aged and infirm, are dumped upon our shores, having been sent from foreign countries here because it is much cheaper to pay steerage fare for them across the waters than to keep them, and they spring up in our jails, prisons, poorhouses, and asylums, and are supported by the tax payers of our State. While I believe it is for the best interests of this country to invite people, no matter how large the numbers, to come here from foreign lands, provided they are healthful in body and in mind, capable of earning a living, and of making good citizens during time of peace, and who would be willing in time of war, should that ever come, to take up arms to defend this country, yet I would for ever exclude the class first referred to, and would not allow a person to immigrate to this country who cannot present a consul's certificate as to soundness of body, mind, and character. As I said before, this land of ours should not be a dumping ground for these paupers, nor should disturbers of the peace, such as Nihilists and Anarchists, from other countries be tolerated here. These are the disturbing elements, and an element that is growing in strength in our midst. I recommend that a joint resolution be adopted, asking our congressmen to urge that laws be enacted carrying out these views.

Another matter should receive your attention. There is, as you well know, on the western shores of this great country a horde of Chinese Pagans. They come from a country where the whole population of the United States in numbers could be taken from and scarcely missed. Their immigration to this country should be for ever stopped. They are not fit subjects to become citizens, they have no interest in this government, they send all their earnings back to their native land, and when they have accumulated a small sum they return there only to send out, to take their places, hordes of similar people. They disgrace labor; they will work for wages— and lay up the greater portion of their earnings—that will not support a white man. They are a "upas tree" [sic] to the growth of this country. I recommend that you urge upon our members of Congress the necessity of the enactment of a law that shall for ever forbid another one of that race from landing in this country. We have no use for them, and the sooner stringent laws are passed prohibiting them from coming here, the better it will be for the country.

The mormon question ought to be settled at once. Polygamy should be strangled now, and I hope you will urge our members of Congress to take immediate steps to consummate this much desired object. It is a blot upon our flag and a disgrace to the nation.

3: Michigan Matures:
Life Before the Turn of the Century

U. P. Hedrick, in an affectionate memoir of his boyhood, captures much of the essence of nineteenth-century rural and small-town life in his book, *The Land of the Crooked Tree*. The setting is Harbor Springs, a beautiful small town situated very near the top of the lower peninsula on Lake Michigan. He describes the coming of the railroad to Harbor Springs, a major event in the history of the town, and the depot that became the focus for social life in that community.

The Coming of the Railroad

U. P. HEDRICK

The children in our family came to think that a railroad was the mainspring of the world. An engine and the cars it pulled, we thought, would bring the grists of the world to our doors. There could be no peace in the family until my brother and I had crossed Little Traverse Bay to see a railroad.

At last a day was appointed, and Father set about preparing our minds for what we should see. The engine was an iron horse that breathed out smoke and steam. We should hear the whistle, the neigh of the iron horse, long before we saw it. No, a car was not like a big wagon box, but like a long room, furnished with seats, lighted by lamps through which ran a rope that rang a bell, the bell cord to be touched only by the conductor.

'Where does the train come from?' we asked.

'The train,' Father said, 'comes from Fort Wayne, through Kalamazoo, Grand Rapids, Big Rapids, Reed City, Cadillac, Kalkaska, and Mancelona.'

Father called the names in the manner of a train announcer.

From *The Land of the Crooked Tree*, pp. 91-94, 96-98. Copyright 1948 by Oxford University Press, Inc. Reprinted by permission.

We had to cross the bay on the little steamboat, *North Star.* Riding on a boat seemed a mean and contemptible way to travel, so slow that we were afraid the train would have come and gone before we landed. At last we were on the wharf, up the bank, through the town, and at the railroad station. The rails shone in the afternoon sun, two glistening tracks of steel. On either side newly thrown banks of sand gleamed like heaps of gold. The arrival of the train was the event of the day in the village, and now a crowd was gathering.

Before the long-drawn, quavering shriek of the engine ended, we saw the monster coming, emitting an enormous smudge of black smoke, a cloud of steam trailing behind, unfolding into wreaths of gold and silver in the hazy afternoon sunlight. I held my breath and could scarcely keep tears of fright from my eyes as, with grinding, whining wheels, clanging bell, and hissing steam, the engine came to a stop.

Father tried to point out the parts of the engine: boiler, steam cylinders, pumps, whistle, headlight, governor, valves; but I was more interested in the engineer and fireman than in the engine. When the train had stopped, two sooty, grimy creatures stepped down from a little boxlike room in the engine and began to pour oil into glistening valves and to rub the outer organs of the iron horse. Were they a part of our world? They spoke to no one, looked neither to right nor left, were concerned only with the monster in their charge.

At last Father succeeded in pulling us away from the engine and led us wonderingly from car to car, explaining as best he could brakes, couplings, and bell ropes. We gazed with amazement at the shining wood, the red plush, the hanging lamps, the big panes of glass, and the brass fittings. To me, coming from a wilderness home, a passenger car seemed like a room in a gorgeous palace; the conductor and brakeman with blue uniforms and brass buttons were high court officials.

A few weeks before, *Uncle Tom's Cabin* had been on the stage in our village. A month of bright sunshine had not erased from my mind the whipping of Uncle Tom. The gray old porter on the Pullman at the end of the train was to me another Uncle Tom, and I wanted to see if his back was scarred with the cruel lash of some Simon Legree. Father, as a Southerner, rather contemptuous of *Uncle Tom's Cabin,* had said that the Uncle Tom in the play was not a 'nigger' but a white man 'made up.' The porter on this train, therefore, was the first Negro I had ever seen.

Long before we had inspected the whole train, the engine, with a series of coughs, snorts, and bell-clangings, started jerkily to back, and my brother and I raced down the track to see a switch work.

It had been a great day. It was marred only by our forgetting to put coppers on the rails.

A few years later the railroad came to Harbor Springs. To children in this little nook before the railroad came, the great world beyond had been 'the outside.' With the coming of the railroad we became part of a world of which we had heard much, but of which very few had firsthand knowledge. For centuries life in the Land of the Crooked Tree had been unhurried; now there was a hurly-burly of activity.

The railroad quickly transformed our whole region. Good roads were built; at every four corners there was a schoolhouse, mill, or shop; the population multiplied apace; frame houses began to take the place of log structures; people dressed better; and a barefooted man with long hair was called a 'mossback.' Everyone talked about railroads, steamboats, mills, stores, town lots. We children in the forest thought there were few places in all America that could offer so many and so great attractions as our town.

Harbor Springs became notable overnight. Stores were built along streets yet without sidewalks. Soon we had a courthouse and a hall. Three hotels and six saloons could not keep the fleshpots filled; much eating and drinking were required to lubricate business. Two newspapers spread knowledge, thus depriving us of the bliss of ignorance; and four new churches were organized to give the town various doctrines.

. . . .

The railroad brought to our little village a station that we all called the 'dee-po.' Quickly the station became a community center. It was a place where those of us who came from the country could rest at all times and warm up in winter; a place where people came to take the train, and where those who had been 'outside' again reached home; tourists, drummers, land buyers, and businessmen of all descriptions came on the train, preferring to travel by rail rather than by water. The telegraph office was in the railroad station, and the first telephone in town was put in the depot a few years after the railroad came.

This small-town depot was a near relative of the big-town railroad station, but it was as different as a countryman is from his city cousin. It was not a place where people rushed in and out at train times, a driving, bustling place of business. As a news exchange and a village forum it was a rival of the store, the hotel, and the saloon.

Without the depot, we should all have been more nearly hermits and introverts.

The depot was a beautiful bit of architecture. It was rectangular in shape, perhaps 25 by 50 feet. It was built of lapped, planed lumber, and the roof overhung the walls on all sides, the overhanging parts being supported by elaborate, heavy cornices. The windows and windowpanes were larger than those of any other building in town. It made very evident that the G. R. & I. had money to burn. The building was painted dark green.

The depot was heated by a large acorn coal stove, a most wonderful heating apparatus. The fuel box was several feet high, its fat belly at least three feet in diameter. This fuel container sat on a highly ornamental base a foot high; the base, in turn, on three curved legs. Around the belly, standing out several inches, was a bright half-round fender on which you could have put your feet had there been chairs. Above the fuel box was a metal canopy that reflected the heat downward, so that the lower half of the room was as warm as the upper. The rectangular door had small panes of isinglass, its edges crimped like a pie crust. The door bore the legend, in big bossed letters, Jewel Stoves & Ranges, Detroit, Mich. Under the door was a projecting iron bar over which you fitted a shaker to shake down the ashes; under this another door opening into the ash pit. My description does not do justice to this depot stove, because from top to bottom it was corrugated up and down and round and round, with much ornamental scroll-work—truly a work of art.

This stove stood in the exact center of the waiting room, and rested on a heavy zinc-covered thickness of hardwood planks to keep the floor from catching fire when the stove was red hot. To me, the most wonderful thing about the stove was that it burned coal, the first I had ever seen. Occasionally I was permitted to shake down the ashes and put coal on the fire, feeling as I did so that I was well on the way to becoming a railroad engineer.

Besides the stove the only other furnishings in the station were heavy board benches, part of the building and immovable. Here one might sit and, if the station master did not object, lie and take a nap. There were a front and back door, and a third one by which the agent and trainmen entered an apartment reserved for them; in it a large case held tickets and on a table were telegraph instruments and eventually a telephone. In this sanctum there were several chairs in which the agent, his assistant, trainmen, and privileged friends sat.

The greatest days for the railroad were in the late 1880's when the excursions came toward the end of summer. Season after season, there were several of these bringing thousands of people from regions far to the south. Friends and relatives came to stay with nearly every white family in the land. Excursion rates to the north were only half the regular rates; but not those to the south; the G. R. & I. wanted the northern country settled. Everyone expecting guests was at the station to meet excursion trains. Hotel runners, hackmen, and the pursers of waiting steamboats were on hand for customers. The boats at neighboring wharves were waiting for excursionists who wanted to go to Charlevoix, Mackinac Island, Beaver Island, points in the Upper Peninsula, or westward to northern Wisconsin.

Hedrick was not a resident of Harbor Springs but a farm boy. In his reminiscences of his boyhood, he captures accurately and without any self-pity the hard yet satisfying daily routine of the farm in upper Michigan.

A Day on the Farm

U. P. HEDRICK

My day began with building fires. At five o'clock every day in the year, Father called:

'Boys! Boys!' to which we were supposed to answer, usually in chorus: 'Yes!'

If a second call was needed, it came as an ominous:

'Wilbur! Ulysses!'

After the second call, I pattered downstairs in bare feet and shirt tails past Father's bedroom door.

Before even putting on socks, I built the kitchen fire.

All was in readiness. The night before, however late I had gone to bed, or however tired I may have been, preparations for the morning

From *The Land of the Crooked Tree*, pp. 175-189. Copyright 1948 by Oxford University Press, Inc. Reprinted by permission.

fire were made. In front of the stove, a pile of shavings, whittled from a pine stick, were laid out; in another pile were a dozen kindlings of pine; and in a third heap were sticks of dry maple wood. It took less than a minute to put all in the stove, and touch the shavings with a match.

Our kitchen stove was a small furnace. It was big enough to warm half the house, and had a fire box that burned twenty cords of wood in the course of the year. The oven was commodious enough to bake a small pig. Its back part was a reservoir to heat water. On wash days water was also heated in a washboiler. The stove had three rows of holes, two to a row, over which there were kettles, either on uncovered openings or on the round lids. The lids were removed with a stovehook, a most important implement, which Mother was always losing.

Much of the successes of the coming day depended on my success in making the morning fire. Mother would be down in a minute. Her teakettle and coffeepot were ready to boil on the back of the stove. On the kitchen table was a pan of sliced potatoes ready to fry; a jar of buckwheat batter stood on a small stand near the back of the stove from November to May—from May to November, batter for flour or corn-meal pancakes; eggs, sausage, ham, or bacon were ready to fry. At half-past five work stopped for breakfast. Long before half-past six, we were again at the chores; by seven, all hands must be in the fields.

Before the kitchen stove much of the life of our family was enacted. There the children of the household came after school, from work, and from doing chores in the icy cold and blizzards of winter. Never was the living room so cheery, nor had one the pleasant smells of cooking, or a singing teakettle. There, one of us on each side of the stove rested our stockinged feet on a stick of firewood, to thaw or toast. Behind the stove and the wood box, Flash, the dog, snored, and the cat purred away her nine lives. No gas, or electric, or any other than a wood stove was ever as dependable and comfortable as our kitchen stove.

The kitchen was quite large enough to serve as a living room. Mother did not bother her head about saving steps and would have suffocated in a modern kitchenette. In it were chairs for all the family. After the evening meal we went to the living room, a family group until Father and Mother went to bed.

In the living room, Father and Mother had special chairs in which we children seldom sat. Father's was a heavy armchair of curly maple; Mother's a low rocking chair, in which she could gently rock back and forth; it, too, was of polished curly maple; both had cushions—once soft. As a tiny child I was permitted to sit in ream was stubborn and churning might

d days, butter 'came' in large golden
d out with the cream skimmer and then
he milk was squeezed out; the butter was
d compact cylinder, and stored in a cool
hbors liked unsalted butter; we liked it

lk and on churning days, if he was not too
e, came in and finished with pleasure the
ed. Before Mother could take the butter out
had lifted the lid and with a long-handled
ull quart of creamy buttermilk with flakes of
He drank the dipperful to the last swallow.
radise!' he would say.

ly one chore as unpleasant as churning; he had
calves how to drink milk out of a pail—he
her of young bovines. The first three days in its
milk from its mother as nature intended; then it
drink from a bucket so that humans may have
er 'broke' a calf into feeding itself, the belliger-
g her emphatic disapproval. The calves were kept
ning the cowyard. In this pen my brother began
is calves.

calves got only the skimmed milk and this had to
warmed the milk on the kitchen stove and poured
n bucket, at which point my brother took over,
messy, ill-smelling enclosure, and began 'breaking-
ose the cleanest corner and backed the calf tightly
dled the infant bovine and called for the milk. This
nded him, he placed it in front of the calf and forced
n into the pail, all the while keeping an eye on the
er. Lastly he stuck two fingers in the youngster's
ushed its head into the milk so that it drank or
eanwhile the calf was anything but quiet; it struggled
kward, sideways, up and down. Only strong arms and
e juvenile cow from breaking loose or upsetting the
as few as three or as many as six lessons the calf's
as completed; at least, fingers were no longer inserted in
In a week, the calf eagerly awaited the coming of the
two weeks a little corn meal or wheat 'shorts' was added
k diet, all this to be followed in a month by a transfer to
e.

Mother's comfortable rocker. Death had left no vacant chairs in our household, and there were none until my brother and I went to college.

The living-room stove also played its part in the life of the family. By the time supper was ready in winter we had thawed out and toasted our feet, put on our foot wear, and taken our places at the kitchen table. After supper, my brother and I scrambled for the best reading place at the round table in the living room, never taking Father's throne nearest the double-burner kerosene lamp. After the supper dishes were done, Mother and my sister joined us; during winter evenings, we children read or studied. If the kitchen stove was the heart of the family, surely the living-room stove was its brains.

Our living-room stove was an expensive luxury; it cost the enormous sum of $60, as much as our Singer sewing machine. It was in shape a huge acorn and was called the 'Acorn,' made in Dowagiac, Michigan, as we were told by the silver letters on the nickel foot rest. It was roomy enough to hold several chunks of wood, from which, through the square of mica in the door of the stove, we could see flames curling from chunk to chunk. This sturdy stove sat on a heavy square of figured zinc, and, since every winter's night it was red-hot, it must never stand too close to wooden walls. Mother kept the body black and the nickel scrollwork shining. At the top, a brightly gleaming spire pointed heavenward. In early morning, when I shook down the fire, the nestled chunks of maple, beech, or birch burst into bright orange-red flames with bluish curls, popping and shooting sparks, each of the three woods burning a different colored flame.

It was always Mother who wound the one-day clock. Its power was heavy iron weights; its works were brass; it struck the hour with a pleasant musical sound, very comforting to sick children lying awake at night. The clock was made in Waterbury, Connecticut, in 1864, and was encased in beautiful mahogany; under the large, Roman figures was a very good picture of George Washington.

The two stoves called for other chores than building fires. Mother reserved May Day and the first day in October for her sons to move stoves and clean stovepipes. Half of our woodshed, all winter wood having been burned, was turned into a summer kitchen, the other half was kept for storage. Into these rooms the stoves were moved. If the weather was bright and sunny, the stoves were moved and stovepipes cleaned one at a time, just after the midday meal, taking two or three hours for each. If the weather was rainy, an afternoon sufficed to move the two.

Our stoves were heavy. We had to move them on hardwood rollers. First the rollers were properly placed under a stove. Then with strong handspikes, with a chunk of wood to give leverage, the stove, one corner after another, was pried up, the stove legs removed, and the stove lowered gently on the rollers. Then we moved it with tugs, grunts, and as strong words as Mother would let us use, to its new resting place.

Now, of course, was the time to clean stovepipes. Moving the stoves required a little heavy work but was not so bad. Cleaning the stovepipes was a nasty, dirty job. Our stovepipes did not run straight up and down. From the stove the pipe went up to within a foot of the ceiling, then made a right-angle turn to the middle of the room, then passed into the room above into a large drum which held heat. Father's and Mother's room, and the one in which my sister slept were warmed by drums; the room in which my brother and I slept was pretty close to the temperature outside. It was this complicated system of pipes and drums that had to be cleaned.

The first step was to spread newspapers wherever soot might fall or tracks might go. Next the wires that held the horizontal pipes to the ceiling were untied. Then each of us tackled a right-angle turn. Eventually a strong tug brought the pipes apart, there being no way to prevent soot from dropping below. Next the pipe was taken from the short neck of the stove.

Wood for our house fires came from the forest in thick slabs a foot wide and eighteen inches long, and was corded up to dry through the summer for the next winter. Nothing but straight-grained, knot-free beech, maple, and yellow birch went into our stoves, though several cords of knotty chunks were saved to keep fire overnight in the sitting-room stove, which Father regularly chunked before going to bed.

The firewood was split into slabs as it was sawed in the woods, and it was my work to split these slabs for the kitchen stove all through the winter. It was a rather pleasant chore to split slabs of wood into pieces small enough for the kitchen stove. A single blow of an ax split a slab; a tough slab went into the chunk pile. Of all the chores I had to do, day in and day out, splitting wood and filling the wood boxes were as agreeable as any.

There were good fat pine kindlings in plenty. In clearing our land we found on every acre several old pine stumps belonging to a century or more before, when a forest fire had burned great pine trees to the ground. These ancient remains had to come out and were cut up for kindling. Every stump was full of pine fat and from them we split the best kindling wood in the world.

One of our luxuries was a commodious woodshed. It was not

Before we leave butter and milk, something must be said about two other milk products, ice cream and cottage cheese. Once every two or three weeks, we made ice cream. In our sub-Arctic land, ice was plentiful, summer and winter; with several cows, cream, too, was always on hand. Our freezer was a wooden pail holding three or four gallons, in the middle of which a heavy metal can, holding a gallon, stood upright, supported top and bottom; in this can was a flanged dasher. With the can well covered, an ingenious device permitted a crank to be fastened to the dasher so that it was turned round and round.

First, a smallish cake of ice was brought from the ice house, doused with water to wash off the sawdust, then broken into chunks and put in an old grain bag, in which it was hammered into crushed ice with the woodsman's maul kept in the woodshed. This crushed ice was tamped about the cream container in the freezer with a liberal supply of coarse salt.

Just what Mother's mixture was for ice cream, I cannot say; it may have been pure cream, flavored with coffee, caramel, or vanilla. Chocolate we did not have. I doubt if she used eggs or a custard, as modern cooks do. When a little short of cream, Mother made an ice cream pie, in which pure cream was frozen and put in a pie crust such as she made for lemon or pumpkin pies. This was a favorite pie in our family the year round.

There was never trouble in getting a boy to turn the crank of an ice-cream freezer, especially if, as sometimes happened, he could stay at home from church to do it. Besides, there was always a reward. Whoever froze the cream could 'lick the dasher.' When the crank of the freezer could no longer be turned, ice and salt were carefully removed from the top of the cream container; the dasher, with its four wooden flanges, was pulled out, always thickly covered with ice cream, very delicious an hour before dinner.

The making of cottage cheese was work wholly for Mother, a product she always called by its Pennsylvania Dutch name, smear-case. When skimmed milk was left over, after feeding calves, Mother made smearcase. A two-gallon crock of sour milk was set in a warm place near or on the back of the stove. In a day or overnight, little curds formed and floated in the whey. The curds were strained out and put in a muslin bag to drip for a few hours—after which they had become smearcase. After being seasoned with salt, a little pepper, and a generous touch of sweet cream, smearcase was ready for the table. Our family ate it mixed with about half as much apple butter. Whey that dripped from the smearcase bag, when flavored with a little lemon juice and sugar, was a frequent drink, as has been said, for workers in the field and for threshers.

My brother gave the cows their hay and grain. Cows gave little milk in winter unless fed some green food; as we had no silo, instead of ensilage our cows were fed carrots, rutabagas, and pumpkins. These had to be cleaned and cut. The pumpkins were easily prepared; we took an ax and cut them in chunks as large as eggs, discarding the seeds, and fed them with a little chopped grain to the animals. But pumpkins lasted only until the middle of December, after which, until spring, the cows had to have carrots and rutabagas.

Cutting these root crops in winter was most disagreeable. The work had to be done in the root cellar, as close and dark as the Black Hole of Calcutta, lighted only with a smoky kerosene lantern. The roots had been cleaned when they were stored, but each one had to be rubbed with a coarse cloth and then cut in pieces small enough to keep the cows from gulping them down and choking. To be sure, we wore grain-bag mittens, but our hands were always cold, always so chapped and cracked that we were ashamed to have them seen in school. This chore had to be done morning after morning all the winter through, before breakfast. What a chore!

Other odd jobs every boy bred in the country had to do before the advent of power machinery were turning a fanning mill, a corn sheller, and a grindstone. There are worse chores than shelling corn and cleaning grain, though few worse than turning a grindstone on a farm that is being carved out of a forest. Shelling corn and cleaning grain with a fanning mill are infrequent chores, not to be dreaded day after day, as is turning the grindstone. We shelled corn and cleaned grain only for seed sowing, and when corn and grain were to be taken to the mill to be chopped into coarse meal.

There were special times for cleaning grain. Wheat had to be run through the fanning mill soon after threshing, to provide clean seed for fall seeding. The second and main time came on cold, rainy days in late autumn when the weather prohibited work out of doors. At this time we usually had a hundred or more bushels of wheat and about the same amount of oats, and some years half that quantity of rye. All grain was cleaned preparatory to grinding at the mill for stock food. Turning the crank of a fanning mill hour after hour was terribly monotonous. Because of poor threshing machines, our grain had much chaff and dust, which covered one from head to foot after even a short turn at cleaning it. One man, more often two, handled the grain, which was brought in grain bags just as it had come from the threshing machine; a second man put the grain in bags to go to the mill. Another operation in cleaning grain was to remove, every hour or two, the chaff, weed seeds, dust, and dirt that the mill had separated from the grain. This refuse was kept for poultry.

Shelling corn was much more pleasant than cleaning grain. It was harder to turn the crank of the sheller than to furnish power for the fanning mill, but there was much less dust and no chaff at all. Besides, it was a rather pretty sight to see husked ears of corn, each ear with exactly as many rows as any other, go into the sheller. The brightly colored bushel box that came with the sheller slowly filled with the golden dented kernels of the dent corns or the reddish-yellow smooth flint corns, each kernel a nugget of gold, either kind the most beautiful of all grains. There were always more bushels of corn than of all other grains put together. Some farmers sent it to the mill to be chopped, cob and all, for cows. This the farm papers of that day told us made fat, sleek cattle.

Another farm chore was oiling the harnesses. Late in the autumn, before steady cold weather came, a day was set, usually a Saturday, for this annual event. The real work was done in the woodshed, but water and oil had to be heated in the kitchen. Father superintended the work and the hired men did the greasing. Mother made an awful fuss over 'harness day,' when four or five males tramped into her kitchen with dirty feet and oily hands to borrow her kitchenware; she scolded one and all, and we all took it meekly.

Father made his own harness oil from a formula that called for tallow and unsalted lard, made black as pitch with lampblack. Always the harness oil was made a day or two in advance, and on the day when operations began was warmed up to a temperature as hot as the hands could stand.

The work on 'harness day' started with taking harnesses apart. Woe betide the person who mixed the parts of sets!

What boy, in these days of automobiles, can name the parts of a harness and tell at sight a single from a double harness, a buggy harness from one used in farm operations? Whatever the kind of harness, there were for the head, bridle, blinds, check reins, bit, lines with numerous buckles; the breast harness included breast-band, or a collar and harness with yoke straps and traces for a single or tugs for a double harness; the parts of the body harness were the saddle, bellyband, crupper, hip straps, and breeching. In a double harness there was the complicated crossing of the two guiding lines held in the driver's hands to the four ends attached to the two bits in the horses' mouths. It was quite a task to take a harness apart, and there might be much trouble if the parts of each harness were separated.

Mother's wash tubs were brought into service for the first operation in greasing harnesses. They were half-filled with hot water into which a half pound of soda had been added. The leather parts of the harness then went into the tubs and were scrubbed with a stiff brush on a washboard until all the grease and dirt were removed. When the leather had been hung for a few minutes for the water to drip off, the hot harness grease was rubbed in. Meanwhile, my brother and I had been polishing the metal parts, chiefly buckles, to silver brightness. By the end of the long day the half-dozen harnesses for the farm's horses had been washed, greased, repaired, and put together for another year's service.

One naturally passes from greasing harnesses to greasing footgear. All the year, excepting the four or five cold months of winter, the men on our farm wore shoes and boots made of leather. In the rains, snows, and dews of the warmer months, all leather footwear became hard, stiff, and foxy red, unless greased once a week. The same harness oil of tallow, lampblack, and unsalted lard was used, but the routine of greasing was much different. We sat near the warm kitchen stove, oven door open, one hand thrust into a boot or shoe, the other applying the grease. It required quite half an hour to do a good job of greasing a pair of shoes. We rubbed and squeezed the leather as the warm grease was applied, and then held the boot in the oven to 'warm in' a minute or two, repeating the process three or four times until the leather was soft and the inside of the boot moist with grease. The greased shoes were put near the stove to dry overnight. Since greasing boots was a hot, sweaty operation, we waited until bedtime to do the work and at its finish took a rub down with warm water.

Winter footwear of heavy rubbers was spread under the kitchen stove at night, and the next morning found them warm and dry— except when the fire burned low or on a cold night went out. In that case, the next morning the soggy boots were stiff with ice. Until long after breakfast on such mornings, the conversation, too, was frigid.

Another annual autumn chore, about the last before winter set in, was banking the house. Our earliest houses did not have stone foundations. Their framework rested on pillars of sturdy logs down to the bottom of the cellar, and stood perhaps a foot above the surface of the ground. The part aboveground was solidly planked in, but planks, doubled and tripled, could not keep out the searching cold of a northern Michigan winter, and the house had to be 'banked up' to keep frost out of the cellar and from working through into the house to chill feet and legs in spite of red-hot stoves.

For banking some of our neighbors used straw, others manure. We found sawdust cheapest and best. Stakes were driven eighteen inches from the house in sufficient number to support heavy planks a foot wide. When the planks were put in place, and the space so made was filled with sawdust, well tramped down, a second layer of planks was put up and a second filling of sawdust made. With such a covering encircling the house, we could feel comfortable indoors when the days grew short and Arctic gales raged outside.

Until after I left the farm there were no bedsprings in our house. Our solidly made beds had slats, on which were homemade bed-ticks. (We did not know, or at least never used, the word mattress.) Mother made her bedticks out of bedticking cloth, which could be purchased at dry-goods stores. The flattish bedtick was filled with oat straw, the tick being closed with a long stout drawstring. For the first few nights the ticks seemed mountain high, but soon flattened down to two feet, and by the end of the year to several inches. An autumn chore for my brother and me was to fill the bedticks.

There were never enough beds in our home for the visitors who came for a night or longer. In winter, when the house was overrun with guests, my brother and I gave up our beds and slept on a 'shakedown.' A 'shakedown,' in our house, was a blanket spread on the floor of the living room or kitchen. In summer the hired men and the two boys in our family slept on 'shakedowns' in the haymow.

Asked to name her most arduous work, I am sure my sister would have said 'cleaning lamp chimneys and lanterns,' a daily task as long as she was in her father's house. We burned kerosene oil and lots of it. Lamps and lanterns had to be filled and their globes cleaned, lamps one day, lanterns the next.

There must have been eight or ten lamps in the house. There were three large double-burner lamps: one in the living room, another on the dining-room table, and a third in the kitchen. There was a single-burner for each bedroom. Common items for Saturday's trading in the village stores were a five-gallon can of kerosene oil, a potato stuck on the spout to keep the oil from spattering, and lamp chimneys and lantern globes. As often as lamps and lanterns were filled with oil, the splotches of black smoke on the inside of chimneys and globes had to be cleaned; remnants of old dresses, sheets, aprons, and shirts were always saved for this work.

It was amazing how many lanterns were used on our farm. For eight months in the year every male on the place had to have a lantern to do early morning chores and to finish up in the evening.

Whoever drove out at night, except when there was a full moon or in the snow whiteness of winter, hung a lantern beneath the front of the vehicle. Each of the two or three persons who worked about a sick animal in the barn needed a lantern. Whoever went to visit a neighbor on a moonless night carried a lantern. Wherever a flash-light would be used now, a lamp or lantern was needed.

Many a time the sight of a light from a lamp or lantern brought cheer to my heart. A gleaming lantern, coming or going, far down a lonely road was a most welcome sight; and a lantern in hand was a most comfortable companion. When I was coming home late on a dark night, especially in a gale in winter, its tiny wick all aglow warmed me all the way through. There was nothing comparable to lamps and lanterns in our isolated home to raise the morale of its inhabitants, whether they were outside or inside the house.

The dentists of Michigan, seeking to improve their profession, to eliminate untrained quacks, and to stabilize the fee schedule for dental work, formed an association in 1856. Their meetings were not marked by any notable scientific advancements, though they afforded the dentists an opportunity for a rare outing and perhaps a time to enjoy special entertainment, for which the 1890s became famous. A Victorian-styled banquet, including an elaborate menu with all the trimmings, sentimental music, and lengthy speeches, was the highlight of the annual meeting and reflected in general a life style of the times.

The development of professions and their impact on shaping society has received only modest attention from historians on the national level and even less on the state level. C. B. Burr's compilation, *Medical History of Michigan* (Minneapolis, 1930), has some information on Michigan's doctors, while R. M. Warner's *Profile of a Profession, A History of the Michigan State Dental Association* (Detroit, 1964) discusses dentists. A glimpse of the life style of the 1890s can be seen in the photographs of Vol. II of George S. May's *Pictorial History of Michigan* (Grand Rapids, 1969).

A Victorian Banquet

In the evening the Association was the invited guest of the dentists of Saginaw, at the beautiful Hotel Vincent. The following

From *The Dental Register,* XLVI (December, 1892), 602-604.

account of the proceedings is taken from the Saginaw *Courier-Herald*.

The handsome dining room of the Hotel Vincent was last evening turned into a floral bower. The room was banked and filled with potted plants and palms; from every conceivable nook and corner hung festoons of roses and handsome vines. In the rear of the room Boos' superb orchestra was stationed. Some 18 small tables were set for the guests; at each place a buttonhole bouquet was to be found and one of the handsomest menu cards ever offered to a banqueted party. Thus arrangements were made for the banquet tendered by "The Dentists of Saginaw" to "The Michigan Dental Association." At 8:30 the guests were seated and partook of the palatable repast which the management of the Hotel Vincent had prepared with great care, and which consisted of the following menu:

New York Counts, Broiled Whitefish, Saratoga Chips, Beef Tenderloin, Mushrooms, Spring Chicken, Water Cress, Fried Frog Legs, New Potatoes, Vienna Rolls, Tea Biscuit, Plain Bread, Assorted Cake, Strawberries, Fruit, Crackers and Cheese, Tea and Coffee.

During the discussion of the eatables the orchestra rendered several selections and all were placed in a good humor. At the end of the last course the Arion quartette, composed of Messrs. Evans, Watrous, Bostwick and Mearns, rendered "Hark! The Trumpet Calleth," in such an acceptable manner that the dentists demanded another song, when they sang "Who Built the Ark?" which pleased the audience immensely.

President Corns then arose and in a brief speech returned thanks for the elegant supper and for the courteous treatment which they had all received from the management of the Hotel Vincent. He then called upon Rev. George F. Warren, who spoke a few words, and who was followed by Dr. J. Taft, Dean of the Michigan University. Dr. Taft responded to the toast "The Progress of our Profession." He said: "The progress that has been made in the dental profession can only be realized by those who have taken part in the great work." He cited the time when the blacksmith or the cobbler could extract a tooth as well as a dentist, and when a dentist was considered but little better than a thief, when the medical profession looked upon the dental profession as a miserable art. He then showed how at the present day they rank high in the professional walks of life and how the medical fraternity invite dentists to become members of their associations. In conclusion he said: "The progress has been upward and onward, and as the responsibility has increased so has the profession advanced to meet all requirements."

He was followed by Dr. N. S. Hoff, of Ann Arbor, who responded to the toast "The Young Members." He entreated the young men of the profession not to give up their studies on the completion of their college course; nor to develop their business ability to the detriment of their professional ability. His remarks furnished much food for thought for the young men of the profession, and were well received.

Dr. George L. Field, of Detroit, responded to the toast "Our Lady Patients." The doctor soon had his listeners in a roar of laughter and kept them in good humor throughout his remarks.

Dr. A. T. Metcalf, of Kalamazoo, responded to the toast "Our Saginaw Friends." The doctor did not confine himself much to his subject, but he told a number of good anecdotes which enlivened the dentists.

Dr. J. A. Robinson, of Jackson, was then called upon. Dr. Robinson is one of, if not the oldest practicing dentist in the United States, being 80 years of age, and having been in active practice for the last 57 years. The old gentleman is as hale and hearty as can be, and his short talk was of great interest to all. He told of his early practice and the contempt he was held in. His talk was bright and wholesome throughout and showed that the doctor is a great lover of his profession.

The quartette then sang "Good night," after which the Orchestra played "Auld Lang Syne," and the banquet was brought to a close by all singing the old familiar song.

4: Progressivism

Hazen Pingree, mayor of Detroit from 1889 to 1896 and governor of Michigan, 1897 to 1901, was always outspoken in presenting his views. In his excellent biography, *Reform in Detroit: Hazen S. Pingree and Urban Politics* (New York, 1969), Melvin G. Holli analyzes Pingree's pioneering role as an urban reformer of major significance. While Pingree was governor, the Michigan legislature was a recipient of his messages, often sharp attacks phrased in acerbic language against members of the legislature who had opposed his reform measures. His final opportunity to evaluate his administration and to criticize those who had opposed him came in his final message to the legislature at the conclusion of his last term as governor. In a lengthy message, he called particular attention to his long struggle for equal taxation in the state, criticizing the opposition to this reform. He sought fair evaluation of the railroads, and although his term did not see the realization of this goal, as a result of his efforts the legislation was ultimately passed.

The following excerpt from Pingree's final message captures some of the flavor of the man, notes his attacks on the railroad interest, and calls attention to his other reforms: direct election of United States senators, municipal ownership of public utilities, and conservation.

A Record of Reform

HAZEN S. PINGREE

I enlisted as a private at the commencement of the civil war and have two honorable discharges, which I prize. I have been a citizen and taxpayer of Detroit since 1865. My ancestors fought for their country in both the Revolution and the war of 1812. I mention these facts to show that there is nothing in my record to indicate that I should not be treated with proper respect as an individual.

From Governor Pingree's message to the Legislature, January 9, 1901, in George N. Fuller (ed.), *Messages of the Governors* (Lansing: Michigan Historical Commission, 1927), IV, 291, 234-238, 248, 252, 254, 279-281, 308-311.

The office which I have held for the last four years should have commanded the respect of every loyal citizen in the State, whatever the opinion of myself may have been. That it did not command the respect of the people of Lansing is proved by the fact that during the whole four years of my term as Governor I have only once been invited to the home of a single resident of the capital city of Michigan. Can you point to a place in the whole United States where a Governor has been so treated by the citizens of a capital city?

I speak of this to show the conspiracy which has been entered into between the people of this city and the State. It is a well established fact that the people of Lansing live upon the State institutions and officers. They think that a man who does not empty his pocketbook here should have no respect shown him. Like parasites, they have fed so long upon the public officials and State institutions that they have no respect for any one except for what they can get out of him. The principal part of the population of Lansing lives upon the tips which they receive from the men who have been elected to office and the indirect emoluments which the State institutions bring. They have grown so accustomed to toadying to the wealthy interests which have conspired to ruin me that they have become a part of the conspiracy itself. Had I bowed down to the golden calf of wealth, this conspiracy would never have been formed and I would have had the entre [sic] to the social circles of Lansing.

I am glad to know, however, that the criticisms aimed at me have induced our new Governor to take up his residence in the capital city. He has my sympathy.

. . . .

During my public life, prior to my election as Governor in 1896, I was particularly impressed with the inequalities which existed in the assessment of property for purposes of taxation. The unequal distribution of the burden of taxation as between the large and small owners of property, was brought most forcibly to my attention. As I studied the question, it became more and more apparent to me how skillfully and stealthily the large property owners, especially incorporated companies, had manipulated the laws of the State, so as to shift this burden of taxation from themselves to the small property owners.

There has always been more or less complaint against the inequality of our tax laws, but never any persistent effort made to remedy the trouble. I resolved to make the problem of equalizing taxation the principal effort of my administration as Governor, appreciating full well, at the beginning, that it would be a hard and relentless contest against the most powerful and the richest interests in the State.

I found no difficulty in enlisting many bright and resourceful public men in this cause. Although long strides have been taken, and an immense amount of good accomplished, and while the problem is nearer solution than it has ever been, yet I cannot help but feel that if Colonel John Atkinson, the head and brains of the contest for equal taxation, had remained alive, the principle for which the people have fought today would be firmly established in the law of the State.

History of the contest.—While mayor of Detroit, my attention was first attracted to the methods by which large corporations escaped taxation, by the fact that, in that city, millions of dollars worth of real estate of railroads paid no taxes at all. I made efforts to place this property upon the rolls, and the contest was carried to the Legislature of 1891, before which body, in June, 1891, Hon. Don M. Dickinson made an able and unanswerable argument, as counsel for the city of Detroit.

This contest resulted in the disclosure of the fact that the railroads, throughout the State, were among the grossest offenders in tax-dodging. It was plainly apparent that, if equality in taxation was to be made possible, these corporations must be brought under the same laws as to taxation as other corporations and individuals.

Accordingly, during the regular session of the Thirty-ninth Legislature, which convened in January 1897, the "Atkinson bill" was first introduced. It provided for assessment by a State board of assessors of the property of railroad, telegraph, telephone, and express companies, at actual cash value. From that day to this the bill has been fought and its progress stubbornly contested by the corporations affected by it, with all of the agencies and methods which it is customary for such corporations to use.

The bill passed the House of Representatives, which was then, and always has been since then, immediately responsive to the wish of the people of the State in this matter. It met with defeat in the Senate. I had discussed the matter of railroad taxation somewhat in my message delivered at the commencement of the regular session of the Thirty-ninth Legislature. Upon May 6, 1897, later in the session, I transmitted an extended special message to the Legislature upon this subject, the matter then being under discussion.

On March 22, 1898, I convened the Thirty-ninth Legislature in special session for the purpose of enacting a law providing for ad valorem taxation of the property of railroad, telegraph, telephone, and express companies. Again the "Atkinson bill" was passed by the House, and again it was defeated in the Senate.

Equal taxation was the principal issue during the fall campaign of 1898, and a Legislature was elected with all of its members pledged absolutely to the enactment of the "Atkinson bill." In spite of this, a considerable number of members in both houses violated their pledges by employing filibustering tactics against the bill. It finally passed the House by an overwhelming majority. Action upon it was delayed in the Senate until just before the spring State election. Fearing the effect of failure to pass the bill upon the chances of the Republican party's nominees, the Senate passed it.

The constitutionality of the measure having been questioned, I caused a test case to be instituted in the State Supreme Court, upon the existing telephone tax law, which was identical in principle with the Atkinson bill, so that, if defective, the defects could be cured before the adjournment of the Legislature. The Atkinson law was declared unconstitutional by the court on April 26, 1899.

An effort was at once made to prepare a law upon substantially the same principle of ad valorem assessment as the Atkinson bill, but it was found impracticable to do so, under the decision of the Supreme Court. I transmitted a special message to the Fortieth Legislature upon this phase of the subject, on May 17, 1899.

In order to meet the universal demand for some legislation which would contribute to the solution of the vexed problem of "equal taxation," the last Legislature enacted a law (Approved June 23, 1899, Act No. 154, Public Acts 1899) creating a Board of State Tax Commissioners, charged with the duty of exercising supervisory control over officers administering the general tax laws of the State, and empowered in certain cases to review assessment rolls and correct the same and add thereto, and to provide for the assessment and taxation of property omitted from the assessment rolls. Among the duties of this board is the determination of the valuation of the properties of railroad and other corporations paying specific taxes.

I strongly recommended and urged the enactment of this law, and it passed during the last few days of the session. I regard it as the most important law ever enacted by a Michigan Legislature. It has certainly been more far-reaching in its consequences and more beneficent in its results, thus far, than even its most enthusiastic friends and advocates anticipated. I will discuss the results of the law and the work of the commissioners in another part of this message.

When it was finally determined that a bill along the lines of the Atkinson bill could not be framed to meet the constitutional objection pointed out by the decision of the Supreme court, a joint resolution was prepared and introduced providing for the submission to the people, at the next general election, of a constitutional amendment, so that when the Atkinson bill, or one similar to it, should be again enacted into law it would be a constitutional measure. This joint resolution passed the House, but received in the Senate the same treatment which all of the preceding equal taxation measures had received. It was defeated there and the Legislature adjourned without any further steps being taken towards the solution of the railroad taxation problem.

I convened the Fortieth Legislature in special session on December 18, 1899 for the purpose of passing a joint resolution for the submission to the people, at the next general election, of an amendment to the Constitution which would permit of the enactment of a law which would provide for the equal taxation of all property by the assessment of the same at its cash value. At this session the House passed the joint resolution by a vote of 86 to 8, but it was again defeated by the Senate, that body declining to permit the people to even express their wishes in the matter. At this session the House also passed measures providing for an increase in the rates of specific taxation of railroads, for the taxation of the property of copper and iron mines and for amendments to the special charters of railroads as to taxation, but all of these measures were defeated by the Senate.

I again called the Fortieth Legislature together in special session on October 10, 1900. At this session the House again passed the joint resolution providing for the submission to the people of equal taxation constitutional amendments. Fearing the effect of another refusal to comply with the wishes of the people, at the general election to be held in the succeeding month, the Senate passed this joint resolution.

The call convening this special session also included the subject of the repeal of the special charters of railroads. These special charters granted to certain railroads special privileges over all other railroads, among other things, in the matter of taxation and rates of passenger fare. At this special session the Legislature passed laws repealing all of these special charters and took, in so doing, a long step forward towards the equal taxation of railroad property. The railroads which were being operated under these special charters were the Michigan Central Railroad Company, The Lake Shore & Michigan Southern Railway Company, and the Detroit, Grand Haven & Milwaukee Railway Company.

At the general election on November 6, 1900, the constitutional amendments were submitted to the people and were approved and

.ratified by a majority of 383,672 votes. This majority was so overwhelming and its meaning so significant that I determined to call another special session of the Legislature in order that it might obey the mandate of the people. It would have been an economy of time and money, and advisable from every standpoint, for this Legislature, the members of which were thoroughly informed upon the subject, to enact a law providing for the taxation of the property of railroad, telegraph, telephone, and express companies upon its actual cash value. I, therefore, called this extra session to meet December 12, 1900, so that there might be ample time before the end of the year for it to enact such a law. The house passed a bill upon substantially the same principles as the Atkinson bill, by the customary large majority. The Senate, however, as it has always done in the past, defeated the bill without assigning any reason for its action. This action of the Senate is too idiotic and boyish to discuss.

. . . .

There is probably no reform, as to the necessity for which the people of this country are more generally agreed, than that of the election of the United States Senators by direct vote of the people. They are united in their demand for this.

The House of Representatives of the United States has four times passed a joint resolution for the submission to the legislatures of the states for their approval, of an amendment to the constitution of the United States, providing for the popular election of the United States Senators, and on every occasion, the Senate has rejected or defeated it. The manner in which the Senate has defeated these resolutions is a matter of no consequence. Their action makes it plain to the people of the country that there is absolutely no prospect that Congress will take the initiative in providing for the submission of such an amendment. The "pigeon-hole" is the only argument which the Senate has offered against the election of United States Senators by vote of the people.

. . . .

Municipal ownership of public utilities, such as supply of water, gas, electric light, telephone service, and the furnishing of street railway transportation, is fast becoming a State issue. A short time prior to the convening of the special session of the Legislature on December 18, 1899, I was requested by the League of the Michigan Municipalities, representing twenty-two (22) of the largest cities of the State, to send a special message to the Legislature covering the subject of municipal ownership so that the Legislature could submit to the people the proposition to amend the Constitution so that cities could own and operate all their public utilities. The same request was made of me by the common council of the City of Detroit.

I believe thoroughly in municipal ownership myself, and it gave me pleasure to comply with these requests. The Legislature, however, declined to submit the question to the people.

. . . .

If the Constitution of this State stands as an obstruction across the pathway of wise legislation, it should be changed. If half the time of courts must be taken up with discussions as to the meaning of words, those words should be written so plainly that the skilful hairsplitter will be compelled to abandon his profession. If the Constitution of this State will permit cities to pave streets and build sewers and own and operate plants for furnishing water and light, and to spend millions of dollars for parks, boulevards, menageries and aquariums, and is such a weak and uncertain thing that it will not permit cities to furnish the most necessary article of all, namely, rapid transportation, at cost, a little modern civilization should be injected into it, and it should be brought down to date.

It may be that upon this subject, I am considered radical. It is a subject which has occupied my serious thought and earnest study for ten years. It is a growing question, and its growth cannot be stopped. I present these suggestions to you for your calm consideration, believing that the time has come for the State of Michigan to permit its citizens to own and operate their own public utilities.

. . . .

There is nothing of more importance to the people of Michigan than the preservation of the forests of the State. The Legislature of 1899, upon my recommendation, passed a law creating a forestry commission of three members. (Act No. 227 of the Public Acts of 1899.) As the president of the commission said, in his letter transmitting the report of the commission to me, this "is purely a business proposition for the State to take care of its own property and make it profitable."

It is, in fact, more than this. It is a question which vitally affects not only the interests of the farmers, but of the thousands who are employed in the mills and factories which cut the timber and utilize the product for manufacturing purposes. It affects all of the industries, and the thousands of people dependent upon them, which are in any way related to the timber interests.

Scientists and experts all unite in the statement that destruction of the forests, both by cutting the timber and by fires, ultimately diminishes and dries up the creeks and rivers, kills the seedlings and saplings, destroys the vegetable mould which holds the moisture, and in general impoverishes the land and renders it useless for agricultural purposes.

The work of the Forestry Commission thus far has been chiefly educational in its nature. The principal step which it has taken has been the setting aside and reservation of certain State tax lands for the establishment by the State of a permanent forest reserve. As a beginning in the work, the Commissioner of the State Land Office has withdrawn from sale and homestead entry the tax, homestead and swamp lands in the west half of Roscommon county and certain lands in Crawford county. This is a beginning of a new policy as to State lands for forestry purposes, and I trust that it will meet with your confirmation and approval.

. . . .

Michigan should understand this question. No state in the Union has so many million acres, from which the forests have been stripped, now lying waste. Where trees have grown, they will grow again. But the problem how best to proceed is new. Thus far the work has been experimental. I have always contended that the State University should take hold of practical questions of this kind, and help the State to solve them. The German universities have established schools of forestry, which accounts for the practical knowledge Germany has on this subject. I am informed that the H. M. Loud's Sons Co. have volunteered to deed to the university something like 100,000 acres of cut-over land, provided the university will undertake to assist the Forestry Commission in retimbering it. The university has shown a disposition to accept quit-claim deeds to such waste lands and undertake the work, providing the Legislature will co-operate to the extent of cancelling the back taxes, and assist in policing the lands so as to prevent fires, which heretofore have proved so destructive. This last could very properly be made the duty of county officials, and the game wardens, one of whom is appointed in every county.

In my first message to the Legislature of 1899, I urged the importance of providing for the appointment of fire wardens. Either that should be done, or the force of the Game Warden increased, so that forest fires and timber thieving could be suppressed. I am aware that there is a disposition to vigorously oppose laws providing for the creation of additional offices, and in a measure I sympathize with this sentiment. Where the material interests of the State are at stake, however, I do not think it is judicious to observe a parsimonious policy. There is infinitely more necessity for fire wardens in the State than for many of the State boards which have been created during the past few years.

If the State should conclude to cancel the back taxes on such lands as lumbermen would voluntarily deed to the university, the State should require, in consideration therefor, that the university establish a school or department of forestry, under a competent professor who, I would suggest, should be brought from Germany, where such startling results have been attained.

It has heretofore been the practice of lumbermen as soon as they have stripped the land of the timber, to convey the land to some irresponsible person, so as to escape liability for the taxes. The State, therefore, will not lose anything by cancelling the back taxes.

Within a lifetime, under wise supervision, at very slight cost, the vast barren tracts of the north could again be made to reproduce the great forests which have been cut off. New York, Wisconsin and Minnesota are all grappling with this problem, and Michigan has more at stake than any state in the Union. Other lumbermen will emulate and follow the example of the Loud company if the State will but do its part, and I most earnestly recommend that this Legislature solicit the co-operation of the State University and the Forestry Commission and adopt a policy which will redeem the waste lands of the State.

. . . .

Concluding, I wish to briefly review the principal accomplishments of the past four years in legislation. The intangible benefits of an awakening of the public conscience, with relation to the inequalities of our tax laws, and the exposure of the methods which have prevailed in the past, of securing special favors in legislation, cannot be accurately measured. But those benefits exist, nevertheless, and it rests with future State administrations, and with the people themselves, to cause this aroused and enlightened public sentiment to be crystalized into good laws.

1. Atkinson Bill Passed.—After a stubborn fight with the representatives of the railroads in the State Senate, lasting through the regular session of 1897, the special session of 1898, and part of the regular session of 1899, the "Atkinson bill" was passed and became a law by my signature on March 15, 1899.

2. Constitutional Amendment Resolution Passed.—After the Supreme Court of the State had indicated that this law was unconstitutional, the friends of equal taxation succeeded, in the face of an opposition on the part of the State Senate, which lasted through a part of the regular session of 1899 and the special sessions of

December 18, 1899, and October 10, 1900, in securing the submission to the people, at the general election of November 6 last, of amendments to the Constitution so that a law similar to the "Atkinson bill" would be constitutional.

3. Constitutional Amendments Ratified by People.—Our course throughout this contest was endorsed by the people, when they ratified the constitutional amendment by the overwhelming majority of 383,672 votes.

4. Special Charters Repealed.—The special charters of the railroads, comprising three of the great systems of the State, the Michigan Central, Lake Shore & Michigan Southern, and the Detroit, Grand Haven & Milwaukee railroads, were repealed at the special session of October 10, 1900. Efforts have been made to do this for a quarter of a century, and it was finally accomplished in the four years of hard fighting just ended. The beneficial results to the people in proper increase of railroad taxes and in reduction of passenger fares are incalculable. The Lake Shore Railroad reduced its passenger rates to two cents at once, and the other roads must soon follow.

5. Taxes of Express and Telegraph Companies Increased.—As a result of the efforts of this administration, the tax rate of the express companies has been increased from one to three per cent, and of telegraph companies from two to three per cent upon the gross amount received by these companies in the State.

6. Railroad Taxes Increased.—As a result of the effort made at the beginning of my first term of office, the Legislature of 1897 passed a law increasing the rate of specific taxation upon the earnings of railroads. It was a beggarly increase, and was only a short step in the direction of equitable taxation. But, nevertheless, under this law, the taxes which railroads have been paying have increased from about $750,000 then, to nearly a million and a quarter of dollars at the present time.

7. State Tax Commission Law Passed.—I have always claimed that if the property which is escaping taxation, or is under-assessed, should be placed on the tax rolls, the taxes of the small property owners would be materially lessened. The people have appreciated the force of this, and the discussion of the subject resulted in the passage, against the opposition of the State Senate, of the State Tax Commission act, which received my approval on June 23, 1899.

8. Property Added to Assessment Rolls.—As a result of the work of the Tax Commission, $350,000,000 of property, which has heretofore been under-assessed or has escaped taxation entirely, has been added to the rolls. Almost all of this increase has been upon property of the large corporations and wealthy individuals who

have avoided their share of taxes in the past, and not upon the property of the owners of small homes.

9. Tax Rate Reduced.—During this administration the average rate of taxes in the State has been reduced from $21.17 on each $1,000 assessed valuation of property in 1899 to $15.47 in 1900, a reduction of $5.70 upon each $1,000, or a decrease of over 26 per cent. In some counties the tax rate has been cut in half—reduced more than 50 per cent.

There were a number of minor reforms accomplished, and abuses corrected, during the past four years, with which you are familiar and which it is not necessary for me to recite in detail. In no four years of the State's history have so many beneficial results been accomplished in the interest of the whole people. The principal credit for them belongs to those members of the House of Representatives, during that period, who fought persistently and courageously for what is right. The odium for the delay in accomplishing these things, and for what extra expense has been caused, belongs to that organization which named itself the "Immortal Nineteen," and the Supreme Court of the State.

My experience during my political life, extending over a period of twelve years, has convinced me that in order to secure the full commendation of those who consider themselves the "better classes," the Governor and other high officials must do nothing to antagonize the great corporations and the wealthy people. I am satisfied that I could have had the praise and support of our "best citizens" and our "best society," and of the press of the State generally, if I had upheld those who have for years attempted to control legislation in their own interests, to the end that they might be relieved from sharing equally with the poor and lowly the burden of taxation. I would have been pronounced a good fellow and a great statesman.

. . . .

Every large interest that I have antagonized has been arrayed against me, and the allies of those interests, the newspapers of the State, have lost no opportunity to attempt to draw the minds of the people from the real issue by making personal attacks on me and publishing malicious and wilful libels, and to belittle my efforts and bring me into disrepute, in order that the present system of unjust, inequitable and iniquitous laws might still remain in force, to the detriment of the great masses of the laboring classes and farmers and those of small properties who are unable to speak and act for themselves.

I make the prediction that, unless those in charge and in whose hands legislation is reposed do not change the present system of inequality, in less than a quarter of a century there will be a bloody revolution in this great country of ours.

I have no apologies to make for my course. I have done what I took the oath of office to perform. I have attempted to secure legislation which the people have demanded, and am willing that whatever of failure there may be in the future should rest where it belongs.

Chase S. Osborn was an ideological if not a direct successor to Hazen Pingree. Osborn, who had served as a member of the railroad commission, made the first real test of Michigan primary election reform when he sought Republican nomination for governor in 1910. His campaign, led by an able fellow townsman from Sault Sainte Marie, Frank Knox, lacked some substance in meeting the issues of the day, but was unusually colorful, reflecting the personality of the gubernatorial candidate and introducing a new means of campaigning—the automobile. This section from an article by Robert M. Warner portrays the excitement of a vigorous campaign in the progressive era.

Cowpath Campaigning

ROBERT M. WARNER

Frank Knox, as Osborn's chief political lieutenant, played the major role in organizing the campaign. His principal duties were to carry on a voluminous correspondence all over the state, to stimulate local Osborn organizations, to coordinate the major divisions of the Osborn campaign, and to raise money. Knox was aided in the Upper Peninsula by State Representative William R. Oates of Laurium and in western Michigan by Calvin A. Palmer, an old-line politician from Manistee. Both of these men were paid for their

From *Michigan History*, XLIII (September, 1959), 351-353, 370-376. Reprinted by permission of the History Division, Michigan Department of State. Footnotes in the original have been omitted.

services. Eastern Michigan was unofficially managed by [Walter J.] Hunsaker, aided by Knox, while Detroit had its own organization run by a "strategy board" of experienced politicians instead of a single manager. Unlike other sections of the state, Detroit was largely independent of Knox's control.

The Osborn campaign staff employed a number of highly imaginative vote-getting techniques. For example, Knox asked to be put in contact with the census supervisor of a certain district to have him influence enumerators under him to work for Osborn. "Of course," Knox explained, "I have no such foolish thing in mind as making their appointment contingent upon . . . [supporting Osborn], but if the supervisor is friendly . . . that friendliness could be used to very good advantage. . . . " In another case, Auditor General Oramel B. Fuller, whose nomination for that post in 1908 had been largely Osborn's doing, was prodded to influence the political affiliation of a member of his department and to award the printing of tax lists to friendly papers.

The technique most frequently used to capture the potential Osborn voter was to flatter his ego by a personal letter from the gubernatorial candidate. From the extensive files of correspondence in the Osborn Papers it would seem that almost anyone in Michigan who showed the slightest inclination to support Osborn received a personal letter from him.

Osborn's friends also did their share of letter writing. For example, hundreds of Michigan doctors, probably most of the doctors in the state, received letters from Dr. Fred Townsend of the Sault urging support of Osborn.

No group was small enough to escape the attention of the Osborn campaign crew. Austrian, Finnish, and Italian national groups were singled out for organization into Osborn clubs. A newspaper editor favorably mentioning Osborn in his German-American publication received a flattering thank-you from the gubernatorial candidate praising the German character and influence. An Osborn worker was reported as "getting along well with an organization among the Polish priests."

The Negro population in Michigan, though small, was not overlooked. Osborn was quick to endorse James Bromley, a Negro, for a Federal appointment, since Bromley was reported to have more influence with the colored vote in the state than any other person and had promised to swing this vote to Osborn in the primary.

Various religious denominations also received an individually tailored appeal designed to garner their votes. The local priest in Osborn's home town wrote a letter for publication in the Michigan *Catholic* praising his fellow townsman's high character, intelligence, and qualifications, and urging support of him. Another Sault resident, the pastor of the Presbyterian Church to which Osborn belonged, sent letters to prominent members of that denomination urging a vote for his parishioner. A segment of the Jewish population of Detroit was enlightened with regard to Osborn virtues by Abraham Berger, a "blind Jewish cigar-maker" who was to spend two months in the city working for Osborn for a fifty dollar fee.

. . . .

A significant and colorful part of Osborn's campaign was his extensive stump-speaking tour of the state. The extent of Osborn's junkets is truly amazing. One newspaper reported that he traveled twelve thousand miles during the campaign and made over seven hundred speeches. Osborn himself said that he made over one thousand speeches. Even during the hot weeks of July and August the peripatetic candidate was averaging eleven speeches daily, with a minimum of seven and a maximum of nineteen. The general plan was to have Osborn tour in those counties where he was least known, which in effect meant spending all of his time in the lower peninsula of Michigan.

A "Cutting-40" auto was the chosen vehicle to carry the indefatigable campaigner over Michigan's rough roads. Knox testified that "as a hill climber and on sandy roads it never met its superior." Sometimes the candidate's car would be joined by others, as was the case in Eaton County, where the Osborn cavalcade consisted of "fifteen big touring cars filled with representative Republicans . . . including ten cars of Charlotte Civil War veterans."

Nearly every nook and cranny of lower Michigan received a bit of Osborn oratory. Knox reported that on one trip meetings were held "wherever we found a crossroads, a blacksmith shop and a bird's nest." To cover the ground much of the traveling was done at the hair-raising speed of "30 miles or more an hour." Knox did not share Osborn's enthusiasm for the "cow-path campaigning," as he called it. He complained that this vote harvesting was "all Gen. Sherman said war was, and then some." When the touring candidate reached a town an hour or two behind schedule, Knox found himself having to "organize the gang" and "drum up a crowd and then Chase would tell 'em how to run the government (prolonged applause)."

This type of automobile campaigning had its quota of hazards. Knox told of one instance of trouble on a trip from Albion to Niles. "The auto I rode in," according to the tired campaigner's account, "got lost in a cornfield and had a bumpy sort of time. Also a mule tried to kick us off the track and in his effort to avoid Mr. Mule our driver nearly dumped us in the ditch." On the same trip Knox was imperiled a second time when he attempted to remove some of the accumulated grime of the day's travel in the open car. According to Knox: "I tried to take a swim this morning with the aid of a patent gas heater, alleged to be instantaneous, and nearly blew myself up. This actorine [?] life is awful."

Automobile campaigning occasioned some unusual expenses. Knox had to send ten dollars to a man whose fence was damaged by a car in Osborn's party, and in another instance he had to pay fourteen dollars to a man whose buggy was damaged when his horse was frightened by Osborn's car. Knox was assured in this latter instance that "a heavy Finn vote [was] depending on this adjustment."

What did Osborn say in these multitudinous speeches he made on his campaign tours? There are only a few manuscripts of his speeches among his papers since he seldom bothered to write out his addresses. Except for a few occasions such as his platform speech at Greenville, his speeches were extemporaneous. Even when he thought through a speech in advance, he frequently discarded it at the last moment and let the most immediate conditions determine the nature of his address. For example, when the Osborn party drove into the village of Maple Rapids, a ball game was in progress; but the players stopped their game to listen. "In his preliminary remarks here Mr. Osborn told of the games he had witnessed in Athens, almost the cradle of athletic sports and said that the boys of this country were not only the equal but the superior to all other athletes. He said that baseball was the greatest of all games and then launched into his political discussion." Often he would praise the town where he was visiting or the beauties of nature before getting down to anything political, which often would be an attack on corruption in the incumbent administration plus mention of a few planks in his program.

One can glimpse something of the nature of Osborn's personality and of the character of his campaign technique in the record of his visit to Omena, a little resort town on the narrow finger of land between Lake Michigan and Grand Traverse Bay. A group of young men—resorters—were lounging around when a small car came up in a whirling cloud of dust and an excited individual announced that "the Governor" was coming. The motorist exhorted the young men to round up a band or make some kind of demonstration to herald Osborn's arrival. The youths responded enthusiastically. They gathered up a few instruments, and when Osborn arrived, they made an "unearthly din" including firing off of an old Civil War rifle by the self-appointed one-man militia. Osborn was so taken with the demonstration that he invited all the boys into the local "sody" fountain for a treat. He then invited them down to Northport, nine miles away, where his next appearance was scheduled. They agreed to join him there.

Osborn went ahead in his car; the Omena boys followed by boat. Osborn promised to persuade the Northport people to have dinner ready for them when they arrived. On the trip down the boys had a chance to become a little better organized. They disembarked with flags waving, the impromptu band playing, and marched up Main Street to the convention hall where the promised meal was waiting. The townspeople and the candidate himself pitched in to serve. The group then adjourned to the meeting hall where Osborn delivered his speech, not on politics, but on the glories of Kentucky, since he found that several of the Omena boys were from that state. This was greeted by great cheering from the boys. The cheering proved contagious, the entire audience joined in the heavy applause, and Osborn had scored another triumph.

This frequent ignoring of state issues was not always well received. An auditor of Osborn's speech at South Haven complained that the candidate gave a good speech but that he barely touched on issues of the campaign, as his voice gave out before he got around to these. Knox agreed with this general criticism and advised Osborn to pay heed to it.

Sometimes Osborn would be very pleased with his speechmaking, and he did not hesitate to say so. For example, he wrote his secretary that in St. Johns "the crowd rose to me like a storm," and in Lansing "It was a hostile audience but I aroused it to frenzied approval." But he also had his bad days when he would deliver "only a fairish speech" or, as he even admitted, "a very poor speech."

One of his biggest triumphs, which Osborn took great relish in relating, was a speech at Ionia at the end of January. As happened frequently in the campaign, all the gubernatorial candidates were present at the Ionia meeting. Personalities had entered the campaign by this time, and Osborn admitted that he had "twitted" genial Pat Kelley in particular "quite unmercifully" several times in personal conversation. In the Ionia speech Osborn told Kelley "that he ought to take up some legitimate work or something of that sort, hoe corn, chop wood and make good. I did say . . . he reminded me of a great big, fine, good-natured, tail-wagging, child-saving Newfoundland dog, which, by the way, I interpolated, wasn't much of a watch dog." Understandably this caused Kelley to erupt in a geyser of anger, and the not-so-genial Pat bitterly denounced Osborn. The result was hisses and catcalls for Kelley—seven minutes of this according to Osborn's reckoning.

Osborn made no such blunders as losing his temper, although there were other mistakes, as when he upset many voters in a Jackson speech by advocating the use of the Bible in the public schools. Osborn's western Michigan manager, "Puss" Palmer, complained: "It raised H . . . l Frank [Knox] and I hope he don't let another one fall like that or I am afraid it will undo all the good that he has done up to date." The resourceful Knox, however, reassured Puss that even this slip could be turned to the candidate's advantage. He was having the priest at Sault Ste. Marie put his stamp of approval on the statement and send his endorsement of it to every priest in the state.

Osborn was a natural campaigner—energetic, colorful, highly egotistical but very warm-hearted. He had a genuine interest in people and loved to meet the crowds. His vivid speeches and vigorous stump tours, though containing touches of the comic and ridiculous, contributed to the victory. In Barry County, for example, a Kelley backer was told that the sentiment against the Lieutenant Governor was stimulated

> by the favorable impression made by Mr. Osborn's speech which was a very good one. . . . There is just enough insurgency everywhere so that Mr. Osborn's sassy talk was rapturously applauded. Everybody felt he was "The Man of the Hour."

Knox was convinced of Osborn's superior ability as a stump speaker, believing it to be a decisive factor in helping to bring victory. As one listener summed up the situation:

> We have heard little Osborn boosting until today but through a particularly magnetic personality and a brilliant speech at a republican banquet given last night, the whole town this morning is saying that Chase Osborn was head and shoulders above any other candidate.

On Monday afternoon the fifth of September a very weary Osborn returned to his home in the Sault to vote the next day and to learn the results of the primary. His spirits got a big boost when his home town accorded him a "most touching reception." Whistles on the steamers sounded a noisy greeting. Over three thousand of the town's citizens turned out to greet its favorite son, and a band escorted him to his home.

The following day Osborn scored a resounding victory at the polls. When all the votes were tallied, Osborn had received 88,270 ballots, not a majority of Republican votes cast but a substantial margin over Kelley's 52,337 and Musselman's 50,721. Of great personal gratification to Osborn was the overwhelming vote given him by his own county—2,482 to a combined opposition vote of 258. As was to be expected Osborn carried his home region of the Upper Peninsula with a majority in every county. He also won a decisive victory in Saginaw County, where his paper, the Saginaw *Courier-Herald*, was located. Wayne, Michigan's most populous county, went for Osborn—very nearly giving him a majority. Kelley's votes were scattered. Musselman's votes were centered in western Michigan around his home county of Kent.

The success of Osborn's campaign can be ascribed to several factors. Fundamental, of course, was the fact that the nominating was done by primary election rather than by convention. "Where, O where," Knox exclaimed, "would we be in this fight if it wasn't for the direct primary?" Under the convention system the Warner administration with its patronage powers would have been in an excellent position to throw the nomination to Kelley or at least to continue the unbroken record of past conventions in denying the sparsely populated, always Republican Upper Peninsula the top place on the ticket.

Save for the existence of the primary system itself, the most important factor in Osborn's success was the careful organization and contacts built up by Osborn and his exceedingly capable manager, Frank Knox. Knox, to be sure, deserves much credit for Osborn's victory. Other factors, however, must also be taken into account. Osborn capitalized on the sectional pride and interest of the Upper Peninsula and kept the area strongly for himself. His colorful, aggressive stump-speaking campaign and a program that was more concrete and appealing than that of any of the other candidates also helped him to win the prize. Certainly, an important element in the campaign was the fact that Osborn identified himself with the progressive spirit of the time. These factors, coupled with vigorous attacks on an unpopular state administration, gave Osborn Republican Michigan.

Osborn's autobiography, *The Iron Hunter,* not only summarizes some of his accomplishments but also captures the spirit of Osborn himself and his very personalized approach to governing. He was a strong leader giving direction to the legislature in promoting progressive measures such as workmen's compensation, his most important act. His program did not make major alterations in the system; it preserved the system through modest reform. But this was the essence of progressivism.

In Michigan the political ramifications of the progressive era are covered in several articles and in a nearly contemporary account by Arthur C. Millspaugh, *Party Organization and Machinery in Michigan Since 1890* (Baltimore, 1917).

The Fight Against "The Human Bloodsuckers"

CHASE S. OSBORN

The first of January, 1911, I was inaugurated as Governor of Michigan. In order to devote every energy to the program of accomplishment I had outlined, I had determined that I would leave the office at the close of my two-year term and would not be a candidate for reëlection. There was much to do and I realized that I would have strong opposition to the passage of the measures I advocated. The political organizations of Detroit were powerful at the state capital. Detroit control had passed long before into the hands of a local Tammany that would stop at nothing. The organization, unwritten, but understood, included men in both the Republican and Democratic parties, grading up from convicts to semi-respectables and connected with men on both sides occupying positions of trust and prominence, but ready at all times to profit by their political relationship to this tong, and just as ready to be parties to questionable political practices that they might not think of resorting to if proposed in their professions. This gang was "The Vote Swappers' League," named such by E. G. Pipp, manager at that time of the *Detroit News*. Most of the men had double standards of practice; one for politics and another for business. Most of those who aided the crooked league in the work were well known. The Republicans were even worse than their Democrat partners, because they presumed to hold their heads a little higher, cloak themselves in a bespotted mantle of respectability and patronize the town clubs and the golf links, and even go so far as to identify themselves with a church if it served a purpose. These fine bucktails divided the offices among their faithful, controlled the Council, boasted of their standing in the several judicial strata and most thoroughly removed the political viscera from any reformer or

From *The Iron Hunter* (New York: The Macmillan Company, 1919), pp. 280-288.

citizens' movement that started any Taiping revolution. I had to decide whether I would serve Michigan or the Vote Swappers' League. I chose the flag of Michigan. The word was passed to the Detroit gang that I could not be controlled. This started a war upon me that has gone the length of bitterness.

The fight was staged first in the Legislature. I found myself as Governor at first unable to secure a majority for anything for which any credit or responsibility attached to the Governor's office. Gradually the legislative opposition wore down. Finally I had a certain majority in the House and soon after in the Senate. The failures in legislation were few and only of measures that required a two-thirds majority.

A multitude of things came up in the executive office. I had succeeded an administration unfriendly to me, and things were not made easy for me, which did not alarm or dissuade me. I had been accustomed to long hours and there was keen delight in putting them in now.

The very day I was inaugurated a plot was discovered to blow up Jackson prison with dynamite. The warden was new and there was much nervousness. Dependable guards were not known from the ones in league with the convicts. I counseled with Warden Russell, of Marquette prison, and Warden Fuller, of the Ionia Reformatory, both officials of long experience and high ability. I succeeded in getting a line on the bad men in Jackson. I had them brought to the executive office one at a time and between two and four o'clock in the morning, so that absolute secrecy might be secured. I succeeded in obtaining enough information to locate and remove quantities of high explosives, and to break up the convict gang, distributing the members among other prisons. While at this task I learned many other incidental facts. My greatest surprise was caused and my indignation was particularly aroused by the indisputable knowledge that a traffic in pardons and paroles was going on. I forced at once the resignation of the Board of Pardons and a new Board was appointed. I appointed a complete, new bi-partisan Prison Board of big men.

I learned that one of the Tax Commissioners of the State was also the retained attorney of a big manufacturer of automobiles. Of course the lawyer could not serve two masters for conflicting interests. I asked him to resign and he did so. Another Tax Commissioner gave very little time to the work and his performance was very unsatisfactory. In fact, the Commission was in a rut. I asked this man to resign. The epidemic phrase was "Go to hell." This fellow applied it and I removed him. This removal made completely new three important boards. I cleaned out every vestige of the old administration that seemed to be necessary to wholesome state administration. In doing so I only kept faith with the people. It was what I had promised them I would do.

When I became Governor a deficit existed in the state treasury of about a million dollars. I was determined to wipe this out. Many economies were inaugurated in the management of state institutions. In this work I was aided by every institutional superintendent in Michigan and by all the appointive heads of departments. It was easy to save the State's money if one managed with anything like the same care with which private business is conducted.

The new constitution of Michigan gives the Governor unusual fiscal authority. In fact, it imposes in him the power and responsibility practically of financial manager. The Governor can veto all or any part of an appropriation bill. I carefully went over every bill with those interested in it. As a result I cut out nearly enough to pay the state indebtedness. This financial use of the veto constitutes a precedent.

But it was in saving through economies introduced everywhere that the big results were obtained. At the conclusion of my administration the State was out of debt and the treasury contained a surplus of more than two million dollars. This was achieved and at the same time more money was appropriated for good roads than the estimate and more for the state university than ever before. The tax rate was also reduced. Also this saving improved the conditions at all state institutions, because the very care that made economy possible naturally conduced to improvements in every detail of service.

The regular session of the Legislature adjourned.

Early in 1912 I called a special session and followed it immediately with a second special session. Under the Michigan constitution the Governor is empowered to summon the Legislature in extraordinary session. At such only those measures submitted in message by the Governor may be considered. The effect is to compel legislative concentration and to focus the eyes of the public upon important measures. At a regular session there is pulling and hauling and trading and confusion, until the public is lost in a muddle of vexatious circumstances and the legislators are nearly as badly off.

Very near to my heart I had the matter of a workmen's compensation law. I had given the subject considerable study in Germany and England and had talked it over often with my intimate associates and many others. The Legislature in regular session had empowered the Governor to appoint a commission to study the question and draft a form of a bill embodying a suitable law. The commission appointed, serving without pay, had given earnest attention to the important subject and had submitted a report of indubitable value. To obtain action upon this was my chief first purpose for a special session. Also I wished to utilize this meritorious measure to further define and stiffen partisan lines in the Legislature, so that I might feed in good measures that otherwise would not carry. The workingmen's compensation act passed. The Legislature empowered the Governor to appoint an Industrial Accident Board to administer the law. The success of the new law might largely depend upon the practical foundation laid for it in its earliest application and interpretation. I secured for the board the only two members of the commission that framed the law who could be secured for state service. By virtue of the understanding and administration of this law by the first board, it came to be recognized as one of the best compensation enactments in America. It has been copied by many other States. Gradually it will undoubtedly be brought nearer to perfection.

Police Commissioner Croul, of Detroit, an official of rare courage and capacity, had told me that of some seventeen hundred saloons in Detroit quite twelve hundred were owned by brewers and distillers. It was their practice to start a booze joint on every likely corner they could obtain and especially near factory doors. Brewery-owned saloons were the worst of all. I saw to it that a bill was introduced making it illegal for brewers and distillers to own or encourage saloons. Forthwith fell upon me the liquor people. The Royal Ark, an association of saloon keepers in Detroit, endeavored to intimidate members of the Legislature. Conditions of much bitterness arose. But the bill became a law.

I found the Michigan Bonding Company to be the most hurtful and the boldest source of evil in the State. It was organized under a law that gave it the practical control of all the saloons in the State. If a saloon keeper did not obey its behests, his bonds were refused. It charged big fees and was strong financially. It had one or more agents in every county and cleverly selected them from among the best-equipped attorneys. By means of a retainer it secured the services of lawyers who would not naturally line up with it. Thus equipped, the Michigan Bonding Company became a dangerous entity. Of it men were afraid. It was the core organization around which was built the opposition to woman suffrage, prohibition and all related reforms. I asked the Legislature to repeal the law giving it existence and I made a fight against it that was nearly successful.

The fight at Lansing while these bills were pending became a vicious one, with enough bad feeling and personal passion almost to obscure reason for a time. I received as many as ten letters in one day threatening my life. To these cowardly messages I paid no attention. They only indicated the feeling that existed among the whiskeyites. Dynamite was placed under my house but it did not explode. My residence was on fire twice mysteriously. One of these fires occurred at two o'clock in the morning. I was attacked on all sides. Throughout all the conflict I did not worry nor lose sleep. My wife stood it bravely but confesses now she was deeply worried and wearied. But only words of cheer and courage came from her then. As for myself, I thought I was right and I think so now when the embers of thought are colorless from fire. Perhaps I took on some of the spirit of the crusader. At least I placed my trust in God and calmly asked divine approval and direction.

Those who were advocating woman suffrage were not united. Some of them, including most of the women propagandists who came to Lansing, were fearful that a measure submitting the question to the people could not pass the Legislature and that its failure would prove a setback. After discussing the matter with Representative Charles Flowers, a veteran partisan of the cause, and with several others, I decided to present the question. It carried nicely. Later, when it was submitted for popular consideration, it undoubtedly carried in the State. However, the liquor interests succeeded in obscuring and invalidating the result. Its next submission was in the spring, when the country vote is light as compared with that of the cities, and suffrage was then unquestionably defeated.

When the returns of the vote began to indicate that the measure had passed at the first plebiscite, those opposed held back the reports from polling precincts that they controlled, giving the impression that whatever totals were necessary to accomplish the defeat of the women would be supplied. There were signs of a sharp practice that was used by the vicious elements to obtain a momentary end. Apparently the only adequate redress for such is an aroused public that will finally act so decisively as to brook no resistance or trickery.

I do not say that all of those who oppose votes for women are vicious, but I do say that wherever I have been familiar with conditions, the management of the campaign against suffrage has been controlled either above the surface or below it by those who are inclined to lawlessness and who make it their instinctive business to fight anything that tends to improve the public tone or widen the zone of influence of those who would be most likely, in the nature of things, to endeavor to cure those evils that are eating cancerously at the foundations of the human family.

Women are the matrix of the race. They occupy a sphere that man, a mere fertilizing agent, never enters. Consequently woman knows instinctively when her own is imperiled. Fundamentally this is the *raison d'être* of the woman movement. All talk of liberty and equality is incidental. Nature, always operating to make life dominant over death, and in ways often most obscure and indirect so far as man's vision and comprehension are concerned, is the author of the activity that has for its purpose the bringing to bear of the powers of woman directly against the jeopardy of her children. The tendency may be delayed or misdirected but it cannot be defeated, any more than the precession of the equinoxes can be controlled by human agencies.

My messages to the Legislature, in special sessions, are a true guide to my state of mind, my thought processes and convictions at that time. I had not yet convinced myself that there could not be some compromise with alcohol. I hoped that if there was any good in it that it might be separated from the much that was bad, and the desirable retained and the objectionable rejected. I had visions of state control that would be more successful than the dispensary experience by the State of South Carolina. It was my nebulous hope that the whiskey traffic might be completely taken out of trade whereby man's degeneracy was made a source of profit. It was a passing dream in which I saw pure whiskey, beers and wines served at cost in temperate quantities in clean environment to those who might be cheered but not poisoned.

But I was nearing the time when I became convinced that life and alcohol cannot exist together any more rationally than life and death. I saw the constant struggle of nature against death and all of the agencies of decay; the finely maintained equilibrium of wild animal and vegetable life; the self-pruning processes of primeval forests and many of the visible efforts of the war of life against death. Because of the limited visual powers of man, there are more invisible activities than those that we can see. But there are also many that we are slow to see because we do not wish to see. So I saw in the world's growing social array against alcohol simply a great movement of life against death. As such it will succeed in spite of man's blindness and opposition, just because the world-old truth that man is ever the weak proponent and God is forever the mighty disponent.

Michigan voted in favor of state-wide prohibition at the election of November, 1916, and in favor of woman suffrage in 1918.

As progressivism achieved many of its goals, it concentrated more and more on what it regarded as one of the prime evils of the day, the saloon and the entire liquor industry. Alcohol was regarded as a corrupter of politics, a destroyer of the home, and a contributor to idleness and poverty. Chase Osborn made it a major topic in his autobiography, *The Iron Hunter*. The panacea presented by reformers was the elimination of alcoholic beverages. Typical of the vigorous campaign carried on by the Michigan prohibition forces is this excerpt from a campaign manual that attempted to relate the problem of alcohol to some of the major social problems facing the state, including insanity.

Though the document is a quaint period piece from our perspective, it does reflect a thinking that was widely disseminated and seriously read by Michigan citizens of the period and helped push Michigan toward prohibition.

The Evils of Alcohol

"The statistics of every state show a greater amount of crime and misery attributed to the use of ardent spirits obtained in these retail liquor saloons than to any other source."—United States Supreme Court.

Alcohol was the direct cause of the insanity of 150 individuals who were admitted to the Michigan state hospitals in the years 1913-14. Alcoholic insanity constituted 8.4 per cent of 1,773 patients admitted during that period.

The greater proportion of alcoholic insanity comes from cities of larger population. Those having a population of 10,000 or more furnish 66.6 per cent of the cases of insanity due to alcohol or drugs.

The indirect influence of alcohol is shown in the occurrence of alcoholism of more than ordinary degree among the ancestors and families of 9.9 per cent of all cases of insanity admitted for treatment.

The comparative frequency of insanity due to alcohol is considerably less in Michigan than in those states in which the population is largely centered in cities. Alcohol was given as the sole cause in 13.9 per cent of the cases of insanity admitted to the state hospitals for the insane in Massachusetts in 1914 and in New York 15.1 per cent of the admissions were due to alcohol.

From *Michigan Campaign Manual for a Dry State* (Lansing: Michigan Dry Campaign Committee, 1916), pp. 8-11.

As regards the general use of alcohol among those admitted to the insane hospitals, an investigation of the habits of 846 males admitted to the Michigan state hospitals for the period of one year showed that 62 per cent were users of alcoholic drinks and 25.7 per cent were total abstainers.

Of those who drank, 23.8 per cent were classed as occasional moderate drinkers; 7 per cent drank steadily in moderate amounts; 3.2 per cent drank steadily, but occasionally to an excessive degree; 9.7 per cent could be classed as occasional excessive or periodic drinkers, and 18.3 per cent drank steadily in excessive amounts. Of all those who used alcoholic drinks, 31.2 per cent were more than moderate in their use.

Of the 809 boys, (studied in the Lansing Industrial School) 273 or 34 percent had used alcoholic beverages. There were 105 or 13 per cent who had been drunk one or more times.

There were 422, or 52 per cent, of the fathers of the 809 boys who drank, 20 per cent excessively. Fifty-seven of the mothers of the boys drank.

In view of the known influence which alcohol has in the production of insanity, and conditions of physical and nervous degeneracy, it is urged that the public be educated to an appreciation of the dangers of intoxicating drinks.

Saloons and Poverty

County poor houses of Michigan, now known as infirmaries, furnish universal evidence that liquor is responsible for more than half of poverty.

Statistical tabulations showing the effect of the license and no-license systems in individual counties of Michigan are of little value as evidence. Many inmates of infirmaries are permanent occupants, whose entry or exit bears no direct relation to social conditions. A lapse of years, possibly of a whole generation, would be necessary to produce any radical change in pauperism as a class following the abolition of saloons.

Two facts stand out: One is that the authorities and citizens in dry counties are unanimous in their opinion that from the standpoint of the county poor the dry regime is far superior. The other fact is that many counties report officially that about three-fourths of the poverty which requires county aid to individual or family, is due to the use of alcoholic beverages.

Official statements written by superintendents of the poor include the following:

"This county is in the dry column, and we find that while the cost of everything is much higher, the Supervisors are not called upon to furnish us more money now than they did while the county was wet."

C. C. HALLENBECK,
Eaton County.

"We are pleased to inform you that there are few cases in this county which are receiving relief that have been caused by alcoholic beverages. We have a clear slate, are now dry and expect to remain so."

O. O. FRICK,
Oscoda County.

"Midland county has been dry eight years and people like it. Two old-timers is all we have left in the county home whose condition is due to drink."

K. M'KAY,
Midland County.

Confidential statements to the same effect are as follows: "Drink is the almost universal cause of poverty while for temporary assistance it is probably the main factor in at least one half the cases." "In my best judgment about 50 per cent of poverty in this county can be attributed to the use of drink, if not more. In fact, nearly all the crime we have can be laid to the same cause." "I am quite sure that three-fourths at least are caused by the liquor traffic."

Following are a few more definite statements:

Alger county—"About 75 per cent."

Genesee county—"About 70 percent from liquor directly or indirectly."

Huron county—"Most of the inmates of the county farm here have come to the institution because of intemperance and the use of liquor."

Mason county—"Thirty-five per cent directly and 20 per cent indirectly, or 55 per cent of all poverty in our county is caused by alcoholic drink."

Iron county—"Ten years as poor Commissioner leads me to say that fully 95 per cent of male inmates at our county farm have come here either directly or indirectly because of liquor."

Kent county—"Of 500 families helped during the year ending March 1, 1916, liquor was the direct cause of poverty in 25 families and an indirect cause in 53 families. Of 103 persons in Kent County Detention Hospital last year, at least one-half were caused by intemperance. In Kent county home were 136 persons, of whom 85 per cent can easily be traced to intemperance as a direct cause."—L. De Payter.

"To the best of my judgment, I would say that 80 per cent of the poverty is caused by alcoholism. It would be a number of years after its passage before we could get the full benefit of state-wide Prohibition. The effects of the past years would stay with us until the rising generation took its place."—V. H. Billings.

Montmorency county—"Four of the six men in our poor house were forced to come here on account of drink."

Oakland county—"Seventy per cent or more of the cases here are due to drink. We are going through the second dry time and we find it helps very much. I hope for state-wide Prohibition."

Arrests in Dry Cities

In every city and county local option or Prohibition invariably results in reducing the number of arrests. There is also a definite and often large reduction in the expense of conducting jails, courts, etc.

The actual relationship between the license system and number of arrests for drunkenness, misdemeanors or crime cannot be determined absolutely. Any conclusions reached are influenced to a greater or less extent by the local policy in making arrests. Sometimes local officials, either policemen, Judges or politicians, start out to make a record for arrests either under a wet or dry regime.

"When is a man drunk enough to be arrested?" This question is answered variously, but the answer in nine counties out of 10 in Michigan proves that the license system produces from two to five times as many cases of public intoxication as the no-license system. In Michigan dry counties, as in Kansas, Iowa and other dry states, the local jail frequently falls into entire disuse. In Michigan wet counties, as in Ingham county during the last period of saloons, the jail is often full of "drunks" and in some cases has had to be enlarged.

5: Automobiles and Urbanization

John J. Carton was a prominent Michigan attorney, president of the Constitutional Convention in 1908, and a major force in establishing General Motors Corporation. In his papers appears a contract drawn up by the Imperial Wheel Company in Flint. All workers were required to sign this contract, which regulated working conditions in one of the new automobile factories that were springing up in the state. Management was not inhumane but paid slight attention to the rights and comforts of the workers.

The literature of the automobile industry is the most extensive of any phase of Michigan history. Arthur Pound tells the story of General Motors from the company's viewpoint in *The Turning Wheel: The Story of General Motors* (New York, 1934). Ford's major biographer is Allan Nevins, whose three volumes (New York, 1954, 1957, 1962) discuss both the man and the company he founded, while John B. Rae in *American Automobile Manufacturers* (Philadelphia, 1959) and *Road and the Car in American Life* (Cambridge, 1971) gives an overview of the automobile industry and its impact on society.

Rules for Workers, 1906

FACTORY REGULATIONS

IMPERIAL WHEEL COMPANY

Please do not accept employment unless you are willing to abide by the following regulations.

From "Factory Regulations," a handbill in the John J. Carton Papers, Michigan Historical Collections, Bentley Historical Library, University of Michigan.

1 . . . . *WORKING HOURS.*—6:30 a.m. to 11:30 a.m. standard time; 12:30 p.m. to 5:30 p.m., standard time, except on Saturday when the day ends at 4:30 standard time. First whistle blows at five minutes before the beginning of working hours. Second whistle on working hours. Over time 6 p.m. to 9 p.m.

2 . . . . Employees shall be in their respective departments prepared to begin work when second whistle blows, and if frequently or habitually late may expect dismissal.

3 . . . . Each employee will be given a number on the time clock. He will always ring same when he begins work, also when he ceases work, and he will not ring any earlier than fifteen minutes before the hour for commencing work, except by special arrangement with his foreman. Should he by mistake ring the wrong number or neglect to ring his own number he will at once report it to the time keeper. It is not expected that oversights of this character will occur often.

4 . . . . An employee known to ring in or out for another will be dismissed.

5 . . . . Employees will remain at their work until the whistle blows, and *all changing of clothing, washing, or cleaning up will be done after working hours.*

6 . . . . SMOKING in any buildings or about the yards is not allowed at any time except in the Boiler Room, and not there during working hours.

7 . . . . REGULAR PAY DAYS occur as follows: For work performed from first of month to and including the 15th, we pay the 23d. For work performed from the 16th to and including the last day of the month we pay the 8th of the month following, except when the pay days fall on Sunday, in which case we pay the day prior. No money will be advanced between pay days.

8 . . . . All bicycles, clothing, shoes, etc., must be kept in places provided for that purpose in each department.

9 . . . . All persons, except those authorized, are strictly forbidden to use elevators and then for freighting purposes only, and all employees are warned against meddling with electric motors or any electrical appliances in any way, save as authorized by their foremen.

10 . . . . Each employee will attend strictly to his own work, and no one will permit himself to indulge in any loud talking, profanity or undignified conduct during working hours.

11 . . . . *SUBSCRIPTION PAPERS.* The passing of subscription papers

through the factory in the interest of disabled employees will not be encouraged for the reason that every employee may protect himself against such a necessity by becoming a member of some association, which will provide for the payment to him weekly of a given sum of money in case of sickness, accident, or death.

12 . . . . All persons accepting employment may become members of the Flint Vehicle Manufacturers' Mutual Benefit Association upon signing an agreement to that effect.

We trust each and every employee of this Company will heartily co-operate with us in making the above regulations effective.

IMPERIAL WHEEL COMPANY,
C.B. HAYES, General Manager.

Flint, Mich., April 1, 1906.

In accepting employment from the Imperial Wheel Company I hereby agree to observe all of the above regulations.
Signed . . . .

During the auto boom in Flint, John Ihlder described the transformation that the rapid growth of General Motors was to bring about in this small midwestern city. The rise in property values, poor housing, and the appearance of new millionaires, like Charles S. Mott, are reflected in this perceptive account of the urbanization of Flint.

Flint, When Men Build Automobiles Who Builds Their City?

JOHN IHLDER

"This," said one of the young mechanics as our car entered Flint one day in the early summer, "is the town where they sleep them so thick that their feet hang out of the windows." In Flint it is difficult to avoid exaggeration. Yet they do "sleep them pretty thick"—a family of seven in a two-room shack on the river bottoms,

From *The Survey*, XXXVI (September 2, 1916), 549-557.

a family of five in one inside room of a downtown block, three shifts in a Polish lodging-house in the North End.

Flint denies that it is a boom town. It admits that it had a boom in 1909-10. Then people lived in tents all winter. But along in the summer they folded those tents and stole away, leaving behind in the hands of the real estate dealers thousands of carefully worded contracts which obligated them to pay for building lots. But the present growth is different; it is permanent. Of this the stranger is assured time and again. For one thing this prosperity wave has been gradually—but rapidly—increasing for three years. For another thing it is based on no such temporary condition as the war in Europe, but on the permanent and insatiable demand of the American people for automobiles and still more automobiles. Flint does not sell to Europe; its interest is in the American market. And it believes the American market will continue irrespective of wars. If any Flint cars go to Europe Flint does not send them. What will happen when those manufacturers who do sell to Europe are forced to seek American consumers again, it awaits with confidence, believing that it has the inside track.

Meanwhile Flint is rich; that is, it feels rich, it talks rich and it has a rich income. There is a list of 182 local men (this 182 is one of the few local figures upon which local statisticians seem to be agreed) who have made from $50,000 to $3,000,000 within the past year. Some say that these 182 have made from $100,000 to $6,000,000. The 182 give evidence that they believe there is more where the first came from. They have not yet begun to spend—on this there seems to be agreement, except that some of them are building fine homes in the city and that others, joined by hopeful fellow townsmen, are still investing.

And why shouldn't Flint believe? All that is necessary is to forget 1910 and concentrate the attention on later years. Less than two years ago General Motors was 24. A year and a half ago it was less than 100. Last September it was 265; in December 490. Then it was exchanged for Chevrolet at 5 to 1. Chevrolet was then quoted at 70 to 90. Now Chevrolet is 244. These are the figures given me by local men and not checked up. They are repeated merely to show what Flint believes and why.

So Flint feels rich and is confident of the future. If the visitor questions the second article of its creed he is shown the new factory buildings, acres of them and all of substantial construction. Then he is invited to consider such figures as these: In 1913 General Motors earned $7,459,471.36; in 1914, $7,249,733.76; in 1915, $14,457,803.42, and in 1916 it will earn $25,000,000. That is, it will if enough workmen can be secured. But that "if" is serious because there is no place for those workmen and their families to live. Which brings us from the realms of high finance to the every-day question of securing a roof over one's head.

Flint is a pleasant little city of the kind typical of the Middle West. Its retail business district, built before the first automobile, utterly belies its present importance. But that is a detail of small significance and one that will soon be changed. Already there is one nine-story "modern" office building covering 100 per cent of its lot, with windows on one side overlooking its neighbors' roofs, such as New York built before it awoke to its folly.

From the business district stretch wide tree-shaded streets lined with comfortable frame houses, each surrounded by its wide yard. This is the real Flint of the past and it explains why some of those who have made the most money during the past few years are building their new homes here. Flint has been a pleasant town to live in, roomy, comfortable, genial, neighborly, the kind of town which holds its people, except those young men who want greater opportunity.

Now it is changing. It offers opportunity to its young men, it is attracting men young and middle-aged from all over the country, from foreign countries. It still keeps its pleasant dwellings on their shady streets, but it is building new houses of different types. A few apartment houses have appeared, as usual filling their lots and borrowing light and air from its neighbors, some of them with dark interior living- or bed-rooms and with water-closets that have no means of ventilation. With these has come that invention of the Pacific coast, one or two samples of which have appeared in nearly all our growing cities, the apartment house with convertible rooms. Flint's sample is known as a "five in three" since the kitchen and the bath-room remain kitchen and bath-room while the other rooms are transformed at will by turning panels from living-room or dining-room into bed-rooms.

But it is not these types of dwellings that have aroused Flint's indignation. They are comparatively large and impressive, they look well from the street, they represent considerable capital, consequently they are "improvements" and to be welcomed, whatever the longer experience of the East may have to show as to their later social and economic effects. What Flint rages about is the construction of shacks and the diminishing size of lots.

A House Famine

In Flint there are two great industries, the manufacture of automobiles and the selling of land. The manufacturers of automobiles, so far as the stranger can learn, are pulling well together. The sellers of lots are divided into two hostile camps, the insiders and the outsiders. These terms may be taken to have a double meaning.

The insider is usually a local man and his subdivisions lie within or close to the city limits. The outsider is from another city— Cleveland, Chicago, anywhere except Detroit, where the real estate men have enough work to keep them at home—and his subdivisions usually lie outside the city limits, sometimes a mile and a half or two miles outside. As Flint has not yet built up to its corporate boundaries, and its street improvements, water mains and sewers are far behind in the race to occupy new territory, some of these outside plats do not look very good to the sophisticated eye. Especially do they fail to please the eye of the insider who sees them being divided into smaller and smaller lots which are sold without restriction for $1 down and 50 cents a week.

The insider so far has kept his lots 35 feet wide at least and stipulates that the houses erected on them shall cost not less than $600. Therefore, he is indignant at the loose methods of the outsider. Moreover, he has been holding his lots for six long, lean years, for not since 1910, when the tent dwellers silently stole away, has business been really good. And he is doing what he can to stimulate actual building.

The methods by which local real estate operators aid home builders to erect dwellings are almost as various as the number of firms. One that seems to promise best, though the operator himself admits that it is still but a promise, is to sell to a lot buyer building material valued at $500 on a 10 per cent commission, stipulating that none of this material is to be used for interior finish. The buyer pays $80 down and $15 a month. In this way he gets the most possible house for the least possible initial outlay. When he is through he has a house, built by himself, which consists of foundation, floors, walls and roof. Then he is expected to lath and plaster it. The plan is less than a year old and none of the houses erected has yet been lathed. On the outside, however, they look better than the tarpaper shacks and, unlike the shacks, they do not involve throwing away material and labor in the realization of the home-builder's ultimate purpose. So far as they go they fit into the final plan.

But with all that the local real estate operators can do, there is still a house famine. There are 1,500 Flint factory workers who live in Saginaw, 30 miles away; 1,200 more live in Bay City, 40 miles away. The factory managers say they would add 2,000, 3,000, 5,000 to their payrolls if houses were provided. The number varies according to who tells it. William Crapo Durant, who organized General Motors, is quoted as saying that he would take on 5,000 men if they could be induced to come to Flint, which they can not do until there are more houses. Then one is told of the number of houses built and building: 2,500 since January 1, 85 a week which will soon increase to 125 a week—if material and workmen can be secured. The record in the city clerk's office shows that building permits for structures to cost $100 or more were issued as follows:

1912	181
1913	290
1914	416
1915	1398
1916 (to June 1)	1046

Of the 1,398 permits in 1915, 1,204 were for houses, 24 for flats, 20 for stores with flats, 88 for barns and garages, the rest for business buildings. Barns and garages require special mention because they are frequently either heralds or substitutes for the houses which are later to appear on the same lots.

So serious has the house famine become that last fall the Board of Commerce sought to organize a $250,000 company to build houses. The project started well and some $60,000 was subscribed. Then there arose a difference of opinion as to method. Some wished the company to build and sell, some to build and rent, others to put the money into the local building and loan association. The result was that several individuals undertook to build houses on their own account.

Charles S. Mott, head of one of the factories, was one of these. He erected thirty ready-cut, five-room bungalows in the North End where the immigrant laborers congregate. At once there was an outburst of indignation. The houses are small, the bed-rooms tiny. But they are attractively designed and they are widely spaced. They are of fairly substantial construction, but they do not come up to expectations. The street on which they face is not graded, they have no water or sewer connections, they were built by outsiders.

It is agreed, however, that this effort of the Board of Commerce did stimulate building by giving others confidence. One man in describing it used himself as an illustration. He bought four lots for $700, sold the two rear lots for $300, built a house on one of the remaining lots for $1,100, sold it for $1,750 and then sold his fourth lot for $400. He is satisfied.

Now it is again proposed to organize a company, some say it will be capitalized at $100,000, others at the old figure of $250,000.

Meanwhile there are rumors that Mr. Durant has employed one of the local real estate men to erect 1,000 houses, others say 100. The real estate man in question will neither confirm nor deny. All he will admit is that he has sold Mr. Durant $57,500 worth of land, that every one of his houses for the past year was sold before it was plastered, that 600 families have their goods in storage, and that there is a demand for from 6,500 to 7,000 houses.

The building and loan association still hopes that any money raised will be turned over to it. This association was organized in 1911 with a capitalization of $250,000. In December last the capitalization was increased to half a million. It is confining its loans to construction work and has every cent out. It pays 5 per cent on its capital and charges borrowers something over 7 per cent.

Strange as it may be to strangers, people here do not seem to be concerned over the increased cost of land. They tell one casually that lots have doubled and trebled in price during the past year, that a lot which two years ago went begging and a year ago would have brought $100 now sells for $300 and $400. But that is merely incidental. What bothers them is increased rentals, or no rentals at all. Any kind of a house will now bring $20 a month. The janitor of a church pays $20 a month for two rooms. Families who never before thought of such a thing are taking in lodgers.

Buildings which offer no attractions even to a confirmed flat-dweller are proving to be gold mines. One big concrete structure which has called down the wrath of the health officer upon the head of its owner earns $6 per week per room. Each room is equipped with a gas plate and there is a hydrant and dark water-closet in the hall. Even the basement rooms are rented except when the health officer vacates them.

The owner of this particular house has proclaimed her fondness for children. In that she differs from many Flint owners who refuse to rent to families with children. So her house overflows with them. In one room there is a family with five. The husband is a contractor who is sharing in Flint's prosperity. He has offered $40 for a house, but no children were wanted. He hopes to find time to build for himself.

Later in the morning we visited this house the city health nurse showed me some cheap houses in another section of town. We were attracted by a new structure built of odds and ends of board which occupied the rear of a lot. Near it were two Negroes hitching a skeleton-like horse to a rickety wagon. "Who lives there?" asked the nurse. "Nobody," replied one of the darkies, "that's jest a chicken coop." Then the door opened and a Syrian came out. "How much rent do you pay for this house?" I asked. "Seven dollars a month."

"And who owns it?" "One of them fellers." "Well," said the darky, "I built it for a chicken coop, anyhow."

So when one begins to talk housing in Flint he is at once asked, How can we build more houses? Beside that every other question fades to insignificance. It is of immediate and vital importance, much more immediate and vital than most of the questioners realize. They see an opportunity for profit postponed if not lost, while unseen by them the character of the city is changing. Flint, with the possibility of becoming one of the finest industrial cities in the country, seems destined to go through the same deterioration as have the older industrial cities of the East. To meet in some fashion the need of the moment is absorbing all the thoughts of those who can and should be thinking of the needs of the future. The men who are building Flint are practical men, keen and alert, but few of their thoughts go beyond the end of the fiscal year.

I have said that the real estate operators are divided into two camps, the insiders and the outsiders. Among the insiders there are further divisions. There are those who are appealing to the high-class trade. They make their lots 40 to 50, some even 100 feet wide. They stipulate that a house shall cost at least $2,500 and not be nearer than 6 feet to the side lot line—leaving space for an automobile roadway between dwellings. There are others who make only a $600 limitation and permit the buyer to erect a garage or a kitchen in which his family may live until he can build a house.

There are some who erect houses for sale and use posts for foundations, who have convinced themselves that 2 x 4 rafters are extravagant, and so saw them in two. It is said that a shingler fell through the roof of one of these economical houses not long ago. For such parsimony as this there is scorn. But when a man erects a $65,000 block on North Saginaw street, with a good-looking brick front and plate-glass windows for the stores on the ground floor, and arranges the upper floors so that each family has bed-rooms whose only light and air come from windows on a gloomy common hall, and water-closets whose only ventilation comes from a register arrangement near the ceiling, there is no indignation. Flint looks at the outside.

And yet this is not quite a fair statement, for there are those in Flint who look also at the inside, who understand what land crowding and dark rooms will mean to the future city and who are fighting valiantly for good standards. They too are somewhat confused by the rapidity of recent changes, by the desire for good appearance, by the unprecedented demand for shelter. Yet in spite of all this they are holding their ground.

The old business blocks of Flint, like those of most cities of its size, are arranged for dwellings above the stores. Sometimes these are let out for light housekeeping, sometimes they are used as lodging-houses. As the store buildings are deep and are erected in solid rows, the middle rooms on the second and third floors have no windows.

Flint has done what few cities have done, and that in the face of a demand such as few cities have met—it has vacated these dark rooms and kept most of them empty. Of course, so long as they remain in their present condition there is danger that they will be reoccupied, but in several buildings which I visited they are now empty or used only as store rooms and have been so for a year or more. These were the worst. Still occupied are suites where the bed-room gets its only light and air from a small dingy skylight, where the water-closet is a dark corner of the bed-room that has been partitioned off. Flint's standards are not yet high, but it deserves credit for keeping them from being lower.

The great trouble in Flint is that things move so fast that people become confused. There are few standards, each gets what he can. In one of the large downtown blocks where the interior rooms are lighted by triangular openings and windows to a common hall, above which is a skylight, there is a family consisting of father, mother and a year-old baby, paying $5 a week for a single room. They do their cooking on an oil stove and share a hall hydrant and water-closet with other families.

On the same floor, on the other side of the building, a woman rents five rooms for $22 a month and sublets each room at $2 a week. These rooms have windows over a neighboring roof.

In the Jungle, a dumping place on the river bank, one owner charges $1.50 a month for the site of a shack built by the tenant, another charges $2. The second owner also owns one of the shacks. For this he charges $3 a month. A better shack next door was bought by the present tenant two months ago for $30 and sold within the past week for $35. He is going to move his family to another neighborhood where he has rented two rooms.

This is an American family, as are all but one of the others in this shack colony. Asked where her people came from, the mother mentioned another town in the state. Asked if her husband's people were also Americans, she replied, "No, they are Indiana folks." Different was the point of view of the building inspector. He said that nearly all the foreigners live in the North End, one colony of Italians in the south being the exception. As there are many English, Scotch and Canadians in Flint, he was asked if they live in the North End. "No," he said, "by foreigners I mean only those who don't speak English."

As to the number of these foreigners, estimates vary, but apparently it is a little under 15,000. For these people very little is being done except through the public schools. Fortunately, Elizabeth Welch, the principal of the Fairview school in the heart of the foreign colony, is of the type that starts things. She was the leader in night school work and now is utilizing the old building, out of which the school moved this spring, as a day nursery, to be supported by the King's Daughters. Except for this, the "foreigners" are left to help themselves become Americans.

The Wage-Earning Population

In this they are assisted by the circumstance that as yet they have not formed separate colonies—with the exception of the South End Italians—though the Poles are beginning to segregate themselves and Miss Welch says that in school the Polish boys tend to keep in a group separate from the others. Near the Fairview school I found two three-story houses sheltering five families—one of whom kept 17 lodgers—each of a different nationality: German, Hungarian, Slovak, Syrian and Servian. Their only means of communication was English, so all but one of the women could speak it well enough to answer simple questions while several of the lodgers were quite fluent.

As it is impossible to get more than an estimate of the population of Flint, so it is impossible to get more than an estimate of the number of wage-earners. The big factories, aside from their office workers, have 16,500 employes, of whom 500 were added within the month. The smaller factories are believed to employ about 2,000 more. Then there are the building trades with an unknown number of workers. Several of the factories employ women in the trim shops, and in making spark plugs, cores, mouldings, carburetors, etc. But the number of these, as of the women employed in the offices and at telephone switchboards, has never been totaled.

In the building trades the unions have entered and, of course, the printers are organized, but otherwise this is not a union town. Stories are told of the futile attempts of the railroads to hold their construction gangs, who disappear in a day on learning of the wages paid by the factories or by the city government which has need of a considerable number of unskilled laborers as it does all its own street paving and laying of sewers and water mains.

As to minimum wages there is again difference of opinion, some asserting that unskilled labor can get $3 a day, others putting the figure at $2.30. The city pays 27½ cents an hour for a ten-hour day to its sidewalk layers and 28 cents to its sewer diggers. Probably like rent, it is a question of what one can get. For though the manufacturers have a gentleman's agreement that they will not hire away from each other, they do. Necessity knows no agreements.

As to skilled workers, their wages are said to run up to $18 and $20 a day for the drop hammer men. But, of course, these men can not work steadily, the labor is too exhausting, and though one of my informants said he had known hammer men to average $14 a day, he admitted that most of them work only two or three days a week.

The factory managements are interested in welfare work. Several have opened lunch rooms and one has a "charity department." This is supported by contributions from the employes which are doubled by the corporation, the fund then being turned over to a committee of the employes for administration.

But their chief contribution has been the Flint Factories Mutual Benefit Association and its subsidiary, the Vehicle Workers' Club. These were organized in 1901 by J. D. Dort, one of the leaders among the manufacturers and perhaps that one who has shown the most public spirit. Eighteen factories are interested in the association, the same eighteen that support the efficient Manufacturers' Association which looks after their labor needs. The Mutual Benefit Association is supported entirely by the dues of members, 10 cents a week entitling the member to $1 per day for eighteen weeks in any one year, beginning five days after he has fallen sick or been disabled, and to a funeral benefit of $50; 15 cents per week entitling him or her to $1.50 per day, and a funeral benefit of $75. Only those employes whose pay amounts to $12 per week or more are eligible to the second class. This distinction casts some light on the question of minimum wages, though wages have been raised since it was adopted.

The Manufacturers' Association supplements these benefits for employes of its factories whose dues to the Benefit Association are paid in full by extending the period 104 weeks when the need of assistance is shown to the satisfaction of its executive committee. This supplementary assistance may begin at the end of thirteen weeks after the beneficiary became incapacitated, and ranges from $7 to $9 per week. It is expressly stated, however, that maximum compensation, both as regards amount and time limit, "will be paid in exceptional cases only, as our intention is simply to relieve suffering and distress temporarily, not to provide support for two years or any part thereof."

This organization antedated the passage of a workmen's compensation law by eleven years. In 1912 an elective law was enacted providing half of the previous wages for not over 500 weeks in case of total disability, and half the previous wages for 300 weeks to the dependents in case of death. Partial disability entitles the injured person to one-half of the amount by which his earning capacity is decreased. Weekly payments in case of death not to exceed $6, nor $10 in case of total disability.

Membership in the Benefit Association is limited to employes of the eighteen factories, but upon them it is strongly urged. The statement is made that at one time membership was a requisite to securing employment. But this is denied, though it is admitted that the advantages of the association are forcibly presented to every applicant for a job. If he or she joins he signs an application blank and his dues are deducted from his pay at the factory. Age and physical condition are not considered, all members paying the same dues. The thirty-one trustees who direct the association are elected by the members and it is claimed that all but two are shop workers.

Subsidiary to the Benefit Association is the Vehicle Workers' Club which occupies all of a large building except those ground floor corners in which the Benefit Association and the Manufacturers' Association have their offices. Dues in the club are 10 cents a week extra and membership is confined to male members of the Benefit Association. The building is admirably suited to its purpose, with a lunch counter and a large lounge or reading-room and billiard room, on the ground floor, bowling alleys and baths below and bed-rooms in the upper stories. Each bed-room accommodates two men who pay $1.50 to $2 a week rent.

Despite these evidences of interest in the welfare of their employes, especially the Benefit Association and the club, which though fifteen years old still are the high-water mark, the men at the head of Flint's industries have not yet awakened to their responsibilities or their opportunities. Their inter-relations bind them so closely together that they can make not only their plants but their city what they desire. They are the men who made Flint and who are making Flint. There is no question here of competition, of lack of means or of power. If Flint degenerates into a typical factory town it will be simply because these men lacked either the vision or the will to interfere.

One of them gave me what is probably a prevalent point of view among them. He said that several years ago there were few calls upon him for semi-public service, but that lately these calls have been increasing at such a rate that he has had to draw the line.

"Parks and playgrounds, children's welfare, Board of Commerce, housing. They are beginning to take up so much of my time that business suffers. They are all good things, the men who originate them are splendid men, but somehow they don't go through. To the men who undertake them they are side issues, not the serious business of life. I believe we should re-organize the city government and put all this work under one department. Put at the head of that work a big man and give him a big salary, a man with power to stir and inspire us, not a routine man. Then we shall have all these things done."

Beginning of Concerted Action

One of the leading lawyers of the city expressed almost the same thought and both, as others had previously done, said that if they could get a man like Dan Reed [sentence incomplete in original].

For Dan Reed has been here to re-organize the Board of Commerce. He aroused Flint's enthusiasm. The big men of the town responded to his demand for an organization through which they could render effective service to the community. They took ten, twenty, fifty twenty-five-dollar memberships in the board. One of them made a special trip to New York and induced Mr. Durant to take 200 memberships. These memberships are to be distributed through the factories, shops and stores. Then with new blood and fresh enthusiasm the Board of Commerce is expected to do great things for its city. Meanwhile the members are sending in suggestions as to what the board should take up and these are being classified by Wayne D. Heydecker, Reed's assistant, who has remained to help get the new organization well started.

It is interesting to note that of the suggestions sent in by the first 70 to respond—all that have responded to the date of this writing—only 11 have to do with business in its narrower sense. One wants more good hotels, two more stores of an up-to-date kind, three a diversification of industries, two a public market for farmers, three improved railroad facilities.

The rest want things which will make Flint a better town to live in. They ask for housing regulation and especially for funds to build workingmen's houses, for a new high school, for more parks and playgrounds, for the extension of sewers and water mains, for an adequate auditorium, for music, for law enforcement, early closing of stores during the summer, for a community house, for river improvement, a committee on vacant lot gardens. One man even suggests getting a city plan and then building to conform to it. By the time all the suggestions are in there will evidently be enough to keep the new committees and their new secretary busy separating the wheat from the chaff and then grinding the wheat.

Flint expects great things from its re-organized Board of Commerce. The question is whether it does not expect too much, and expect that much without a great deal of work on the part of the men who alone can get results. If the big men, having assigned their ten, twenty and fifty memberships, now sit back, the proposed housing code will have as hard sledding this year as it did two years ago, the proposed building company will get no further than that of last fall. These things, which it is so easy to suggest and which "everybody" wants, run counter to the private interests of individuals who do not sit back.

When the best subdivision in town requires only six feet between building and lot line, when apartment houses cover nearly 100 per cent of their lots, when families come crowding in as fast as any sort of shelter can be provided for them, it will take more than a suggestion to keep Flint from becoming an overcrowded tenement house city or to secure enough money at low rates of interest to build good dwellings or to keep lot prices within the means of the working-man. If Flint's growth is permanent there is serious work ahead for the best organizing ability in the city. For at present everything outside the factories is unorganized, a go-as-you-will-and-the-devil-take-the-hindmost affair, with the result that the future is forgotten and standards are lowered.

Civic Consciousness in Embryo

In judging Flint one must always remember that it is a village grown overnight into a city. In it the social and civic activities of a city are just beginning. There is as yet no charity organization society, though one is planned. The nearest approach to it is a child welfare association which sends children to the country for vacations. There is only one playground, an athletic field where the factory baseball and soccer teams play their league series.

The schools have large grounds where the little children can romp, but the children in their teens are left unprovided for. There are pleasant little parks scattered through the city and one on the shore of diminutive Thread Lake for those who take the open air from benches. There is one commercial amusement park which is said to be well regulated. These comprise Flint's provision for outdoor recreation, if golf and motoring for the well-to-do and vacant lot baseball for the boys are excepted.

As for indoor commercial recreation, it is represented by the movies and the dance halls. There are fifteen movie theaters, an ample supply except on Saturdays and holidays when one has to wait his turn to enter. There are perhaps half a dozen dance halls, visited regularly by the police matron whose chief task seems to be sending young girls home.

On the whole, Flint, despite its great influx of strangers, seems to be an orderly town. It has no red light district or recognized houses of prostitution, though it has prostitutes and street walkers who ply their trade unobtrusively. But it is the wettest dry town in Michigan. Prohibition has closed some saloons and changed others into soft drink places where hard liquor is sold by boot-leggers and washed down by five-cent glasses of water sold by the proprietor. It has led to the opening of blind pigs, especially in the foreign North End, where beer is delivered openly and where cases of empty beer bottles stand on the back porches. The trouble has been that the law requires proof that the proprietor of the place sold the liquor.

The mayor hopes to overcome this difficulty by an ordinance already drafted which requires proof only that liquor was drunk on the premises. If the ordinance goes through it is expected that the police department's labors will be considerably lightened as more than half the arrests now are for drunkenness.

Naturally the number of arrests has increased with the increase of population, though the police statistics seem to indicate that the people of Flint are strong on New Year's resolutions. In January, 1915, the total number of arrests was 78 of which 49 were drunks and disorderlies. This number increased steadily until October when it reached a total of 350; of this number 215 were drunks and disorderlies. Then it decreased somewhat until January when came the New Year drop to 151, including only 74 drunks and disorderlies. Since then it has been mounting again more rapidly than before.

As substitutes for the saloon Flint offers the wage-earner the Vehicle Workers' Club, already described, and the Y.M.C.A. This has approximately 900 members, of whom, it is claimed, a large proportion are factory workers. It has a large, new, well-equipped building with reading-room, gymnasium, showers and swimming-pool. On the upper floors are bed-rooms which rent for $2 a week up.

Several of the churches are active in civic and social work, especially St. Paul's, whose rector, the Rev. J. Bradford Pengelly, is one of the chief advocates of a housing code. This church is about to build a parish house, a feature of which will be a school of civics.

There are several women's organizations: the Columbian Club, the Federation of Women's Clubs of Genesee County, the Art Club, the Y.W.C.A. and the Women's Council. Of these the last takes a definite interest in civic questions but it is too young to have had much influence. The King's Daughters have already been mentioned. This list would be incomplete without the name of Lucy Stewart, who, though unorganized, has agitated for a housing code until she has made the question one of very practical importance to busy men who would prefer to spend their time on other things.

The government is the old-fashioned mayor and ward elected aldermen form. There are proposals to change this form, but no definite propaganda is now under way. The present mayor, Earl F. Johnson, is forceful and respected. The president of the council is one of the leading real estate men, one who is dealing in high-class property. Both are definitely interested in housing and the latter expressed confidence that the housing code will go through this year. He would forbid all building on streets which do not have water and sewers.

A City Which Has Outgrown Its Shoes

When reminded that Flint has many built-up streets without these and asked if it may not prove impossible to extend them fast enough to meet the need, he declared that Flint won't admit there is anything it can't do. When told of one lot on which six houses are now being erected and asked if Flint could do the most important thing, prevent land overcrowding, he was not so confident.

The statistics of the city engineer's office indicate that his confidence regarding sewers and water-mains may not be justified, even though Flint has shown itself more progressive than the armies of Europe by using machinery instead of spades to dig its trenches. There are some 200 miles of streets in the city. Of these 24½ miles are paved. The paving is now going on at the rate of from 8 to 10 miles a year.

Of sewers there are 80½ miles with 25 miles more proposed for 1916. These are partly storm water, partly sanitary and partly combination. The water-mains do not cover as much territory as the sewers, but there is a proposal to bond for half a million dollars so that they may be extended more rapidly. The city has already spent $400,000 for pumping station, filtration plant and mains.

Of one city department the people are very proud, the fire department. All of its apparatus is of the latest design and is motor driven except one piece which is kept in the North End where a motor vehicle might get mired in the mud roads. For this fire department the city pays $61,385.32 a year. For the police department it pays $27,336.29. For health conservation and sanitation it pays $9,169.09. For building inspection $506.65. These are figures from the auditor's report issued February 29, 1916. Since then there have been some changes; for instance, the building inspector, who also has charge of the electrical fire-alarm system, has been given an assistant. But his work has increased out of proportion.

The Health Department, too, is undermanned. Besides the health officer who gives but part time to the work, there are three inspectors and a municipal nurse. The health officer has been trying for years to get a system of garbage collection, the purpose of which should be the removal of garbage instead of the feeding of pigs. The present contract with the owner of the pig farm expires this year, and Dr. Knapp hopes he can now bring his six-year campaign to a successful conclusion and retiring from office leave behind a large monument in the form of a reduction or incineration plant and several thousand little monuments in the form of clean back yards.

The week before my visit was clean-up week in Flint and the city paid several hundred dollars to cart away refuse. No one who saw the back yards the following week would have guessed there had been a clean-up week without being told—that is, unless he knew what those back yards had been like two weeks before.

As to its schools, Flint is not quite sure. They have been subjected to a fearful strain this past year and the employment of extra teachers alone has caused an unexpected expenditure of nearly $20,000. But the president of the Board of Education declares that a place has been found for every child of school age. This is something of an achievement, even though it has necessitated the use of thirty basement rooms (though heated and adequately lighted) and of four two-room temporary buildings.

The total attendance at the public day schools in 1914-15 was 6,363; at the night school, 265. The total attendance at the day schools in March is this year, [according to] the latest figures available, 8,799. The younger teachers are all normal school graduates who have had practical experience before coming to Flint.

So far the school buildings have not been used generally as social or neighborhood centers though the Board of Education permits clubs to use them if they will pay the janitors for overtime.

In addition to the public schools there are three Catholic parochial schools, in one of which instruction is partly or wholly in Polish.

To the visitor in Flint who has studied the older industrial cities of New England the first impression is almost wholly agreeable. Instead of barren, dusty streets lined with dingy three-deckers, he sees green, shady streets lined with little cottages set in pretty yards. And beyond these streets stretches a fertile almost level country with room for indefinite expansion. Then he begins to note details significant of coming change. Houses are being put on the rears of lots, multiple dwellings are going up.

When he examines some of the new houses more closely, he finds that they are of flimsy construction which in a few years will cause discouragement to the owner and lead to neglect and dilapidation. He, of course, sees the tar-paper shacks, but they do not impress him as much as the others, for they are, or may be, only temporary. The city can well limit their life to three or four years by granting licenses for that length of time. Yet they are the things against which local opinion is most directed, for their undesirableness, especially to those who wish to keep up land prices, is obvious now, and to the most casual observer, while the greater and the enduring menace of the large, crowded tenement or the pretentious but flimsily built dwelling will become obvious only after the mischief can not be remedied.

Flint is thinking of today, with scarcely a thought of tomorrow. Like the kings of Prussia and the emperors of France, what its dynamic citizens want and want now is a city that will look well from the street. And by well, they mean impressive. Big buildings fill their eye. They have seen the larger cities from the street and would like to have Flint resemble these larger cities—look metropolitan. The men who are doing the building know of high land values in the larger cities, and being interested primarily in land, they see only good in the increasing price of lots.

In other words, those who are controlling the development of Flint have only one angle on its future development, profits for themselves. They can be reached to some extent by showing them that over-intensive use of land will prove a boomerang, that crowding buildings so close together that they darken each other's windows will depreciate values. But even this touches them only lightly, for they believe that this overcrowding cannot soon become serious and their concern is the present. Let the buyer beware of what his neighbors may do five or ten years hence.

Meanwhile the real makers of Flint, the men whose ability has built up the great industry upon which all else depends, sit back. They are occupied with other and even more profitable concerns. They have an affection for the town in which they made their wealth, but it is rather cool and platonic. It expresses itself in words, it leads them to give their "support" to "worthy" movements, it leads them to give two hours a day for five days to securing members for the Board of Commerce, it leads them to speculate on what a better form of government might do for the city; but so far it has not led them to give the city that keen and whole-hearted service which alone can save it, can make it all that it is capable of being.

Flint Needs Builders—As Well as Buildings

Yet upon them rests the responsibility. They found Flint a pleasant little country town, they are changing it into a city. They found it an American community, they are changing it into a cosmopolitan community. New and vital civic and social problems are arising as a direct result of their work, of the work which is bringing them great wealth, and they find that the calls upon their time because of these problems interfere with their work of getting more wealth, so they are drawing the line.

Have they a moral right to draw such a line? Have they a moral right to concentrate upon that part of their work which yields the greatest profits and either disregard or give only shreds of attention to the other part, the part which means the making or the wrecking of their city? For the building of Flint, every phase of it, is their work. They made the town grow from 13,103 population in 1900 to 38,550 in 1910; to 65,000 or 70,000 in 1916. They have made a city. But ten years from now they will have small cause for pride in their achievement unless they make the development of their city a serious part of their work. Perhaps, through the re-organized Board of Commerce, they will. Not that they can become autocrats and impose their will upon the community, but that they may identify themselves with the community in all its aspirations and endeavors. A group that stands aloof may have great power though there are limits to that power even in a legalized autocracy. But a community deprived of the active and earnest cooperation of its leaders, its "big men," as are some of the eastern manufacturing towns whose "big men" are absentees, progresses haltingly.

It is leadership, vision, confidence that the "big men" of Flint can give their city. But they can give these only if they admit they have no monopoly of them, that while they are leaders, have vision, inspire confidence, there are others, not so successful in a business way, who also possess the qualities of leadership and vision and the ability to inspire confidence in ways that supplement theirs. The building of a city is a work for all its people.

By 1920 Detroit was clearly established as an automobile city characterized by a rapid expansion of its work force and the spread of the city
into surburban areas. Henry Ford was a major force in the state with his
five dollars a day attracting a working population to Detroit, which, as
Webb Waldron's article makes clear, was regarded as a town of high
wages. Waldron identified the rise of the automobile with the American
way of life and the triumph of individual entrepreneurship.

As he viewed the boom activity in the city, Waldron posed a key
question, which is still to be answered in our present years of urban
crisis: "What is the significance of Detroit?"

Boom Days in Detroit

WEBB WALDRON

Detroit, Michigan, U.S.A.
January 15, 1920.

My Dear Roberval:

You remember that last day after luncheon at your delightful
club, as we sat on the terrace looking down into the gardens that
stretch to the Avenue Gabriel?

You speculated on what impressions America would make on an
American who had been away through the most exciting period of
her history—an American who saw the armies in action, who saw
Germany and Hungary in revolution, who was bored and disillu-
sioned by the bickerings and intrigues of the peace conference, who
saw Europe everywhere on the brink of economic smash-up, and
who through it all had looked back to America as a comparative
heaven of sanity, health, and safety. You wondered whether the
war had affected America essentially or only superficially. You
wondered what America was thinking about, where America was
going. You said that was the most important question in the world.

Well, I'm going to give you a picture of America as I find it.
Perhaps, after I've seen a little more of my country, I'll be able to
tell you where it is going.

I do not think I could begin any better than with probably the
most amazing city in America—Detroit.

One day last summer I heard an American officer in Paris say to a
prominent French woman: "You'd enjoy America. We aren't so
crude, you know. We have several cities with distinctive atmo-

From "Where Is America Going?" *The Century*, 100 (May, 1920), 58-64.

sphere; San Francisco, for example, and New Orleans, and that charming old French town, Detroit." Maybe the American's reference to Detroit was facetious. Maybe, on the other hand, he had never been in Detroit. Charming old French town! When I saw Detroit first, in 1899, it was a sleepy middle-Western city, rather like an overgrown village; possibly a whiff of its eighteenth century French atmosphere did cling somewhere about it. But today! There is atmosphere, yes; but its single characteristic is a smell of gasoline. Imagine this. A cluster of new sky-scrapers thrusting gawkily up out of a welter of nondescript old buildings. A big open square crowded with automobiles; great radiating streets teeming with crowded trolley-cars, radiating outward like the fingers of a Brobdingnagian hand through a vast dreary waste of crisscross streets lined with rows of soot-blackened wooden houses, on and on, mile after mile, till they reach stupendous palaces of steel and glass that suck in and disgorge hundreds of thousands of workmen morning and night. Automobiles are everywhere—automobiles in solid ranks along the curbs, automobiles parked solidly in public squares and vacant lots, automobiles rushing up and down in unbroken streams. Automobiles! automobiles! Such is Detroit. Yet, despite all this, Detroit is still in many ways a village. It has a village transportation system, village newspapers, a village society, a village point of view. This is a very typically American thing, Roberval, that villages become metropolises and yet remain villages. A village of one million people! For Detroit is making over half the world's automobiles.

What are these people thinking who rush up and down in trolley-car and motor, who crowd these sidewalks and shops, who pour in and out of these steel-and-glass palaces where automobiles are wrought? What has the war done to them? I fought my way into a trolley-car that already contained twice as many people as it was built to carry.

"We thought they'd sold us out to the bosses," one workman was explaining to another.

"How's that?" asked his companion.

I edged nearer, listening. It seems that the men in the department of the automobile plant in which the first speaker was employed recently decided to ask for an increase of wages. The entire department belonged to the union; so the men asked their union officials, "What increase shall we demand?" "Demand an increase to one dollar an hour," was the reply. The men delegated the union officials to put this demand up to the plant management. But before the demand had been passed upon, the men made a startling discovery. The non-unionized employees of another plant, doing exactly the same kind of work, were already getting a dollar and a half an hour. The unionized men turned on their union representatives and charged them with treachery. But there had been no treachery. The non-unionized men had simply asked for a dollar and a half, and got it without question.

"What's the good of belonging to the union?" the speaker concluded.

I dropped off the car. That phrase, "What's the good of belonging to the union?" stuck in my mind. Let me explain, Roberval, that I've come back to an America torn by industrial conflicts. Strikes, rumors of strikes, industrial conferences that more often fail than succeed, fill the newspapers. From the newspapers one gets the impression of two giants, the labor union and the capitalist, facing each other with set jaws and bared teeth.

In a telephone-book I found the address of the headquarters of the Auto Workers' Union, whose full title is the United Automobile, Aircraft and Vehicle Workers of America. In a small office I discovered William A. Logan, international president of this organization.

"What are your aims in Detroit?" I inquired. Mr. Logan, in answer, started to lecture me on the iniquities of the new law of the State of Michigan which forbids sabotage, and exclaimed that the courts will probably interpret sabotage to mean striking or anything they please.

"But," I insisted, "what are your specific aims and grievances in Detroit?"

He hesitated.

"Well," he said finally, "I guess we haven't anything to complain of. Everything's all right."

Think of it! Could any one go into the offices of any labor organization in any other industrial capital of the world at the present moment and get such an answer? Perhaps one could. I do not know. Here in Detroit, at least, labor organizations are apparently unable to raise an issue because they know that any group of men, unionized or not, can go to an employer and get almost anything they want. Why?

I took a car for one of the steel-and-glass palaces.

"Labor troubles?" the manager repeated in answer to my question. "In the ordinary sense, no. We haven't time to fight out wage disputes. Good Lord! man, we're six months behind in our orders!"

"What do you mean by in the ordinary sense?"

"Why should we pay twice as much as before the war for men who do only a little over half as much work?" he demanded. "That's what hurts. Do you know that labor efficiency has slumped thirty-five per cent in this plant in the past year?"

Employers in England, France, Germany, and Hungary complained to me of a like slump in labor efficiency. Over there the explanation I got was "war weariness." But was America in the war long enough to grow "weary"?

"Why the slump?" I asked.

"During the war," the manager replied, "the Government spread posters broadcast telling the working-classes they were 'it,' that victory over Germany depended on them alone. Well, that propaganda simply gave them a realization of their own power, and they're acting on it. They work at the rate they please."

No labor troubles, but plenty of troubles with labor, I saw. Detroit emits a cry of industrial discontent, but it comes almost entirely from one end of the horn—the employers'.

I went on to another plant.

"Yes, we have a serious loss in efficiency," the president of the company admitted. "Almost forty per cent in some departments. Cause? The war, of course. But I couldn't agree that it is conscious shirking. Here's an incident that illustrates what I mean. The boy who was my chauffeur before the war came back a few weeks ago and took his old job. I'd had seven or eight different drivers in the last year, and now I congratulated myself. Ken was a good, skilful man; he'd been with us for years, was like one of the family. But I realized immediately that he wasn't doing his work as he should. And a couple of days ago he came into my library, deeply troubled. 'I want to work for you,' he said. 'The wages are right, and you treat me fine; but I'm doing my work rotten and I know it. I've had about fifty jobs since I got out of the army, and either got fired or quit every time. Now I've got to quit you. If I don't, you'll fire me sure. I'm sorry. I don't know what's wrong.' I urged him to give the job another chance, but he wouldn't. He's a perfectly honest, ambitious fellow; but the war did something to him; he doesn't know what, I don't know what. It's done something vital and destructive to a lot of us." He mused a moment. "Maybe," he said at last, "that very restlessness is the sign of some ultimate good. How can we tell?"

I went on to still another office, and here I got data about the alarming increase in the waste of material.

"For every dollar we spend on productive labor," the president of this third plant read from a report of his controller, "we must set aside forty cents for scrapped material due to careless workmanship." He looked up from the paper. "You can't discipline a workman any more," he explained. "If you do, he quits. He knows he can get another job right away, and you know you have to have another man right away, a man who may not be as good as he is."

This company builds one of our highest-grade automobiles; careful workmanship is imperative. Some time ago the company erected and equipped an apprentice school at a cost of $350,000. Here a boy got a course of expert shop instruction; he was paid at the full rate for work he did while training. The company figured that the school would pour a constant stream of expert workmen into the plant, men trained on just its type of work, and that these graduates would be attached to the plant by a certain loyalty, thus reducing the labor turnover. "Every time a new man comes on a machine, there is almost sure to be a temporary drop of efficiency on that machine," the president reminded me. "The first output of the machine may be unfit to pass our inspection, even if the man is a conscientious worker, because he isn't accustomed to our standards yet."

Recently, however, this concern found that its apprentice school was costing eight hundred dollars each for every graduate who stayed with the plant. "Some of the graduates never entered the shop at all," the president said. "Others would stay a few weeks, then drift on to another plant. Sometimes they had no apparent reason for quitting, sometimes they went because another plant offered half a cent or a cent more an hour, for the time being, on a certain class of work. So we've shut down the school. We couldn't afford it."

It must be explained that the working conditions in this shop are excellent, and the wage-scale quite up to the high average in Detroit. In New England I have visited machine shops where a large number of the workmen have, as it were, grown up with the plant. Such a condition is almost unknown in Detroit. Few of the automobile shops are more than ten years old, of course, but you wouldn't find many mechanics who have been continuously in the same shop through even half of the shop's history. Workmen move restlessly from shop to shop as the mood strikes them or as this or that concern bids slightly higher. In a plant like Ford's, where multiple manufacture has been pushed to the last degree, so that most men's jobs consist in performing one very small operation over and over in endless monotony, the sense of attachment to the concern is naturally at a minimum. "Nobody would work for Ford's five minutes except that he pays a little more," a workman informed me. "Ford's makes a machine out of a man."

Watching the driving routine on the assembly-floor at the Ford plant, one is reminded of the protest put into the mouth of the French workman Pierre, in Brieux's new play, "Les Américains chez nous": "L'économie des mouvements, le rendement maximum, le taylorisme, comme vous dites—moi, j'appelle ça le *terrorisme*...."

Toujours et toujours faire le même mouvement, prendre un bout de métal par ci, le donner à la bête, en reprendre un autre et le lui redonner et toujours, toujours, toujours. Je vous ai dit que c'est à devenir fou!"

Later in the day I interviewed the manager of still a fourth plant.

"They're talking down in Washington about restricting immigration, especially alien enemy immigration. Do you know what we'd do if we were wise? We'd offer a bonus of a hundred dollars to every German workman who would come to this country and settle. One German is worth half a dozen Polacks or Dagoes. Dangerous? Nonsense! Think of the trouble the Germans in this country could have kicked up during the war if they'd wanted to! But they didn't. The trouble was all made by a few hired agitators. The German, next to the Anglo-Saxon, is the best citizen in the world, and the best workman."

"What do you think of the League of Nations out here?" I asked irrelevantly.

"Oh, it's all right. We're for it. And we wish those fools down in Washington would hurry up and ratify the peace treaty so we could cut loose from Europe for good."

You, Roberval, one of the few men I met in France to whom the League of Nations seemed a realizable or even a reasonable idea, how often you emphasized your belief that if the League of Nations was a reality to America, America could impress that idea on the world!

"The really important thing"—the manager came back with relief to more vital matters—"is the question whether we can get enough labor to fill our orders."

He, too, is swamped with orders. He, too, is crying for men, men, men.

Some of the results of this demand for men will astonish you, as they astonished me. And here comes a matter that has never been fully realized—the profound effect of the machine tool. It isn't an industrial effect only; it is ultimately an economic, social, and political effect, also. The same effects have been observed in Europe, I imagine, but probably not to the same degree. I am not saying, mark, that all jobs in automobile plants are machine-tool jobs; rather, I want the machine tool to typify the vast majority of jobs in these plants. They are highly specialized jobs on expensive material, where the profit is high to the employer even at the amazing wages paid here, and they are jobs which may be learned in a few days or a few weeks at most by any man of ordinary intelligence.

Now, why should a man dig sewers, even at seven dollars a day, when in a few days or weeks he can learn a job in an automobile plant and earn almost twice as much with half the exertion? The city government of Detroit has been offering seven dollars and more per day for men to dig trenches for sewers and water-mains, with no comers, or else with "comers that might as well be goers," as one city official puts it. Why should a man work for an ice company? Why should a man get up at three o'clock in the morning to drive a milk-wagon? People in Detroit complain that their ice and milk fail to come half the time because the men do not stay on the job long enough to learn the routes. Why should a man work on a farm when he, too, can get a job in an automobile shop and triple his pay? I remember that ten or fifteen years ago twenty-five dollars a month was thought good wages for a farmhand in southern Michigan. Eighteen dollars was often the year-round wage. One day a man who had been working on a Dakota ranch turned up at one of my uncles' farms and asked for a job; he wanted thirty dollars a month. "Go chase yourself!" my uncle exclaimed. "No mother's son's worth thirty dollars a month." Now, farmers around Detroit and Jackson and Flint are offering seventy-five and one hundred dollars a month and board for help, also with no comers or else "comers that might as well be goers." A farmer near here told me that he is paying his man four dollars a day, and not only boarding the man, but the man's driving horse as well. "And he ain't worth shucks," the farmer added. Farmers in this district say that this year they're going to farm only what they can care for with their own hands without hired help. This draining of the farm is happening everywhere in America around industrial centers, but probably nowhere so acutely as here. And the natural query is, What will happen if even one quarter of the country's farmers act on that principle this year? That again leads on to another question. If farming is a business, as its defenders say it is, why can't it compete with other businesses in the labor market? Is the price of the farm product too low, or is there something the matter with the farmer? The man who answers that question must fix his eye on the machine tool and what the machine tool typifies.

But is labor any better off in Detroit with all these soaring wages?

"It's harder to live on seventy dollars a week now than on thirty-five before the war," a die-maker at the Ford plant told me.

There's a curious compensation in these things. High wages draw swarms of people; a congestion of people brings profiteering in food and property values and rents. Government statistics show that the cost of living has gone higher in Detroit than in any other American city. And it's not only the high cost of living, but the inability to find any roof at all under which to live, that confronts thousands of people here. Housing is a world problem. A distinguished Japanese told me a few days ago that it is as acute in Tokyo as I found it in Paris and Berlin and Budapest, but Detroit has the worst situation of any city in America.

Mayor Couzens, the Jim Couzens of Ford fame, tells me he is in favor of building a wall around Detroit and keeping people out for six months, or, at least, of strongly advising people to stay away. "Of course," he said, "it would be hard to get the newspapers to handle any such appeal, because the merchants and their advertisers wouldn't like it." He added: "Human nature's such a contrary thing, that we'd probably have twice as many people piling in here just to find out why we didn't want any more people."

Neither merchants nor industrial men can see the Chinese wall idea, but they have evolved another idea—"The Detroit Idea," the House Financing Corporation.

Once you called my attention to the impossibility of Bolshevism or any sort of revolution in France, because you are preëminently a nation of small landowners. Detroit's business and industrial leaders know that individual ownership is the surest way of making social and political conservatives out of their men, of quieting the restless spirit that is undermining their efficiency. Besides, there is a real desire among Detroit mechanics, as in most American industrial centers, to own their own homes; the desire needs only stimulus and direction. The House Financing Corporation is a sort of specialized bank whose sole aim is the rapid building of houses and individual ownership of houses. The $3,000,000 capital stock has been subscribed by Detroit employers on the basis of $25 per employee for concerns having up to 500 on the pay-roll, and a decreasing scale down to $10 for concerns employing 20,000 or over. It is no more a charity affair than a bank is; it returns six per cent on all money put into it.

To understand its working, let me explain how houses are usually built in American cities. A builder buys land and puts up a house or a block of houses, then sells them on the instalment plan. Suppose the builder sells a certain house for $6000. The buyer signs a contract to pay, perhaps, $1500 down and the remainder in monthly fractions. You assume, I suppose, that this $6000 is the cost of the house and land to the builder plus the profit he wants to get out of it; but it includes much more than that. Let us see. After the builder has made his contract with the buyer and received his $1500, his next move is to get all the rest of his money out of the house, for he is usually a man of small capital. So he secures a mortgage on the contract; for $1500, maybe. Then he takes the contract, with the mortgage attached, to a concern that buys such contracts and sells it, probably at an enormous discount, perhaps fifteen or twenty per cent. I should interpolate that it is very difficult to sell these contracts even at such discounts. As a result he may get $4500 cash out of a house that he has sold for $6000. The land and house may have cost him $4000. But if he hadn't put the price up to $6000, he wouldn't have made any profit at all. Who loses? The buyer, of course.

Now, the House Financing Corporation is backing responsible builders so that they can erect houses rapidly. As soon as a builder finishes a house or a block of houses, he can get all of his money out of them through the House Financing Corporation, and so go right on building. The price of the houses to buyers includes only building price, plus a reasonable builder's profit. Also, the House Financing Corporation advances to individual owners up to four fifths of the value of their land and prospective house; banks and trust companies will advance only one half. By enabling the home-builder to pay cash, the contractor in turn can pay cash, get material cheaper, and so make a better price on the house.

But it's in the promotion of rapid building rather than in the saving of money that this scheme has been serviceable in helping solve the housing problem in this amazing city. Despite complaints about the high cost of living, no one seems very much interested in trying to force prices down.

"People don't ask the price any more," a Gratiot Avenue merchant declared. "They just say, 'Send up the goods.'" A friend of mine was waiting one day in a cigar store near one of the automobile shops. During that time about twenty mechanics came in.

"Only six of the twenty bought two-for-a-quarter cigars," he said; "the rest took twenty-five-cent cigars." If capitalists smoke twenty-five-cent cigars, why shouldn't mechanics smoke them, too? No reason in the world; and yet this free, lordly attitude to the humble "fifty-cent" dollar isn't likely to decrease the dollar's humility. Rather the opposite, don't you think? You know, Roberval, what effect our doughboys' loose and easy way with their money had on prices in French villages.

Make, spend—that is the spirit of the moment. How dumfounded a French mechanic would be at a glimpse into the home of the lathe-hand I am just visiting. In the parlor are a new piano and an expensive talking-machine. In the dining-room a new and expensive set of silver dishes. In the kitchen a new electric washing-machine that cost over one hundred and fifty dollars. When the mistress of the house goes out calling or shopping, she wears a new sealskin coat. The master of the house rides to and from his work in his own automobile; on holidays the family motors to the country. Is this man interested in national, political, social, or economic problems? He is not. He is interested in making all he can now, while the making is good.

"Bolshevism?" he says. "I think it's mostly a lot of newspaper bunk. But if Bolshevism is coming, I guess it's up to me to make all I can before it arrives."

And making means spending.

There seems to be no immediate danger of an end to the opportunities for making. Once some very, very wise men set 1909 as the date of automobile "saturation." By that time, we were told, every one in the world who could possibly afford an automobile would have one, and the only thing necessary henceforth would be to manufacture enough cars to take the place of those that wore out. Then the saturation date was advanced to 1912, with appropriate explanations. The war advanced it still further. Now wiseacres equally wise fix 1921 or 1923 as the period of saturation.

But the automobile men I talked with in Detroit aren't so wisely sure as all that. When I asked Roy D. Chapin, president of the Hudson Company, about saturation, he drew my attention to the billions that will be spent on highways in America in the next ten years, "every mile of which will mean more cars and a greater intermingling of people," and then spoke of the export field "in which America will always be able to undersell foreign builders because our vast production will keep our costs down." When I asked Alvan Macauley, president of the Packard company, he called me to the window of his office and pointed to a whole city block adjoining his plant parked solidly with cars of every kind and price.

"Do you know whom those belong to?" he asked. "Mechanics in this plant. The day is coming when every mechanic and every farmer and every professional man in this country will have his car." (All except editors, school-teachers, and preachers, I mentally reserved.) "That day is a long time off."

Yes, it is a long time off, even in America, to say nothing of Europe, and then Siberia, Nigeria, and Polynesia.

Automobiles and washing-machines and sealskin coats as anti-dotes for Bolshevism—this seems to have become the theme of my first letter. What is the significance of Detroit? Is all this half-satisfying plenty in the midst of a world that has destroyed and wasted and underproduced only a strange local magic? Is the peculiar chance for profit in automobile production, in contrast to the food production and clothes production by which communities live, alone responsible? Yet the demand which makes automobile production profitable comes from the food-producers and clothes-producers of those other communities. Then what, if any, relationship is there between plenty in Detroit and want in Vienna? Are they facets of the same phenomenon? And what, if any, relationship is there between the things which force themselves upon me here—these expensive, sometimes evil-smelling, but exceedingly comfortable things—to our dreams and our fierce concern over international policies and national ideals?

My next letter will treat of an altogether different phase of our life, as I find it now. In the meantime, from this city of conspicuous peace, I send you greeting. Who would have thought that four thousand miles or so of water and land could make me feel so far from the Avenue Gabriel!

Yours sincerely,
WEBB WALDRON

6: World War I

Although Michigan's role in World War I was not unique when compared with some other states, it did have its repercussions in shaping the history of the times. Michigan had its share of anti-Germanism, as James D. Wilkes exemplifies in his article "Van Tyne: The Professor and the Hun," *Michigan History*, 55 (Fall, 1971), 183-204. It also supplied its share of troops that went off to war and expanded industries to provide the materials to fight the Germans across the seas. Sidney Fine gives us an example of the more conventional response to the war in his *Frank Murphy in World War I*, Michigan Historical Collections Bulletin No. 17 (Ann Arbor, 1968). But Michigan also provided men for one of the almost forgotten side issues of the war. This episode was particularly unfortunate, fought by men who were confused as to why they were there and producing no positive results and only bitter memories. This was the abortive expedition organized by the allies in the closing months of World War I to shore up their fast-disintegrating Russian allies by sending an expedition to combat the growing strength and success of the Bolsheviks. The expedition, composed of French, British, and a small number of Americans, ultimately failed. Michigan soldiers filled the major part of the American contribution to this ill-fated expedition. Richard M. Doolen, citing in part from documents created by Michigan soldiers themselves, captures something of the feeling and frustration of this expedition in his article, "Michigan's Polar Bears."

Michigan's Polar Bears

RICHARD DOOLEN

For most members of the American armed forces in Europe, the signing of the armistice with Germany in November, 1918, meant the end of combat and the realization that soon they would be

From Michigan Historical Collections Bulletin No. 14 (The University of Michigan, 1965), pp. 3-20. Published by permission of the Michigan Historical Collections, Bentley Historical Library.

reunited with their families at home. But for one contingent of United States servicemen, the end of fighting in western Europe signified very little at all, for its work had only begun. These were the men of the American Expedition to North Russia, the "Polar Bears," who, with their British, French, Canadian and assorted other allies, still faced many months of combat before they too could return from the war. Sent to Archangel in the early days of September, 1918, these Americans would remain for some nine months before finally being withdrawn in June, 1919; yet during that time few if any would ever understand precisely why they were there.

Although the exact nature of the Polar Bears' mission was unclear, there was never any question as to the identity of their opponents, the armies of Soviet Russia. When the Polar Bear Regiment arrived in Archangel, the Bolshevik government had been in power for less than a year, had withdrawn Russia from the Allied side by making a separate peace with Germany, and was now involved in civil war with several anti-Communist "White" Russian armies. President Wilson, previously committed to a policy of non-intervention in Russia's internal affairs, had opposed American participation in the expedition. However, under heavy French and British pressure, and with the understanding that the expedition would have only certain limited objectives related to the successful conclusion of the war with Germany, he at last consented in July, 1918, to the use of American soldiers. These were to number approximately 5,500 men who would join smaller detachments of English, French and other Allied troops under British command in the Archangel region. A large proportion of the American troops were men from Michigan, members of the 339th Infantry Regiment. In addition to the 339th, the American force comprised the First Battalion of the 310th Engineers, the 337th Field Hospital and the 337th Ambulance Company, all from the 85th Division, which had been trained at Camp Custer, near Battle Creek, Michigan.

. . . .

Many of the difficulties encountered by the Polar Bears were the problems of all combat soldiers. Supply and shelter, weather and sanitation are considerations in the operations of any modern army, and the expedition to North Russia was no exception. In a December memo to his platoon commanders, Captain Otto Odjard requested that all men be told to bathe and change their underclothing at least once a week. This order, he noted, was to be complied with "in spirit as well as in letter," but it is questionable whether men at the front were often able to execute either the spirit or letter of this type of order as the campaign wore on.

On arrival in Archangel, those Americans destined for the Dvina front were transported upriver on old coal scows. Numbers of the men on board were seriously ill, a situation not surprising in light of Clarence Scheu's description:

> Suffering Sea Cooks, what a rotten hole they have dumped us into now, coal dust 2 inches thick, damp, filthy dungeon. We are sleeping on bottom of scow, no light, ventilation, or anything. . . .

A two-day issue of rations for the American troops, as described by one participant, included one can of corned beef, one can of meat and vegetables, an ounce of tea, three and one half ounces each of sugar and rice or beans, eight ounces of bacon, and hardtack. However, when on the move, or under severe battle conditions, the soldier's diet might be reduced to hardtack and bully beef, or whatever he could obtain from the peasants in the way of smoked fish, black bread or vegetables.

Weather conditions were unusually severe; temperatures of fifty degrees below zero were recorded by some of the men in mid-winter, and in December and January daylight lasted for only a few hours. Attacking Russian soldiers wearing white smocks in order to blend with the snow-covered landscape, might creep close to the Allied lines before being observed, and difficult terrain often combined with the Russian climate to make the soldier's lot particularly uncomfortable. One veteran recalled that in September, 1918, he had "slept in a swamp all night and it was raining so we had no place to lay, so we did not do any sleeping but walked back and forth all night to keep from freezing." When weather conditions became most severe in the coldest winter months, frostbite was added to the list of customary army medical problems, and deep snow made troop movement not only cumbersome but hazardous. Near Chenova, in March, 1919, American and British troops were described as "thoroughly overcome with fatigue" after advancing five hundred yards in the face of heavy enemy machine gun fire, through snow up to their waists.

To a considerable extent, however, the expedition into northern Russia was trying, not because of the combat dangers, or other predictable problems associated with military operations, but rather because of the uncertainty as to the purpose of the mission. E. M. Halliday entitled his account of the Polar Bears' exploits *The Ignorant Armies*, and the title is singularly appropriate, for it calls attention to the sheer frustration experienced by men trying to understand why they had been dispatched to Russia in the first place. Officially, they and the other Allied detachments had originally been sent to the Archangel region to guard the military supplies stored there and keep them out of German hands; or to prevent the establishment of a German submarine base in the area. There was also talk of reconstructing a second front in the east, and of somehow restoring Russia to the coalition of nations fighting the Central Powers.

However, after the armistice with Germany was signed, the expedition could only take on more and more of the character of an anti-Bolshevik force, seeking to aid the White armies in breaking the Communist hold on Russia. Since this latter aim was never clearly expressed, it is not surprising to find American soldiers wondering why their services were needed in this remote corner of the world when the fighting in western Europe had ended. That the expedition had never really captured the imagination of the men involved is indicated by a portion of a letter written home in February, 1919, by an American lieutenant:

> [I] suppose that by this time the country is swarming with returned soldiers. They must be getting them out of France, at a pretty good rate. They certainly did some fine work over there. How I wish that I had been fortunate enough to get over there. How would you like to take a day off to go to the circus, get as far as the big tent, then be turned around and spend your day in one of the sideshows. . . ?

This same lieutenant, Charles B. Ryan, attended a lecture by DeWitt Poole, the American chargé d'affaires. The title of Mr. Poole's talk was "Russia: Why We Are Here," but the American lieutenant thought it might be summed up in the familiar expression: "We're here because we're here." "I sometimes wonder," another American soldier noted in a diary entry, "if the US will ever wake up to the fact that they have a regiment over here, on guard."

The problem of maintaining morale was further complicated by the propaganda activities of the Bolsheviks, who piled leaflets where American soldiers might find and read them, and on occasion used more direct means. Sergeant Gordon Smith recorded in September, 1918, that a "Bolo" had come out under a white flag to deliver a lecture on Bolshevism and to tell the Americans that the Russians did not want to fight them. According to Lieutenant Harry Costello, a Bolshevik orator appeared in the darkness one November night and shouted to the Americans, asking why they were fighting them and declaring that they were fellow-workers.

In Costello's opinion, the Soviet propaganda efforts were quite unsuccessful, because the hardworking men from the farms and factories of Michigan saw the Bolshevik leaders not as fellow "toil-ers," but as cruel and shiftless men "who turned the evils of Romanoff rule into anarchy, murder, rape and pillage." American soldiers in the expedition realized the dangerous nature of Bolshe-vism, he believed, and expected that at some time in the future they might again be called upon to play their part in crushing the Communist menace.

An abhorrence of Communism and a conviction that it must never become a danger to the United States were doubtless shared generally by these American soldiers. It did not follow, however, that each man would feel altogether sure of his own immediate role as an opponent of the Russian Revolution on Russian soil. "Now is the time," wrote Lieutenant Ryan in a letter of April 7, 1919, "to finish off the Russian Communists, and incidentally, get a few of our homegrown Bolsheviks." The men of the 339th had seen what Communism meant and "it ought to be unhealthy for any agitators to start their propaganda in the shops around Detroit." But what if the Russian people themselves were either apathetic or actually in opposition to this western effort to save them from Communism? In February, Lieutenant Ryan had noted in his diary:

> There is a rumor that they have arrested 300 civilians in Archangel. What are we doing here anyway? The people won't help themselves. They are nearly all Bolsheviks. If this is not interfering with Russian politics I miss my guess.

If the Lieutenant found the Russians' lack of enthusiasm disap-pointing, another American soldier took a perhaps more realistic point of view. Running through the diary of Sergeant Silver Parrish, there is a deep feeling of sympathy and understanding for the Russians, a feeling which he apparently took no pains to hide. He saw them as industrious but downtrodden people, seeking only to throw off the yoke of their oppressors: "After being up here fighting these people I will be ashamed to look a union man in the face, for the way they have been treated by their government and the Cossacks is a dirty crime." Parrish was sure that the majority of the people were in sympathy with the Bolsheviks, and he did not blame them for that. In fact, he admitted, he and his platoon had been called Bolsheviks themselves because they signed a petition "protesting against conditions and fighting the Bolo after the Ger-mans had quit."

These were not the words of a malingerer or slacker, for men like Parrish obeyed their orders even when they seemed to bring tragedy to innocent people. Told to destroy a Russian village in November, 1918, because of possible danger from snipers, Parrish relates that he and his men carried out the order even though "My heart ached to have the women fall down at my feet and grab my legs and kiss my hand and beg me not to do it. But orders are orders, . . . so I done my duty." Nor could there be any question of this man's courage; Parrish boasted that his platoon had "the best fighting record of any platoon in the battalion," and he himself was decorated in the course of the campaign by the British government.

As the long, frustrating winter months drew to a close, there were exaggerated reports in late March, 1919, of mutiny among the American soldiers. The difficulty hinged upon a certain amount of grumbling among members of Company "I" who had been away from the front on rest, and were being ordered to load sleds for their return to combat. The men believed, as did many of their comrades, that the Russians themselves were not making a sufficient effort on their own behalf, and could not see why they had to do their fighting for them. The men did carry out the orders after only a short delay, and were the next day in battle with the Bolsheviks, but newspapers in the United States played up the story with a considerable amount of sensation. What is significant in the incident is not that discontent should begin to be manifested, but rather that no more serious incidents were reported; for at this same time there were far more dangerous cases of actual mutiny among the other Allied soldiers, including both the French and British.

There is, however, some evidence that discontent among the Americans had become a major consideration by the end of winter. The protest petition to which Sergeant Parrish referred and which he apparently authored was drawn up in the early days of March. He reports that he was called on the carpet before his colonel, who read the articles of war to him and informed him that his offense was punishable by death. In describing this petition in his diary entry for March 4, Sergeant Parrish noted that it requested the reason why Americans were fighting the Bolsheviks; why there was not better treatment with regard to food, mail and medical attention; why there was no heavy artillery; and why the Americans were under British command. The petition may also have contained, or was accompanied by, a second statement by the men, threatening to refuse to advance any farther after March 15. In the back pages of the Parrish diary such a statement is included in a petition headed Resolution Number One, and directed to "the commanding officer of Archangel district." The two may be quite distinct documents, and the second, perhaps, was never actually submitted, for it is difficult to reconcile such a threat and its effect upon the British command, with the award to Parrish on March 18th of the British Military Medal. Still, we have the testimony of Lieutenant

John Cudahy that either this or a similar incident occurred involving a threat by the American soldiers at Toulgas to "walk out." He placed it in February, but he was speaking from several years hindsight, and may have confused the exact date. Cudahy was not critical of the men involved, for he saw them as individuals who were familiar with peacetime industrial strikes used as weapons for expressing disapproval, and who, when told the implications of mutiny, realized their error and never again engaged in such a protest.

The attitude of the men becomes more understandable when placed in the context of other events at the time. In late February, President Wilson had announced his intention finally to withdraw the American troops from Russia. This news very quickly reached the men at the front. Now it was but a question of awaiting British replacements and adequate transportation home, and thus further bloodshed must have seemed particularly senseless. In the back of the Kenneth Skellenger diary, there is the following entry, dated March 9, 1919, and addressed "to the Bolsheviki soldiers":

> officially we Americans know we have been ordered out of Russia by our President.
>
> We are under the damned British control until May 17th. This we do not understand. We are only fighting for our lives. There are practically no English soldiers in the front lines or in Russia.
>
> We would join hands with you to down crowned heads. It is all for the majority of human beings.
>
> The US soldiers hear many stories about the inhuman "Bolo" but we do not believe *all* we hear.
>
> Homes and dear wives wait for us and no doubt for you.
>
> We won't make an attack on you. If you wait 2½ months we will be out of Russia.
>
> Signed Soldier Boys of the U.S.

Both the Parrish petition and the entry cited above evidence the antipathy which American soldiers in the expeditionary force felt toward the British command. Colonel George Stewart, the highest ranking American officer present, was himself not popular, but the subordinate American officers appear generally to have been liked and respected by their men. On the other hand, only General Ironside, after November the overall Allied commander, seems to have escaped the almost universal American censure of British officers, too many of whom, it was believed, perhaps unfairly, had found snug office jobs behind the lines in Archangel while Americans did all the fighting at the front. It was also charged that the British soldiers sent to Russia were not physically fit, but rather worn-out veterans from the western front, and this belief, along with incidents like the accidental shelling of Allied lines by British artillery, made the situation very tense at times.

. . . .

Relations between the French and American soldiers were on quite a different plane. Here there were both respect and comradeship transcending any language difficulties, and nurtured by a mutual dislike of the British. Probably, only the valiant units of Canadian artillerymen rivalled the French "poilus" in the hearts of the American troops.

Toward the Soviet soldiers, the Americans seemed to hold a certain measure of respect, quite apart from any dislike of their Communist leaders. These were no cowardly opponents, declared Lieutenant Ryan, and all that was necessary to be convinced of that was to see them coming at you as you waited behind your machine gun. The Americans came to believe that stories of Bolshevik atrocities perpetrated against captured Allied soldiers were much exaggerated. In their account of the expedition, Joel Moore and Harry Mead noted that the atrocity stories were often part of the British propaganda efforts, designed to arouse American soldiers against their opponents. But, as they pointed out, "Brave men do not need to be fed such stuff. Distortion of facts only disgusts the man when he finally becomes undeceived."

More than respect was involved in the Polar Bears' regard for the Russian peasants, with whom they were often in close contact, to the extent of being quartered with them under the same roof. There were unpleasant aspects to living in the moujiks' houses, particularly the ever-present cockroaches and the absence of adequate ventilation; but on cold winter nights, complaints were probably very few as the men bedded down around the huge brick ovens, a prominent feature of rural north Russian homes. Residents of Archangel, and Russian urban dwellers generally, may have been suspect in the eyes of the American soldiers as shirkers or Bolshevik sympathizers, but for these simple peasants there was kindness and understanding.

On Christmas eve, in the village of Chemova, some of the men of "B" Company decorated a fir tree with packages containing canteen items of cigarettes, sugar and tea, then invited in the peasants to share in the celebration. Clarence Scheu, in describing the festivities, remarked that in the middle of the party, "seven or eight Russians approached us and swore fidelity to the Americans present, and boy how they can swear. We reciprocated likewise and passed the cigarettes, stripped the tree to the children, bid all 'da da' . . . and turned in a tired but happy lot." Scheu also remembered giving money toward the rebuilding of a Russian schoolhouse.

American doctors, too, made their own contribution to the peasants' welfare. Captain Henry Katz noted that a Shenkursk newspaper had commended American medical men for visiting the villages around that city and caring for the people during an influenza epidemic in November.

Sergeant Parrish's interest in the Russian people was particularly keen. Much of his diary is devoted to vivid descriptions of battle-field encounters with the Bolsheviks, but there are also informative and amusing accounts of the day-to-day activities of the peasants with whom he so deeply sympathized. These were simple, hard-working people, he noted, and with hearts of children. Neither moral nor immoral, they were "nearly unmoral," and saying things which would embarrass an American but which were customary for them. If one had seen women and children costumed like these people on a stage, said Parrish, it would have been laughable, but here in this context, it brought forth only sympathy for them, and loathing for those who kept them in such poverty and ignorance.

The sergeant devoted considerable attention to the peasants' crops, the appearance of their homes, and their diet, which, as he described it, seems to have consisted primarily of such items as potatoes, fish, berries and mushrooms. One institution he found especially admirable, and thought it might very well be copied in the United States. This was the bathhouse, a log structure similar to the saunas used by the people of neighboring Finland. Tiers of steps or benches were placed near a large kettle of water heated over a stone furnace.

> When the water is hot, they get in there and throw water on the hot rocks and it makes hot steam. They then get on this bench or steps and if they want to perspire very freely they get up to the top and if not they stay down low. Then they wash and pound each other with some little leafy twigs. The whole family together, men, women, girls and boys. (I guess we will have to start Baths like that in America.)

Russian marriages, the sergeant decided, were more business propositions than sacred undertakings. "If you are a man and want a woman, you go to her parents and if you have enough money to put with hers you get her whether she wants you or not." Women had the same privilege of purchasing husbands if they desired and had the money to do so.

For amusement, the peasants sometimes made use of a "teeter-totter affair," which Parrish had observed in operation and which he wryly described:

> One girl gets on one end and one on the other and one jumps up and comes down on the board which throws the other one up in the air 2 or 3 feet high. She then in turn lands on her end and away goes the other girl and they keep it up until they get tired or break a leg.

Not all the Americans involved, perhaps not even most, were deeply interested in the daily life of the peasants. Probably few grew so attached to them as did Sergeant Parrish. But shared Christmas celebrations, the work of American medics in the villages, kindnesses to Russian children, and living under the same roof with the peasants were experiences not soon to be forgotten on either side.

On the other hand, if the expedition's underlying purpose had really been to save the people of Russia from Communism, there can have been little satisfaction felt by these American soldiers who had given so much under such trying circumstances, and who were at last taken out of Russia in the summer of 1919. What had they really been able to accomplish in their nine months' tour of duty? How long would the shaky anti-Communist North Russian government in Archangel be able to last once the British too had withdrawn? Not long, as events were to show. What value, then, did the intervention in Russia by the western powers actually have? "When we came away," wrote Sergeant Costello, "many of us wondered if we had not succeeded by our failure to crush it [Communism] in translating this whole Bolshevist business into a national movement."

Combat in Russia had been an experience testing not only fighting abilities, but, to an unusual degree, the stamina and morale of the soldiers involved. If the task was left unfinished, it was surely not the fault of these who had served at the front. In any case, it was good to be going home. Gordon Scheu described the Polar Bear troopship's arrival in Boston harbor:

> We are all set and ready to disembark at a moment's notice, everyone on edge on deck, and [the] rails are crowded with troops watching; [we] pass Boston lighthouse at 8 p.m. Sight Revere Beach, brightly illuminated at 9 p.m. A mighty cheer goes up from the ship. It's all over now, we're home.

Part III

1920-1973

Introduction

During the years from the end of the first world war to the present, Michigan's history was marked by increasingly accelerating change in almost every realm of human endeavor. Rapidly recovering from a post-World War I recession, the state continued its development, particularly in automobile manufacturing, an industry that had already become by 1920 Michigan's most significant business enterprise. Led by such captains of industry as Henry Ford, James Couzens, William C. Durant, Walter P. Chrysler, and the Dodge Brothers, among others, the word automobile and Michigan became synonymous for many people in the nation, while Detroit quickly became known as the Motor City, or, as rock music fans now call it, Motown.

The growth of automobile manufacturing and other industrial developments also served as a magnet for immigration, both internal and external. With the promise of jobs and a better life in mind, thousands of foreigners (at least until the implementation of the quota system in the mid-1920s), southern whites and Negroes, as well as vast numbers of Michiganians who could no longer make a living off the land, flocked to Michigan's cities, places where opportunity for increased upward mobility and material rewards seemed greater. Interestingly, the lack of planning at this stage of the state's urban growth did not become apparent to most people until the sixties; in the seventies and beyond, all of us will be forced to pay some type of price for the view of unlimited progress that dominated the thinking of the twenties. Yet even in the twenties and thirties such rapid urban development created fear and uncertainty in the minds of many. Such hate groups as the Ku Klux Klan and the more notorious Black Legion provided a small number of the state's most confused citizens with an outlet for their pent-up frustrations.

Because of its industrial base, the Great Depression of the 1930s hit Michigan particularly hard. In some ways, however, the depression was a blessing in disguise for the workingman. With a Democratic administration in Washington that was at least somewhat sympathetic to their demands, workers went out on strike or sat down in the plants in an attempt to win, among other things, recognition of their unions and the right of collective bargaining. By the end of this decade, the automobile industry had made major concessions to the United Auto Workers, and, in the years after World War II, unions in other industries also began to win major victories for their members. From these early beginnings less than four decades ago, organized labor in Michigan as well as in the nation has become the political equal of the people on the other side of the bargaining table. Now facing the reality of increased automation in many industries, both labor and management will be forced to make serious reappraisals of their positions on many issues, economic, political and social, in the years ahead. Leaders of the caliber of Walter Reuther and Frank Murphy would be most welcome in the Michigan of the seventies.

In the social, educational, and cultural spheres, Michigan's development since World War I may also be summed up in the phrase rapid growth, much of it by design, but an equal amount of the patchwork variety. Whether or not this growth represents progress will be left for the readers of this volume to decide. During the past half century, Michigan's educational system has become one of the best known in the country; its network of roads and highways is now second to few; the tourist and resort industry has emerged as a gigantic bonanza while at the same time providing a "wilderness experience" for millions; and the state's museums and libraries, although always in need of more financial resources, are excellent in most respects. Such rapid growth, however, has brought equally great problems. To any thinking citizen of the state, it has become brutally apparent that giant strides need to be taken in such areas as air and water pollution, race relations, and urban growth. If some of these pressing problems are not solved in the next half century, what has been accomplished in the last fifty years will have been for nothing.

1: The Twenties: Roaring and Otherwise

Few people in Michigan's history have symbolized the state's development during a particular period as well as Henry Ford symbolizes the turbulent years from 1917 to 1930, a time of great economic growth and equally great social dislocation. As social historian David D. Van Tassel points out in his "Editor's Preface" to Roderick Nash's *The Nervous Generation: American Thought, 1917-1930*, "the decade of the twenties was full of paradoxes, not readily describable or easily characterized. Great changes were occurring beneath the surface, occasionally roiling to the top in strikes, riots, depressions, and crusades. And a generation of Americans, 'nervous Americans,' underscored change as a character of the new age in their vigorous efforts to affirm and maintain older values." In the following chapter from his book cited above, Professor Nash sees Henry Ford as the best example of a man in whom the old and new mingled: "on the one hand Ford was a builder and bulwark of the modern, mechanized nation; on the other he devoted a remarkable amount of effort and expense to sustaining old-fashioned America." Obviously this view of Ford as a symbol of this age is only one interpretation of a man who is undoubtedly Michigan's best-known native son. Among the other worthwhile book-length studies on Ford and his times are: Keith Sward, *The Legend of Henry Ford* (New York, 1949; Atheneum paperback, 1968); Roger Burlingame, *Henry Ford* (Chicago, 1954); the multi-volume work by Allan Nevins and Frank Ernest Hill; and most recently Reynold M. Wik, *Henry Ford and Grassroots America* (Ann Arbor, 1971).

Henry Ford: Symbol of an Age

RODERICK NASH

Few names were better known to Americans from 1917 to 1930 than that of Henry Ford. Whether one read his publications, or followed his headline-making public life, or merely drove the car his

From *The Nervous Generation: American Thought, 1917-1930*, pp. 153-163. Copyright © 1970 by Rand McNally & Company. Reprinted by permission.

company manufactured, Ford was inescapable in the twenties. Indeed it is possible to think of these years as the automobile age and Henry Ford as its czar. The flivver, along with the flask and the flapper, seemed to represent the 1920s in the minds of its people as well as its historians.

Cars symbolized change. They upset familiar patterns of living, working, recreating, even thinking. Much of the roar of the twenties came from the internal combustion engine. While providing portable bedrooms in which to enjoy the decade's alleged sexual freedom, cars also assisted gangsters and bootleggers in getting away. The image of two of them in every garage helped elect a President in 1928. The rise of widespread use of the automobile, in a word, contributed significantly to setting the twenties apart. And Henry Ford, calling machinery the "new Messiah" (as he did in 1929), seemed to herald the new era.

Beneath the surface, however, such generalizations ring hollow. Neither Ford nor the twenties merited the clichés with which each has been so frequently discussed. In the case of the man, both old and new mingled in his mind. On the one hand Ford was a builder and bulwark of the modern, mechanized nation; on the other he devoted a remarkable amount of effort and expense to sustaining old-fashioned America. In fact, the nostalgic, backward-looking Henry Ford repeatedly deplored the very conditions that Ford the revolutionary industrialist did so much to bring about. This ambivalence did not signify a lack of values so much as a superfluity. His faith was strong if bigoted and contradictory. His prescriptions for America were clear if simple-minded. He seemed to the masses to demonstate that there could be change without disruption, and in so doing he eased the twenties' tensions. "The average citizen," editorialized the *New Republic* in 1923, "sees Ford as a sort of enlarged crayon portrait of himself; the man able to fulfill his own suppressed desires, who has achieved enormous riches, fame and power without departing from the pioneer-and-homespun tradition." In this nervous clinging to old values even while undermining them Ford was indeed a "crayon portrait" of his age.

But was Ford typical of the twenties? Can he really be said to symbolize the age? He was, after all, in his middle fifties when the decade began. However, a great many Americans were also middle-aged in the 1920s, far more in fact than the twenty-year-old collegians who have hitherto charactized these years. And at one point even a group of college students ranked Ford as the third greatest figure of all time, behind Napoleon and Jesus Christ.

The Dearborn, Michigan, into which Henry Ford was born in

1863 was a small farming community only a generation removed from the frontier. Both sides of the Ford family had agrarian backgrounds, and the children grew up on the farm. Henry's formal education began and ended in the Scotch Settlement School which he attended for eight years. The staple of his academic diet was the McGuffey reader with its moral-coated language lessons. When Ford left school to become an apprentice mechanic in Detroit, he also left the farm. But the farm never left Henry. Agrarian ideas and values shaped his thought even as he became an industrial king.

The 1880s for Ford were a time of aimlessness, his only real interest being in tinkering with watches and other engines. In 1892[1] he joined the Edison Company in Detroit as an engineer. During his spare time he struggled with the problem of building a gasoline engine compact enough to power a moving vehicle. By 1896 Ford had his automobile. Soon he had it doing ninety miles per hour![2] It required seven years more, however, for him to secure the necessary financial and administrative backing to launch the Ford Motor Company. The rest was pure Horatio Alger.

The first Model T appeared in 1908, and it soon made good Ford's boast that he could build a car for the masses. Six thousand sold the first year. Six years later, after the introduction of assembly line production, the figure was 248,000. From May to December 1920 almost 700,000 Model Ts rolled out of the Ford plants. The total for 1921 was one million. In 1923, 57 per cent of all cars manufactured in the United States were Fords. Three years later the Ford Motor Company produced its thirteen millionth car. From the perspective of efficient production the Ford organization was also something of a miracle. In 1913 it required twelve hours to make a car. The following year, after the introduction of the assembly line techniques, the figure dropped to ninety-three minutes. In 1920 Ford achieved his long-time dream of building one car for every minute of the working day. And still he was unsatisfied. On October 31, 1925, the Ford Motor Company manufactured 9,109 Model Ts, one every ten seconds. This was the high point, and competition was rising to challenge Ford's preeminence, but by the end of the twenties Henry Ford was a legend, a folk hero, and reputedly the richest man who ever lived. Transcending the role of automobile manufacturer, he had become an international symbol of the new industrialism. The Germans coined a word to describe the revolutionary mass production techniques: *Fordismus.* At home

[1]Ed. Note: Ford actually began his employment with the Edison Co. in 1891.

[2]Ed. Note: The car Ford built in 1896 never went 90 miles per hour. Ford's cars did not reach that speed until 1904, after the formation of the Ford Motor Company.

Ford's popularity reached the point where he could be seriously considered a presidential possibility for the election of 1924.

Fortunately for the historian of his thought, if not always for himself, Henry Ford had a propensity for forthrightly stating his opinions on a wide variety of subjects outside his field of competence. He also had the money to publish and otherwise implement his ideas. The resulting intellectual portrait was that of a mind steeped in traditional Americanism. For Ford agrarian simplicity, McGuffey morality, and Algerian determination were sacred objects. Nationalism was writ large over all Ford did, and America was great because of its heritage of freedom, fairness, and hard, honest work. Ford's confidence in the beneficence of old-fashioned virtues verged on the fanatical. The "spirit of '76," equal opportunity democracy, rugged individualism, the home, and motherhood were Ford's touchstones of reality. He deified pioneer ethics and values. "More men are beaten than fail," he declared in 1928. "It is not wisdom they need, or money, or brilliance, or pull, but just plain gristle and bone." A decade earlier "Mr. Ford's Page" in the *Dearborn Independent* stated that "one of the great things about the American people is that they are pioneers." This idea led easily to American messianism. "No one can contemplate the nation to which we belong," the editorial continued, "without realizing the distinctive prophetic character of its obvious mission to the world. We are pioneers. We are the pathfinders. We are the road-builders. We are the guides, the vanguards of Humanity." Theodore Roosevelt and Woodrow Wilson had said as much, but Ford was writing *after* the war that allegedly ended the nation's innocence and mocked its mission.

Ford's intense commitment to the traditional American faith led him to suspect and ultimately to detest whatever was un-American. The same loyalties compelled him to search for explanations for the unpleasant aspects of the American 1920s that exonerated the old-time, "native" citizen. The immigrant, and particularly the Jew, were primary targets of Ford's fire. In editorial after editorial in the *Dearborn Independent* and in several books Ford argued that aliens who had no knowledge of "the principles which have made our civilization" were responsible for its "marked deterioration" in the 1920s. They were, moreover, determined to take over the country if not the world. Spurred by such fears, Ford became a subscriber to the tired legend of an international Jewish conspiracy. When he couldn't find sufficient evidence for such a plot, Ford dispatched a number of special detectives to probe the affairs of prominent Jews and collect documentation. The search resulted in the "discovery" of the so-called "Protocols of the Learned Elders of Zion," an alleged exposition of the scheme by which the Jews planned to overthrow Gentile domination. Although the "Protocols" was exposed as a forgery in 1921, Ford continued to use the spurious document to substantiate his anti-Semitism until late in the decade. Everything wrong with modern American civilization, from the corruption of music to the corruption of baseball, was attributed to Jewish influence. Unable to admit that America as a whole might be blamed for its problems, unwilling to question the beneficence of time-honored ways, Ford searched for a scapegoat. He found it in the newcomers who, he believed, had no conception of or appreciation for American ideals.

The tension in Henry Ford's thought between old and new, between a belief in progress and a tendency to nostalgia, is dramatically illustrated in his attitude toward farming and farmers. On the one hand he believed farm life to be a ceaseless round of inefficient drudgery. Indeed, he had abundant personal evidence, remarking at one point, "I have traveled ten thousand miles behind a plow. I hated the grueling grind of farm work." With the incentive of sparing others this painful experience, Ford addressed himself to the problem of industrializing agriculture. The farmer, in Ford's opinion, should become a technician and a businessman. Tractors (Ford's, of course) should replace horses. Mechanization would make it possible to produce in twenty-five working days what formerly required an entire year. Ford's modern farmer would not even need to live on his farm but instead could commute from a city home. To give substance to these ideals Ford bought and operated with astonishing success a nine-thousand-acre farm near Dearborn.

Still Ford, the "Father of Modern Agriculture," as he has been dubbed, was only part of the man. He also retained a strong streak of old-fashioned, horse-and-buggy agrarianism. Farming, from this standpoint, was more than a challenge in production; it was a moral act. Constantly in the twenties, even while he was helping make it possible, Ford branded the modern city a "pestiferous growth." He delighted in contrasting the "unnatural," "twisted," and "cooped up" lives of city-dwellers with the "wholesome" life of "independence" and "sterling honesty" that the farm environment offered. In Ford's view the importance of cities in the nation's development had been greatly exaggerated. Early in the 1920s the *Dearborn Independent* editorialized: "When we all stand up and sing, 'My Country 'Tis of Thee,' we seldom think of the cities. Indeed, in that old national hymn there are no references to the city at all. It sings

of rocks and rivers and hills—the great American Out-of-Doors. And
that is really The Country. That is, the country is THE Country.
The real United States lies outside the cities."

As such a manifesto suggests, a bias toward nature and rural
conditions was an important element in Henry Ford's thought.
"What children and adults need," he told one reporter, "is a chance
to breathe God's fresh air and to stretch their legs and have a little
garden in the soil." This ideal led Ford to choose small towns
instead of cities as the sites of his factories. "Turning back to village
industry," as Ford put it in 1926, would enable people to
reestablish a sense of community—with nature and with men—that
urbanization had destroyed. Ford believed that cities were doomed
as Americans discovered the advantages of country life.

Ford's enthusiasm for nature did not stop with ruralism. From
1914 to 1924 he sought a more complete escape from civilization
on a series of camping trips with Thomas A. Edison. John
Burroughs, the naturalist, and Harvey Firestone, the tire king, also
participated. Although the equipment these self-styled vagabonds
took into the woods was far from primitive, they apparently shared
a genuine love of the outdoors. In the words of Burroughs, they
"cheerfully endure wet, cold, smoke, mosquitoes, black flies, and
sleepless nights, just to touch naked reality once more." Ford had a
special fondness for birds. With typical exuberance he had five
hundred birdhouses built on his Michigan farm, including one with
seventy-six apartments which he called, appropriately, a "bird
hotel." There were also electric heaters and electric brooders for
Ford's fortunate birds. The whole production mixed technology
and nature in a way that symbolized Ford's ambivalence. When he
could not camp or visit his aviary, Ford liked to read about the
natural world. Indeed he preferred the works of Emerson, Thoreau,
and Burroughs to the Bible. Ford so admired Burroughs' variety of
natural history that even before becoming acquainted with him he
sent him a new Ford car.

As for roads and automobiles, Ford saw them not as a threat to
natural conditions but rather as a way for the average American to
come into contact with nature. The machine and the garden were
not incompatible. "I will build a motor car for the great multitude. . . ," Ford boasted, "so low in price that no man . . . will be
unable to own one—and enjoy with his family the blessings of hours of
pleasure in God's great open spaces." In *My Life and Work* of 1923
Ford again confronted the tension between nature and modern
civilization. He declared that he did not agree with those who saw
mechanization leading to a "cold, metallic sort of world in which
great factories will drive away the trees, the flowers, the birds and
the green fields." According to Ford, "Unless we know more about

machines and their use . . . we cannot have the time to enjoy the trees and the birds, and the flowers, and the green fields." Such reconciliations only partially covered Ford's nervousness about the mechanized, urbanized future. Contradictions persisted in his thinking. The same man who envisaged fenceless bonanza farms could say, "I love to walk across country and jump fences." The lover of trees could state in utmost seriousness, "Better wood can be made than is grown."

Ford's attitude toward history has been subject to wide misunderstanding. The principal source of confusion is a statement Ford made in 1919 at the trial resulting from his libel suit against the *Chicago Tribune.* "History," he declared, "is more or less the bunk. It is tradition. We don't want tradition. We want to live in the present, and the only history that is worth a tinker's dam is the history we make today." On another occasion he admitted that he "wouldn't give a nickel for all the history in the world." Complementing this sentiment is Ford's reputation as a forward-looking inventor and revolutionary industrialist unsatisfied with the old processes. Here seems a man fully at home in the alleged new era of the 1920s. But in fact Ford idolized the past. His "history . . . is bunk" remark came in response to a question about ancient history and Napoleon Bonaparte and had reference to written history. For history itself—what actually happened in his nation's past and its tangible evidence—Ford had only praise.

The most obvious evidence of Ford's enthusiasm for history was his collector's instinct. He began with that bastion of his own youth, the McGuffey readers. Sending agents out to scour the countryside and putting aside considerations of cost, Ford owned by 1925 one of the few complete collections of the many McGuffey editions. Hoping to share his treasures with his contemporaries, Ford had five thousand copies of *Old Favorites from the McGuffey Readers* printed in 1926. The book contained such classic stories as "Try, Try Again" and "The Hare and the Tortoise." It dispensed an ideal of individualism and self-reliance at the same time that Ford's assembly lines were making men cogs in an impersonal machine.

From books Ford turned to things, and during the 1920s amassed a remarkable collection of American antiques. He bought so widely and so aggressively that he became a major factor in prices in the antique market. Everything was fair game. Lamps and dolls, bells and grandfather clocks made their way to Dearborn. Size was no problem. Ford gathered enough machines to show the evolution of the threshing operation from 1849 to the 1920s. Another exhibit traced the development of wagons in America. Eventually the entire heterogeneous collection went into the Henry Ford Museum at

Dearborn, a pretentious building designed to resemble, simultaneously, Independence Hall, Congress Hall, and the old City Hall of Philadelphia. Ford delighted in showing vistors around the five-acre layout. Asked on one occasion why he collected, Ford replied, "So that they will not be lost to America." Later, on the same tour, Ford played a few bars on an antique organ and observed, "That takes me back to my boyhood days. They were beautiful days."

This sentiment undoubtedly figured in Ford's 1920 decision to restore his boyhood home. Everything had to be exactly as he remembered it. Furniture, china, and rugs were rehabilitated or reconstructed. Ford even used archaeological techniques to recover artifacts around the family homestead. The ground was dug to a depth of sixth feet and the silverware, wheels, and other equipment used by his parents in the 1860s were recovered. In 1922 Ford purchased the Wayside Inn at Sudbury, Massachusetts, to preserve it from destruction. Celebrated by the poet Henry Wadsworth Longfellow, the old inn appealed to Ford as a symbol of pioneer days. He opened it for the public's edification in 1924. But a new highway ran too near. Roaring cars disturbed the horse-and-buggy atmosphere. So, turning against the age he helped create, Ford had the state highway rerouted around the shrine at a cost of $250,000. He also bought and restored the schoolhouse in Sudbury alleged to be the site where Mary and her little lamb gamboled. Naturally the shop of the "Village Blacksmith," also in Sudbury, had to be included in Ford's antique empire.

Beginning in 1926 with the construction of Greenfield Village near Dearborn, Ford embarked on a career of large-scale historical restoration. This time not a building but a whole community was the object of his attention. Greenfield, named after the Michigan hamlet in which Ford's mother grew up, was a monument to his agrarianism as well as his reverence for the past. "I am trying in a small way," Ford explained with unwarranted modesty, "to help America take a step . . . toward the saner and sweeter idea of life that prevailed in pre-war days." Greenfield Village had gravel roads, gas street lamps, a grassy common, and an old-fashioned country store. The automobile mogul permitted only horse-drawn vehicles on the premises. The genius of assembly line mass production engaged a glass blower, blacksmith, and cobbler to practice their obsolete crafts in the traditional manner. Ford dispatched his agents to seek out, purchase, and transport to Greenfield the cottages of Walt Whitman, Noah Webster, and Patrick Henry. In time they even secured the crowning glory: the log cabin in which William Holmes McGuffey had been born and raised.

History, then, was not "bunk" to Henry Ford. The speed of

change seemed to increase proportionately his desire to retain
contact with the past. As Ford declared in 1928, a year before
completing Greenfield Village, "Improvements have been coming so
quickly that the past is being lost to the rising generation." To
counter this tendency Ford labored to put history into a form
"where it may be seen and felt." But values and attitudes were also
on display. Ford looked back with nostalgia to the pioneer ethic.
With it, he believed, the nation had been sound, wholesome, happy,
and secure. "The Old Ways," as the *Dearborn Independent* declared, "were Good."

Ford's opinion of the new morality of the jazz age was, not
surprisingly, low. He deplored the use of tobacco and even went so
far as to publish for mass circulation a tract, entitled *The Case
Against the Little White Slaver,* which excoriated cigarettes. When
Ford had the power he went beyond exhortation. "No one smokes
in the Ford industries," their leader proclaimed in 1929. As for
alcohol, Ford was equally unyielding. Twice he threatened to make
his international labor force teetotalers at the risk of their jobs. In
his American plants Ford enforced a policy of abstinence. Any
workman detected drinking publicly or even keeping liquor at home
was subject to dismissal. The prohibition policy of the 1920s, in
Ford's estimation, was a great triumph. "There are a million boys
growing up in the United States," he exulted in 1929, "who have
never seen a saloon and who will never know the handicap of
liquor." When confronted with evidence of widespread violation of
the Nineteenth Amendment, Ford had a ready explanation. A
Jewish conspiracy was to blame for illicit booze. The mass of real
Americans, Ford believed, were, like himself, dry by moral conviction as well as by law.

Sex was too delicate a matter to be addressed directly, but Ford
conveyed his opinions through a discussion of music and dancing.
Few aspects of the American 1920s worried him more than the evils
of jazz. The new music clashed squarely with his ruralism and
Bible-belt morality. In 1921 Ford struck out in anger at "the waves
upon waves of musical slush that invade decent parlors and set the
young people of this generation imitating the drivel of morons."
Organized Jewry, once again, was blamed for the musical degeneracy. "The mush, the slush, the sly suggestion, the abandoned
sensuousness of sliding notes," declared the *Dearborn Independent,*
"are of Jewish origin." The problem, obviously, was not only
musical but sexual as well. The loosening of morals in the 1920s
appalled Ford. He expressed his feeling in reference to jazz: "Monkey talk, jungle squeals, grunts and squeaks and gasps suggestive of
cave love are camouflaged by a few feverish notes." What Ford

could only bring himself to call "the thing" appeared also in song titles such as *In Room 202* and *Sugar Baby*. Pointing to the Jewish origin of these tunes (Irving Berlin was a frequent target of attack), Ford called on his countrymen to crush the serpent in their midst.

The reform of dancing fitted nicely into Ford's campaign to elevate the nation's morals to old-time standards. His interest began with the collection of traditional folk dances. Not only the scores but the backwoods fiddlers themselves were invited to Dearborn to play *Old Zip Coon* and *Arkansas Traveler*. To Ford's delight, here was something both wholesome and historical. He also manifested concern over social dancing, publishing in 1926 a guidebook entitled *"Good Morning": After a Sleep of Twenty-five Years Old-Fashioned Dancing is Being Revived by Mr. and Mrs. Henry Ford*. The book also endeavored to revive old-fashioned morality. It began by condemning as promiscuous the newer dances such as the Charleston and the whole flapper syndrome. "A gentleman," the book explained, "should be able to guide his partner through a dance without embracing her as if he were her lover." Proper deportment, according to Ford, minimized physical contact. "[The gentleman's] right hand should be placed at his partner's waist, thumb and forefinger alone touching her—that is, the hand being in the position of holding a pencil." There were also rules regarding gloves, handkerchiefs, and the way to request a partner for a dance. Ford's dance manual, in short, was a monument to the old conceptions of morality, decorum, and order, and the dances he and his wife hosted at Dearborn were implementations. Precisely at nine Ford's guests convened in evening dress in a lavish ballroom for a paean to Victorianism.

Ambivalence is the key to the mind of Henry Ford. He was both old and new; he looked both forward and backward. Confidently progressive as he was in some respects, he remained nervous about new ways. The more conditions changed, the more the nostalgic Ford groped for the security of traditional values and institutions. He was not lost; on the contrary, he had too many gods, at least for consistency. Neither was he dissipated and roaring. And he hated jazz. But Ford was popular, indeed a national deity, in the twenties even if his senatorial and presidential bids fell short. As a plain, honest, old-fashioned billionaire, a technological genius who loved to camp out, he seemed to his contemporaries to resolve the moral dilemmas of the age. Like Charles A. Lindbergh, another god of the age, Ford testified to the nation's ability to move into the future without losing the values of the past.

Among the more sordid chapters in Michigan's social history of the 1920s is the story of the Ku Klux Klan and its hostility toward Catholics, Jews, immigrants, and Negroes—not necessarily in that order! Until the late 1960s, most historians viewed this second edition of the hooded empire as primarily a rural and small-town phenomenon. The growth of the Klan was seen as one expression of the decline of an older, rural America and the recognition of a new, more confused, urban society. However, following the publication of Kenneth T. Jackson's study of the KKK in the cities in 1967, the historical community suddenly became aware of the urban dimension of the Klan's activities. No longer were all Klansmen dismissed as a bunch of yahoos and yokels. More often than not, rank-and-file urban Klansmen were viewed as interested local citizens who were genuinely concerned about problems that seemed beyond their ability to control.

Although a number of the Wolverine State's villages and towns had klaverns, as Klan locals were known, their activities usually consisted of a number of well-publicized cross burnings, marches down main street, and other Klan fraternal functions. However, unlike these smaller areas, by 1920 Detroit had become a multi-ethnic, multi-religious, multi-racial metropolis and a classic model of urban uncertainty. In the following essay Professor Jackson focuses on the history of the Klan in the Motor City, or to put it another way, the KKK in Michigan's largest urban dimension.

The Ku Klux Klan in Michigan

KENNETH T. JACKSON

The era of the Model T was a boom time in Detroit. Attracted by the relatively high wages of the automobile industry, Negroes, immigrants, and southern whites flocked to the city of Walter P. Chrysler, Henry Ford, John and Horace Dodge, William C. Durant, and the seven Fisher brothers. Between 1910 and 1930, the population of the motor capital tripled; in 1920 it stood at 993,000 and qualified Detroit as the fourth largest city of the United States. Housing, transportation, schools, and movies were overcrowded; jerry-built homes on business lots twenty feet wide were sold as rapidly as they could be constructed. Fully 25 per cent of the labor force worked at night, and census takers revealed that beds in all-male boarding houses were being rented in eight-hour shifts.

From chapter entitled "Detroit: The Write-in Challenge" in The Ku Klux Klan in the City, pp. 127-143. Copyright © 1967 by Oxford University Press, Inc. Reprinted by permission. Footnotes in the original have been omitted.

Everything was in short supply; everything except alcohol. Because of its proximity to Canada, Detroit was an important center of the bootlegging industry. On the Canadian side of the river, speedboats took on cargoes of whiskey and, avoiding the United States Customs Patrol, slipped back to the American side under cover of darkness.

Among the newcomers to Detroit, more than 25 per cent were foreign-born. Canadians, Italians, Poles, Scots, Hungarians, and Yugoslavs were the most numerous, but practically every ethnic group was represented. They crowded into the lower east-side ghetto or, if they were Polish, into Hamtramck, a city completely surrounded by Detroit. Of particular importance to "one hundred per cent Americanism" was the fact that most of the "aliens" were also Catholics.

Religious intolerance was not a new phenomenon in the Motor City. In the 1890's it had been the home of both the national president and national secretary of the anti-Catholic American Protective Association, as well as the location of a thriving chapter of that organization and the seat of publication of *The Patriotic American,* which created a sensation by printing a spurious document ascribed to Pope Leo XIII in which American Catholics were absolved from their allegiance to the United States government. In 1920 when the city's Catholics numbered more than 350,000, traditional fear of the Pope took new form as a concentrated effort in Michigan to abolish parochial schools. However, this proposal, spearheaded by James A. Hamilton of Detroit, was defeated, 610,699 to 353,817.

Although not so firmly rooted in the Detroit past, the "Negro problem" became increasingly important during and after World War I. In 1910, there were only 5741 colored persons in the city, but between 1915 and 1925 no city approached Detroit in the number of Negroes arriving to work and live. Numbering 40,000 in 1920, the total skyrocketed to 80,000 in 1925, and to 125,000 in 1930. There was work for them in the foundries, mills, and factories, as garbage collectors, elevator operators, and laborers. But decent housing was denied them and tuberculosis was common in the segregated slums. Cramped into a tiny east-side ghetto, Negroes were forced by the crush of physical necessity to seek expansion in white neighborhoods.

The vast population influx dramatically affected the sedate homes and tree-lined streets of the older residents as well as the new because the pace of neighborhood transition accelerated, moving white to Negro, Protestant to Catholic, and German to Italian. Lower- and middle-income whites, jealous of such social status as was theirs, were disturbed at the resulting destruction of neighborhood tranquility. As a result, Detroit became the unquestioned center of Klan strength in Michigan. Although the secret order had active chapters in Grand Rapids, Flint, Bay City, Jackson, Lansing, Kalamazoo, Saginaw, Pontiac, and Muskegon, approximately half the Wolverine state's 70,000 Klansmen resided in Detroit.

The first kleagle in the Motor City was C. H. Norton. Arriving in the summer of 1921, he made little headway until the September exposé of the New York *World* publicized the Klan in the city. Copies of the eastern daily were snatched up at prices ranging up to fifty cents on Detroit newsstands. Norton saw his opportunity and placed an advertisement in *The Detroit Free Press* inviting white Protestant citizens to membership in the Invisible Empire. Local Negroes immediately called for an investigation by the United States District Attorney, and John C. Lodge, president of the city council, instructed the police department to regard Klan demonstrators as disturbers of the peace. The Invisible Empire chose not to challenge the city administration and canceled its scheduled Thanksgiving Day parade.

After attaining a membership of three thousand in the fall of 1921, Wayne County Provisional Klan experienced relatively slow growth in 1922. Kleagle Norton, who was not an adept salesman, was hampered by the regional Klan emphasis upon recruitment in Ohio and Indiana and a lack of interest in the Wolverine state. Such activities as the Detroit klavern undertook were usually secret, insignificant indoor affairs. Klanswoman Esther Tansel, who with her husband earned a living by distributing anti-Catholic literature in the metropolitan area, reported that she had to go through three sets of locked doors to get into the meeting hall. While speakers harangued the membership about Nordic superiority, men stood around the exits with revolvers in their belts.

The fortunes of the Wayne County Klan improved early in 1923, when Manly L. Caldwell became the chief Detroit organizer. In eighteen months he increased membership from 3000 to 22,000 and earned $76,000 in the process. His most effective confederate was the Reverend Sam White, a Klan lecturer so devoted to the cause that he returned payment for fifty special appearances (at ten dollars per speech) to the Invisible Empire "because I believed in it." With the additional membership thus generated, the Detroit Klan no longer felt impelled to schedule sessions behind locked doors. Yet the membership was still hesitant to demonstrate publicly within the city.

The first outdoor muster of the Ku Klux Klan in Detroit came in a snow-covered wood a few miles from Royal Oak near the Wayne County line on April 4, 1923. On the same Oakland County farm, thirty-five miles northeast of downtown Detroit, a reporter from the *Free Press* witnessed a similar cross burning on the evening of June 13, and noted that "Sentries allowed no machine to pass unless the countersign was given." Before dining on hot dogs and coffee, eight thousand Knights listened to a diatribe by the grand goblin of the Domain of the Great Lakes on the mental and physical superiority of Nordic peoples.

The scene of the Detroit Klan's initiation ceremonies shifted the following month to a farm adjacent to the Detroit Riding and Hunt Club, a half mile west of the junction of Snyder and Seven Mile roads. On July 12, 1923, "patrols of Klansmen" shielded the farm as five thousand hooded Knights inducted eight hundred new members. More seldom used than the Seven Mile Road location was a field near John R. Street and Fifteen Mile Road, where 792 proselytes were initiated on August 18, 1923. That the initiations habitually occurred in such rural and suburban locations obscured the fact that most of the celebrants were city dwellers.

Probably typical of Klan propagation attempts in the Detroit area was a meeting in suburban Royal Oak on September 21, 1923. In response to notices of a public lecture by C. S. Townsend of New Jersey, about two thousand persons gathered in a vacant lot near the center of town. Three avowed Klansmen were present; two on the platform and one passing out membership applications and selling copies of Klan newspapers.

With the passage of the Burns Law in the summer of 1923, the Michigan State Legislature prohibited public meetings of masked men. At first the Detroit Klan failed to heed the legislation. On August 29, nine Wayne County deputy sheriffs accidentally stumbled upon an assembly of three thousand hooded Klansmen on Seven Mile Road, one hundred of whom were accepting congratulations for raiding two roadhouses. Although the law officers informed the Klansmen that their regalia violated the law, the white-hooded figures refused either to unmask or to leave the field. Because the deputies had no warrant, no action was taken. But the Detroit klavern did not always defy the Burns Law. On October 20, 1923, at a demonstration featuring an electric cross at the Seven Mile Road location, not one of five thousand Klansman was masked.

As the Klan blossomed in Detroit, public criticism of the secret order was persistent. At the Century Theater on January 22, 1923, Thomas Dixon, author of the novel on which *The Birth of a Nation* was based, praised Reconstruction Klansmen as "the bravest and noblest men of the South," but berated their modern counterparts as unprincipled marauders. In July prominent Detroit Methodist

Lynn Harold Hough, a former president of Northwestern University, dubbed the secret order, "the most diabolical institution this country ever saw, an absolute contradiction of everything for which America stands, and the apotheosis of race and religious hatred." His words were echoed by the Detroit Conference of the Methodist Church, which unanimously condemned "any organization which would substitute lawless methods for the appeal to the Court and the ballot." The attitude of an unsympathetic metropolitan press was reflected by the *Detroit News*: "The Klan boasts no saving grace. No man operating behind a mask ever intended to effect any purpose save the violation of law."

Opposition to the Klan later focused on the street vending of the Michigan edition of *The Fiery Cross*. Detroit police confiscated the Klan newspaper, which specialized in the regional and state activities of the hooded order, but in October 1923 public sale of the propagandistic weekly was approved by the city corporation counsel. When the police continued to arrest and detain *Fiery Cross* newsboys, the Wayne County Klan secured an injunction from the Circuit Court preventing further official interference with the newspaper's sale.

Too weak to participate effectively in Detroit politics in 1922, the Invisible Empire took only slightly more interest in the 1923 municipal election. Its primary interest was removing from the city council Dr. Frank Broderick, who was denounced enthusiastically at a hymn-singing Klan demonstration in rural Wayne County on October 29. Placing ninth in a field of eighteen, Broderick narrowly survived the Klan attack, and received fewer votes than any other successful candidate. As the returns were being tabulated on the evening of November 6, a five-foot tall cross blazed on the lawn of the city hall before being quenched by the hastily summoned fire department.

The burning of crosses near public buildings developed into a favorite activity of the Detroit Klan in 1923. On Christmas Eve, a six-foot oil-soaked cross was set afire on the steps of the county building. A pre-arranged Klan rally followed. A masked Santa Claus opened the Cadillac Square ceremony by leading a huge throng, estimated by the *Detroit News* at 4000 and by the Klan at 25,000, in the Lord's Prayer. Further proceedings were interrupted by the arrival of police riot squads. Taunts and hoots met the policemen, but the area was quickly cleared by officers with drawn revolvers.

As was the case in other cities, a visit by the Imperial Wizard usually signaled dissension within the secret order. On February 8, 1924, Hiram Wesley Evans addressed eight thousand Knights at the Armory, the largest indoor meeting of the Klan in Detroit history.

Interrupted six times by cheers, the former Dallas dentist dwelt upon public schools and good government, neglecting to discuss an issue sorely troubling Detroit officials: the Wayne County Klan had not been officially chartered in 1924 despite its large membership and was therefore provisional. Unlike chartered or numbered Klans, provisional klaverns could keep no part of the ten-dollar "klec-token" required of all new members. Money went to Atlanta, therefore, which would otherwise have been available for Detroit projects.

Because the charter was not forthcoming in 1924, local Klansmen technically broke away from the national office and formed the Symwa Club (Spend Your Money with Americans). The new organization superseded the local Klan chapter, but it continued to function as part of the Invisible Empire. Most important, it sent only five dollars of each initiation fee to the Imperial Palace in Atlanta. Symwa Club had the same officers, meeting places, dues, and goals as the Wayne County Provisional Klan, and the Symwa kleagle was the official representative of the Ku Klux Klan. Until recognized with a charter, however, the Detroit organization was determined to withhold some financial support from the national body.

James A. Colescott, who was to become the Klan's imperial wizard in 1939, arrived in Detroit from Minnesota in 1924 and eased the unhappy situation. With the aid of Kleagles Daniel E. Rhoads and Charles E. Lewis, Colescott increased Detroit Klan strength to thirty-two thousand, a feat which *The Fiery Cross* labeled, "nothing short of phenomenal." A Junior Klan for boys under eighteen and a local branch of the Women of the Ku Klux Klan were organized. The need for additional meeting halls was alleviated in late 1923, when the local order secured "two whole floors" and 40,000 square feet of floor space at 206 Hancock Avenue East, where the symbol of the cross was hung over the door.

Under new leadership, the demonstrations of the Detroit Klan became even more elaborate. Bands, quartets, and abundant refreshments were the usual ingredients of a successful initiation. At one 1924 gathering of fifteen thousand just north of the city in early May, a fireworks display featured exploding bombs of red, white, and blue and a band playing revival favorites.

With new muscle, the Detroit Klan enthusiastically entered the political lists in 1924. Among important projects were the election of a Klan sympathizer as Michigan governor and the passage of a state law outlawing parochial schools. The battle for governor was fought within the Republican primary, where both of the Klan favorites, James Hamilton of Detroit and the Reverend Frederick Perry of Adrian, were defeated by incumbent Governor Alex J. Groesbeck. Having been condemned by virtually every daily and weekly newspaper in Michigan, the parochial school amendment was equally unsuccessful, losing by almost three to one.

It was in a local contest, however, that the Detroit Klan made its influence most keenly felt. On September 9, 1924, a primary election was held to determine candidates for the remaining one year of the term of Mayor Frank E. Doremus, who had become seriously ill and could not continue in office. John W. Smith and Joseph A. Martin led the voting and were therefore certified for the runoff election in November. But the third-place finisher, attorney Charles S. Bowles, decided to disregard the primary election and run as a write-in candidate against the two successful campaigners. It was an unprecedented move, but with the active support of the Ku Klux Klan the "sticker candidate" almost accomplished a political miracle.

A lawyer trained at the University of Michigan, with offices in the Dime Bank Building, Charles Bowles was the first president of DeMolay (Masonic order for boys) in Detroit and held high office in several Masonic lodges. His platform emphasized subways, economy, and "strict law enforcement." Bowles' support by the Invisible Empire was blatantly expressed at an anti-Ku Klux Klan rally at the Arena Gardens, where Aldrich Blake of Oklahoma was scheduled to expose the "one hundred per cent American" movement. Hours before the October 21 event was to begin, a menacing crowd of six thousand men and boys gathered at the entrance to the Gardens. Police were unable to disperse the mob, which shaped itself into a column, three abreast and several blocks long. Marching up and down Woodward Avenue, the solid chain of humanity shouted, "Bowles, Bowles, Bowles," and effectively isolated the box offices from all who might wish to purchase a ticket to the anti-Klan rally. Several hundred Bowles supporters massed opposite the Public Library and forcibly posted Bowles stickers on the windows of passing cars as they slowed down.

Riot calls to police headquarters brought four squads of fifty men each to the area. Forming flying wedges, the police drove the mob in both directions on Woodward, hastening its retreat with tear gas bombs. Originally scheduled for eight o'clock, the rally was delayed for thirty-five minutes to allow four thousand five hundred persons to purchase tickets. Meanwhile the police lined both sides of the street to prevent any recurrence of the disorder.

Neither of the remaining mayoralty candidates chose to ignore such evidence of Klan influence in the Bowles campaign. Joseph A.

Martin, a clean-government, business candidate with strong support in upper-income wards, charged that in the orgy of un-Americanism, the "Klan accidentally tore the night shirt and pillow case from its hero and revealed to the entire citizenship that Charles Bowles was the Ku Klux candidate for Mayor and general manager of Detroit." He added that in the "riotous demonstration to prevent an anti-Klan lecture, the Ku Klux Klan of Detroit pasted the symbols of the Klan and the symbols of the Bowles campaign side by side the length and breadth of Woodward Avenue from Antoinette Street to Palmer Avenue."

The Klan issue was seized upon even more eagerly by John W. Smith, whose primary support was among Catholics, Negroes, and recent immigrants. Referring to southern whites as "ignorant hill-billies," Smith concentrated his campaign in lower east side wards, where he spoke often of the alleged misdeeds of the Invisible Empire against minority groups. Typical of his approach was an appearance at St. Stanislaus Catholic Church two days before the election. Arguing that the question was not so much one of who was going to be Mayor of Detroit as it was whether the Klan was going to be allowed to say it elected the mayor, Smith stated that Klansmen "have robbed Catholic churches and have attempted to burn them. They have tortured and slain Negroes and Jews." At St. Hedwig's Catholic Church on the day before the election Smith called the Klan an ugly monster from the South, "which is going to the polls tomorrow to put over the parochial school amendment and its candidate for Mayor."

Realizing that he had the "one hundred per cent" vote in his pocket, Bowles was careful to avoid mention of the secret order despite persistent challenges by Martin and Smith. Martin's remark was typical: "If Charles Bowles is not the candidate of the Ku Klux Klan, as I have repeatedly charged, why does he not publicly give the Klan that condemnation which it so richly deserves?" But the "sticker candidate," well aware of the zeal of his hooded supporters, remained silent.

On the Saturday evening immediately prior to the election, the largest meeting of Klansmen in Detroit history congregated in a field in Dearborn Township. Hundreds of women were in the crowd, which began arriving as early as six o'clock under the glare of a huge flaming cross and the lights of thousands of automobiles. Estimates to the number, none of whom were hooded or cloaked, ranged from twenty-five thousand to fifty thousand. Because Klan pickets prevented non-members from entering the field, Bowles' appearance was not officially reported, However, he may well have attended the rally, and his name met the eye wherever it turned.

Most of the automobiles were plastered with Bowles campaign labels and with instructions on how to vote for the "sticker candidate."

On the day of the election the *Detroit News* reaffirmed its endorsement of Joseph Martin, denounced John W. Smith as the machine candidate, and warned the citizenry: "If you want the City of Detroit to be advertised over the nation as a city controlled by the 'invisible empire' of the Ku Klux Klan . . . Vote for Charles Bowles." The vote for mayor was the heaviest in Detroit's history; there were several fights between Smith and Bowles supporters, but no major disturbances. When the returns began to come in, it was apparent that Bowles had cut heavily into Martin's strength. In most of the districts where Smith was strong, both Bowles and Martin were weak; but in districts where Martin was strong, Bowles was also strong and the Smith vote was light. Only in the most "respectable" districts of the city did Martin edge Bowles out, while in the lower-middle-class Protestant sections, Bowles fared the better of the two. Martin supporters felt, therefore, that had Bowles accepted his primary defeat and not entered the general election as a write-in candidate, then Martin would have won by a tremendous majority.

With the ballots counted Smith seemed the winner:

John W. Smith	116,807
Charles Bowles	106,679
Joseph Martin	84,929
	308,415

As was expected, Smith piled up big majorities in the Third, Fifth, Seventh, Ninth, Eleventh, and Thirteenth wards, showing great strength on the lower east side, where many predominantly Catholic or Negro precincts gave him more than 90 per cent of their total vote. Along the present Chrysler Freeway between Napoleon and Willis Streets, anti-Klan sentiment was particularly overwhelming. In one Third Ward polling place at the Ginsburg Library, Smith outdistanced Bowles 699 to 0; at Adelaide and Hastings Streets the vote was 792 to 1; at Russell and Watson Streets the tally was 806 to 1; at Medbury and DuBois, 578 to 0; and at Rivard and Livingston, 718 to 2.

Despite the fact that Bowles was unable to overcome such mountainous leads, he carried twice as many wards as Smith and won an absolute majority in the Twenty-second Ward. The Klan candidate's greatest support was in a triangular area bounded roughly by Grand River Avenue, Philadelphia Street, and the present John C. Lodge Freeway. Additional Bowles strength was noticeable along the Woodward Avenue side of Palmer Park, on the far east and west sides, and in the northwestern part of the city. In the absence of Klan membership records in Detroit, this voting pattern may be presumed a fair indication of the secret order's strength in the city.

The official canvass of the election revealed that while 325,678 votes had been cast, only 308,415 ballots were tabulated. According to the election commissioner most of the 17,000 discarded votes were for the write-in candidate and had been rejected for various mistakes. The placing of a period following the name or the use of the surname only was sufficient for disqualification. On November 7, the *Detroit News* listed 120 ways in which voters had invalidated Bowles ballots, including:

Chas. Bowles	Charlie Bowles
Charles Boles	Charles Bouls
Cha. Bowles	Bowles, Charles
Ch. Bowles	Bowles
Charles Bowls	Charles S. Bowles
Charles Bowels	Charles E. Bowles

Two days after the election Bowles announced that he would ask for a recount, "since unquestionably more persons attempted to vote for me than either of the other candidates." His attorneys argued that numerous precedents demonstrated that absolutely correct spelling was neither essential nor necessary, and that the presumptive intent of the elector was shown in many instances where the ballots were thrown out. Bowles argued for a liberal application of the rule of "idem sonans," or the spelling of a word by sound.

The request for a recount was granted, but the election commission refused to alter the original instructions, and write-in votes not absolutely perfect were again discarded. As a result Bowles found himself behind by more than 14,000 votes. Although Bowles' supporters claimed that 15,545 disputed ballots should have given their man victory, the Board of Canvassers declared John W. Smith mayor. Because a request to the Michigan Supreme Court for a writ of certiorari would have required at least one year to complete, Bowles reluctantly withdrew from the struggle on November 20. Two days later the *Detroit News* commented: "No one will probably ever know whether more voters intended to vote for John W. Smith or Charles Bowles at the mayoralty election."

Although the Motor City Klan suffered defeat, its near victory was a surprise to many. The liberal *Christian Century* expressed dismay and incredulity that, "In Detroit, a Klan write-in candidate, almost totally unknown in the city, whose name was not even printed on the ballot . . . came within a few thousand votes of being elected mayor of the fourth city in the United States." Perhaps the vote for A. J. Brodie, endorsed by the Klan for the city council, offers a better indication of the secret order's strength in Detroit. He polled only 68,887 votes against Robert G. Ewald's 180,618.

Wayne County Klan No. 68 was the new designation of the Detroit klavern when it finally received its charter early in 1925, but decline had already set in. The strenuous election campaign had sapped some of its strength, as did the ill-fated financial ventures of the Symwa Club. The most damaging was a scheme to buy, subdivide, and sell a tract of land on the Middle Belt Road, using the profits to build a temple "like Solomon's" for Detroit Klan headquarters. Known as the "gold brick deal" because contributors were given a pasteboard lapel button in the shape of a brick, the project failed to materialize. Fourteen thousand dollars were invested by Detroit Knights, but the klavern was never built, and the money was never returned. More amusing was a scheme to manufacture and sell Klan phonograph records throughout the country, but the Cross Music and Record Company of Detroit never produced a single record.

As a result of such misadventures, the Wayne County Klan was in frequent financial difficulty. A judgment of $424.60, representing two months' rent, resulted in the temporary removal of furniture from the Klan office at 206 Hancock Avenue East in 1925, and late in 1926 the owner of the property sued the Klan for ten thousand dollars in damages to her building. Apparently the Detroit Klan had very little money, and even that could not be properly accounted for. The Grundy Audit Company, employed to inventory the organization's books in 1925, refused to sign the audit after ninety days of work.

When the Detroit Klan seemed on the verge of collapse, the explosive and easily exploitable issue of neighborhood segregation breathed new life into the secret order. By 1925 the Negro population of Detroit had increased to 80,000, yet they were still confined to three small wards that had been apportioned to them in 1910. As fewer residences became available in the ghetto, many colored business and professional men looked for good houses outside the colored boundaries. The Ku Klux Klan reacted quickly. On July 11, 1925, the Invisible Empire staged a huge meeting on West Fort Street, a mile west of Lincoln Park Village. Standing on a platform illuminated by the red glare of fiery crosses, a speaker advocated laws to compel Negroes to live in certain sections of the city.

The first racial incident in 1925 came when Dr. Alex Turner, a Negro surgeon on the staff of Grace Hospital, was forced by a

Klan-inspired white mob to vacate his recently purchased home in the northern part of Detroit a short distance out of the colored section. Several weeks later a similar result accompanied the attempt of James Fletcher to escape the Negro ghetto. Unquestionably, however, the major crisis came in September, when Dr. Ossian Sweet bought a two-story brick house in a white workingman's neighborhood on Detroit's East Side. According to his wife: "I had in mind only two things: first to find a house that was in itself desirable, and, second, to find one that would be within our pocketbook. I wanted a pretty home, and it made no difference to me whether it was in a white neighborhood or a colored neighborhood."

Even before the young Negro physician took possession of his home, white neighbors, including many foreign-born Catholics, had formed the "Water Works Improvement Association" to preserve segregation. When the Sweet family moved in at 2905 Garland (at Chalevoix), mobs formed on the streets and threw bricks, bottles, and stones at the house. The tragic result came on September 9, when Dr. Sweet's brother Henry shot and killed Leon Breiner, a white neighbor demonstrating in the street. Although Detroit police had made no attempt to protect the Sweet home, the Negroes were promptly arrested and charged with first degree murder.

The trial of Dr. Ossian Sweet and his brother attracted national attention. Chicago attorney Clarence Darrow agreed to defend the accused Negroes. He spent three weeks selecting a jury, carefully excluding known Klansmen. Darrow had to contend with an unsympathetic white population and with "law and order" advocates who demanded that an example be made of the Negroes. He based his defense upon the right of any man to protect his family and his home. In a celebrated decision, the Sweets were ultimately acquitted.

Although the Ku Klux Klan was not officially involved in the incident, it thrived upon and fed the racial hysteria that enveloped the city. Three days after the Sweet shooting, Mayor John W. Smith sent an open letter to Police Commissioner Frank H. Croul. Charging that the Ku Klux Klan was responsible for neighborhood violence and had capitalized on the disturbances, Mayor Smith suggested that the secret order was seeking to establish a "dictatorship" in Detroit. But the mayor, who had been elected with Negro votes, let it be known that he harbored no sympathy for their efforts to escape the ghetto:

> . . . I must say that I deprecate most strongly the moving of Negroes or other persons into districts in which they knew their presence may cause riot or bloodshed.

I believe that any colored person who endangers life and property, simply to gratify his personal pride, is an enemy of his race as well as an incitant of riot and murder. These men who have permitted themselves to be tools of the Ku Klux Klan in its effort to fan the flames of racial hatred into murderous fire, have hurt the cause of their race in a degree that can not be measured.

Mayor Smith's letter won him no new friends among Klansmen, who vowed to frustrate his attempt to win a full term in November 1925. Again the Klan favorite was Charles Bowles, but this time he sought broader support. Although he accepted the Klan endorsement with equanimity, he vigorously denied membership in it and even campaigned actively for the Negro vote.

As evidence of its serious intentions, the Invisible Empire assessed its Detroit membership five dollars per man and brought in Kleagle Ira W. Stout to direct the campaign. Appealing to Protestant solidarity, Klan workers formed Bowles Clubs on most blocks and distributed pamphlets and handbills on the streets. One political observer labeled the secret order a "highly organized, fanatical group," and predicted that the Klan would defeat Mayor Smith unless a heavy vote was recorded.

Two imponderable elements complicated the situation: (1) Henry Ford's endorsement of Mayor Smith, an action which placed Jewish citizens in the position of either voting with the Ku Klux Klan or aligning themselves with the nation's most notorious anti-Semite; and (2) the Klan's endorsement of five candidates for the city council. Councilman Phillip A. Callahan was a former president of the Symwa Club and an obvious Klansman, but another endorsee, Councilman Robert G. Ewald, scorned hooded support: "I am not a Klansman, did not solicit their endorsement, and do not want it." A. J. Brodie and Sherman Littlefield said they were not Klansmen but accepted its endorsement.

The final week of the campaign was predictably the most vitriolic. Both sides predicted victory. A 20-by-5-foot KKK banner was hung from the rotunda of the City Hall, and the secret order arranged for services in many churches. The wife of one minister declared in her husband's church that any woman not voting for Bowles should be tarred and feathered. Many Protestant clergymen objected to this sort of behavior, including Reinhold Niebuhr of Bethel Evangelical Church, who dubbed the Ku Klux Klan "one of the worst specific social phenomena which the religious pride of peoples has ever developed."

The 1925 Detroit election was a disaster for the Invisible Empire. Although Callahan won a place on the city council, Charles Bowles was defeated 140,000 to 111,000, and no face-saving charges of election fraud could be made. Bowles did well in the north end and northwest sections of the city, but could not crack Smith's strength among Catholics, Negroes, and immigrants.

Failure in politics accelerated the demise of Wayne County Klan No. 68, which was down to less than half its peak strength by 1926, and to only a few hundred members in 1928. Its few activities were inoffensive. In 1926 and again in 1929, the secret order promoted indoor circuses, the first in Highland Park and the second at Danceland. Both were financial failures; the Danceland circus particularly so because the performers were stranded in Detroit when their checks were not honored by the bank. Despite the efforts of Exalted Cyclopes W. F. Jackson and Charles Spare, the Detroit Klan had ceased to exist by 1934.

More sinister and violent than the Ku Klux Klan was the Black Legion, which had a brief and infamous career in Detroit and parts of Ohio in the mid-thirties. Formed ostensibly to seek jobs for southern whites, the Legion was anti-Negro, anti-Semitic, and anti-union. Its power was broken in May 1936, when the body of Charles Poole, a young WPA worker, was found on a desolate suburban road near Detroit. Seven Black Legionnaires were convicted of the murder and the authoritarian secret organization soon lost most of its several thousand members.

Between 1939 and 1941 a brief effort was made to revive the dormant Detroit Klan. Meetings were held in a variety of locations: Odd Fellows Halls, the Danish Brotherhood Hall, the Findlater Masonic Temple, and the Klan's two-story frame headquarters on West Forest. Recruiting was desperate and intense and unsuccessful. At a large banquet, on October 19, 1941, members were told by Klan officials: "Bring an eligible American and if we Klux him that night we will refund your dollar." Even with such an uncritical admissions policy the Ku Klux Klan was dead in Detroit before news of Pearl Harbor offered patriots new enemies.

In an age when all of us are continually bombarded by the images on a television screen, it is easy to forget the role that radio once played in the lives of most Michiganians. During the years following World War I, the radio, once viewed by many as a toy, gave Michigan's residents a more intimate contact with the world outside of the local village, town, or city. The following selection by Cynthia Boyes Young details the story of one of Michigan's pioneer efforts in this new medium, the beginnings and early years of the *Detroit News'* radio station, later (and best known as) WWJ. The development of this station also provides an interesting account of what historians delight in calling the entrepreneurial spirit. At the same time the range of programming offers a unique view of the popular culture of the 1920s.

WWJ—Pioneer in Broadcasting

CYNTHIA BOYES YOUNG

No scientific invention during the first half of the twentieth century, except perhaps the automobile, made a more immediate and direct impact on American society than that of radio broadcasting. It is to Detroit's credit as a dynamic and progressive city, that here both radio and the automobile were first made available to the American people on a large scale.

The subsequent results of automobile mass production are readily apparent to all Americans today, but the many implications of radio broadcasting are perhaps not so well known. Programs of an educational and cultural nature have carried the finest music, drama, and public lectures into the most remote sections of our country. Radio has also become important in our national life in such varied manifestations as the promotion of social solidarity, the apprehension of criminals, relief of suffering and distress, the dissemination of accurate news, entertainment of the people, encouragement of interest in public affairs, and the development of skills, vocations and habits.

It appears that these tremendous possibilities for radio were partially foreseen by James E. Scripps, founder of the Detroit *News*. As early as 1901 he listened to the story of a young inventor, Thomas E. Clark, and witnessed his demonstration of wireless communication through the air. Operating from the top of the Banner Laundry Company at 73-75 Michigan Avenue (opposite the present site of the Book-Cadillac Hotel), Clark sent a message to Scripps who was waiting two blocks away in the Chamber of Commerce Building at State and Griswold. So excited was Scripps over the success of the demonstration that he gave Clark a check for $1,000 with which to continue his radio experiments and told him:

From *Michigan History*, XLIV (December, 1960), 411-433. Reprinted by permission of the History Division, Michigan Department of State. Footnotes in the original have been omitted.

> I think you have a good idea there and I want you to have every opportunity to do what you can with it. I don't care whether I ever see the money again. It is my contribution toward helping a little idea become a big, worthwhile fact.

During the next twenty years many technical improvements were made in wireless transmission. Through the efforts of men like Clark, Lee DeForest, and others, the way was paved for wider use of wireless telephony, and in 1920 the people of Detroit were invited to participate in the first experiment in regularly scheduled radio broadcasting.

The actual beginnings of the Detroit *News* radio station, later to be known as WWJ, were not recorded at the time, and the story can only be partially pieced together from the reminiscences of radio pioneers.

There seems to be no question, however, that the enthusiasm of James Scripps about the potentialities of radio was passed on to his son, William E., and grandsons, William J. and James E. Scripps II. Both young men were ardent radio amateurs. It is quite probable that they were partially responsible for convincing their father, William E. Scripps (owner of the Detroit *News*) to install a transmitter in the News building.

In a speech given by Dr. DeForest at WWJ's tenth anniversary celebration, he recalls that about 1917 he and Clarence Thompson approached William E. Scripps with the suggestion that the Detroit *News* should purchase and install a radio transmitter because there were so many enthusiastic amateur listeners. DeForest and Thompson had been promoting this idea among newspaper owners all over the west and south, but had met with no interest until they talked with Scripps.

The fact that no action was taken immediately was probably due to the fact that the United States was on the verge of entering World War I. Strict regulations prohibited any use of radio except for military or commercial purposes.

The recollection of Thomas E. Clark, who maintained a close friendship with the Scripps family, is that in about 1919, William E. Scripps talked with him about the matter of purchasing a transmitter. Clark was invited to a meeting of the Detroit *News* board of directors to present the idea and explain the principles of radio transmission. Though Clark was given an icy reception by the board, Scripps was undaunted and proceeded to send Clark to New York to purchase a transmitter. However, he was unsuccessful in obtaining one and the Detroit *News* later made its own transaction. It was at this point, apparently, that the *News* again made contact with the De Forest Radio Telephone and Telegraph Company.

Though the actual sequence of events leading to the decision to purchase the transmitter are obscure, it seems probable that all of the foregoing were factors influencing William E. Scripps. By 1920 he had agreed to the idea of experimenting with radio broadcasting, thus making the Detroit *News* the first newspaper in the world to install a radio broadcasting station.

The original apparatus obtained by the Detroit *News* in the summer of 1920 and installed in a corner of the sports department, consisted of a DeForest Type OT-10 transmitter, similar to those DeForest had been selling to the navy since 1914. The panel mounted two oscillators and two modulator tubes using a grid modulation circuit. It was operated at a wave length of two hundred meters and had a power rating of twenty watts. The power supply was derived from a 150 watt, 500 volt, *D.C.* generator driven by a one-fourth h.p. motor. Enthusiastic amateur operators who belonged to a group called the Detroit Radio Association put in many hours of time at the new transmitter as volunteer operators.

. . . .

The broadcast range of this first outfit was limited and under the best conditions was not more than one hundred miles. It was estimated that there were about three hundred operators receiving in the area covered, and one hundred privately owned receiving sets in Wayne County. These radio amateurs were among approximately twenty thousand in the entire country. Their apparatus, usually one and two tube regenerative circuits, were used only to communicate with each other.

Though the *News* transmission set was in place and ready for operation on August 20, 1920, no public announcement of it was made until a ten-day series of experimental transmission of opera recordings had been conducted. When these proved satisfactory it was announced that the August 31 primary election returns would be broadcast.

The anticipated birth of newcasting was announced in a page 1 story in the Detroit *News* on August 31, 1920:

> The Detroit *News* tonight will announce the results, as they may be received, of the State, Congressional, and County primaries over southeastern Michigan, using as a medium, its newly completed wireless telephone. . . . So far as is known here, this is the first time in the history of radio development that a newspaper will use the radiophone in the transmission of news. . . . Every wireless operator in Michigan, Ohio, and Ontario is invited to open his receiver and participate in the enterprise. Every community that houses an operator is fortunate; and every man, woman, and child invited by an operator to sit in and listen to tonight's

demonstration will be specially favored, for they are participating in an
event that will be in a sense, epochal.

. . . .

The success of the venture and recognition of its significance
were dramatically reported in the *News* the following day:

> The sending of election returns by The Detroit *News* radiophone Tues-
> day night was fraught with romance and must go down in the history of
> man's conquest of the elements as a gigantic step in his progress. In the
> four hours that the apparatus . . . was hissing and whirring its message
> into space, few realized that a dream and prediction had come true. The
> news of the world was being given forth through this invisible trumpet to
> the waiting crowds in the unseen market place.

So the story began. From that date on, the *News* offered uninter-
rupted service to an increasing audience, constantly enlarging and
elaborating the programs.

In the first week of broadcasting, baseball news, bulletins of
foreign affairs, and campaign proceedings went out over the air. The
results of the Dempsey-Miske fight were broadcast within thirty
seconds of the time the bulletin was received by wire.

The first music concerts were confined entirely to phonograph
music and were broadcast twice daily, at 11:30 A.M. and 7:00 P.M.
On September 4, 1920, a party was held at the Charles F.
Hammond home at 700 Parker, Detroit, where Charles, Jr. and a
dozen of his young friends danced to music from the Detroit *News*
Radiophone. Reported in the society column of the Detroit *News*,
this event was considered to be the local beginning of the social
aspect of wireless.

. . . .

When the scores of the World Series games in Brooklyn were
announced on the radio in October, and the returns of the Harding-
Cox election were broadcast in November, the traditionally scep-
tical man in the street was greatly impressed. What had at first been
regarded as a fad by the public was now being recognized as a great
new medium of communication. The attitude toward radio seemed
to change overnight. Interest grew and dealers reported a big demand for radio material. By November, the *News* was so overwhelmed with requests for information that a radio department
column was included in the Sunday edition of the *News*. The
column offered information to all beginners about "radiophone"
and the methods of achieving best reception. Schematic diagrams
were printed in the paper and the *News* offered further benefits to
its listeners in the forms of assistance by the technical staff of the

station, improved and extended transmission, and a greater variety of programs.

Because electrical shops couldn't supply enough headphones to meet the rush of new radio listeners, there grew up quite an epidemic of pilfering of telephone receivers—mostly from apartment house phones. So enthusiastic were these beginners that many scrupulously honest souls indulged in this petty thievery. With a single wire antenna strung in the room or attic, a coil on an oatmeal box, a piece of silicon or galena with a cat whisker, and a telephone receiver, the would-be radio operator was able to participate in the amazing magic of voices and music on the air.

While listeners grew more and more excited, not all of the executives of the Detroit *News* showed the same enthusiasm. Opinions ranged from coolness, to the attitude that the transmitter was an expensive plaything, to indifference to its future.

Financially, the radio station was not considered a loss to the Detroit *News* in spite of the expense incurred in its operation. Although no radio advertising was sold, the station was popular enough to be considered a good-will medium, and hence of value to the newspaper circulation. Therefore, despite the general indifference and opposition of some members of the board of directors, Detroit *News* owner William E. Scripps, and general manager Herward S. Scott continued to support the radio experiment and saw that it was perpetuated.

. . . .

So ambitious were the plans of the young station that the original transmitting set was soon found to be inadequate and was partially rebuilt. In June, 1921, a two-wire antenna, 290 feet long, was stretched between the Detroit *News* building and the Fort Shelby Hotel. Soon after, reports began to arrive from such distant points as Belleville, Illinois, and Atlanta, Georgia, that *News* broadcasts were being received. At the same time, the *News* receiving set was picking up wireless telegraph messages from such far distant places as Germany, Rome, and Hawaii, and the United States Navy station at Bordeaux, France. At this time two young engineers, Frederick Lathrup and Walter Hoffman, were operating the transmitting equipment.

The program schedule was now expanded to include more musicians and theatrical talent from Detroit playhouses. Members of the Detroit *News* staff: George W. Stark, Robert Kelly, William Holliday, and Al Weeks undertook to book talent for radio appearances. Ernest R. Ball, composer of "Mother Machree," "Love Me and the World is Mine," and other songs, was appearing with the Keith circuit on the stage of the Temple Theater in 1921, and was one of the earliest professional entertainers over the *News* radio. George W. Stark, present Detroit historiographer and veteran member of the Detroit *News* editorial staff, recalled Ball's performance:

> The microphone was almost more than he could bear. At the conclusion of "Mother Machree" he looked at it rather helplessly; then touched his thumb to his nose and wriggled his fingers, the familiar gesture of the frustrated and final answer to all things. It was masterful pantomime. But he sang an encore.

. . . .

For the value of the experience, stage and musical personalities readily appeared on the *News* station with no thought of compensation. To many it was a matter of prestige to have appeared before a microphone and they were eager for the opportunity.

The program expansion in 1921 was also marked by the appearance of the well-known Finzel's orchestra of Detroit and other musical groups, who furnished dance music by radio. The *News'* second Christmas concert on December 24, 1921, was a "peace program" including songs by carollers, and addresses by Governor Alex J. Groesbeck, Mayor James Couzens, and the Rt. Rev. Fr. John P. McNichols, president of the University of Detroit. Another feature of the program was the broadcasting of music played by the chimes in the steeple of the Fort Street Presbyterian Church across the street from the *News* building.

. . . .

On January 28, 1922, the Detroit *News* installed its new Type 1A-500 watt Western Electric transmitter. Since none of the local men were familiar with this equipment, Howard E. Campbell, an engineer from the Bell laboratory, was brought from New York to supervise and train the staff. Edwin G. Boyes replaced Fred Lathrop who had been asked by William E. Scripps to act as supervising engineer of a concern started by Scripps (The Scripps Motor Company) to manufacture nonregenerative receiving sets which would offer better quality reception than the many types of regenerative sets being used by the public.

. . . .

The transmitter and the engineers were in a separate room adjacent to the studio and cables were used to run in microphone lines and signal systems. The microphone used in 1922 was the double button carbon mike produced by Western Electric. Boyes describes this as looking like a squirrel cage with the microphone mounted inside, and recalls that its large, businesslike appearance made it a symbol of radio for many years.

A push-button signaling system devised by the engineers gave visual instructions like, "stand-by," "one minute," "on the air," "closer to the mike." Boyes remembers that occasionally it was augmented by someone running back and forth between control room and studio with more detailed instructions on technique. He notes, however, that even a crude signaling system was adequate then because broadcasting was not yet concerned with accurate mike and talent placements and the split-second timing so essential in radio broadcasting today. Boyes stated also that in those days if you were two or three minutes late getting a program off the air it didn't make too much difference. But there was one important responsibility and that was to protect the audience from something that might be said in the studio if someone neglected to turn off a switch. This required constant alertness on the part of the control engineer.

With new equipment and a larger staff, the *News* began to develop longer and more carefully planned programs and continued to introduce many more "firsts" in radio broadcasting.

On February 10, 1922, the Detroit Symphony Orchestra, conducted by Ossip Gabrilowitch, gave the first complete symphony concert ever presented by radio. Another memorable musical occasion was the first performance, on May 28, 1922, of the sixteen-piece Detroit News Orchestra. The first radio concert orchestra ever assembled, its members were drawn primarily from the ranks of the Detroit Symphony Orchestra.

Another of the presentation of special events in which the *News* pioneered in 1922 was the broadcast of church services. For the forty days of Lent, leading clergymen of all denominations provided sermons that were presented every evening. During the Easter season, beginning on Palm Sunday, the Easter cantata and the sermon of Warren L. Rogers, Dean of St. Paul's Cathedral, were heard on a broadcast of the cathedral services. The morning and evening Easter services were broadcast and a regular presentation of cathedral services was continued thereafter. At the end of the first year, Dean Rogers described the broadcast as "the greatest missionary achievement since the time of Jesus Christ." Other churches without rectors of their own worshipped by radio with St. Paul's. One Presbyterian church in Michigan installed a receiving set and heard the services of St. Paul's while the pastor was on vacation. "These incidents", the Dean said, "are becoming more numerous with the growth of the popular knowledge of radio and with the decline in the prejudice against radio equipment being used for religious purposes."

During 1922, the *News* also offered its readers an impressive and diversified array of stars and programs undreamed of in the earlier days. To name only a few, there were the radio debuts of operatic soprano, Emma Calve; the Shakespearean artists, E. H. Sothern and his wife, Julia Marlowe; the appearance of Will Rogers; the presentation of the University of Michigan and Michigan State University extension courses; and the baritone voice of Thomas E. Dewey of Owosso, singing with the Detroit News Orchestra. One of the most notable achievements of the station that year was the broadcast of appeals resulting in locating a ten-year-old boy missing for ten days in Ohio.

The present call letters of the Detroit *News* station, WWJ, were adopted in March, 1922, replacing the first commercial call letters, WBL. The reason for the change is explained by Edwin Boyes. When the fad was raging to pick up distant stations, people often sent postcards to the transmitting station to inform them that their programs were being received at great distances. WBL was sent hundreds of cards, addressed not only as WBL, but as WGL, WDL and other combinations of letters that sounded the same. Interference on the air waves and noise on the receiving sets made it difficult to hear call letters clearly. Hence, it was decided that letters would have to be chosen that would be more easily recognized through the interference. This need was made known to radio inspector Edwards, who in turn requested the commissioner of navigation to assign new letters to the Detroit *News* station.

. . . .

Competition in the field of radio broadcasting first faced the Detroit *News* in March, 1922, when it was learned that the Detroit *Free Press* intended to begin broadcasting as soon as Western Electric delivered to them the same type of radiophone that the Detroit *News* was using.

The first broadcast by the Detroit *Free Press* station occurred on May 4, 1922, and included the participation of the Hon. Alex Groesbeck, Governor of Michigan; Dr. Marion LeRoy Burton, president of the University of Michigan; and Edgar A. Guest, Detroit *Free Press* poet-humorist.

The Detroit *News* of May 4, 1922, stated their reaction in an editorial:

> For the last two years the Detroit *News* has been building up a nationwide service for the people through its radio broadcasting station. This work is just at its beginning and will be continued on a still larger and broader scale despite the handicaps imposed upon Station WWJ, The Detroit News Radio Bureau. The handicap consists of a temporary, at least, curtailment of hours now used by WWJ by order of the Department of Commerce.

When the wave of popularity of radio swept the nation during the first two years of Detroit *News* broadcasting the government was unprepared in the way of laws to govern the air. Only one wave length (360 meters) had been allotted by law for broadcasting. Other desirable wave lengths were under the control of the navy department and its regulations did not permit re-issuance to other interests. The only thing the department of commerce could do in the meantime was allot hours of transmission until Congress could proceed by law for another wave length. The editorial continued:

> This was the situation when the Detroit *Free Press* decided to break in on the Detroit *News* service and demanded of the government that it too be allotted hours. . . . The *Free Press* frankly stated in its advertising that it preferred to wait until the experimental stage had been passed before getting into it. That is, it preferred to wait until the *News* had done all the pioneering work and had built up a public service which had brought instruction and pleasure to the people, before attempting to interfere with it.

The advent of the *Free Press* radio station was just one local indication of the great impact radio was making all over the nation. The Associated Press saw its enormous potential and recognized a possible rival in the form of news broadcasting. In 1922 it issued a notice to its member papers forbidding them to broadcast by radio telephone or telegraph, any news dispatches received on A. P. wire. A spokesman for the A. P. gave this explanation:

> The free distribution of news by wireless telephone broadcasting stations has been giving many newspaper publishers food for thought. At present the instruments for receiving these messages are more or less of a novelty, but what the result on newspapers would be when receiving sets became more popular and in many more homes is what publishers are wondering.

And well they might wonder about radio's future, not only as affecting newspapers, but as it was to affect nearly every aspect of our lives. Through the years to come, WWJ continued to pioneer in all areas of radio broadcasting and to set high standards for quality that have made it a great asset to the Detroit *News* and a credit to the city.

By 1923 there was no longer any doubt that radio broadcasting was not only here to stay, but was growing rapidly. Recognizing this, WWJ moved to further improve the quality of its transmission by purchasing and installing a Western Electric 1-B 500 watt transmitter in May, 1923. The additional features offered by this instrument enabled the station to maintain greater frequency stability, more effectively suppress harmonics (which might cause interference with other stations), and generally to improve program transmission.

. . . .

Among the popular program offerings of the year 1923 was the broadcast of a talk on the subject, "What is the Matter with the Movies" by movie idol, Rudolph Valentino, who was appearing in a dancing act in Detroit. A picture of the Sheik, seated before a microphone, appeared in the Detroit *News* above the cut-lines: "Generally he is seen and not heard. Here he's being heard and not seen." However, WWJ poet-broadcaster, Anne Campbell, recalls that Valentino was seen as well as heard by great throngs of people who crowded to the Detroit *News* the day of the broadcast to get a look at the famous star.

Two significant events in the development of broadcasting occurred in June, 1923, and both involved WWJ in pioneer undertakings.

Detroit became the first city in the United States to have municipal band concerts by radio in parks when WWJ began broadcasting the music of Herman Schmeman and his thirty-piece concert band which played at the Belle Isle band stand. Four other city parks heard these band concerts through special loud speakers set up by WWJ in cooperation with the department of parks and boulevards. The story in the Detroit *News* announcing this event assured readers:

> There is no danger of crowds being unable to hear the music plainly, as tests have shown that even a fly walking across the sounding board produces a thump that would be mistaken for the footfall of a man.

Of nation-wide interest that year was the expedition to the North Pole of the noted arctic explorer Dr. Donald B. MacMillan. Leaving in June, 1923, MacMillan, for the first time in the history of exploration, carried radio equipment with him, and transmitted accounts of his progress. Thirty thousand radio amateurs, members of the American Radio Relay League, and the North American Newspaper Alliance, of which the Detroit *News* was a member, cooperated in the experiment. The major service provided by WWJ was the use of its broadcast transmitter in the sending of news by code to the expedition. Reports from MacMillan were picked up by key amateur stations around the country and relayed to the Detroit *News.*

. . . .

Another important event of 1924 was the first direct broadcast of the Gold Cup races from the old Detroit Yacht Club. Returns of the races were reported from the judges' barge by direct voice transmission rather than by the method used in 1923 when the first broadcast of the boat races was accomplished through the use of wireless telegraph from the judges' barge to the studio of WWJ. Because no wire facilities were available to the barge in 1923, the reports were received by code, compiled, and then broadcast.

Enthusiasm for sports has always been a characteristic of Detroit and in the 1920's this spirit led Detroiters to flock to Ann Arbor to cheer the University of Michigan Wolverines on the football field. On October 25, 1924, because the Michigan-Wisconsin game at Ferry Field had been sold out far in advance, Coach Fielding H. Yost gave WWJ permission to broadcast the event. Thus, with Ty Tyson at the microphone the first University of Michigan football game was heard over radio. Before the next game the athletic association had received so many requests for tickets because of interest aroused by the broadcast that Yost gave WWJ permission to broadcast all home games.

The following year the station started the New Year 1925 on its way by broadcasting a play by play account of the New Year's Day Leland Stanford—Notre Dame football game in Pasadena, California. By combining broadcasting service with continuous wire service direct from the playing field, the station was able to bring to Detroit homes first hand the game that the Detroit *News* described as being "remarkable" and "full of thrills."

. . . .

In accordance with its pioneer tradition, WWJ participated in the introduction of network broadcasting in February, 1925, by becoming one of the regular outlets in the chain of stations that was later to become the National Broadcasting Company. The chain originated as a result of the plan of the American Telephone & Telegraph Company (AT&T) to experiment in long-line broadcasting transmission. Through their manufacturing division, Western Electric Company, AT&T built Station WEAF in New York City. Using the telephone lines of AT&T's engineering division, the Bell Laboratories, WEAF broadcast programs that were carried by a series of affiliated stations in the East and Middle West.

In 1926, AT&T sold WEAF and rented its long-line broadcast facilities to Radio Corporation of America, which in the meantime was operating its own broadcast stations, largest of which was WJZ in Newark, New Jersey. With the combined facilities of WEAF and its own station, RCA created the National Broadcasting Company. The first network was called the Red Network. Later additional stations covering less populous areas were included in a new network called the Blue Network. The contract between the National Broadcasting Company and WWJ committed WWJ to broadcast a certain number of hours of commercial network programs daily. Since these programs paid WWJ for their time, 1927 marked the first year that WWJ sold time commercially. Besides these required programs, the station could purchase additional sustaining hours from NBC.

. . . .

Public interest in radio continued to be stimulated by such programs as the broadcast of the details of Calvin Coolidge's inauguration ceremonies, which WWJ carried as part of a nation-wide loop.

. . . .

Technological improvements in radio were being made so rapidly and increased services received so eagerly by the public that the Detroit *News* again invested in advanced equipment to improve the quality of its transmission. On June 30, 1925, WWJ purchased its fourth transmitter—a Western Electric 1,000 watt 6-B—which was installed in the fourth floor studios of the Detroit *News*. About six months later the transmitter was moved to the garage of the Detroit *News* on the corner of Lafayette and Third, and in November, 1926, two new antenna towers were built 265 feet above the street; one on the paper warehouse section of the *News* building and the other on the garage. On June 15, 1927, WWJ began the use of the 374.8 meter wave length.

Though these innovations extended the station's area of coverage and improved the signal somewhat, WWJ soon began to face the increasingly complex problem of crowded wave lengths and interference arising from radio's phenomenal growth and the resulting intense competition.

Congress' first attempt to deal with this problem led to the passage of the Radio Act of 1927 and the creation of the Federal Radio Commission, which was made responsible for regulating broadcasting. The Radio Act of 1927, approved on February 23, 1927, was intended to regulate all forms of interstate and foreign radio transmission and communication within the United States, its Territories and possessions; to maintain the control of the United States over all the channels of interstate and foreign radio transmission; and to provide for the use of such channels, but not the ownership thereof, by individuals, firms, or corporations, for limited periods of time, under licenses granted by Federal authority. For the purposes of the act, the United States was divided into five zones (Michigan was in the second zone) and the Federal Radio Commission created, composed of five commissioners appointed by the President.

. . . .

While the technological, financial, and legal aspects of broadcasting were being examined, revised and expanded, innovations in programing also continued. On April 20, 1927, the Detroit Tigers opened the baseball season at Navin Field and WWJ announcer, Ty Tyson, was on hand to give the fans at their radios a play by play account of the game direct from the field. This first broadcast of such an event by any Detroit station also introduced the idea, known in present-day sportscast lingo as "pre-game color." The preceding day's Detroit *News* reported:

> A microphone for the use of the announcer will be placed in the press stands, and in various other parts of the field there will be concealed other microphones for the pick-up of crowd noises to lend realistic atmosphere to the game as heard by radio listeners in their homes. . . . Mr. Tyson from his vantage point high up over the heads of the audience will point out for listeners the colorful aspects of the scene before the serious work of broadcasting every move of the game begins.

One small indication of the success of WWJ's attempts to offer the best possible education, entertainment, and service over the air was provided by the visit to the Detroit *News* in March, 1927, of Mrs. Mae Fisher of Pasadena, California. Calling on the household editor, Mrs. Fisher reported that she and her neighbors in Pasadena always awaited with pleasure the "Dinner Menu By Radio" broadcast (which reached California at 6:30 a.m.). "To myself and others in Pasadena," she said, "the Household Editor of the Detroit *News* has become a personal friend with whom we chat each morninng."

Several years later, veteran Detroit *News* reporter, Rex G. White, recalled the awe with which he realized in the earlier days the tremendous significance radio would surely have when "a single man could sit beside an inanimate thing and talk and his words could stir a nation, lead a cause, awake a public conscience, thrill a million hearts from Maine to California."

2: The Years of the Great Depression: Characters and Crises

There can be little doubt that the Great Depression of the 1930s was a traumatic event in the period between the two world wars. The many ramifications of the social, economic, and psychological dislocation wrought by this, the worst of the nation's "economic downturns," as some economists call such disasters, have only recently begun to be studied by social scientists. Perhaps most fundamental to our even imperfect understanding of the far-reaching effects of this national problem is some basic knowledge of the ways in which local units responded to the depression. In "Flint and the Great Depression" William H. Chafe analyzes the response of one industrial center, an area that was particularly hard hit because of its dependence on automobile manufacturing. Another view of the way in which a Michigan city responded to the depression is David M. Katzman, "Ann Arbor: Depression City," *Michigan History*, L (December, 1966), 306-317.

Flint and the Great Depression

WILLIAM H. CHAFE

Flint, Michigan, was and is a company town. Its economic survival depends upon the auto industry. A manufacturing center for carriages in the late nineteenth century, it became in the twentieth century a central production facility for General Motors, containing branches of Chevrolet, Fisher Body, Buick, and AC Spark Plug. Like the auto industry, the city expanded rapidly, growing in population from 13,103 in 1900 to 156,492 in 1930. At the beginning of the Depression, more than half of Genesee County's 83,000 employed citizens worked for GM. Today the corporation still dominates the city. The largest office building in town, the college library, the child health center, and a recreation park all

From *Michigan History*, LIII (Fall, 1969), 225-239. Reprinted by permission of the History Division, Michigan Department of State. Footnotes in the original have been omitted.

bear the name of a former vice-president of GM, and as late as 1966, when Flint purchased public vehicles, it invited bids only from GM truck makers.

Frequently, community facilities failed to keep pace with the city's rapid growth. Housing was a major problem. In the early years of the century, GM representatives scoured the country urging unskilled workers to journey to Flint. When the workers arrived, however, there was often no shelter for them. Migrants who came during the boom years of 1908-1910 lived in tarpaper shacks, tents, and railroad cars, all without sanitary facilities. Neither the city nor the corporation would invest the capital to lay water mains or sewers, and working-class areas were flooded by spring thaws and heavy rains. In 1919 GM began to construct company housing, but its most ambitious plan—to build a 2,759 person dormitory—was forgotten as a result of the recession which followed World War I. Although 3,200 GM homes had been built by 1933, housing remained a major problem for Flint, and a government survey taken at the beginning of the New Deal showed that one third of Flint's families lived in substandard housing while one tenth lived in structures classified as "dangerous."

Flint was thus not untypical of many industrial boom towns of the 1920's. It had experienced the full thrust of the decade's economic prosperity, and it offered social and economic advancement to aspiring newcomers. Yet the city also faced problems. It lacked stability and tradition. Population increases exceeded the city's capacity to provide adequate housing and sanitation. And the growth of the private sector of the economy had outrun the growth of the public sector. Flint's experience during the Depression and the New Deal may thus shed some light on critical variables which affected similar cities across the country.

In Flint as elsewhere, voluntarism characterized the early response to the Depression. Private agencies dispensed relief to clients whose problems fell within their particular province, although persons who were not widowed mothers or homeless children sometimes had difficulty finding a niche for themselves. Private charity had not traditionally made provision for those who were healthy and able, yet still unemployed. The Flint Community Fund, an umbrella organization of sixteen agencies ranging from the Junior League to the Salvation Army, acted as a central fund-raiser and checked relief recipients to insure that no one got more than his due. It did little, however, to effectively mobilize new resources. An occasional churchman, like the Rev. John E. Zoller of the Methodist church, enlisted religious facilities in the cause of general relief (Zoller fed as many as 1,200 a day at his tabernacle), but most churches restricted their efforts to their own congregations. The weekly potluck supper was a primary means by which the church could provide a form of relief and at the same time bolster spirits among its congregants.

On a city-wide level, the Flint Relief Commission was established in 1931 in response to a request from the President's Organization on Unemployment. Its administration, however, was unwieldy. Consisting of twenty-one leading citizens, the commission divided its responsibilities into twenty-one separate parts with a commissioner in charge of each. The food division collected donations of food, the clothing division solicited clothing, and the odd jobs division assigned six hundred men to areas of the city where, on their own initiative, they might seek temporary employment from local residents. Although a public body, the commission was financed by private contributions. Indeed, so dedicated was Flint to the ethic of voluntarism that even the free milk for 2,500 school children was paid for by proceeds from a benefit band concert sponsored by the Lion's Club.

Public welfare was even less effective and served primarily as a political issue to be used by opposing sides in the faction-ridden City Commission. In the bitter 1932 campaign, two renegades from the camp of Republican Mayor William McKeighan charged his administration with using welfare workers to register voters for his own political machine. When the renegades were subsequently recalled by petition, their counterattack consisted of the charge that the city was shortchanging relief recipients. For both factions, welfare employees and clients were a source of patronage and political power.

Until 1933, then, assistance to the needy in Flint was limited. Its inadequacy rested primarily in the fact that older forms and institutions were unable to cope with a crisis as large as the Depression. In effect, the existing structure of welfare could not adapt to the new demands placed upon it, and no new structure arose from within the local community to assume the task. What happened in 1933 was that from without, the federal government seized the initiative and reordered the older forms and institutions of charity. By injecting an outside influence, the state usurped local power, replaced voluntarism, forged a new structural apparatus to attack the Depression, and in the process fostered significant changes in the administration and philosophy of local relief.

Money was the key instrument of change. The governmental body which held the purse strings also dictated policy. Michigan relief administrator Fred Johnson pointed out to local residents that under Hoover's Reconstruction Finance Corporation, loans were offered to local governments, and administration consequently remained in local hands. Under the Federal Emergency Relief Administration (FERA), in contrast, grants were given to states, and the disbursing agent—the federal government—retained control over their expenditure. As a result, direction of the Flint welfare operation moved from City Hall to Washington.

The cause and effect of federal control were clearly revealed in a controversy surrounding the appointment of Victor S. Woodward as director of the County Emergency Relief Administration (CERA) in August, 1933. Flint politicians preferred the appointment of a local man. Woodward, however, was a former aide of Harry Hopkins in New York's relief administration and was appointed allegedly because the federal government required that every local committee be headed by a trained social worker. When Flint citizens protested such outside control, the County Emergency Relief Committee confessed it was powerless to interfere. Woodward, the Committee declared, "was recommended by the federal agents who have had to do with supplying the funds. . . . The source of support should make significant . . . how far removed . . . supervision is from local control and influences that are not constructive. We primarily are the agents of the United States government and we function virtually at its pleasure." The infusion of federal funds had transformed, for the moment, the power structure of the local government, making jealous local politicians the servants of the federal establishment.

One immediate consequence of federal control was the emergence of a new welfare hierarchy. Relief ceased to be locally initiated and controlled. FERA in Washington mandated the establishment of the State Emergency Relief Administration (SERA) in Lansing, and SERA administered its grants through CERA in Flint. Significantly, two thirds of CERA's members were chosen by the state rather than by local officials. The order of federal bureaucracy replaced the confusion of local voluntarism.

Simultaneously, there occurred a substantial change in Flint's approach to relief. Prior to 1933, welfare applicants had to obtain the endorsement of two taxpayers before they could be considered for assistance. A poorly trained staff spent much of its time referring clients to the proper private agencies. The self-image of welfare employees, according to a 1933 report, was that of detectives and investigators rather than public servants whose responsibility to dependents was as great as to taxpayers. Under the New Deal, in contrast, the local welfare administration recognized the universality of the Depression's impact. People of all classes and backgrounds had been stricken, and every citizen had a right to public assistance until a job became available. It was uneconomic and inhumane, Woodward insisted, to permit people to live in squalor or to provide them with only enough relief to survive. "[E]very human being," he emphasized, "is entitled to live in quarters which are decent."

Under Woodward's guidance, the County Relief Committee discarded old welfare shibboleths and redefined the task of relief:

> The welfare problem is not merely one of doling out relief on the basis of the old-time poor departments; . . . we have a great problem of social rehabilitation; . . . thousands of families never have had to resort to public aid. . . . [For their sake] we are not content with mere investigation.

Woodward's commission attempted to treat each case individually. Trained supervisors were added at the ratio of one for every eight caseworkers. The staff climbed from sixty-five in May, 1933, before the federal takeover, to one hundred eighty in April, 1934. Equipped with more workers, outside financing, and a different conception of the task at hand, the welfare administration set out to meet the needs of Flint's unemployed with new energy and purpose.

A striking improvement in public health represented a major achievement of the new approach. Early in the Depression, Flint ranked third in infant deaths and fifth in maternal deaths in a comparative study of twenty-two cities—a consequence, the study concluded, of grossly inadequate public health services in Flint. By 1936, in contrast, the maternal mortality rate among Flint relief clients had plummeted to two thirds that of the general population, a result of intensive prenatal and postnatal care under government sponsorship. In 1935 alone, public health nurses made 8,053 prenatal and postnatal visits, encouraging patients to see the doctor, teaching personal hygiene, and stressing instructions received by expectant mothers in monthly mailings from the State Health Department. A plan under which each public patient could choose his own doctor further aided the local public health program. In its first year of operation, public monies financed 13,081 office visits by relief clients.

Housing reforms were another major improvement. A special committee abolished rents based on property assessment and tax warrants and instead created a rent schedule geared to the size, condition, and utilities of an apartment. The housing and salvage division of the County Relief Administration made repairs which landlords could not afford and deducted the cost from rents—an interesting forerunner of city rehabilitation of private housing today.

Harry Hopkins' Works Progress Administration financed and in-
spired most of the local improvements. Children bicycled on streets
newly paved by WPA workers, while their parents joined in evening
operettas performed by WPA orchestras in outdoor WPA theatres.
Other federal efforts included modernizing the airport, cleaning the
local lake for recreation purposes, building parks, painting schools,
extending sewers, surveying traffic, and manufacturing sheets, mat-
tresses, and shoes. What Robert and Helen Lynd observed in Middletown was true of Flint also: "In 1933 the city shifted over, with
the interjection of federal planning into the local scene . . . . [and]
was asked to state its civic desires positively, to frame a new series
of axioms and to go ahead and act on them. Having no alternative,
the city began to play the new game . . . and for a brief span of
months . . . had the experience of pressing the buttons . . . to 'see
how it works'." In both Flint and Middletown, the changed atmosphere resulted in the achievement of civic improvements which five
years before would have been unthinkable.

As the Depression deepened, increasing numbers of Flint people
had occasion to experience directly the benefits of the welfare
state. Local unemployment oscillated constantly due to seasonal
layoffs in the auto industry, but 1938 marked the nadir of the
Depression in Flint. During the previous low in late 1934 and
early 1935, the maximum number of families on relief had been
10,561. In the first six months of 1938 the number soared to
19,650.

The backgrounds of the jobless revealed the growing universality
of the Depression's impact. The percentage of native-born whites on
the relief rolls increased from 68.1 in 1934 to 77.1 in 1938. Over a
quarter of the 1938 total had never received relief before. Most
significant, however, was the sharp rise in educational and occupa-
tional level among relief recipients. Whereas in 1934, 28.2 per cent
of the people on welfare had a high school diploma, the figure
leaped to 51.3 per cent of new applicants and 40.4 per cent of the
total in 1938; 40.7 per cent of the new applicants were professional
men, moreover, managers, officials, white collar workers, and
skilled laborers. In addition, more than half of the total applied for
relief during the first month after loss of income.

Clearly the day had passed when welfare was restricted to the
pariahs of the community. Substantial citizens who earlier had
clung to a job or escaped relief by withdrawing savings or doubling
up with relatives had now exhausted their resources and were
compelled to seek assistance. As a result, suffering and want ceased
to be the exclusive domain of voluntary charities or the private
responsibility of individual citizens. "The human care of depen-

dents has gone past private agencies," a prominent Flint citizen observed in 1938, "and is now a public job—a big job."

Significantly, the major regression in public policy toward re-liefers followed the partial withdrawal of the state from direct responsibility for the welfare administration. Federal financing of direct relief ended with the passage of WPA, and the resulting burden placed on local authorities spurred deep resentment of the state's continuing domination of the welfare board. With increased appropriations from the county came insistent demands for more local control—in effect, a repetition of the federal government's argument in 1933 that money means power—and in July, 1936, a new Relief Commission took office, two thirds of whom repre-sented choices of the county instead of the state.

Restoration of local control carried with it a reaction against many premises of the federal program. The County Board of Supervisors charged that adminstrative costs could be slashed by 50 per cent and that many reliefers could find work easily if only they were willing to look. More extreme was the response of new welfare administrator Louis J. Ludington to the recession of 1938. Begin-ning in April with a plan to move 12,000 "unemployables" out of the county, Ludington graduated by August to the proposal that second generation reliefers be sterilized. Too many welfare recipi-ents, he charged, had a "decidedly communistic atti-tude . . . [rooted in their] having too much time to think about themselves and their troubles." When Ludington was removed in September, he claimed to be a "Moscow trial victim" punished by the state and the auto workers union for prosecuting welfare chiselers.

At first glance, it would appear that the administration of Lud-ington represented the undoing of all that had been accomplished under Woodward and that by the end of the Depression the leader-ship of Flint had returned full circle to the individualism and voluntarism of pre-New Deal days. But the statistics of the 1938 recession belie such an interpretation. The impact of the Depression experience had broadened, not narrowed, as time passed. The number of middle-class victims who sought relief almost immediate-ly in the 1938 crisis demonstrated that the welfare state had become during the Depression an indispensable presence in Flint. However much individuals such as Ludington might berate public assistance, more and more Flint people relied upon it in time of need. Thus it seems that the Ludington episode did not signal a community-wide revulsion against relief as much as a political reaction against the New Deal. Given this fact, it might be better to seek an explanation for Ludington's actions in the framework of other conclusions which can tentatively be drawn about the Flint experience.

First, it appears that whatever change in social welfare policy occurred in Flint during the Depression owed its existence to outside intervention from state or federal authorities. In the early years of the crisis, older forms of voluntarism prevailed. New policies coincided with the structural reorganization which accompanied the establishment of the New Deal relief program. State intervention thus emerges as the critical variable in explaining the introduction of progressive welfare policies. The local community did not possess within itself the energy or imagination to forge new forms of relief adequate to the crisis.

Second, money provided the lever by which the change in welfare policy was accomplished. As long as local taxes or charities supplied the financial base for relief, local leaders retained control, and the notion that public welfare was a dole, not a right of citizenship, prevailed. When the federal government became the major source of funds, on the other hand, it insisted that its own personnel take over. Federal administration, with a new and different conception of welfare, was a quid pro quo of financial aid.

Third, the New Deal programs substantially benefited the Flint community. More and more Flint residents received public assistance directly from a welfare administration which considered such aid a right of citizenship, not a symbol of shame. Moreover, the entire community gained indirectly. Public health care and recreation facilities improved drastically. Streets were paved, parks were built, and cultural programs were developed. New Deal funds helped to renovate and modernize the city, permanently improving its physical appearance and public services. By the end of the 1930's, the people of Flint had become accustomed to a level of public services which, in the future, they would not wish to see withdrawn.

Fourth, the gains registered under the New Deal took place at the cost of alienating some local leaders who had previously exercised control and who would return to power when the Depression crisis ended. The major fault of New Deal welfare policies in Flint was that they were imposed from without, with seemingly little effort made to develop a cooperative relationship with local political forces. By taking so little account of local pride—as, for example, in importing a relief administrator from New York instead of choosing one of similar views from Flint—New Deal officials generated resentment among local leaders and diminished the possibility that at a future date the community itself would carry on the programs and philosophy initiated by Washington.

Thus Ludington's attack on the welfare system and the county insistence on retaking control of the relief committee after the withdrawal of direct federal relief funds may be partially explained by the anger local leaders felt at being denied a voice in the earlier New Deal programs. It may be argued that federal authorities could achieve their goals only by imposing them on local communities. But, until evidence from other communities comes in, we may speculate that the failure to consult and respect local leaders represented a major error in the New Deal's attempt to permanently alter the values and structure of American Society.

Whatever the case, the experience of Flint during the Depression suggests how dramatic were the effects on local communities of New Deal programs.

The decade of the Great Depression in Michigan brought previously unknown hardship to a great percentage of the state's citizens. An entirely new range of experiences—soup-and-bread lines, mortgage foreclosures, business failures, apple vendors, bank holidays, and sit-down strikes—now often viewed in a rather nostalgic fashion, became an important part of everyday life in the thirties. However, unlike many other states, Michigan was fortunate to have a governor during two crucial years of the decade who understood the problems of the workingman. As Professor Sidney Fine of the University of Michigan emphasizes in the following selection, Frank Murphy was, in many respects, the best kind of person to have in Lansing when the conflict between General Motors and the United Auto Workers, the best known of many sit-down strikes, reached the crisis stage in January, 1937. Murphy's handling of this and subsequent developments on the labor-management front earned him much deserved praise as a civil libertarian. For the remainder of his two-year term, Murphy continued to be ever mindful of the rights of the individual while, at the same time, inaugurating a far-reaching administrative program sometimes called the Little New Deal. In 1939 President Franklin Roosevelt appointed him Attorney General of the United States and one year later named this Michigan Irish-American to the United States Supreme Court, where he served with distinction. Students interested in examining Murphy's career in greater depth should consult J. Woodford Howard, Jr., *Mr. Justice Murphy: A Political Biography* (Princeton, 1968); the same author's "Frank Murphy and the Sit-Down Strike of 1937," *Labor History*, I (Spring, 1960), 103-140; and Fine's

"The General Motors Sit-Down Strike: A Re-Examination," *American Historical Review*, LXX (April, 1965), 691-713.

The selection that follows Professor Fine's biographical sketch of Murphy is one example of the kind of source material one must use to view history "from the bottom up" as a generation of New Left historians have urged us to do. If it were not for this letter, which is part of the Frank Murphy Papers in the University of Michigan Historical Collections, the grievances of Mrs. Blanche (Foley) Bucher against General Motors would have been lost forever. For Mrs. Bucher, writing to Governor Murphy during that 1936-37 winter of many an auto worker's discontent, an appeal to the state's chief executive seemed to be the last remaining hope to save her husband's job.

Frank Murphy: A Brief Biographical Portrait

SIDNEY FINE

Frank Murphy was born in Harbor Beach (then Sand Beach), Michigan, on April 13, 1890. After completing high school in his home town, he enrolled at the University of Michigan, where he received his law degree in 1914. He then worked for a Detroit law firm until he joined the Army shortly after the United States entered World War I. He served with the American Expeditionary Force in France and Germany, studied briefly in England and Ireland while on detached service, and then returned to the United States in the summer of 1919 to become first assistant United States attorney for the Eastern District of Michigan. He served in that capacity until March 1, 1922, when he entered private law practice with his close friend, Edward G. Kemp. He was elected to the Detroit Recorder's Court in 1923 and served as a Recorder's Court judge until August 19, 1930, when he resigned to run for mayor. He won the mayoralty election in September and was reelected in November, 1931.

Murphy was a supporter of Franklin D. Roosevelt in the 1932 presidential election and was rewarded for his efforts by being designated governor-general of the Philippines, a post that he officially assumed in May, 1933. When the Philippines became a commonwealth in November, 1935, Murphy became high commissioner. He announced his candidacy for the governorship of Michi-

From *Sit Down: The General Motors Strike of 1936-37*, pp. 148-155. Copyright © The University of Michigan Press, 1969. Reprinted by permission. Footnotes in the original have been omitted.

gan in July, 1936, and defeated his Republican opponent, Frank Fitzgerald, in November.

Murphy was a very ambitious person who aspired from an early date to the highest elective office in the land. He believed that the best way to realize his lofty ambition was through dedicated public service rather than through partisan maneuverings. "His creed," a Detroit newspaper accurately observed just after he was elected governor, "is that the politician who gives the best government is the politician who travels the furthest." Murphy's abstemious personal habits—he neither drank nor smoked—were very decidedly related to his ambitions for himself. As he told a reporter early in his public career, "I cherished definite aims in life. I figured I'd need a lot of independence and self reliance and they depend upon self control and firm will. In short I figured I'd go further in attaining my aims if I steered clear of the stimulating influences of alcohol and tobacco." Keeping in trim through boxing, riding, and other exercise was another means by which Murphy sought to fulfill his ambition to be "the best possible public servant my limitations will permit." The gruelling, around-the-clock negotiations during the GM sit-down strike were precisely the sort of endurance contest for which Murphy had been preparing himself from the time of his youth.

Murphy's vaulting ambition for high office did not mean that he was inclined to sacrifice principle to win public favor nor that he feared to challenge accepted views. "I like public office," Murphy wrote to his brother George, "but I am no slave to it and from the first I have practiced and preached the doctrine that I would rather be out than in office if to be in meant surrendering a worthy principle." Indeed, Murphy liked to think of himself as a fighter for unpopular causes who would triumph despite the formidable character of the opposition. "I don't want the odds my way in any race," he wrote his mother from overseas at the end of World War I. "I want the odds to be against me if the race isn't even and I shall expect to win, too. I find that the real zip in life is not in winning but in fighting [,] not in going easily with the current but beating back the breakers." In the sit-down strike Murphy was to be given the opportunity to "beat back the breakers."

As a public servant, Murphy acquired a deserved reputation as a civil libertarian, as a zealous advocate of the freedoms embodied in the Bill of Rights. From the point of view of the leadership of the American Civil Liberties Union, Murphy was just about the ideal government official. Americans, Murphy thought, were "often a little slothful and drowsy about this precious right we call liberty" and were indifferent about "the chains forged for our fellows," but they would do well to remember that "a wrong to the liberty of one citizen is a blow at the liberty of all citizens." As Recorder's Court judge, mayor, and colonial official, Murphy tried to live by this creed. As governor dealing with the sit-down strikes, he was undoubtedly influenced by his belief that the civil liberties of the automobile workers had been violated by their employer.

Murphy had "a deep reverence for human life" that made it impossible for him to accept the idea of capital punishment. The admonition "Thou shalt not kill," he declaimed in a debate on the subject of capital punishment in 1927, came from Mt. Sinai and has been "the cornerstone of civilization" ever since. Because he loathed crimes of violence, he did not wish the state to become "an example of violence and ferocity." For Murphy, the problem of crime was "interwoven with social and economic conditions," and he advised those who wished to solve the problem "to seek its causes at their source, and strive to apply the remedy at the beginning, rather than at the end, of a sordid life-story." It is thus not surprising that when Murphy was confronted with the GM sit-down, he refused to order the forcible evacuation of the strikers and stated that he thought it necessary to consider the social and economic conditions that had led the workers to sit down and not merely to deal with the problem by labeling their action a crime for which they were to be punished.

As a criminal-court judge in Michigan, which forbade capital punishment, Murphy was spared the necessity of ordering the execution of persons convicted of capital crimes, but even the sentencing of the unfortunate to prison caused him some pain. When he was a United States Supreme Court justice many years later, he wrote feelingly to his brother about "expiring a little each time you have to take part of another man's life from him." When he assumed his seat on Recorder's Court, he characteristically stated that he knew that he would frequently "drop into error" as a judge, but "I trust and pray that when this occurs it shall be on the side of mercy." In the sit-down strike the governor of Michigan was influenced by similar considerations.

Murphy had great compassion for the weak, the afflicted, the down-trodden, the flotsam and jetsam of humankind. "To me," he wrote his mother in 1918, "there is deep satisfaction in giving help and relief to the trouble[d] and depressed. I would rather do that than any task I know." Speaking to the Women's Club of Manila in the summer of 1933, Murphy declared, "We are not here for ourselves alone; we are here to do things for those around us. . . ." It was the common responsibility to aid the sick and aged and to heal "broken spirits."

As Recorder's Court judge, Murphy sought to salvage "fragments" of the human wreckage that passed before him by "granting a parole, exercising judicial clemency or handing out advice," and he was a prominent figure in efforts to persuade the Michigan legislature to enact old-age pension and unemployment-insurance legislation. When he was mayor of Detroit during the depression, he did more to feed the hungry than any other municipal official in the nation, and he was, in the pre-New Deal era, one of the most conspicuous and influential advocates of federal relief for the unemployed. In the Philippines, Murphy's "most distinctive accomplishments . . . were the awakening of a new social consciousness . . . and the improvement and extension of government services for the amelioration of the lot of the common people."

Murphy concluded at an early age that the workingman was among the disadvantaged in American society. He worked as a high school and college student in the starch factory in Harbor Beach, and he was later to recall that "it was a slave's life, those long hours and the living by whistles." When asked to write a paper for a sociology course he was taking at the University of Michigan, Murphy chose the subject "Politics and the Laborer." "It is because I lived and worked with the common, ordinary, day laborer and have listened to his complaints and his joys, and feel that I know his wants and needs," the young college student wrote, "that I have ventured upon this difficult problem. I love the subject. I want to make it my life's work. If I can only feel, when my day is done, that I have accomplished something toward uplifting the poor, uneducated, unfortunate, ten-hour-a-day laborer from the political chaos he now exists in, I will be satisfied that I have been worth while." By this criterion, Frank Murphy at the end of his illustrious career had every reason to be "satisfied" that he had indeed been "worth while."

In addition to his personal experience as a day laborer, Murphy was heavily influenced in his stance with regard to labor by his Catholic religion and particularly by the labor encyclicals of Leo XIII and Pius XI. As mayor of depression-ridden Detroit, Murphy, in an interpretation of *Rerum Novarum,* declared that he had been guided by "the signpost set up by the beneficent Leo" to put the welfare of his fellow man above balanced budgets. Leo, Murphy thought, had shown the way to those concerned with "safeguarding the worker" in the contemporary world. The encyclical told them that it was their responsibility, as rulers who must protect the "safety of the commonwealth," to put the idle to work, to remove the causes of poverty and unemployment, to stabilize the worker's income, to care for the destitute and the aged, and to secure appropriate labor legislation. No Christian, Murphy declared shortly thereafter, could be indifferent to depressed labor conditions or to the differences between employer and employee that resulted in strikes. Interestingly enough, he joined the Third Order of St. Francis, whose Rule required its members to cultivate charity, love, peace, and heal discord and misunderstanding. As governor during the GM strike, Murphy was provided with an unparalleled opportunity to practice the Order's Rule of Peace.

Quite apart from personal experience and religion, Murphy was undoubtedly influenced to take a pro-labor position by his conviction that labor and the Catholic church were emerging as the "two strongest forces" in the United States. Few public officials in the entire nation in the 1920's and 1930's were as closely allied with organized labor as Murphy was, and few were willing to accord it the status and recognition that he was.

Murphy first ran for the position of Recorder's Court judge in part out of a desire to break up a court ring allegedly unfair to labor. He received the endorsement of the Detroit Federation of Labor (DFL) in this election as in every subsequent election in which he was a candidate. As a criminal court judge, Murphy conducted himself in a manner that pleased the forces of organized labor in Detroit. He did not assume that labor was always responsible for violence in industrial disputes, and in one case he criticized the prosecutor's office for showing an interest in misdemeanor charges only when they stemmed from a strike, thus creating the dangerous impression that the state was on the side of the employers.

Murphy, in the 1920's, saw organized labor as "the natural nucleus" of a movement to aid the downtrodden and to solve the problem of the "industrial frontier." He advised organized labor in Detroit to work for the five-day week, a living family wage, the right to engage in collective bargaining, the right to strike, unemployment insurance, and limitations on the use of injunctions in labor disputes.

In view of Murphy's record on the Recorder's Court, it is quite understandable that the DFL was the first organization to ask him to run for mayor in the late summer of 1930 following the recall of Mayor Charles Bowles. As mayor, Murphy worked closely with the DFL in evolving his policy to deal with unemployment, and, believing that "labor must have its share in a well-balanced government," he made a large number of labor appointments. When Detroit celebrated Labor Day in 1931, Murphy invited Vice-President Matthew Woll of the AFL to deliver the main address, which Woll declared was the first time that any city government, to his knowledge, had invited the Federation to share in the observance of the occasion. The Detroit *News* unhappily remarked that "Mayor Murphy is a labor union mayor in open shop Detroit. . . . "

"The existence of a strike," Murphy declared shortly after he gave up the Detroit mayoralty, "shows that things are not in their natural order, that something is wrong. The government, therefore, should intervene in such conflicts . . . to protect, first of all, the interest of the public." The only major strike that confronted Murphy as mayor was initiated on January 23-24, 1933, by unorganized workers at the four Briggs plants in Detroit, but since the company would not agree to the city's mediation of the dispute, the Mayor was limited in what he could do to compose the strike. He did, however, appoint a Mayor's Fact-Finding Committee of distinguished citizens to investigate the strike, which deplored the company's refusal to meet with strikers and called for collective bargaining between organized workers and their employers to resolve labor disputes in the future.

The active picketing of the Briggs plant by the strikers and the company's determination to operate despite the walkout brought the Detroit police into the strike and led to striker complaints of misuse of their power by the law officers. Murphy, in this difficult situation, told department heads that it was the city's policy "to maintain the peace" but not "to take sides." Since he did not believe that he could order the company to close its factories, he thought that workers going to and from their jobs were entitled to "a certain amount of protection," but at the same time he ordered the police to protect the strikers from attack and not to interfere with the conduct of the strike. He made it clear that there were to be no "illegal arrests," that no strikers were to be held incommunicado, and that no one was to be deprived of his rights simply because he protested industrial conditions or went on strike. The mayor had to concede, however, that despite his best efforts the police sometimes went "too far." It was far easier for the mayor to outline a strike policy than to ensure that it would be observed by the police.

Privately, Murphy thought that the Briggs management was, to some extent at least, responsible for the strike because of the labor conditions that prevailed in its plants. The city of Detroit refused to use its Free Employment Bureau to provide strikebreakers for Briggs, and it rejected a company request for transportation equipment to move employees into and out of one of the plants. The city, also, as Murphy was to do in the GM strike, made relief available on the basis of need regardless of whether or not the recipient was a striker.

In the Philippines, Murphy manifested the same interest in the condition of the workingman and in organized labor that he had demonstrated in Detroit. His administration was responsible for an eight-hour day law for workers in hazardous occupations or engaged in employments requiring great physical effort, the creation of a department of labor, efforts to control usury, the relief of unemployment, slum clearance, and the provision of public defenders for the indigent; and the governor-general vetoed a bill requiring compulsory arbitration. Murphy also made "the first appreciable effort" in the history of the Philippines "to bring the labor movement into its full dignity . . . [as a] co-operative element in the social and economic life of the people."

When a strike of cigar workers occurred in Manila beginning on August 16, 1934, Murphy, as he had done in the Briggs strike, appointed a Fact-Finding Board to investigate the dispute. He called for the settlement of the strike by arbitration rather than by force; but the policing of the walkout took a violent turn, and in a clash between strikers and the constabulary on September 17, three strikers lost their lives. "This regrettable and unnecessary incident," to use Murphy's phrasing, led to an inquiry about the strike from the American Civil Liberties Union. "At such times of excitement," Roger Baldwin wrote the governor-general, "you know fully as well as we, it is possible for wise policing to avoid the kind of tragic conflict which here took place." Murphy learned in Detroit and the Philippines that police forces tend to have a life of their own and that it was sometimes difficult for the chief executive of a governmental unit to control their operations. In the GM strike he was determined to keep firm control of major policing activities so as to provide the "wise policing" that would prevent the sort of tragedy that had occurred during the Manila cigar strike and that must have weighed heavily on his conscience.

When he campaigned for the governorship of Michigan in 1936, Murphy, who was endorsed by labor organizations throughout the state, emphasized his close ties with organized labor. "I am heart and soul in the Labor Movement," he told the Detroit *Labor News.* "I have yet to go contrary to the expressed wish of Organized Labor in matters that affect it, and as expressed by its official chosen representatives, and you all know that I shall never do so." Speaking to an audience in Muskegon, he declared that it was the "duty" of a public official to avoid strikes, but it was not his "duty or prerogative . . . to permit the use of the police power except to protect the public," nor should he deny welfare aid to strikers. When he won the election, he wrote William Green, "I am certain that you will find that my administration . . . will mark a new day for labor in Michigan"; and he told the Detroit and Wayne County Federation of Labor at a victory celebration, "If I worked for a wage, I'd join my Union."

Although Murphy identified strongly with the unfortunate and with organized labor, he delighted at the same time in the company of the well-to-do, and some of his closest friends were among the social and economic elite of Detroit and Michigan. Murphy was on especially good terms with several of the automobile magnates, including Walter Chrysler, B. E. Hutchinson, and Byron C. Foy of Chrysler Corporation and Lawrence Fisher of Fisher Body and GM. Murphy was also a heavy investor in automobile stock. When he became governor at the beginning of 1937, he held 1650 shares of GM stock, 550 of Chrysler, and five hundred of Packard. The GM stock alone at the end of the year was worth $104,875. On January 18, 1937, during the course of the GM strike, Murphy sold his GM stock at a minimum profit of $52,800. How the parties to the GM dispute would have reacted to this information had it been known to them is an interesting speculation.

Murphy was of medium height and build and had what Russell B. Porter of the New York *Times* described as a "distinctly Celtic countenance." Although not handsome in a conventional sense, he was exceedingly attractive to the opposite sex. He had blue eyes, receding red hair, and very bushy red eyebrows—a cameraman remarked after the strike, "I expected a couple of sit downers to jump out of those eyebrows any minute." The eyebrow-to-eyebrow confrontation of Murphy and John L. Lewis during the strike negotiations must surely have been something to behold. Murphy was gentle in manner, very soft-spoken, and had more than his share of charm, but behind the exterior of charm and affability, there was a reserve that few if any penetrated. It was this man who played so decisive a role in the GM strike.

A General Motors Worker's Wife
Appeals to Governor Frank Murphy

9612 Corunna Rd.
Flint, Mich.
Feb. 19, 1936 [*sic*]
Feb. 19, [1937]

Dear Governor Murphy:

You have been so good in your efforts to help the working people. I come to you in Our trouble. The Methods General Motors is useing now is the dirtiest they've use'd yet.

Fireing men for nothing. My Husband was fired last night. They said He was solicting in the plant. It couldn't be a Biger! lie! Mr. Murphy I swear to God that my husband didnt even talk Unionism for he knew they were fireing them right and left, for nothing anyway. My husband is a quiet person and does very little talking. Hes a good honest sober hard working man. After 7 years of good service G. Motors fire Him—for nothing absoluty—a frame up. The unfairest thing a employer could do. Wouldn't even let him talk. He wanted them to tell him who and he would prove he never solicted no one. He did no talking on the line and eat lunch with two close friends of Ours who have been Union Men for months so He sure wouldnt be solicting them. He left his machine only once for two minutes. He spoke to no one while he was gone. Now either some stool pigeon is trying to make a swell Guy of Himself by lieing. But I honestly believe its a threat of terror they are holding over Our heads in there efforts to break the Union up. I tell you Governor they are doing all they can to stir the men up over such unjust actions till they strike and then Mr. Knudsen will say we broke our agreement. Something must be done if peace is to be maintained in Flint. The workers are so worked up over this fireing—they won't stand much more. Mr. Murphy Im frightened to what this will do to my Husband. He's so bitter about it. Its so unfair. Here we bought four acres last Summer and last fall borrowed from a loan company. Mortgage everything we have to build a small house. Now we will loose it all everything we've worked ten year to buy and our Home besides that we worked so hard to build—lost—thru no fault of our own. Just so G.M. can break the negotiations off. They care not for

Mrs. Blanche (Foley) Bucher to Governor Frank Murphy, February 19, 1936 [*sic* 1937], Frank Murphy Papers, Michigan Historical Collections, Bentley Historical Library, Ann Arbor.

the lives they ruin in there low down methods. This fireing is not all. They are arming men with shotguns, clubs, rifles. Last night 12 men with rifles stood on the roof over the entrance to plant 4. Why? They knew they had fired 3 men, maybe more unjustly. These cops and non union men have orders if the men set down in protest of this awful discrimination to bar the doors. The fact is—all men—will be in the battle—shot down—like a Russian firing Squad! So I ask you Governor if Mr. Knudsen didn't agree there'd be no discrimination. Yet they fire my husband for no reason at all —except He wears a union button. Hes always been a good worker. I can get plenty of His fellow workers, neighbors, Priests to tell you that my Husband does not lie—and is Honest reliable sober—a good worker. Even his boss Ed Richardson said Tony I can't believe you did it. But Mr. Hill, the Supt. there, was no if or ans about it. He was not guilty. Governor Murphy I beg of you to use your High office to stop these awful discriminations. And give my Husband and These other men who have done no wrong there jobs back so they can support there familyes and save there Homes.

My small son came Home from school to-night with fear in his heart for his daddy's life. He said, Mother, Ruphert said that his Dad who works on the line and is one of these Terror cops has a shot gun at work and if those union men try to protest against discrimination they'll all be shot. A nice thing this General Motors company is doing. Feelings are running higher here than any time. During the sit down we excepted the terms and G. Motors word— only for this Terror Movements, discriminations of the worst kind.

Please do something for us.

My Husbands name is Tony F. Bucher. He worked in plant 4. 449-750 his number.

May God Bless You and reward you for your goodness to the working people. Im praying that when President Roosevelt gives up the presidency you will be Our next One! and I feel sure you will if you run. I think this country needs a Irish President. Hopeing you will see in to this matter at once.

Sincerely,
Blanche (Foley) Bucher

In bold contrast to the generally conservative nature of the Western Michigan Dutch stands Albertus Johannes Muste. Born in the Netherlands in 1883, Muste immigrated with his parents to Grand Rapids in 1891. Raised in the stern traditionalism of the Dutch Reformed church, Muste was ordained as a minister in the Reformed Church in America. Dissatisfied with Calvinist doctrines, he began his long journey of the soul that led him into the Congregational church, and later into the Trotskyite branch of American radicalism. But by 1936 Muste had accepted, and begun to practice, a lifelong commitment to pacifism.

In the following essay Muste discusses an attempt by labor unions to institute nonviolent tactics in seeking satisfaction of their demands for better wages and working conditions. Known to his friends as "the American Gandhi," he remained actively opposed to war throughout the 1940s and fifties, and as Chairman of the Committee for Nonviolent Action and leader of the Fellowship of Reconciliation, Muste spoke out continually against the war in Vietnam. Further information about Muste can be found in Nat Hentoff's *Peace Agitator: The Story of A. J. Muste* (New York, 1966) and *The Essays of A. J. Muste* (Indianapolis, 1967), edited by Hentoff.

Sit-Downs and Lie-Downs

A. J. MUSTE

An event of the greatest significance for those who believe in the way of nonviolence occurred recently. A great national labor union, the American Federation of Full-Fashioned Hosiery Workers, which is itself a department of the United Textile Workers of America, and affiliated with the Committee for Industrial Organization (C. I. O.), adopted at its annual convention a resolution providing for the appointment of "a standing commission to study the merits and possibilities of using nonviolent resistance in labor disputes and that the commission be instructed to propagate its findings among the membership, and be requested to continue its study of this philosophy."

This action was an outgrowth of the actual experiment in nonviolent resistance ("lie-down picketing") carried on in December, 1936, under the leadership of a Fellowship of Reconciliation member and another student of Richard Gregg's writings. Both are members of the Hosiery Workers Union and active participants in the strike which has been in progress since October at the Berkshire

From *Fellowship* (March, 1937). Reprinted by permission of the Fellowship of Reconciliation.

Mills of Reading, Pennsylvania. The most encouraging feature of this entire development is that the initiative has at each stage come from the ranks of the workers themselves and not as the result of more or less artificial stimulation from without.

The reference to "lie-down picketing" naturally brings to mind the matter of the "sit-down," which has figured so largely in the news during recent weeks. Many who are ordinarily sympathetic with organized labor are inclined to condemn this method as flagrantly illegal and as a peculiarly unfair device which enables a very small minority to hold up not only the employer but their fellow-workers against their will. I am convinced that this view leaves many important factors out of consideration. Space permits us to mention only a few of them.

As was demonstrated in one instance, in Flint, when the workers in the department in which the sit-down occurs are not pretty unanimously for it, it is impossible to put it into effect. Also, the sit-down technique lends itself in a special sense to furnishing an alibi to workers who are themselves afraid of discharge if they join a union, and who do not know how the strike is going to come out. They often sign petitions indicating that they are anxious to go back to work at the same time when they secretly hope the sit-down may succeed and lead to better conditions! In such a situation, who is subject to judgment and who is doing the coercing—the sit downers, or their less courageous fellow-workers; or is it the corporation which controls a man's job and his family's livelihood and has him so intimidated that he may sign up with a company union at the very time he has joined a bona-fide union? And this of course suggests that in all such situations it is exceedingly difficult to tell how many men are really for or against the union. Or rather I think we can safely say on the basis of experiences in the railroads, the garment trades and many others, that an overwhelming majority of the workers in any industry will almost certainly flock into the union the moment they feel sure that this will not subject them to the displeasure of the employer.

Consider another phase of the problem. The General Motors Corporation for years refused collective bargaining, now the law of the land. It stocked at least some of its plants with gas and guns and spent nearly a million dollars in a couple of years for labor spy service. Do the laws governing private property cover a plant made into a private arsenal? When men sit down inside such a plant, so that these weapons cannot be turned against them, while a dispute over union recognition goes on, are they so obviously violating property rights and breaking the peace? Or are they safeguarding property and preserving peace?

To whom do the G. M. C. factories "belong"? To a few officials who perhaps own very little stock? To the 300,000 stockholders who have practically nothing to say about the labor policy which leads to the sit-down? To the DuPonts who probably do exercise predominant influence over this policy and who raked in $250,000,000 in a few years, on an investment of about one-third that amount? To the municipal, state and national government which help the corporation to function? To the purchasers of General Motors cars, who may not like to have their money spent for labor espionage and resistance to collective bargaining? Or does the worker himself also have some "property right" in his job?

We must surely face the fact that the concept of property rights is in flux. There was a time when any strike, any form of picketing, was regarded as an infraction of property rights, because it interfered with production, with a supposed right of an owner to use his property in disregard of any social restrictions. It is not inconceivable that the sit-down may come to be regarded as no more an invasion of property rights than ordinary forms of strike and picketing.

It must be noted also that the sit-downers observed very strict discipline and that practically no actual damage was done to property, and that on the whole the evidence tends to show that the sit-down method lends itself more readily than other types of picketing to nonviolent techniques.

That so little actual violence and no loss of life occurred in a situation so "loaded with dynamite" (both literally and figuratively) as that in Detroit, Flint and their vicinity, is to be credited in part to the rigorous discipline which the strikers imposed upon themselves. The restraint which General Motors appears to have exercised in not insisting upon having the men driven out of the plants at the point of a bayonet was another factor. Chiefly, however, thanks seem to be due to Governor Frank Murphy. His position—that if the forces of the state are to be used, they shall be used simply to maintain order and to see that private individuals or groups do not use violence against each other, not to weight the scales against the workers—is eminently sound. Above all we can subscribe to his view that violence itself is an evil, a poison which corrupts whatever it touches. Bring it into a situation and all other issues become more complicated and are made harder of solution. Keep it out and all other issues are simplified. Even property will in the long run be safer!

We do not wish to leave the impression, however, that the sit-down is, from the point of view of our Fellowship philosophy, on the same level as the "lie-down picketing" or that it fully exemplifies the spirit of nonviolence. There was, alas, altogether too much readiness to resort to violence on the part of strikers, as well as others, in the G.M.C. situation, even if violence seemed "necessary" and likely to produce "results." It is, in large degree, on physical possession of property and physical coercion of the non-striker that sit-downers depend, though the spiritual qualities of men who will subject themselves for over forty days to the stern rigors of a sit-down must by no means be minimized.

The leaders of the Reading lie-down experiment, on the other hand, were definitely moved by the spirit of love, even toward their enemies. They openly depended upon the appeal to the higher sentiments and feelings of others rather than upon physical means for success. The action of the Hosiery Workers convention therefore opens up a glorious opportunity for all who believe in the way of love and nonviolence to propagate our message in the ranks of the workers. Let us pray that we may make full use of that opportunity. It will require very clear and responsible thinking on our part to devise techniques of nonviolence. It will also involve identification in knowledge, in spirit and in action with the underprivileged and oppressed so that we may, without hypocrisy, speak to them of "a better way" and may win a hearing when we plead that evil means can never lead to good ends.

No state or era is without its extremists. In Father Charles E. Coughlin, Michigan has one of the most vocal critics of American society in the twentieth century. Born in Canada of Irish-American parents, Coughlin rose to a position of national influence in the 1930s with his weekly radio broadcasts from the Shrine of the Little Flower in Royal Oak. Coughlin's attacks on President Herbert Hoover and his handling of the depression which had begun in 1929 gained the "radio priest" a listening audience of hundreds of thousands. While he initially supported Franklin D. Roosevelt, in 1934 Coughlin began to criticize the President for taking too long to institute social and monetary reforms.

The following speech, delivered in 1931, concerns the death of four workers during a labor conflict with the Ford Motor Company in Detroit. Exemplifying Coughlin's polemical style, this speech, like the thousands of others he gave, concentrates on the decline of American standards and the threat of outside influences, in this case Bolshevistic atheism. Although his popularity declined in the early 1940s, he remains active in his angry, but not so frequent, verbal attacks on groups such as the student radicals of the 1960s. Charles J. Tull's book, *Father Coughlin and the New Deal* (Syracuse, 1965), provides a history of Coughlin's rise and his significance in America. Sheldon Marcus, *Father Coughlin: The Tumultuous Life of the Priest of the Little Flower* (Boston, 1973), should also be consulted.

Ballots—Not Bullets!

CHARLES E. COUGHLIN

Yesterday afternoon, a vast throng of Detroiters gathered to attend the simple funeral of four slain men. It was simple, in one sense. In another, it was unique to see a procession of 10,000 marching men, not one of them carrying an American flag. There were plenty of red flags.

As you know, last week there was a demonstration in which some of Detroit's jobless, suffering laborers participated. We since learned that this demonstration had been organized by the communists. However, the thousands of those who marched through the streets of the City of Detroit were orderly and were obedient in every respect to the policemen who accompanied them. By no means were they all communists.

The object of the demonstrators was to march to the Ford automobile factories, which are located not in Detroit but in the City of Dearborn adjacent to Detroit.

It appears that the jobless marchers had determined to send a delegation from their ranks to the Ford executives to ask for part-time jobs. But when they approached the Ford factory, radical leaders urged them to trespass upon private property. Promptly they were halted; greeted with tear gas bombs; covered with ice cold water which was shot at them out of a fire hose; and eventually bombarded with bullets as they persisted in their trespassing.

The four victims of this unfortunate occurrence were buried yesterday afternoon.

Some newspapers referred to this tragedy as a communist uprising. Undoubtedly there were communists who were the chief agitators and organizers. But the fact of the matter still remains that it is difficult for any sane man to comprehend why the communists

From *Father Coughlin's Radio Discourses 1931-32* (Royal Oak: The Radio League of the Little Flower, 1936), pp. 227-239. Reprinted by permission of the author.

should take action against the Ford Motor Company in view of the fact that Ford men and Ford money and Ford machinery probably have done more to perfect the Soviet Five-Year-Plan than was contributed by any other single agency in America.

It is generally understood that Soviet Russia and Henry Ford are on the best of terms. Hundreds of Russians sent here by their Government have been receiving instruction in the Ford plants. Hundreds of skilled American workmen have been sent by the Ford corporation to teach the Russians in their own Soviets.

Just yesterday a member of my own parish who is skilled in the art of processing iron was sent by the Ford organization to Soviet Russia to continue the policy mutually agreed upon some years ago.

I repeat, that it is difficult to comprehend how the communists could be responsible for this attack upon one of their greatest American benefactors.

Two conclusions are inevitable. The first is that if the communists of America profess responsibility and assume the questionable credit for the demonstration which resulted in the slaying of four men, they are not only trying to capitalize upon something which does not belong to them, but they are proving to the world that besides the doctrines of atheism, of irreligion and of internationalism, they also profess the policy of biting the hand that befriends them.

The second conclusion is very obvious: These jobless, hungry, dispossessed workmen were led into the streams of icy water and into the hail of bullets by a captain whose name is poverty. His able lieutenants were the supine legislators who during the three years of this depression, have executed not one single, tangible piece of legislation to benefit directly the American laborer, but who have led them from pillar to post by their rash optimism and by their vicious favoritism extended to the wealthy.

Railroads and banks are not abstract things. Railroads and banks are owned by thousands of stockholders; by men and women who are rich enough not only to possess their own homes and to supply their own needs but who also have a superfluous amount of money which they can invest in stock.

Now, during the last two or three weeks to these railroads and banks, or in other words, to these comfortable men and women who had the money to invest in them, loans amounting almost to a billion dollars have either actually been made or will be made.

More than that: during the past few years, loans totalling approximately $31,000,000,000 have been extended to foreign countries either directly or in bond issues to help maintain the jobless of foreign nations, all of which was accurately cited in a previous discourse over this microphone.

To return to the hunger march: let us not condemn too severely the jobless marchers who were beguiled into following the red radicals who promised them food. While we repudiate such leadership and condemn such methods, nevertheless, pause to consider:

Speaking of these jobless men who, through no fault of their own, have been reduced to this pitiable state and who are seeking jobs, may I quote for you what Mr. Daniel Willard, a thorough American and the President of the Baltimore and Ohio Railroad recently said. His words are these: *"I can think of nothing more deplorable than the condition of a man, able and anxious to work, with no resources but his labor and perhaps with others even more helpless dependent upon him.*

"Unless he is willing to starve and see those who justly look to him for support also starve, his only alternative is to seek charity, and, failing in that, to steal. And while I do not like to say so, I would be less than candid if I did not say that in such circumstances I would steal before I would starve." Pause to consider: these four victims were not trying to steal. Under the leadership of radicals, they were trying to get work. The unfortunate thing is that they turned to follow such leadership—all of which reflects upon ourselves.

Now, what has been foreshadowed at the Ford factory in Dearborn, Michigan, is but the beginning of a tragedy that will be enacted on the streets of America if we permit the radicals to assume the leadership of our discontented and jobless citizenry.

We who in our greed have endeavored to extend our commercial and financial empire to the ends of the earth, remind one of the old fable of the dog crossing the bridge. In his mouth he had a bone. As he glanced into the depths of the waters he imagined that he saw a larger bone. So, into the water he plunged to capture the larger one, with the result that he lost everything he had.

Our Opportunity

Did it ever occur to you that there is no immediate need on the part of some of our capitalists to develop foreign industry and neglect our own opportunities? Nor is there any altruism of magnanimous charity attached to such a policy if there be truth in the old saying that "charity begins at home."

Did it ever occur to you that there is a vast, undeveloped empire bounded by the Golden Gate and the Statue of Liberty, by the warm waters of the Gulf and the frozen shores of the Great Lakes? Quoting from a survey made by the American Federation of Labor, we have here in the United States of America five million families who are living below the minimum of the health requirements of food. There are four million five hundred thousand families with barely enough to sustain life at its level. Here are nine million five hundred thousand families or more than thirty-three million persons who are eager to buy the products of our automobile industry, of our textile industry, or of any other industry if their incomes permitted it.

Add to these seven million families of Americans who own no automobile; the twenty million families who, as yet, possess no efficient radio set; the four million families in whose homes there is not a bath tub; the thirteen million families whose homes are not even wired for electricity. What a stupendous, undeveloped empire within our very midst!

Why need we spend lavishly of our American dollars abroad to develop foreign nations; to build up foreign industries; to alleviate the impoverished conditions of foreign peoples when within our very gates there is a huge, virgin market ready for our products? Multiply these figures above mentioned by four to acquire the number of persons actually affected. Conservatively you have a population greater than that of the British Isles; greater than the population of France; outnumbering the people of the Kingdom of Italy; equal to the one-time German Empire.

The distant fields of internationalism appear all the greener to the greedy eyes of those who are blind to the land of their birth and to the uplifted hands of the fellow citizens who have helped them amass their stupendous fortune. But the immense profits made by cheap foreign labor is the siren song which coaxes the flow of gold from our American institutions.

View the situation from another angle. We have in the great Mississippi Valley an empire of sufficient acreage and square mileage to accommodate a population of one hundred and twenty million people over and above those who already claim that district as their homes. These figures are arrived at by taking the ratio at which the average English square mile is already populated. Or if you take Belgium and its rate per average square mile of population, there is sufficient accommodation in that Mississippi Valley alone for one hundred and eighty million persons. More than one hundred and twenty million potential citizens and consumers of our produce equivalent to the present total population of the United States!

If mass production cannot subsist without mass consumption; if at least ten foreign markets are more or less lost to us by the fact that their own people are beginning to mass produce their own necessities, why need we Americans lose hope and courage when there is at our hand's reach a potential empire almost as great as the ten of them put together?

With a controlled mass production, there is still a sane outlet for American money. Keep American money for American people. It was made by the sweat of American brows. If it must be exported to help wage an industrial war against our own laborers, place an export tax upon it!

Greedily, to gain the domination of the foreign world, our international bankers and international industrialists are tempted to drop the bone of "America First", hoping to possess themselves of the entire world. The result will be that they will have nothing unless they forego the greed that is born of international industrialism.

No wonder the Philadelphia Record says editorially on Monday, February 15th that *"there is every reason why we should place an embargo on gold. Europe is refusing to pay its debts to us but at the same time is draining our gold as fast as it can lay its hands on it."* We have made a mistake with our policy of gold for foreigners; food for foreigners, but none for the American workman.

In the meantime, forty million bushels of wheat valued at approximately $1,000,000 has been the only direct assistance which the Government has given to the millions of helpless Americans who are not only jobless but who are becoming hopeless.

Forty million bushels are only crumbs dropped from the opulent tables of Dives. Crumbs to the jobless, crumbs to the dogs!

My fellow Americans, there is more than a sentiment growing among the people of the United States. Their tears, their sufferings and their poverty have crystallized watery sentiment into the solidity of conviction.

If a shot fired at Lexington or Concord was heard round the world, so the shots fired at Dearborn shall not be easily muffled unless we bend every effort not only to relieve the laborer from his distressing conditions but also to lead him thoughtfully and surely away from the siren voice of destructive communism.

Laboring men, I have a word for you: Place no undue blame upon the shoulders of Henry Ford. Undoubtedly he has done his best during this year of depression to supply work and food and shelter to many thousands.

Were you or I in his place, perhaps, we would have managed less efficiently than he has done. His organization of itself is not able to employ the eight million unemployed.

My friend, the laborer, I have been most outspoken in coming to your defense. Will you hear me and believe me when I tell you of the communism which is dicing for your approval and for your support?

Communism is by no means a product of Russia. It is international. It hopes to amalgamate the workers of the world in one great nation known as the human race. It was the deposed German Emperor, Kaiser Wilhelm, who sent a sealed train which carried the fathers of the Russian Revolution into Moscow. Trotzky from New York, Lenin from Germany, Bella Kun from Hungary. Men from every nation who long since had devoted themselves to the anarchy, the atheism, and the treachery preached by Karl Marx, were those who devised the slaughter of more than 1,700,000 religious-minded Russians and set up a government known as the 'Godless.' Openly they professed their hostility to American imperialism as they termed it.

Openly, at this very instant, they are plotting the overthrow of our Constitution hoping for the realization of an international government. The word 'international' is their morning star of hope and their evening star of achievement.

Listen to what Lenin, the great apostle of communism, has to say. Be intelligent enough to believe him. On page 61, volume 16, of his 'Complete Works' he says: *"It is not in Russia that the complete world revolution will be obtained, but only when the proletariat has won the victory in the majority of advanced countries."* In the same volume, page 102, he writes: *"We exist not only in a state but in a system of states: The existence of the Soviet Republic along side imperialist states cannot long continue."* On page 129 of that same volume he further states: *"That looking at things from the plane of world history there is no doubt that the final victory of our revolution, if there were no revolutionary movements in other countries, would be impossible."* Can plainer words be used to tell you of their ambitions in America? They want revolution by blood, by slaughter. And you want peace and work and happiness gained through the power, not of bullets, but of ballots.

Now, gradually, the Lenin plan has been working out.

Today there is a political upheaval rumbling amidst the springtime breezes of Germany. Today Nationalists and Communists are fighting to overthrow the Von Hindenburg Government.

The political upheaval which is thundering along the banks of the Rhine shall reverberate up the stream of the Thames and along the shores of the Potomac if Christian, common sense does not soon come to replace the policies of pagan greed.

Mr. Laboring Man, no one with intelligence wants to become a communist. Communism is nothing more than an unintelligent effort to escape from the idleness and the poverty; from the political favoritism, from the unjust concentration of wealth in the hands of a few and from the unsupportable taxation which threaten us.

Be intelligent and use the American method of ballots—not the Bolshevik method of bullets.

In 1776, long before communism raised aloft its bloody flag and cried aloud its murderous doctrines, our forefathers fought against these damnable evils. Victory came to them. The Constitution was written. But through your carelessness and my carelessness we have let slip through our fingers the priceless jewel of liberty. Have we not permitted hypocritical gangsters to lead us? Have we not witnessed gangsters dominating our officials? Have we not beheld our country handed over to the policy that the "many exist for the few"?

Every protest against things as they are is not communistic any more than was the protest made in 1776 as intimated by the editorial which I have just read. But things as they are some times are identified with the policy of a King George; some times are identified with pagan stupidities; some times are associated with the usurpation of our political power and of our American liberty by grasping bankers, lobbyists and bureaucrats who have become the chief dictators and counsellors of a financial minded Government.

My friend, Mr. Laborer, God only knows that mine is nothing more than a voice pleading to keep distant from America the terrors of Moscow and the horrors of communism.

God only knows that Americans at heart are not communists and never will be such. Communists are not born. They are made. No man freely chooses atheism; no man relinquishes the hope to own his own home or to cherish his own wife. No man wants to become labeled with a number in a militaristic State. But sometimes the greed and the selfishness of the capitalist drive him to it. I know that you have more intelligence than to do such a thing. You have a ballot. The poor Russian had only a barbaric bullet!

Fellow Americans, if today the communists are promising to the laborer and to the farmer what both Republican and Democrat formerly promised and failed to accomplish, then let our political parties of tomorrow become of the people and for the people and not for the chosen few.

After one hundred fifty years, how proud would we be if today we could report to our forefathers that the Republic is more secure and constant and powerful and great than at any other time in its history!

In potentialities, our country is "more truly great". But in actualities it has sunk to its lowest depths from which we shall rise and, please God, which we shall never see again.

Our Republic is "more secure"! With its navy weakened, its army demoralized and its officers of the law calling upon the gangsters of the land to come to their assistance!

Our Republic "more constant"! And yet we have lived to see the day when the advice of Washington and his foreign entanglements has been torn like a scrap of paper.

Our country "more truly great"! Yes, if greatness is identified with the fact that our banks are choking with gold and hoarding it in their vaults; if our public utilities have made more money during the years of the depression than at any other time in their history; if our churches have been emptied; if our streets have been filled with eight million unemployed; if the ferocity of the Indian savage has been outdone by the ferocity of the rum runner and kidnaper; if taxation has been multiplied to an unbearable degree; if these and a thousand more elements that have crept into our national life are treated as mere fancies and fairy dreams, then we are "truly great".

My friends, there is something deeper, more substantial which has been removed from the foundation of our national life than the mere loss of money and loss of jobs. Although some will blame mass productionism; although others will cry out against internationalism; although a few will trace all our evils to the mockery of prohibition, yet underneath all of these, there is the lack of Christian charity. That is the main foundation which has been destroyed.

How dare I make that assertion in face of the fact of the millions of dollars which have been raised during this past year to feed the hungry, to clothe the naked and to shelter the homeless?

But, my friends, that is not necessarily charity, according to its Christian interpretation.

What does St. Paul say? *"If I should distribute all my goods to feed the poor, and if I should deliver my body to be burned, and have not charity, it profiteth me nothing."*

What does the Apostle of the Gentiles mean by this statement? He means nothing more than this: That charity is not identified necessarily with feeding the poor or with clothing the naked.

Charity is more than that. Define it if you will as the love of God and the love of your fellowman as yourself, and then do you understand its implication? Charity means seeking first the kingdom of God and His justice rather than seeking banks filled with gold. Charity is identified with loyalty to the principles for which Christ lived and died rather than loyalty to the fictitious principles of a political party. Charity towards your fellowman recollects for you the fact that whatsoever you do unto the least of Christ's little ones you do unto Him. Charity means seeing Christ in every Magdalen; visualizing Christ in every ragged piece of humanity; viewing Christ in every human being.

If the promoter and financier and industrialist believed in the doctrines of Jesus Christ he would no more exploit his fellowman than would he sell the Master for thirty pieces of silver.

My friends, today is Passion Sunday. If we and millions more like ourselves have suffered from the lash of poverty, remember that the God Who created us was born in a cold stable; let those who have been dispossessed of their homes remember that the Son of Man had nowhere to place His head. If the laborer or the farmer have been disparaged by a Government erected to defend them, Christ was betrayed by a Pilate who feared the enmity of a Caesar. He, the God of all might, of all wealth, stooped down into the gutter of our infirmities; became like unto the meanest of us in all things save sin.

Although He castigated the Pharisees of His day for having placed unbearable taxes upon the shoulders of His brothers, nevertheless, He did not promise us that the world would be freed of Pharisees until the end of time. He has blessed us a million-fold, however, in that He gave us the privilege of our democratic ballots. Guided by His inspiration, we can rectify any national or industrial evils which appear among us.

Meanwhile, these are days of suffering. These are the days of Calvary which precede the joys of Easter morn.

Thus, on this Passion Sunday and next Sunday, when there will be enacted for us the trial and death of Jesus Christ, I implore you, my friends, not to measure life by the cradle and the grave; not to count as great the mere possession of gold which you cannot take with you into the world beyond, but count that man as great who, despite the vicissitudes of life, can raise aloft the standard of Christ's flag; can sing in his heart the principles of Christ's charity; and if necessary, can trudge beside the Master along the highway of this Jerusalem up the steeps of Calvary and bow his head in resignation while the hands and heart and feet are pierced with the nails of greed and the spear point of oppression.

"Father, forgive them, for they know not what they do!", spoke Christ of old from the throne of His cross to those who murdered Him. *"This day shalt thou be with Me in paradise!"*, spoke He to the good thief and to the ten million good thieves who have courage to suffer and, if necessary, die in order to be born again in the eternal courts of heaven.

Today the name Kellogg means cereal, either the old stand-by, corn flakes, or one of the newer, more "exotic" sugar-coated varieties, to most people in the state. And for connoisseurs of such breakfast fare, cereal means Battle Creek, a city often referred to as "Foodtown, U.S.A.," "The Cereal City," and "Cornflake Capital of the World" as well as several other equally literary descriptions from the minds of Madison Avenue. The story of the way in which Battle Creek came to have this unique reputation and, more specifically, the role of the Kellogg family in this historical process, is one of the most unique chapters in Michigan's social and cultural history. In the 1870s, Dr. John Kellogg, a Seventh Day Adventist and vegetarian, became medical superintendent of the Adventists' Western Health Reform Institute. By 1900, the Institute, now known as the Battle Creek Sanitarium, or "San" for short, had become, in the words of one historian, a vast resort offering "the combined features of a medical boardinghouse, hospital, religious retreat, country club, tent Chautauqua, spa, all carried forward in an atmosphere of moral reform and asceticism." In an attempt to improve upon the "San's" extremely bland diet Dr. Kellogg invented a vast number of grain- and nut-food products including peanut butter and flaked breakfast foods. From this religious and health-inspired beginning, Dr. John's brother, W. K. Kellogg, built one of the state's great fortunes, a fortune largely based on W. K.'s genius for advertising and merchandising corn flakes, as author Gerald Carson emphasizes in the following excerpt from his book, *Cornflake Crusade*. For another view of the Kellogg story see H. B. Powell, *The Original Has This Signature—W. K. Kellogg* (New York, 1956).

The Golden Rule and Other Good Ideas

GERALD CARSON

The first advertisement W. K. Kellogg ever published was about chickens. When he was in his twenties, working fifteen or more hours per day, handling the billing and shipping of Sanitarium health foods, buying printing, filling in as a hospital orderly, W. K. supplemented his slender income (nine dollars a week, three children) by dealing in breeding stock and eggs as a side line. "Regular egg machines," he called his Brown Leghorns.

"As I recall, I did not receive a single reply," W. K. admitted, in looking back at this early venture into advertising. "Since that time I have been responsible for the expenditure of something in excess

From *Cornflake Crusade* (New York: Holt, Rinehart and Winston, 1957), pp. 212-215, 217-228. Copyright © 1957 by Gerald Carson. Reprinted by permission of Collins-Knowlton-Wing, Inc.

of one hundred million dollars for advertising," he said, "some of which did pay."

The first advertisement for W. K.'s corn flakes identified the product only as "Toasted Corn Flakes," and appeared in the Canton, Ohio, *Repository* in a test campaign that cost $150. Within nine years the Company was spending a million dollars a year for advertising. In 1931, its twenty-fifth anniversary year, W. K. put three million dollars into advertising. This was the first year, incidentally, in which extensive use was made of radio, which was quickly to become as essential to the conduct of a cereal business as corn grits or cardboard and glue.

Especially through "The Singing Lady" program broadcast over the NBC network, Kellogg led the way toward a major shift in emphasis which focussed the attention of the cereal promoters upon the dream world of the younger set. Capable men, to glance ahead for a moment into the longer future, have carried on the sizzling pace of Kellogg's salesmanship since the Founder passed on. In television they have found the ideal medium for instructing American youth in their breakfast duty.

"With television, we can almost sell children our product before they can talk," says Howard M. List, advertising manager of the Kellogg Co. "They know who the TV heroes are before they can talk full sentences. In the old days, children ate what their mothers bought; now the kids tell their mothers what to buy."

Although W. K. Kellogg liked to remark that he was "an old man" before he struck out in business for himself, the rapid expansion in the assets of the Toasted Corn Flake Co. had a tonic effect upon him. He seemed to get younger with every million. And each million needed another to keep warm by. W. K.'s pleasure lay in acquisition, not in distribution.

. . . .

Nearsighted from boyhood, when he could scarcely see the schoolroom blackboard, W. K. Kellogg experienced a gradual loss of vision in later life. In July, 1935, he underwent a first operation for glaucoma. A second unsuccessful operation was performed in 1937. Thereafter, he had only partial vision, decreasing until he could barely see a hand held close in front of his face, or recognize an old associate. During his last years he was totally blind, unable even to walk from his car to the door of his apartment without the aid of his white cane and his faithful German shepherd dog, a son of Rin-tin-tin.

The impression is held generally that W. K. didn't get much fun out of life.

"I've tried to recollect if I ever saw W. K. smile," one associate has said. "I believe he tried to one day when about twenty men were crowded into a small conference room for a meeting and his Seeing Eye dog developed a resounding flatulence."

. . . .

W. K. went to the movies as long as he could see the pictures. Sometimes, on lodge night, he attended Battle Creek Masonic Lodge, but the boys froze up when they saw him coming. W. K. was not the gabby type. Perhaps, before his sight failed he had read the books in his library, its four walls filled from floor to ceiling with standard sets and special bindings. He must have consulted his Mark Twain because he quoted Twain in support of the dim view he took of a possible biography of himself: "When I was young I had difficulty in remembering anything with accuracy, from day to day. Now, it seems, I am able to remember everything—whether it ever happened or not."

The hard-driving old cornflake king in the black, baggy suit and neat bow tie, was not a brilliant conversationalist. His reliance upon the cliché was notable even among corporation presidents. "Once seen, never forgotten," he would say; or, "What cannot be cured, must be endured." Perhaps his abiding sense of his own inadequacy dried up the springs of a freer communication. At any rate, he was a man of few words, and those mostly borrowed. The only subjects Kellogg would talk about with animation were Kellogg Co. plant problems and the grocery trade. W. K. did not inquire after the comfort of his advertising men when they came to Battle Creek. But he never failed to ask where they were staying, and financed the construction of a hotel so that people in town on Kellogg business would not spend money at the Post Tavern. W. K. was a voracious reader of sales figures and balance sheets, and liked nothing better than to chew the fat with some visiting jobber. When he mentioned the product of a competitor, W. K. always cited the price per case.

. . . .

Perhaps W. K.'s most human side is illustrated in a little game he liked to play when making important financial decisions. For example: there was a time when the Kellogg Co. had an all-bran product. W. K. believed that the opportunity was limited. However, he asked his advertising agency, N. W. Ayer and Son, to work out a merchandising plan under which bran could be sold in interesting quantities. The result was a well-reasoned proposal which deeply impressed W. K. But the cost was six hundred thousand dollars. This sum appeared to be as much as the total sales would amount to in a year. The cost was high, perhaps too high. W. K. went over the plan with a fine-toothed comb, then reached in his pocket, flipped a coin. He covered it with his hand, leaned over and peeked. He announced it was heads. Clarence Jordan, the Ayer representative in the meeting, spoke of the incident to Arch Shaw. Shaw explained that W. K. always flipped, always peeked, always announced the turn of the coin as he wanted it to be. R. O. Eastman used to say that he was going to eliminate the monkey business by getting Mr. Kellogg a nickel with heads on both sides.

During the early years of the Corn Flake Co., Kellogg got out a lively, brash house organ, called *The Square Dealer*, edited by able, uninhibited, young Eastman. Its character was that of "a monthly message of good cheer from the Home of 'The Sweetheart of the Corn' to the sales force of the Company and their customers." It was devoted to "a Business Application of the Golden Rule and Other Good Ideas." When W. K. told the sales force that the factory could manufacture so many cases daily if the sales department could only sell them, Eastman's little magazine rubbed the point in. If the Postum Company was caught in some misbehavior, the dereliction was reported by Kellogg's censorious *Square Dealer*. If the Quaker Oats plant had a fire, Kellogg sadly reported the fact to the grocery trade. The magazine publicized the vital connection between a healthy agriculture and a healthy breakfast-food company, by stories about the annual award of the W. K. Kellogg National Corn Trophy for the Grand Champion ear of corn. The trophy was a thirty-inch-high urn of no great usefulness, but turned out handsomely by Tiffany in gold, silver, bronze and enamel, with a picture of the Sweetheart of the Corn on the side. . . .

"During several years there were more orders than we could fill," says George C. McKay, who rose from the ranks to become vice-president and treasurer. "We cut down the orders, not as a scheme, but from necessity."

With short supplies and quick turnover, the corn flakes were always crisp and fresh, and that kept the stocks continually turning. W. K. filled his magazine with business-building ideas for retailers—counter-display suggestions, layouts for advertisements. He conducted an idea exchange. In return he expected a *quid pro quo* from the retailers—adequate display of Kellogg's Corn Flakes, eye-level shelf position, the maximum of "front facings." The bigger the display the greater the sales. And the less room there was left for competing cereals. It was a practical application of The Golden Rule.

. . . .

W. K. "retired" on numerous occasions, a little drama of renunciation and withdrawal which was played out in a series of repeat performances between 1924 and 1939. There was in him a fanatic drive to work, to amass, to dominate, which even blindness and four score and seven years could not subdue. Various men had risen in the Company since the early days—Andrew Ross, followed by the younger "Lenn" Kellogg, George and Eugene McKay, Lewis J. Brown, James F. O'Brien, Walter Hasselhorn. "Lenn" Kellogg and Brown each had borne uneasily and briefly the title of President. In the end, none were chosen. The parade of ex-officials from the Company never disturbed its progress. Perhaps that was why W. K. never felt it necessary to give credit to other men for contributions to his success.

The old President or Chairman of the Board, or whatever he called himself at any particular time, would come to the victim and sit and twitch. He would finger his old-fashioned watch chain and fidget, darting glances to the right and the left, nervous as a witch, talk of this and that. Finally he would whisper in a weak voice, "I've bad news for you. You've lost your job."

After much tribulation, W. K. Kellogg found his man in Watson H. Vanderploeg, a vice-president of the Harris Trust and Savings Bank of Chicago. "Mr. Van" became president of the Kellogg Co. in 1939 after a two years' preparatory period of service and continued as the operating head of the Company until his death in May, 1957. In 1946, W. K. declined re-election to the Board of Directors, but, as it said in his obituary, "retained an active interest in the administrative affairs of the Company." That was a euphemism for saying that the old food manufacturer would die, but never surrender.

There is reason to suppose that the passing of the nonagenarian, when it finally occurred, brought relief and refreshment to the Company's management. The best evidence is that the progress of the Kellogg Co. has been accelerated. A new vitality showed itself when it was no longer necessary to reckon with the founder's opinion on each advertising idea, his requirements on package design, on new products, his viewpoints on executive salary and titles. Wall Street pays its own special kind of hardheaded tribute to the Kellogg Company's latter day progress in words such as these: "Common stock is of good quality. Leading breakfast cereal company. Good management. Sales growth above population growth."

"Nothing succeeds," as John Finley once said, "like successors."

W. K. always kept a sharp watch over his personnel, encouraged private confidences about his executives and even second-string employees. It is related of him that once, when his train was crossing Iowa on the way to California, he looked out of the car window as the train passed through a town. It was nearly evening. He saw a Kellogg Co. automobile parked on a street. At the next stop a telegram was sent back to Battle Creek. It called for identification of the salesman who operated the truck and a check on his next expense account to see if he charged up garage rent that particular night. . . . The more he saw of men, the better he liked German shepherds. A sparrow couldn't fall, a heart interest couldn't blossom on a packaging line, the wife of a Kellogg white-collar employee couldn't smoke a cigarette in public, but what W. K. would hear of it.

Perhaps the quality of this granitic man can be wrapped up in a single incident. The time: 1932. The directors of the Kellogg Co. were in a dither. They decided to pull in their horns, cut the advertising, the house-to-house sampling, the premiums, pare all costs no matter what the cost. Word of the decision reached W. K. in California where he had settled down for the winter. He wired that he would be back in Battle Creek on a certain date, called a meeting of all directors, executives and advertising men. W. K. walked in, spoke to this effect:

"If we knew this entire country was going bankrupt on Saturday, we would fight right through Friday night, wouldn't we?"

And walked out.

The meeting voted to *add* a million dollars for advertising and a full-throttle selling drive. Once more W. K. had demonstrated solid-rock courage in a long career of pluck and luck. The greatest development of ready-to-eat cereals came *after* this dark time.

W. K.'s fond hope of developing a successor in the Kellogg family line to carry on after him was never realized. His family relationships ended in disorder, disharmony and disaster. One son, Karl H. Kellogg, a physician, lacking both physical robustness and the characteristics of a businessman, spent his life in California. W. K. quarrelled with "Lenn," the other surviving son, who tried to make a go of it with his father. W. K. became estranged from his second wife, the former Dr. Carrie Staines, a one-time physician at the Sanitarium, whom he had married in 1918. The aging capitalist tried to bring a grandson into line for the succession; but the business relationship ended up in a tangle of lawsuits. Loneliness was W. K.'s final portion.

John L. Kellogg made many contributions to the business. He once took a wax-paper wrapper off the outside of the corn flakes package and put it on the inside. This eliminated an inner paper bag and required about two inches less of paper than had the outer wrapping. A trifling innovation, it would seem. But wax, ink, glue, cardboard and paper rank high in the costs of a breakfast food factory. Two inches less of waxed paper meant $250,000 saved in a year. On another occasion John L. suggested treating bran with the Kellogg malt flavoring. Out of the suggestion came a valuable product, Kellogg's All-Bran. Here again the humble kitchen stove, so often encountered in the Battle Creek story, comes into prominence. "Lenn" said he read every book extant on the human colon at that time: a book in one hand, a spoon in the other, a health-giving mixture bubbling on the back of the kitchen range.

Less fortunate was "Lenn's" experience with a hot cereal called New-Ota. The American Hominy Company was in bankruptcy. Among its assets was a comparatively new rolled-oats mill at Davenport, Iowa. At a time when W. K. was in Europe, the mill was up for auction. J. L. bought it in his own name, persuaded his father when he returned to have the Kellogg Co. take over the oatmeal mill. But W. K., a cornflake man through and through, wanted nothing to do with the oats game. The Company took a heavy loss on this operation and the plant was sold finally to the Ralston Co. For this mistake, and for divorcing his wife to marry a girl in the Kellogg office, W. K. threw "Lenn" out of the Company.

John L. Kellogg was a reasonably good businessman, but a thought on the risky side. Like Edsel Ford, he never really had a chance. Perhaps he just didn't measure up. His subsequent career suggests that this was so. He went to Chicago where he started several promotional ventures. These enterprises went into receivership and disappeared. John L. died in California in 1950, suddenly, while standing by Dr. Karl Kellogg's fireplace. His body was returned to Battle Creek for burial, not in the place prepared for him by his father but at Memorial Park, in the Roman Catholic faith of his second wife, farthest removed of all Christian creeds from the ancestral Kellogg Adventism. But so it was; John L. Kellogg came to see the hand of Our Lady guiding the Cereal City on its high road of destiny, and found in Rome a balm and solace after the extraordinary rigors of being W. K.'s son.

The old cornflaker then turned his attention to a grandson. He would bring him up in his own image. John L. Kellogg, Jr., was the apple of W. K.'s eye. Tall, slender, attractive, artistic, somewhat diffident in manner, John L., Junior, prepared for his business vocation, became a lively participant in the social activities of Battle Creek's horsy set, and made the grand tour. He entered the Kellogg Co. where he was quickly elevated to a seat on the Board of Directors and a vice-presidency. The theory was that he was to learn the business from top to bottom. It turned out to be more top than bottom. His duties were chiefly those of "assisting" his grandfather

folklore of Battle Creek capitalism. But George Darling understood the old lone wolf better than most. He found the deeply buried id.

The bulk of the Kellogg cornflake fortune passed to the W. K. Kellogg Foundation; to which may be added W. K.'s personal "out of pocket" benefactions approaching three million dollars. The Foundation's program was the application of knowledge rather than research or relief. The variety of the approach is suggested in such projects as a tuberculosis control program for Detroit, diagnosis of speech defects in children, the construction of schools, pools, hospitals and gymnasiums, camps and playgrounds, the enrichment of life in rural areas. The majority of the expenditures during Mr. Kellogg's last years, and since, have gone into national and international activities through seven operating divisions: Dentistry, Education, Medicine and Public Health, Hospitals, Nursing, Agriculture and the International Division. The W. K. Kellogg Foundation is now one of the largest in the United States, with assets of $128,670,144, ranked only by the Ford and Rockefeller Foundations and the Carnegie Corporation.

Without denying the possibility that W. K. was moved by a simple, warmhearted desire to extend a helping hand to his fellow man, one cannot but notice other circumstances which help, at least, to explain a benevolence which was atypical. First of all was a great unsolved problem of gerontology—You Can't Take It With You. W. K. felt, certainly, no disposition to leave fifty million dollars to the family with which he had quarrelled and feuded and which he had already largely survived. Especially as he had long before made what he considered to be adequate provision for them. He could not, in good conscience, see the cornflake millions gobbled up by the government. He certainly could not allow John Harvey to go down in history as *the* humanitarian Kellogg. In this context, then, there came into being the Ann J. Kellogg School, the W. K. Kellogg Bird Sanctuary, the Kellogg Experimental Farms, a Kellogg Reforestation project, the Kellogg Radiation Laboratory at California Institute of Technology, the Kellogg Center at the then Michigan State College now Michigan State University, the School of Dentistry at the University of Michigan, the W. K. Kellogg Municipal Airport, and special research programs and fellowships in various universities abroad and at home.

The minister who committed W. K. to his last resting place said that Mr. Kellogg's monument was "the numberless men and women, boys and girls, and little children whose lives were enhanced by Mr. Kellogg's plans." The plans included a high per capita consumption of corn flakes and the return of most of the profits, for a complex mix of reasons, to socially useful projects serving the people who ate the flakes—a kind of gigantic cereal premium on a world-wide scale.

"There was a lot of good in W. K. Kellogg," mused a leading citizen of Battle Creek, looking out over the winking lights of the cereal city, "buried way down deep."

3: Since World War II: Culture and Society

By 1945 Michigan had earned an enviable reputation as a primary midwestern mecca for those who desired to escape from the drab routine of their dreary daily lives, or to be more precise, tourists and/or vacationers bent on refreshing themselves with a weekend, or the rapidly becoming standard two-week vacation, in a wilderness or near-wilderness area. Realizing the unlimited financial potential in this annual invasion, such organizations as the West Michigan Tourist and Resort Association and the East Michigan Tourist Association urged the state to prepare for what Arthur W. Stace, author of the following short selections, called "Escape Day," that time when thousands of veterans of World War II would return to the state and region seeking escape from their arduous wartime existence. At the time that he wrote these editorials Stace was editor of the *Ann Arbor News* and a special feature writer for the Booth newspaper chain; but he was also a member of the Tourist and Resort Advisory Committee, a fact that probably accounts for some of the rather flamboyant phraseology he used in *The Present and Future of Michigan's Tourist Business.*

The Present and Future of Michigan's Tourist Business

ARTHUR W. STACE

Escape Day Will Bring Mighty State Invasion

Vacationland, 1945—Michigan, "Tourist Empire of the Inland Seas," is looking to a new "day"—Escape Day.

Escape Day when her own war-weary fighting boys and the fighting boys of all the Mid-Western area flock back from battlefields and camps and seek escape from their labors, their hardships, their danger, and their memories on Michigan lakes, Michigan

Pamphlet published by West Michigan Tourist and Resort Association, 1945, pp. 1-12.

streams, Michigan beaches, amidst Michigan woods, Michigan wilds, Michigan scenic beauties, Michigan natural wonders.

Escape Day when war-weary workers, business men, professional men, housewives, and civilians in all walks of life will join in the rush to the joys and relaxations of recreational Michigan.

Escape Day when there will be no more shortages of gasoline, tires, automobiles, foods, lodgings, services, and conveniences; when all Michigan, land of outing delights, again will offer fullest measure of satisfactions to body, mind, and spirit.

Tremendous Rush Seen

Escape Day—which like the Biblical days of Creation may be a period covering months or years rather than the 24-hour round of the sun—is expected to bring a tremdous rush of visitors to Michigan's richly endowed recreational areas. A rush to the southern county lakes, rivers, and Great Lakes borders. A rush to the more extensive waters and the vaster wilds of the North Country. A rush to the Land Beyond the Straits, with its far-flung seas, its craggy shores, its mountains, its hills of iron and copper, its forests, its foaming waterfalls, its scenic drives, its lonesome spaces where chief dwellers are the timid deer and the elusive bear.

Looking forward to the rush of Escape Day—a rush already under way despite wartime barriers to travel, despite growing difficulties in providing desired food and lodgings—Gov. Harry F. Kelly and the new Michigan Tourist Council have sounded a warning to the state's second biggest industry.

Warned to Prepare

"Prepare!", they urge with prophetic zeal. "Prepare for the greatest inflow of visitors from other states Michigan ever has known! Prepare for a mass vacation migration from our own Michigan industrial areas! Prepare facilities to feed, to house, to transport, to entertain dollars-bearing legions! Prepare greater facilities, improved facilities, favor-winning facilities, profit-deserving facilities! Prepare—make Escape Day the dawn of a new era in Michigan hospitality, an era that will be marked by better care of our guests and by such satisfactions of their desires that they will be eager to return again and again! Prepare, that Michigan may avoid the disasters visited upon neglect and greed! Prepare that Michigan may reap the golden crop that is ready for the harvesting—a crop that means growing returns for the recreational business and richer living for all of us."

The Michigan Tourist Council is doing more than sounding a warning and a call to action: it is taking definite steps to carry out Gov. Kelly's directive to "place emphasis upon developing adequate, attractive accommodations, and upon drawing capital into the territory to furnish proper facilities."

. . . .

Autos Change Picture

In the early days when summer visitors came by boat and rail there was not much trouble taking care of them. Many had their own cottages and stayed all seasons. Others could find accommodations in the big hotels—mostly owned by transportation lines—in boarding resorts, or in private homes. Outings then were on a more simple scale; guests expected less—and got it. The guests, too, were confined to small segments of the social-economic ladder.

The automobile and a highway network covering the two peninsulas has changed the whole picture. Resorters and tourists now (in non-war times) come in tens of thousands where they came in hundreds. They include all degrees of wealth and culture. All sorts of facilities have sprung up to serve them—or to profit off them. All sorts of facilities and all sorts of operators. Some are of highest standard, sources of pride to the state and real assets to its recreational business; some of passing grade; some so tawdry that they are blotches on the landscape and drawbacks to the industry.

. . . .

Should the State Build Public Lodges in Its Parks?

Vacationland, 1945—We're going to be hungry to see the sights of Michigan when Escape Day comes. We're going to be hungry for the Big Waters, hungry for inland lakes and streams, hungry for the woods, hungry for the wilderness.

And supposing we want to get all this in Michigan's newest state-owned recreational domain—the Porcupine Mountains! Supposing we want to climb to the heights above the Lake of the Clouds, to linger amidst the pines and hemlocks, to gaze afar over Lake Superior, to wander over forest trails, to fish in gurgling streams, to clamber beside roaring waterfalls! Supposing we want to do this, where would we stay?

That's the big question. Where would we stay? And, unless we have our own camping equipment, there isn't any answer.

And if we wait to visit Tahquamenon Falls, and to tarry in its interest-filled vicinity for days or weeks, where would we stay? And again there isn't any answer unless we have our own lodgings and carry our food with us. It's the same with Wilderness Park, jutting out into Lake Michigan between the Straits of Mackinac and Sturgeon Bay.

Here's Real Problem

This lack of accommodations for ourselves and for our visitors from other states presents a real problem for the Michigan Tourist Council which is charged with the job of promoting the interests of the state's second largest industry. As a solution of the problem, the council has proposed to the State Conservation department, which has control of the Porcupine Mountains, Tahquamenon Falls, and Wilderness Park areas, that it erect experimental lodges or hotels in these public outing lands.

It has been suggested that these might be of the lodge-and-cottage type, each costing around $125,000, and with accommodations for 100 or more persons.

The lodges would have the double purpose of supplying accommodations in areas now lacking them, and of providing models that might be used to demonstrate to private interests how such resorts should be built, what they should offer in facilities and services, and how they should operate. They might serve, also, to stimulate private investment in similar projects in other localities.

The question has been raised, of course, as to whether the state should go into the hotel business. The Michigan Hotelmen's association, which naturally is vitally interested in the promotion of the tourist industry, has approved the experimental building of lodges in public parks where hotel facilities are not now available, but makes the reservation that they be leased for private operation by professional hotel men.

. . . .

Modern Means of Travel to Boost Touring in State

Vacationland, 1945—Getting to Michigan's playplaces and back home again is now the chief worry of Mr. and Mrs. Tourist-Resorter and their youngsters. In the Big Recreation Days coming after we finish walloping Japan, that promises to be the least of their outing worries.

Then, with war restrictions lifted on gas, tires, and new cars, automobiles again will swarm over the state's splendid network of highways, now far-extending and giving easy access to rich recreational resources, many of which were unreachable less than a dozen years ago.

On the highways, too, will be buses: long-distance buses, local service buses, special tour buses.

On the rails, if the lines servicing Michigan are as wise as may be expected, will be a revival of the old-time deluxe resort trains. Only in this revival instead of slow, wearying travel in outmoded sleepers and coaches of a passing era, there will be comfortable, even luxurious journeyings on swift stream-liners, equipped to make vacationing begin when one boards the train instead of at the end of the trip at a Michigan lake, stream, shoreplace, scenic wonder, or outing spot.

In the air will be passenger liners, private planes, and helicopters. On the water will be passenger boats, cruisers, yachts, and runabouts.

. . . .

Air Travel Will Help Recreational Business

Vacationland, 1945—"Let's fly away to Michigan!" That may be a popular vacation slogan after the war. And it may be meant very literally.

"Let's fly away to Michigan and go fishing," says John Business Man in Chicago to his buddy after a hard morning's work. So they hie themselves to the airport and grab a seat on the Northland Flyer. Within two hours they are set down on the big army-developed field at Alpena, in northeastern Michigan, or at Pellston, mid-way between Petoskey and Mackinaw City. In a few minutes they are whisked by auto to the lake or stream for which they are bound. The evening fishing hours find them in boat or waders, glorying in the joys of battling with gamey bass or elusive trout.

Or says hot and weary Mr. St. Louis on a Saturday morning. "Guess I'll grab a taste of Michigan invigoration by spending the weekends with the family at Northport"—or it may be Charlevoix. So he, too, grabs a plane and after a magic-carpet rush through the air he arrives in time for lunch with "Mother" and the kiddies, and for an afternoon game of golf, or a sail, or a swim.

Pioneers Already Flying

In these imaginary instances we are a little ahead of the facts—but not far. Already venturesome pioneers are flying in private or chartered planes to the Northland on outing trips. They will be followed after the war by increasing numbers. Airplanes promise to open up a new phase of recreationing in Michigan. By wiping out distance and slashing time they will bring the Straits of Mackinac as close to Detroit as is Lake Huron to Port Huron, as close to Chicago as are the orchards of St. Joe.

Building of military airfields has advanced recreational aviation possibilities in Michigan by many years. Splendid fields have been constructed at many points—by the navy at Traverse City, by the army at Pellston, Alpena, Grayling, and in the area of Sault Ste. Marie. We have no assurance that all these fields will be turned over for civil aviation, but that would seem to be a natural outcome, hooking up with the desire of the military authorities to keep them always ready for emergency use.

Other fields are under construction by municipalities that are looking to the future. For instance, Charlevoix, which witnessed a shocking tragedy two years ago when an army plane crashed in trying to take off from a meadow used as a makeshift landing field, is now constructing a real airport on another site.

Flying boats have thousands of landing places now awaiting them on lakes, on bays, on arms of the Great Lakes.

When Gen. Marshall, head of the army, and Admiral King, head of the navy, came to Michigan last month to attend the governors' conference at Mackinac Island, military planes landed them at the Traverse City airport. From there a navy flying boat took them to the island, where a smooth landing was made in the breakwater-protected bay. From their offices in Washington, D. C., to Mackinac Island was a half-day jaunt, though possibly in this case, they took a little more time than that.

Helicopters promise to play a large part in post-war recreational travel in Michigan. The Greyhound Lines are now planning regular passenger routes in Michigan. They will make comparatively short air jumps at 90 miles per hour. Their great advantage is that they will need only a small space in which to land and take-off. A fair-sized vacant lot or clearing will do. The Army Air forces have done much in developing practical helicopters, but have not yet released them for civil use. When they do, the whirlaway buses will become familiar sights in the Michigan air.

Boating Increasing Fast on Great Lakes Waters

Vacationland, 1945—What part will boats play in Michigan's post-war recreational business—a business that with proper development is bound to reach new "highs" in activities and dollar-values?

The answer is, of course, a big part. But it will be along new lines.

Time was when boats were vital to Michigan resorts—to the pioneer "watering places," such as Mackinac Island, Petoskey, Charlevoix, Ludington, Grand Haven, Macatawa, South Haven, and St. Joe. They were a principal means of getting to many spots. They continued to serve when the railroads become dominant in Michigan transportation. They went into a decline when summer visitors began to scamper all over the state in their own automobiles; when trucks began to haul the freight the steamship lines depended upon for an added margin of profit.

Gone are the day and night boats that used to carry resorters across Lake Michigan from Chicago to St. Joe, South Haven, Saugatuck, Grand Haven and Muskegon. Gone are the weekly or semi-weekly boats that ran up to Ludington, Portage Lake, Charlevoix, Harbor Springs and Mackinac Island.

Cruises vs. Trips

In the place of these passenger boats that carried vacationers to Michigan for summer stays, or for vacation periods, or for weekends are cruise ships, most of them booked up weeks or months in advance, which carry their loads of pleasure-seekers on definite tours lasting from several days to a week or more. They have little or no room for trip passengers going from port to port. These cruise ships serve a definite important function in the Michigan recreational picture, as do excursion boats, but they do not bring "staying guests," who are profitable because they stay to lodge and eat and trade in Michigan.

Perhaps, the war-born revival of the popularity of lake boat trips may be followed by a revival of port to port service. Perhaps when the St. Lawrence seaway opens the way to ocean boats, passenger craft engaged elsewhere at other seasons may come to the Great Lakes to share in the summer business.

Regardless, however, of what happens to the large passenger boats, the end of the war promises to bring a further boom in small-craft boating. Yachts and cruisers of all sizes, runabouts, sailboats will ply Michigan waters in ever increasing numbers.

. . . .

War Started to Free State from Winged Pests

Vacationland, 1945—Imps are sometimes present in the Michigan recreational paradise. Winged imps that tease, annoy, and damage, taking away something of the fullness of the joys that belong to a vacation in the peninsular state. Mosquitoes that hunt one's blood by day and night. House flies seeking to share (and taint) one's food. Horse flies that pester with stinging bites. No-see-ums that hide within the skin.

Banishment of these pests is one of the objectives immediately ahead of the Michigan Tourist Council in its campaign to establish here a new recreational era. And real progress is being made, with a definite promise of ultimate success.

MSC Gives Help

Michigan State College is helping in this matter, and its work thus far is far more substantial in results than the "plans" indicated in previous articles in this series. A "secret weapon"—that is no longer a secret—has gone into experimental action against the pests, with such success that we may, without being over optimistic, vision a day when mosquitoes, flies, and other noxious insects will be among the least of our vacation worries.

The secret weapon is DDT, which is short for dichloro-diphenyl-trichlorethane. This magic preparation, which kills every insect that comes into contact with it, is a war-developed product. It has been used by the Army sanitary experts in killing insect pests encountered by soldiers, sailors, marines in Pacific islands.

It was brought to the attention of the Michigan Tourist Council by Prof. Hutson of the Department of Entomology at MSC. Prof. Hutson has been working on insect control on Michigan farms, and the knowledge acquired working for Michigan's third largest industry is now being applied to the state's second largest industry.

Sprayed Everywhere

Wonder-working DDT can be sprayed on the walls, ceilings and floors of a room, it is stated, and any fly or mosquito that touches it is a "goner." Yet it is not poisonous to humans nor to animals. Neither is it injurious to clothing or room decorations. The effects of one spraying will last six weeks or more.

Following up on Prof. Hutson's work, the Mackinac Island Park Commission is this summer engaged in fly-killing experiments on a big scale—and heaven knows no better spot could be chosen. With Prof. Hutson directing the job and resident Commissioner William F. Doyle managing it, engineers have done wholesale spraying throughout Mackinac Island village, on the docks, and along the trails followed by the horse-drawn rigs for which the island is noted.

Some 500 pounds of DDT, manufactured by the Michigan Chemical Company at St. Louis, and released for this purpose by the WPB, have been sprayed through a hose on 32 horse stables, along 30 miles of roadway, on streets, alleys, and dumps. It has been sprayed, too, on eating places and in stores.

"We just can't believe the results we see," declares Commissioner Doyle. "The flies are disappearing. No longer do they rise in swarms on the woodland drives, nor in the outer drive where in spots they were particularly pestiferous. Many of the drivers have removed the fly nets from their horses.

"We started the first spraying on July 5, the day after the

governors left. We were told by Prof. Hutson that we should spray twice a summer, so we started the second spraying on August 1."

Mackinac Island has two kinds of flies, the common house fly, which is only a bother, and the hard biting horse fly, which inflicts sharp pain. The horse fly breeds in decaying vegetation or in any decaying matter. It has been the "curse of the woods" on the island but has swarmed everywhere. If DDT drives the flies and the mosquitoes from Mackinac as St. Patrick drove the snakes from Ireland, it will prove a blessing, indeed.

Not everything is known about DDT yet, whether the damage it does to beneficial insects offsets the destruction of those that are evil, and whether there are other serious drawbacks connected with its use. But this much is known—it is a potent weapon. And it may rid us of foes that have marred many a vacation and set back our recreational development.

Most of the People Are Seekers of Outdoor Fun

Vacationland, 1945—In the "new Michigan recreational era" now dawning, the two peninsulas will be called upon to entertain far greater numbers of vacationers than ever before. These will include not only hosts of dollar-bearing pleasure seekers from other states, but also mounting legions of summer migrants from Michigan itself.

In the older days of Michigan resorting, economic conditions were such that only comparatively small segments of the population could avail themselves of the outing joys offered by our waters, our wilds, our scenic wonders. Now with higher wages, shorter hours and the spreading habit of taking vacations at least once a year the recreational business base has broadened.

A large proportion of Michigan residents now tear themselves away from their working lives periodically, at least annually, and seek fun and relaxation in touring, fishing, hunting, or "just getting close to nature" in the great outdoors. Week-end trips have multiplied in number. So have spring trips, autumn trips, even winter trips. Michigan is no longer a recreation paradise in summer only—it holds an all-season allure for growing thousands. Nor does it reserve its choice offerings for the wealthy and the particularly well-to-do. It extends them to all the people.

Larger Crowds

So in preparing itself for the post-war "new recreational era," Michigan will have to provide accommodations both for larger crowds and for persons of diversified social and economic standings. The state has gone far already in establishing facilities both for those who can afford luxury and those of more modest means and requirements. It has its deluxe resorts and it has its tourist camps. It needs, according to the Michigan Tourist Council, more of both, a raising of standards of both, and a filling in between of sound-quality accommodations that will meet every taste and every purse.

Who should go into the recreation business?

Only those who are qualified, say the advisers of the Michigan Tourist Council. Only those who have adequate investment capital and working funds. Only those who are capable, efficient, and energetic. Only those of sufficient physical or mental vigor to meet the shifting demands of a business that is often difficult and exacting. Only those who can provide satisfying service on whatever level they propose to operate.

It is no business, say these advisers, for those who want to "retire and take it easy." It is no business for the lazy and indifferent.

Is it a business in which a discharged service man, even if partially disabled, might establish himself? Yes, say the wise ones, provided he is able to get a start on his discharge allotment and borrowing ability; provided, too, he has the necessary personal qualifications; provided, also, that he is capable of giving proper service and management.

Will Get Figures

The Tourist Council plans to get figures on the costs of establishing and operating various types of facilities, together with estimates of the returns that might normally be expected. This matter is, however, still in the planning stage.

Meanwhile, there are in Michigan plenty of operations that might be studied by any person seriously and intelligently considering on embarking upon any phase of service to tourists or resorters. There are examples of outstanding success, and examples of dismal failure. There are examples of places so well run that they draw paying, satisfied, returning patronage; and of places so badly operated that they drive patronage away, not only from themselves but even from their neighbors or communities. There are examples of rewarded enterprise, initiative, and imagination; and examples of punished indifference, dullness, and mediocrity.

The Michigan Tourist Council need not worry overmuch about getting people into the state's recreational areas with the coming of Escape Day and with final victory over Japan. It has to worry and busy itself about providing proper facilities for these people as they come. And that is going to require prompt action, energetic action. Michigan, as Governor Kelly has pointed out to the Council and to the people of the state, is in a "race against time" to prepare proper facilities for its own touring population and for its visitors from outside.

Michigan has produced many individuals who have helped mold and shape national policy in an increasingly confusing post-World War II epoch. Such a man was Arthur H. Vandenberg of Grand Rapids. Born in the Furniture City on March 22, 1884, Vandenberg graduated from high school in 1900 and immediately went to work for the Grand Rapids *Herald*. In 1901 he attended the University of Michigan but returned to the *Herald* the same year when his money ran out. Two years later he went to New York City but stayed less than a year. By 1904 he was back on the *Herald* staff, and, in 1906, when the ownership of the paper changed hands, Vandenberg became managing editor. A lifelong Republican, Vandenberg was a member of the GOP's state central committee in 1912. At the age of 32 he was chairman of the state convention and a state Republican power. Elected to the United States Senate in 1928, Vandenberg served in this capacity until his death in 1951. For much of his senatorial career, as his biographer C. David Tompkins points out, Vandenberg sought to impose limitations on New Deal programs and championed American isolationism. "Yet, by 1945, Vandenberg had demonstrated a large capacity to grow and salvage what he could from defeat." On January 10, 1945, he delivered the following speech in which he publicly reversed his earlier isolationist position and called for support of an internationalist, bipartisan foreign policy as the only kind of policy that could hope to succeed in the postwar world. In the years from 1945 until his death, Vandenberg was the GOP's leading spokesman for this new spirit of cooperation. To best understand the various aspects of this many-sided man's public career one should read Tompkins' *Senator Arthur H. Vandenberg: The Evolution of a Modern Republican, 1884-1945* (East Lansing, 1970) and Arthur H. Vandenberg, Jr., *The Private Papers of Senator Vandenberg* (Boston, 1952). Tompkins is presently at work on a second volume on Vandenberg, which will cover the years from 1945 to 1951.

A Speech Heard Round the World

ARTHUR H. VANDENBERG

Mr. President [Vice-president Henry A. Wallace, President of the Senate], there are critical moments in the life of every nation which

"A Speech Heard 'Round the World"—Senator Arthur H. Vandenberg announces his support for a bipartisan foreign policy and an internationalist position. Speech delivered in the United States Senate, January 10, 1945.

call for the straightest, the plainest and the most courageous thinking of which we are capable. We confront such a moment now. It is not only desperately important to America, it is important to the world. It is important not only to this generation which lives in blood. It is important to future generations if they shall live in peace.

No man in his right sense will be dogmatic in his viewpoint at such an hour. A global conflict which uproots the earth is not calculated to submit itself to the dominion of any finite mind. . . . Each of us can only speak according to his little lights—and pray for a composite wisdom that shall lead us to high, safe ground. It is only in this spirit that I speak today. . . .

The United Nations, in even greater unity of military action than heretofore, must never, for any cause, permit this military unity to fall apart. . . . We not only have two wars to win, we also have yet to achieve such a peace as will justify this appalling cost. Here again an even more difficult unity is indispensable. Otherwise, we shall look back upon a futile, sanguinary shambles and—God save the mark—shall be able to look forward only to the curse of World War III.

. . . .

I hasten to make my own personal viewpoint clear. I have always been frankly one of those who has believed in our own self-reliance. I still believe that we can never again—regardless of collaborations— allow our national defense to deteriorate to anything like a point of impotence. But I do not believe that any nation hereafter can immunize itself by its own exclusive action. Since Pearl Harbor, World War II has put the gory science of mass murder into new and sinister perspective. Our oceans have ceased to be moats which automatically protect our ramparts. Flesh and blood now compete unequally with winged steel. War has become an all-consuming juggernaut. If World War III ever unhappily arrives, it will open new laboratories of death too horrible to contemplate. I propose to do everything within my power to keep those laboratories closed for keeps.

I want maximum American cooperation, consistent with legitimate American self-interest, with constitutional process and with collateral events which warrant it, to make the basic idea of Dumbarton Oaks succeed. I want a new dignity and a new authority for international law.

I think American self-interest requires whole-hearted reciprocity. In honest candor, I think we should tell other nations that this glorious thing we contemplate is not and cannot be one-sided. I think we must say again that unshared idealism is a menace which we could not undertake to underwrite in the post-war world.

. . . .

The real question always becomes just this: Where does real self-interest lie? Here, Mr. President, we reach the core of the immediate problem. Without remotely wanting to be invidious, I use one of many available examples. I would not presume, even under these circumstances, to use it except that it ultimately involves us. Russia's unilateral plan appears to contemplate the engulfment, directly or indirectly, of a surrounding circle of buffer states, contrary to our conception of what we thought we were fighting for in respect to the rights of small nations and a just peace. Russia's announced reason is her insistent purpose never again to be at the mercy of another German tyranny. That is a perfectly understandable reason. The alternative is collective security.

. . . Which is better in the long view, from a purely selfish Russian standpoint: To forcefully surround herself with a cordon of unwillingly controlled or partitioned states, thus affronting the opinions of mankind . . . or to win the priceless asset of world confidence in her by embracing the alternative, namely, full and whole-hearted cooperation with and reliance on a vital international organization. . . ? Well—at that point, Russia, or others like her, in equally honest candor has a perfect right to reply, "Where is there any such alternative reliance until we know what the United States will do?". . .

I propose that we meet this problem conclusively and at once. There is no reason to wait. America has this same self-interest in permanently, conclusively and effectively disarming Germany and Japan. . . . It should be handled as this present war is handled. There should be no more need to refer any such action (use of force to keep the Axis disarmed) back to Congress than that Congress should expect to pass upon battle plans today. The Commander-In-Chief should have instant power to act and he should act. I know of no reason why a hard-and-fast treaty between the major allies should not be signed today to achieve this dependable end. We need not await the determination of our other postwar relationships. This problem—this menace—stands apart by itself. . . . I respectfully urge that we meet this problem now.

From it stem many of today's confusions, doubts and frustrations. I think we should immediately put it behind us by conclusive action. Having done so . . . we shall be able, at least, to judge accurately whether we have found and cured the real hazard to our relationships. We shall have closed ranks. We shall have returned infinitely closer to basic unity.

Then, in honest candor, Mr. President, I think we have the duty and the right to demand that whatever immediate unilateral decisions have to be made in consequence of military need . . . shall all be temporary and subject of final revision in the objective light of the postwar world and the postwar peace league as they shall ultimately develop. . . . Indeed, I . . . would write it in the bond. If Dumbarton Oaks should specifically authorize the ultimate international organization to review protested injustices in the peace itself, it would at least partially nullify the argument that we are to be asked to put a blank-check warrant behind a future status quo which is unknown to us and which we might be unwilling to defend.

We are standing by our guns with epic heroism. I know of no reason why we should not stand by our ideals. If they vanish under ultimate pressures, we shall at least have kept the record straight; we shall have kept faith with our soldier sons; and we then shall clearly be free agents, unhampered by tragic misunderstandings, in determining our own course when Berlin and Tokyo are in Allied hands.

Let me put it this way for myself: I am prepared, by effective international cooperation, to do our full part in charting happier and safer tomorrows. But I am not prepared to guarantee permanently the spoils of an unjust peace. It will not work. . . .

Mr. President, I conclude as I began. We must win these wars with maximum speed and minimum loss. Therefore we must have maximum Allied cooperation and minimum Allied frictions. We have fabulously earned the right to be heard in respect to the basis of this unity. We need the earliest possible clarification of our relations with our brave allies. We need this clarification not only for the sake of total Allied cooperation in the winning of the war but also in behalf of a truly compensatory peace. We cannot drift to victory. We must have maximum united effort on all fronts. We must have maximum united effort in our councils. And we must deserve the continued united effort of our own people.

I realize, Mr. President, in such momentous problems how much easier it is to be critical than to be correct. I do not wish to meddle. I want only to help. I want to do my duty. It is in this spirit that I ask for honest candor in respect to our ideals, our dedications, and our commitments, as the greatest contribution which government can now make to the only kind of realistic unity which will most swiftly bring our victorious sons back home, and which will best validate our aspirations, our sacrifices, and our dreams.

Michigan has long been regarded as a stronghold of organized labor, particularly in its heavily industralized eastern section. Led by such well-known union figures as Victor and Walter Reuther, August Scholle, and James Hoffa, the state's AFL and CIO locals fought hard for higher wages, shorter hours, and expanded fringe benefit programs for their members in the years after World War II. Yet success in these "meat and potatoes" areas also brought problems not the least of which was what might be called "the curse of bigness"—the fact that the unions grew so large that they began to lose touch with the rank and file. However, paying little heed to such matters as the loss of identity of the average worker, in the mid-1950s the national leaders of the AFL and the CIO decided to merge their already huge organizations into one giant union. The success of this merger on the national level was accomplished without many problems; but on the state level, the story was somewhat different. As Dr. Jacqueline Brophy tells us in the selection that follows, the merger of these two state union organizations was a difficult process. Professor Brophy's analysis of the intriguing interplay between old rivals also gives us much insight into the state dimension of labor history, a field that will hopefully attract more scholarly attention in the future. For those who wish to read further on this general subject two recently published biographies of Walter Reuther—Frank Cormier and W. J. Eaton, *Reuther* (Englewood Cliffs, New Jersey, 1970) and Robert L. Tyler, *Walter Reuther* (Grand Rapids, 1973)—should prove rewarding. For a brief survey of the labor movement in Michigan one should consult Doris B. McLaughlin, *Michigan Labor: A Brief History from 1818 to the Present* (Ann Arbor, 1970).

The Merger of the AFL and the CIO in Michigan

JACQUELINE BROPHY

When in December, 1955, the American Federation of Labor and the Congress of Industrial Organizations merged nationally to form

From *Michigan History*, L (June, 1966), 139-157. Reprinted by permission of the History Division, Michigan Department of State. Footnotes in the original have been omitted.

a united labor movement, it might have been supposed that their subordinate state branches would quickly have followed suit as a matter of course. In fact they did not do so; nor did the new national American Federation of Labor-Congress of Industrial Organizations (AFL-CIO) expect them to. The constitution of the AFL-CIO anticipated for the states the same kind of difficulties which already had been confronted in the national merger struggle, and it extended to the state federations of labor and the state councils of the Congress of Industrial Organizations a two-year period of grace in which to effect their consolidations.

Even so, by the December, 1957, deadline, the labor movement remained unreconstructed in fourteen states, including Michigan. Personal rivalries and conflicting interests among unions threatened in some states to delay the merger indefinitely. At this stage, George Meany, president of the AFL-CIO, turned from a program of persuasion to one of coercion, and he chose Michigan as the first state upon which to enforce his authority. In February, 1958, he cancelled the charters of both the Michigan Federation of Labor and the Michigan CIO Council and he called a state convention which substantially completed the merger by the end of the month.

State labor bodies had a structure, a function, officers, and a life of their own. The speed with which the state organizations of the American Federation of Labor and Congress of Industrial Organizations merged corresponded to the degree of advantage which the respective leaders could discern either for themselves or for their own organization.

In states with comparatively small numbers of organized workers, the advantage of a unified labor group was so obvious that in nineteen less industrialized states, the AFL and CIO central bodies completed merger within a year. In areas where state labor bodies were more powerful, formal integration came much harder.

While the failure of the AFL and CIO state organizations in Michigan to merge involved various issues and interests, the primary reason was undoubtedly the effort of leaders of the International Brotherhood of Teamsters and the building trades unions to prevent it.

At the time of national merger, James R. Hoffa of Detroit was head of the Teamsters' powerful Midwestern Conference; before the two-year grace period had expired, he was elected provisional president of the entire International Brotherhood of Teamsters, succeeding Dave Beck. Beck had been forced from the presidency by revelations of his corrupt activities brought out by the United States Senate's Select Committee on Improper Activities in the

Labor or Management Field. During this period, the Teamsters were also under pressure from the AFL-CIO Executive Council to conform to its newly adopted ethical practices code or face expulsion. According to some analysts, Hoffa tried to use his power in the Teamsters, and his resultant influence in state and local labor federations, to dim the enthusiasm of the leadership of the AFL-CIO for enforcing labor's ethical practice codes, and to prevent the Teamsters' expulsion from the AFL-CIO.

In hindering state and local mergers, Hoffa found ready cooperation from leaders of the building trades unions, both on a national level and in Michigan. The top officers of the Michigan Federation of Labor were conservative old-line craft unionists under whose leadership the MFL had done little more than hold monthly executive board meetings and allot small amounts for political action, mostly for support of various Republican candidates for state office. A notable example was the $1000 contribution to the campaign of George W. Dean, president of the Michigan Federation of Labor, for the State Board of Education on the Republican ticket in 1957.

The fact that the leaders of the Michigan Federation of Labor and the Michigan CIO Council were at opposite poles in political outlook made prospective merger no easier. The Michigan CIO was the bulwark of the state Democratic party. It was militant and active in its support of liberal Democrats. The name of August Scholle, president of the Michigan Congress of Industrial Organizations, held the same horror for Michigan's conservative Republicans as Walter Reuther's held for their counterparts on the national scene. In contrast, George W. Dean and John H. Thorpe, president and secretary-treasurer respectively of the Michigan Federation of Labor, were longstanding Michigan Republicans. Thorpe was regularly a delegate to the Republican national conventions, and Dean had served as the Michigan commissioner of labor for several years in Republican administrations.

Since the membership of the American Federation of Labor in Michigan was less than half that of the Congress of Industrial Organizations in the state, it was inevitable that it would play the lesser part in a merged Michigan labor movement. Not only would officers of the Michigan Federation of Labor personally lose positions of some prestige, but they would be submerged in an organization whose political principles were to a great extent contrary to their own.

It is little wonder then that the leadership of the Michigan Federation of Labor responded so eagerly to any sort of lead to go slow on state merger provided from either the national Building and Construction Trades Department of the AFL-CIO or from the Teamsters.

Another factor which may have played a part in the difficulties of merger in Michigan was the personal animosity between James R. Hoffa and Walter Reuther, two of the strongest personalities in the American labor movement. Their major roles were played on stages beyond the state level, but their impact, direct or indirect, on the Michigan situation was considerable. Both made their headquarters and their homes in Detroit. Hoffa's International Brotherhood of Teamsters was the union with the largest membership in the Michigan Federation of Labor; Reuther's United Automobile Workers the largest in the Michigan CIO.

Hoffa and Reuther were accurately described by A. H. Raskin, veteran New York *Times* labor reporter, as

> polar opposites in their associations, their methods of operation, their concepts of union morality and, most important, their ideas of what the labor movement is all about. . . . For Hoffa, unions are a business, in which anything goes as long as the organizations keep delivering. . . . Reuther rejects this cash register estimate of unionism, even when it does not involve racketeering. He views unions as instruments for effecting basic social and economic reforms. His mind skips . . . far beyond the bargaining table in its blueprints for a better tomorrow.

Each man despised what the other stood for in labor circles.

In spite of all these unpromising factors, there was a moment when it seemed that merger in Michigan of the two labor organizations would be accomplished within a few months of the national merger itself. This was during the exciting and inspiring days of the unity convention of the AFL-CIO in December, 1955, in New York.

The executive board of the Michigan Federation of Labor had decided that the national merger convention was a historic occasion worthy of the presence of its entire membership, that is, of Dean, Thorpe, and the ten board members. In the heady atmosphere of the merger convention in New York City, they were apparently carried away with the events taking place. Informal conversations occurred between Dean and Thorpe and their CIO counterparts, Gus Scholle and Barney Hopkins. When the leaders of the Michigan Congress of Industrial Organizations suggested that Michigan labor, both AFL and CIO, together sponsor a cocktail party at the convention hotel, a meeting of the executive board of the Michigan Federation of Labor was hastily called on December 6 to ponder these weighty developments. It was duly moved and seconded that the MFL co-operate in a joint get-together of the Michigan Federation of Labor and the Congress of Industrial Organizations, "provided it is co-sponsored by the State AFL and the State CIO, and is so announced." Also formally approved by the Michigan Federation of Labor executive board was a motion directing its officers to meet with the officers of the Michigan CIO council to arrange an initial meeting of both executive boards to consider Michigan merger problems. As Gus Scholle recalled the party later, "There were a good many hearty handshakes there and a lot of pictures and profession of good will all around." In addition, the officers of the two organizations met informally and reached tentative agreement that each organization would set up a committee of ten to explore the problems of merger.

Things were moving along sufficiently well that the *Michigan CIO News* was able to quote Scholle on December 8 as saying:

> I see no major obstacles on the road to merger in Michigan. I feel that the problems faced by both our organizations can be worked out in a month's time. Under such circumstances I can't see why there cannot be a joint state convention of the AFL and CIO in June,

when both groups had their regular conventions scheduled.

But the warmth of good fellowship that pervaded the New York convention soon vanished in Michigan's cold winter climate. As the next meeting of the Michigan Federation of Labor executive board got underway January 12, 1956, the minutes of the recent executive board meeting in New York were read. Teamster Frank Fitzsimmons moved that they be rejected. There was a question, he said, whether the Michigan Federation of Labor executive board constitutionally could hold a meeting outside of Michigan. But he put his major emphasis on the fact that not all members of the board had been notified of the meeting. Fitzsimmons and two others had not taken advantage of the decision to go en masse to New York City. When the board was hastily summoned to meet during the convention, only those in the city were contacted; those back in Michigan had not been notified.

With this enlightenment on the niceties of orderly procedure, the members of the executive board readily agreed to reject the minutes. Objection came from only one member, George Murphy of the UAW-AFL (later renamed Allied Industrial Workers). But it was decided the New York meeting had been out of order; its minutes were rejected; and the position of the Michigan Federation of Labor on merger reverted to the decision taken at its November executive board meeting, that is, to advise the Michigan CIO Council when the MFL was ready "to jointly discuss this matter."

. . . .

The Teamsters' victory was complete at this meeting when the executive board was moved to positive action on one item: it agreed to support the Teamsters in that organization's co-operation with the International Longshoremen's Association, a union expelled from the American Federation of Labor two years earlier for corruption and racketeering along the New York waterfront.

A week or two later, the officers of the Michigan CIO Council wrote the Michigan Federation of Labor that they were prepared to meet to work out problems of integrating the two state organizations. The MFL did not reply. Nor did it take any action a few weeks later on a letter from the directors of the Committee on Political Education, the new committee of the national AFL-CIO which replaced the CIO Political Action Committee and the AFL Labor's League for Political Education. The letter suggested that immediate steps be taken to integrate the political action committees of the state CIO and the state AFL. Scholle and Hopkins, in receipt of the same communication from the Committee on Political Education, wrote the officers of the Michigan Federation of Labor that they were willing and ready to meet on this proposal from the national office. The Michigan Federation of Labor did not respond.

In the months that followed, the Michigan Federation of Labor did name a merger committee of twelve people, including James Hoffa. The members met regularly to talk with one another about merger difficulties, but made no move to meet with the CIO.

During the first six months of 1956, the Michigan Federation of Labor certainly would have had no difficulty in observing the signals from the national level to "go slow" on merger, even if it had gotten no lead directly from Hoffa. In March, Dave Beck, still the national president of the Teamsters, advised his locals not to rush to support mergers of state and city bodies. A month later, a meeting was held of the Building and Construction Trades Department of the national AFL-CIO. This department was composed of nineteen union presidents, including Beck, whose International Brotherhood of Teamsters was represented through its national Division of Building and Construction Drivers. The Building and Construction Trades Department formally adopted a resolution opposing merger of state and local bodies until "such time as a satisfactory written understanding on jurisdiction is reached between the Building and Construction Trades Department and the Industrial Union Department." The Industrial Union Department was newly created when the American Federation of Labor and the Congress of Industrial Organizations had merged nationally. It was headed by Walter Reuther, former president of the Congress of Industrial

Organizations, and provided a center for the former CIO unions, and for those AFL unions which had members organized on an industrial basis.

Jurisdiction, or which union has the right to organize which type of worker, had long been an unresolved problem among unions, especially those in the building trades. Twenty years earlier, it had been a disrupting factor which had helped to bring about the formation of the CIO, for to a great extent the skilled trades' dog-in-the-manger attitude about their "jurisdiction" over certain types of workers in industrial plants had hampered organization of the mass-production industries.

Now, two decades later, jurisdictional rights were again being raised as the major impediment to labor unity. It is hard to take this argument seriously as an obstacle to state mergers of the AFL and CIO, because jurisdictional frictions were not confined by any means to those between the building trades unions and the former unions of the Congress of Industrial Organizations. Some of the most virulent jurisdictional disputes were those between the various building trades unions themselves; yet this had not prevented them from all belonging to the same federation, nor indeed had it prevented them from the even closer relationship in the Building and Construction Trades Department. But regardless of the irrationality of the jurisdictional argument as a real impediment to merger, it was an old battle cry that could raise an automatic response in many an old-line craft unionist throughout the country.

The Building and Construction Trades Department sent its resolution opposing state mergers to all state and local building trades councils. All the international union presidents "signatory hereto" (which included all but one of the nineteen unions in the department; Harry Bates of the Bricklayers International Union had not been present at the meeting) were to take action also, each instructing "by wire or letter all of its local unions to use every facility at their command to postpone merger of AFL-CIO state and local central bodies."

For the forces in Michigan opposing merger, the department's formal stand was made to order. The Detroit Federation of Labor and the Detroit Building Trades Council both quickly passed similar resolutions and forwarded them to the Michigan Federation of Labor, which thereupon sent copies of each, as well as copies of the Building and Construction Trades Department resolution itself, to all American Federation of Labor city and county central bodies and building trades councils in the state. For good measure, the Michigan Federation of Labor executive board formally adopted a similar resolution at its May 24, 1956, meeting. In contrast, a resolution the Michigan Federation of Labor received from another of its affiliates, the Michigan Council of the International Association of Machinists, which pressed for state merger, got no such circulation; the board merely voted to accept it as information.

In a letter to the Lansing local of the United Brotherhood of Carpenters, Michigan CIO President Scholle, recognizing the jurisdiction argument as a red herring, patiently spelled out why such problems could not interfere with merger of state bodies. The local had adopted a resolution urging "no merger until settlement of jurisdictional problems," and had forwarded copies to both the state CIO and the state AFL. "Your resolution seems somewhat strange to us," wrote Scholle,

> due to the fact that you surely know as well as we do that county and state organizations have absolutely no authority over questions relating to jurisdiction of international unions. We have felt that unity and solidarity should be achieved before trying to resolve every question of a controversial nature which may presently confront our mutual parent body.

Jurisdictional problems are never finally settled, Herbert Mc-Creedy, regional director of the AFL-CIO, told the Michigan CIO convention in June, in an explicit description of the irrationality of the jurisdictional argument as an obstacle to merger. Even if it were possible at any given time to settle all jurisdictional problems, "modern technology, automation, the change of industry, the technical progress [in] methods by which we produce, would create tomorrow other jurisdictional problems that we would then have to sit down and deal with."

Walter Reuther addressed the same convention: "There has been a lot of talk in the papers about the controversy between the Building Trades and the Industrial Union Department. Well, that's not the argument." At a recent meeting the AFL-CIO Executive Council had reviewed

> grievances that the Building Trades Department has with other unions. We found there are as many AFL unions who have disagreements with the Building Trades as there are former CIO unions. But it's always easier to make it look like the industrial unions are fighting the building trades.

It was true that as recently as the 1954 convention of the Michigan Federation of Labor, the Kalamazoo Building and Construction Trades Council had been complaining that some AFL unions did work "rightfully belonging to the different trades of the Building and Construction Department."

In Washington, the Building and Construction Trades Department announcement had brought forth an immediate condemnation from President George Meany and the AFL-CIO Executive Council. The Council found the action of the Building and Construction Trades Department "to be in direct violation of the letter and spirit of the merger agreement and the constitution" of the AFL-CIO.

Meany, who had been president of the plumbers' union and therefore a former member of the Building and Construction Trades Department himself, met with the nineteen union presidents a few weeks after they had adopted their resolution. In plain language he dressed down the instigators of the resolution. Then he told them he was prepared to appoint a committee of AFL-CIO Executive Council members to deal with complaints of the building trades against the industrial unions. The building trades agreed to abandon their official opposition to state mergers.

During the same month of June, 1956, both the Michigan CIO and the Michigan Federation of Labor at their conventions adopted high-sounding resolutions in favor of unity. The MFL, perhaps prodded by pro-merger locals, went so far as to recommend that the merger committee meet with one from the Michigan CIO within thirty days and at least once every thirty days thereafter.

Not to be outdone, the Michigan CIO executive board named an eighteen-man merger negotiating committee. The two groups met for the first time on June 29, 1956, in Detroit. During a three-hour session the MFL committee, almost as numerous as the CIO group, made it clear once again that the problems of jurisdiction in organizing must be resolved before it would talk about any details of merger. Hoffa insisted that merger would be meaningless unless jurisdictional questions were resolved first: "We do not want to enter a marriage that will end in a quick divorce." Scholle, while still maintaining that local bodies had no authority regarding jurisdiction, at length agreed to go along with the ambitious proposals of the Michigan Federation of Labor. Each side was independently to draft proposals to eliminate jurisdictional strikes. Then the two committees would meet to see if they could combine the two documents into a single proposal to submit to the parent AFL-CIO for adoption as national policy.

When the two committees next met on October 3, 1956, Hoffa suggested that there be a six-man committee, three from each side, "to draft up rules of organization, rules on strikes, rules respecting picket lines, and rules on jurisdiction" and that they should then report back to the entire group. Scholle, saying this was an entirely new proposition and that he would have to find out whether his committee thought it a good procedure, suggested that decision be postponed until the next meeting. Hoffa agreed and the meeting ended. The group did not get together again until the national AFL-CIO stepped in a year later.

Meanwhile, although the national Building and Construction Trades Department had agreed to withdraw its official policy of opposition to state mergers, its sentiments remained the same, if now unofficial. The Teamsters continued to muddy the waters. Dave Beck in January, 1957, was reported to have offered the building trades unions $500,000 as an initial contribution to a war chest for the construction unions to use in organizing in competition with former CIO unions.

Meany, still trying to find a formula to keep peace in his labor family, presented a plan for arbitrating interunion disputes and outlawing boycotts by one union of products made by members of another. "The Reuther group looked upon the program with cordiality. The building trades have shown no enthusiasm for it," reported the New York *Times*.

In June, 1957, Meany, once again seeking a means of settling the jurisdictional problem that would be satisfactory to both sides, came up with another suggestion. The Industrial Union Department and the Building and Construction Trades Department would each select three persons who would then be put on the payroll of the AFL-CIO. From these six, three teams of two persons each would be dispatched to the site of any dispute to try to work out a solution. If that failed, the team would then take the problem to a three-man committee in Washington composed of the president of the Building and Construction Trades Department, the president of the Industrial Union Department, and a person designated by Meany.

The Detroit Building Trades Council announced it was against Meany's plan and would fight it at the forthcoming convention of the Building and Construction Trades Department, August 5, in Atlantic City.

Before both this meeting and another which the building trades held in late November, rumors were rife that the construction unions would fight the policy of the AFL-CIO and would even secede from the federation. Both times, thanks to Meany's efforts, they decided not to follow such a drastic course.

The turmoil on both national and state levels was ostensibly about jurisdictional problems, but in fact, as Joseph Loftus of the New York *Times* observed, the work day involved few jurisdictional disputes, and the building trades had rejected a variety of proposals which could have dealt with the problem. The jurisdictional question was a surface argument, hiding discontent which went back to the 1955 merger that many building trades leaders had sullenly opposed. The discontent was worsened by the federation's efforts to clean up corruption within the labor movement. The corruption issue touched the three biggest unions in the Building and Construction Trades Department: the International Brotherhood of Teamsters, the United Brotherhood of Carpenters, and the International Union of Operating Engineers. The building trades were the chief complainers against Meany's policy of accepting the Senate investigation, and of expelling corrupt unions. Pressing the jurisdiction issue was one way of putting pressure on Meany and the industrial union leaders who supported his policy.

With a year and a half of the two-year period to achieve state unity already gone by, only two meetings had been held between the negotiating committees of the Michigan AFL and the Michigan CIO.

The Michigan Federation of Labor at its June, 1957, convention faithfully reflected its teamster-craft union domination by voicing its support of Hoffa, whose questionable activities were under attack by the AFL-CIO Executive Council. "The Michigan labor movement has benefitted through the years" from Hoffa, read a convention resolution passed with a rising ovation. "He has always stood side by side" with us; let us "give him a unanimous vote of confidence" and "support him in every way in his present difficulties." Michigan Federation of Labor President Dean claimed Hoffa was the most outstanding labor leader he had ever met in Michigan; "I know nothing detrimental about him."

Michigan Federation of Labor Secretary-Treasurer Thorpe interpreted the lack of progress toward unity in this way: "After we brought up the question of jurisdiction, the CIO officers disqualified themselves as having no authority to discuss matters of jurisdiction. So we felt," he reported to the Michigan Federation of Labor convention, "that it would be a waste of time to meet further until we could discuss the things that have kept us apart, namely jurisdiction."

The Michigan CIO had another viewpoint: "It is unfortunate that Hoffa and others are injecting the spurious issue of jurisdiction even after it has been clearly pointed out that this question is not within our province," said Gus Scholle. The "arbitrary refusal" of the Michigan Federation of Labor leaders "to discuss anything on the merger outside of jurisdiction indicates that they want to prevent unity for reasons best known to themselves."

When the AFL-CIO met in Atlantic City two years after merger, the big news of the convention was the expulsion of the Teamsters union from its ranks. But, in the excitement created by that issue, the AFL-CIO leaders were not unaware of the other duties imposed upon them by the merger constitution. Reviewing the more than a dozen states where merger had not been achieved on the state level, the Executive Council empowered President Meany to extend the deadline, but also authorized him to proceed against affiliates which had failed to merge in accordance with the 1955 convention agreement. The constitution's "sudden death" provisions gave the president of the AFL-CIO power to revoke charters of the recalcitrant state bodies and order special conventions to which he could dictate unity terms.

Michigan was chosen as the first of the recalcitrants to receive special treatment from the national office. First Meany assigned special representatives to assist the Michigan state bodies in an attempt to reach voluntary unity terms. They were Peter McGavin, formerly of the AFL, and R. J. Thomas, one-time president of the CIO United Auto Workers. McGavin and Thomas arranged a meeting December 19 in Detroit with the merger committees of the two organizations. The eleven-member Michigan Federation of Labor group included four members of the Teamsters whom McGavin and Thomas said they "would not and could not" allow to participate because of the expulsion of the Teamsters from the AFL-CIO two weeks earlier. The Michigan Federation of Labor committee walked out.

John Thorpe, secretary-treasurer of the Michigan Federation of Labor, said he had never been informed officially that the International Brotherhood of Teamsters was out of the Federation. The next day in Washington it was announced that the AFL-CIO was mailing formal orders to state and city central bodies to expel the International Brotherhood of Teamsters, the Bakery and Confectionary Workers' International Union, and the Laundry Workers International Union, all of which had been ousted for corruption by the AFL-CIO convention earlier in the month.

A hearing was then set up for January 13, 1958, in Detroit in accordance with the "Rules Governing Merger of State Bodies" to make one last determination whether there was a possibility of voluntary merger. Meany named two vice presidents of the AFL-CIO, Joseph Keenan, secretary-treasurer of the International Brotherhood of Electrical Workers, and L. S. Buckmaster, president of the United Rubber Workers, to be in charge of the procedure.

At the hearing, a representative of the Michigan Federation of Labor read a prepared statement accusing the Michigan CIO of stalling merger talks; the Michigan Federation of Labor asserted that jurisdiction was not the main question in the dispute "as has been reported." Scholle in turn presented a record of correspondence and verbatim minutes of the two merger meetings to show the contrary. Keenan suggested that there be a meeting of five from each side to make one more attempt to work out a voluntary merger. When the Michigan Federation of Labor named a member of the International Brotherhood of Teamsters as one of the five, Keenan ruled him unacceptable. The MFL representatives thereupon left the room for a long conference with members of the MFL executive board who were waiting outside. At length, they announced that they would not remove the teamster, and were calling a special meeting of all affiliates of the Michigan Federation of Labor for February 1 in Lansing to rally forces against merger.

With all hope of voluntary merger thus dashed, plans went forward for the first shotgun wedding of state central labor bodies. On February 4, AFL-CIO President Meany cancelled the charters of both the Michigan Federation of Labor and the Michigan CIO Council and issued a charter for a new Michigan labor organization to be set up at a special convention called for February 24 in Grand Rapids.

Meanwhile the anti-merger meeting of the Michigan Federation of Labor on February 1 brought out more than five hundred delegates. The organization's merger committee recommended that affiliates boycott the convention called by Meany to begin February 24. Only six were counted against the recommendation when a standing vote was taken.

The meeting further agreed that the Michigan Federation of Labor should "refuse to disclose the membership of affiliated local unions to President Meany or his representatives for the purpose of calling a meeting for merger with the Michigan CIO." And a further resolution was adopted ordering MFL officers to take steps to protect the resources and assets of the Michigan Federation of Labor and not to surrender them without convention approval or a court determination.

In spite of this apparently overwhelming opposition by the Michigan Federation of Labor to the unity convention, officials of the AFL-CIO were confident that the meeting would take place with a good representation from AFL unions. Credentials were sent from Meany to all locals in Michigan on the basis of information provided by international unions. Complete co-operation was obtained from some AFL unions which had long favored merger but had had no opportunity for an effective voice in the ruling body of the Michigan Federation of Labor, its executive board. Largest of these were the Allied Industrial Workers, the American Federation of State, County and Municipal Employees, and the International Association of Machinists. Some of the building trades unions, such as the Bricklayers International Union, the Operative Plasterers' and

Cement Masons International Association, and the International Hod Carriers, Building and Common Laborers Union, urged participation. In addition, some locals of unions which officially opposed merger had never agreed with their spokesmen and were eager to come. And finally, many locals which had been willing to abide by the policy of the Michigan Federation of Labor up to this time were loathe to be left out of the big event.

In an effort to forestall attendance at the merger convention, the Michigan Building and Construction Trades Council called a meeting in Lansing for Monday evening and Tuesday, February 24 and 25, the first two days of the gathering in Grand Rapids. But some of the delegates said they would go on to Grand Rapids as soon as the Lansing meeting ended.

During the first two days of the convention in Grand Rapids, Peter McGavin, Meany's personal representative, served as chairman, and R. J. Thomas as secretary. They had appointed a constitution committee consisting of sixteen members, ten from the Congress of Industrial Organizations and six from the Michigan Federation of Labor, and other committees in about the same proportion, with an attempt made to get a distribution of members throughout the state and from different unions.

Scholle and Hopkins, president and secretary-treasurer of the old Michigan CIO Council, were elected to the same posts in the new organization. The new constitution created a third major office, that of executive vice-president, which was filled by George Murphy of the Allied Industrial Workers. He had been the only member of the executive board of the old Michigan Federation of Labor who had consistently advocated merger of the two state bodies.

When the convention objected to accepting the complete slate for the forty-man executive board recommended by the committee, the chairman opened the field to nominations and twenty-three additional names were on the final ballot. Results were as the committee recommended, however, with approximately one-third of the seats going to those from former AFL unions and the rest to those from the former CIO.

Considering the unhappy history of negotiations between the AFL and the CIO in Michigan, the turnout for the unity convention was impressive: 1,125 delegates from 531 local unions and six county labor councils. Former AFL locals represented at the convention numbered 223 from forty-five international unions. Former CIO locals totaled 308 from twenty-six internationals.

Not all details were tidily disposed of by February 26, 1958, the final day of the merger convention. Most of the building trades unions continued their refusal to become dues-paying members of the state organization, though it was far from a 100 per cent boycott. And the MFL officers continued to resist the Meany directive that they, like the CIO officers, should turn over for the new organization the "funds, properties, books and assets" of the now defunct Michigan Federation of Labor. Legal proceedings were begun, but in May, 1958, the matter was settled out of court. The Michigan State AFL-CIO established its Lansing offices in the building that was once the property of the Michigan Federation of Labor, and its Detroit offices in former property of the Congress of Industrial Organizations.

Upon the dissolution of the Michigan Federation of Labor, George Dean retired and the International Brotherhood of Teamsters hired John Thorpe as its legislative representative in Lansing.

While the creation of a merged labor federation in Michigan did not solve all the internal problems of the Michigan labor movement, it did bring the state structure into line with the structure of the national AFL-CIO. It provided the vehicle for locals of all internationals to work together in the state. Many building trades local unions continue to remain unaffiliated with the state organization, but there is by no means a complete boycott. And nearly all the former AFL unions which were not in the building trades became part of the merged state federation in substantial number.

The national AFL-CIO had demonstrated its authority to enforce state mergers in compliance with its constitution, and the resultant Michigan State AFL-CIO has been no less effective than most state labor bodies in the country.

Few would dispute the fact that Michigan's cultural accomplishments compare favorably with those of other states in the Midwest. Yet while all of the middle western states can boast about their fine museums, universities, libraries, and symphonies, only Michigan can point with pride to one of the most unique institutions in the history of the fine arts in this nation, that example of the artistic vision of one amazing individual, Interlochen. In 1928, Dr. Joseph Maddy of the University of Michigan's School of Music founded the National Music Camp at Interlochen. Today Maddy's dream "has grown into an internationally famous educational center for the arts, touching the lives of some 2,300 young people each summer in the National Music Camp and providing quality education to over 300 students each winter in the Arts Academy." As the eminent concert pianist and member of Interlochen's Board of Trustees Van Cliburn notes in this reading, Interlochen is more than another educational institution; it is a triumph of mind and spirit.

The Spirit of Interlochen

VAN CLIBURN

Suddenly each summer on the lake shores of northern Michigan a living truth is rekindled. I have felt its glow all the way around the world, across continents and across borderlines that let down their barriers only for those who know the universal password.

In Berlin, Moscow, Helsinki, Munich, Vienna, I have watched in wonder, and often with a throb in my throat, as the glorious music of Brahms or Beethoven or Tschaikowsky or Richard Strauss suspended national enmities and softened the look in men's eyes.

I am no politician. I am a pianist, an American from Kilgore, Texas, who has had the privilege and the responsibility of playing for many peoples of the world. And of this I am sure: If there is a universal language, it is music.

Nowhere in the world, in my opinion, is there a place—or a man—turning out more musical missionaries for peace than Dr. Joseph Maddy's summer music camp at Interlochen, Michigan. On my concert tours I am constantly meeting former Interlochen students. Interlochen is a magic word in the music world and I have felt its impact long before I became personally acquainted with it.

In the winter of 1961 while I was in Chicago making a recording, my mother telephoned me to ask a special favor. Would I agree to play a benefit concert at Interlochen the following summer? I knew, of course, that Interlochen was the home of the National Music Camp. And though I was well aware of its fine reputation and influence on American youth, I frankly was not enthusiastic over the idea of a summer camping trip. I would have to interrupt a concert tour for the benefit performance. And I was scheduled to leave for another European tour that summer; I simply could not afford the time.

But my mother, who taught me until I was seventeen and who is passionately interested in her own pupils as well as all young

From Van Cliburn's "Foreword" to Norman Lee Browning, *Joe Maddy of Interlochen* (Chicago: Henry Regnery, 1968), pp. xv-xxi. Reprinted by permission of the Trustees of the Interlochen Center for the Arts and President Roger E. Jacobi.

people, is also a very persuasive woman, and she has a sixth sense about such things. Several of her own pupils had attended Interlochen. And she had just met Dr. Joseph Maddy, who, she told me, had come all the way to Kilgore to invite me to Interlochen. My mother is an excellent buffer for me, a strict disciplinarian, and not given to burdening me with extra work in the middle of a concert tour. She said, "Please, won't you do this for Dr. Maddy? I just have a good feeling about it." It was her sixth sense in action.

I didn't know Dr. Maddy. The telephone bill was mounting. I finally compromised, with great reluctance. "I'll do it for you," I said.

That summer, just before the music camp opened, Dr. Maddy telephoned me to discuss the program. He said the students wanted me to play the *Tschaikowsky B Flat Minor Concerto*, and he told me I would be accompanied by a hundred-and-eighty-piece high school orchestra.

After recovering from the shock, I managed to inquire, "Did you say one hundred and eighty?"

"That's right," he said matter-of-factly.

"What are you going to use for amplification—for sound?" I asked, thinking of one piano amidst the din of nearly two hundred amateur musicians.

"Oh, don't worry about a thing," Dr. Maddy replied. "Everything will be all right."

Between then and the time I arrived at Interlochen I was frantic. I had never had occasion to play with a high school orchestra. Never had I been accompanied by a throng of young student musicians. So it was with the greatest trepidation and bewilderment that I sat down for our first rehearsal, taking my place at the piano in front of those earnest and silent hundred and eighty youngsters in their blue corduroy uniforms.

When it was finished, I knew that here was something quite extraordinary. These young musicians, still in their teens, would do credit to some of our professional symphony orchestras. I felt like sitting down and immediately writing recommendations for some of them.

We played the Tschaikowsky that summer; and the following summer, 1962, I needed no persuasion to interrupt a busy schedule once more and return to Interlochen for another benefit concert. This time they especially chose the *Rachmaninoff Third Piano Concerto* because it is difficult and rarely played. I knew it would be a challenge to these young players, and I thought they would enjoy playing it. With only one week of rehearsals before I arrived, and only two rehearsals with me, those youngsters came through as if they had been seasoned troupers. It was one of the most memorable experiences of my professional career.

If I live to be ninety I will never forget the way they played. I doubt whether any other high school orchestra has performed the *Third Rachmaninoff*. Yet the youngest member of that Interlochen orchestra was only thirteen. He was a little second violinist and looked barely out of swaddling clothes. Five others were fourteen, and the oldest one was only eighteen. Believe it or not, there was no supplementation by even one faculty member. . . .

But how can one express the wonder of Interlochen? No one can truly translate it for others. I can only say that in a world which deals so much, for expedience's sake, in tinsel and material values, there is something fine and wholesome and splendid and altogether overwhelming in the euphony of sixteen hundred young boys and girls delighting in the wonders of great music. Any man who can do this for young people bears the mark of genius, and a nation fortunate enough to have an arts center like Interlochen can look to the future with hope.

For it is not in the least necessary that all young people with a talent for music become professional musicians. It matters little whether or not Interlochen students use their musical training professionally in their later life. They had been trained, with discipline and trust, for leadership in life as well as in the arts. And somehow you can always spot them. They may be doctors, lawyers, businessmen, or civic leaders. They're usually prominent in their communities, performing in local orchestras or chamber music groups and helping guide the cultural life of the community.

I think what has impressed me most about Interlochen is that it is so uniquely American—a music center for youth operating within a framework that gives daily expression to the God-fearing ideals and traditions held by our forefathers. It always fills me with indignation to hear anyone call America a cultural wilderness. Part of the reason we have acquired this reputation is because of our political persuasion not to have any interference from a central government. Our cultural achievements have traditionally come about mainly under private auspices, and this is good. I feel it is very much to the credit of the American people that they can contribute to the cultural life of their communities without government subsidies. I am not for government support of the arts. The national workshop of music at Interlochen is, of course, a privately sponsored institution operating without the helping hand of government, local, state, or national. And its over-all theme, boldly emphasized in every facet of this mammoth organization of music for youth, is strictly and refreshingly American. It is simply: in order to make progress one must keep working.

These young musicians learn very quickly that today's achievement does not assure tomorrow's success. The orchestra, for example, holds competitive examinations each week to determine each player's ability and qualifications to hold his position. Age and tenure make no difference. When a fifth chair player thinks he is good enough to challenge a second or first chair player he may do so, and the best man wins. A player may move up or down only one or two or maybe a dozen chair positions at a single competitive tryout, depending on his ability—and probably the length of time he has practiced the previous week. It may be a nerve-wracking procedure, but the young musicians soon learn a lesson that they definitely must know before embarking on life's greater competitions.

Equally important, after the weekly competitions are over and the coveted chair positions are won, it then dawns on these youngsters that the winning of their goal was not the end but only the beginning. For next week they must strive for greater objectives.

For most of these youngsters their first love is music. Their enthusiasm, their energy, and their consequent skill evoke the attitude of seasoned professionals, but without the professional's ofttimes blasé or jaded world-weariness. No finishing school has dampened their enthusiasm. No critic has made them cautious. The spirit of the invincible conqueror is with them, and when they look at you, they look not only with their eyes, full face, but with their hearts, and a smile and a maturity quite uncommon for teenagers. This was one of my most memorable impressions on my first visit to Interlochen, and I noticed it again, even more acutely, during my return. These youngsters look back at you full in the face, in the eyes. They never appear cowed or timid or shy like so many this age. They are gracious, mature, and human. I think music does this for them.

You will never find the young musicians at Interlochen discussing music in a spirit of pseudo-intellectual snobbery to impress others. They're discussing it because they love it. And they sing and play and practice music from dawn to dusk partly because it's the rule of the school—but chiefly because they want to.

No guest artist or conductor ever appears on the Interlochen concert stage in the usual formal attire, white tie and tails. It is traditional for guest artists to wear the Interlochen uniform. The boys wear blue corduroy trousers and the girls wear blue knickers. They wear blue shirts on weekdays, white shirts on Sunday. I never thought I would live to see the day when I would play a concert in corduroys and shirtsleeves! The outdoor Interlochen stage is the only place I have ever performed not in full formal concert attire. I can't tell you what the audiences—and they were huge—thought, but I can tell you how I felt. The workshop spirit of Interlochen was so *present*, and the seriousness of those young people was so inspiring that formal concert dress could not have made the performance more dignified, for it already had achieved its own dignity.

In this spirit Interlochen has become a special corner of America that is kindling sparks in the youth of our land, and even in distant parts of the globe. For its influence is felt throughout the world: former students appear as far away as the Vienna and Munich Youth Symphony Orchestras; they contribute notably to our fourteen hundred professional orchestras; and they hold first chair positions in many of the world's major symphonic groups. Other music camps have mushroomed, patterned after Interlochen. One of these, the Transylvania Music School at Brevard, North Carolina, was founded by a former Interlochen student.

With my own feeling for music and for all people who share it, I have no hesitancy in saying that America should be proud and grateful for this vital training ground where our nation's youth learns not only music but universal values. Interlochen is a proving ground of responsibility, endurance, and growth. It is a significant example in our time of youth at its best, and of individual, competitive freedom. Too much of this has vanished from the American scene. We should cherish these young people who can look you straight in the eye, and at the same time I take great pleasure, as we all should, in saluting this extraordinary man, Dr. Joseph Maddy, whose dreams and pioneering spirit keep the thread of music and youth fastened to the stars.

The story of the Detroit sound is that of Motown, and the story of Motown is the story of Berry Gordy, Jr. Gordy started out as a worker in a Detroit auto plant and a part-time song writer and, with the help of his family and a $700 loan, built Motown into a million-dollar industry. His success is at least partially responsible for the introduction of Negro music, sung by Negroes, into the white music market. For a greater part of the 1960s, the Motown sound, sung by the Supremes, the Temptations, Stevie Wonder, and many others, was one of the best selling types of music in America. Yet this story of success has had its unhappy side for Detroit. By July of 1972, Berry Gordy and company had moved at least half of their operation to the West Coast, and had branched out into films and other entertainment fields. The Motown sound can still be heard on the radios of Detroit listeners, but this model of black capitalism at its best is now a memory for the Motor City.

The Big, Happy, Beating Heart of the Detroit Sound

RICHARD R. LINGEMAN

At night as I stand on the other side of East Jefferson Street in Detroit, the Ford Auditorium, a long, low, blue granite-faced building with a vertical latticed metal front, suddenly looks to my wondering eyes like a gigantic hi-fi amplifier. A hallucination, no doubt, caused by my having spent two days at Motown Records, the big, happy, beating heart of the Detroit sound.

Those who think of "Detroit sound" as referring to the din of the auto assembly line intermingled with the muted wall of manufacturers announcing price increases on their 1967 models may be surprised to learn that in the pop record business the Detroit sound means the kind of music made by Motown Records, a relatively small company which sells more singles than any other company in the country.

What is more, Motown is a Negro-owned business, with mostly Negro performers and composers, whose musical style stems from what is called rhythm-and-blues music—in the past a trade euphemism for a kind of music performed by Negroes and sold mainly to a Negro market. Due in great degree to the popularity of a Motown singing group called the Supremes, Motown's records have attained national, as opposed to racial, best-sellerdom; and the company has become sort of the compact giant of rock 'n' roll, standing in relation to the real giants as George Romney's Rambler once did to the Big Three.

Why am I going to the Ford Auditorium? Why, damn it, man, I am going to the Soul Show, starring Jackie "Moms" Mabley and also a rhythm-and-blues group called Smokey Robinson and the Miracles, which happens to be the very first of many such groups

From *The New York Times Magazine*, November 27, 1966, pp. 48-49, 162ff. Copyright © 1970 by The New York Times Company. Reprinted by permission.

formed by Motown and has been with the company ever since it was founded in the late fifties by a young Negro auto worker and part-time song writer named Berry Gordy, Jr.

A word about "soul," a vogue word among Negroes having had a number of transmogrifications these days. Soul can mean a mild manifesting of race pride and social solidarity—"our thing"—a shared emotional bond of unity and good feeling. In the early sixties there was a "soul music" movement among Negro jazz musicians, most of them conservatory-trained, advocating a return to the roots of Negro music for inspiration, a return to field hand chants, work songs, funky blues and gospel rhythms on what was a rejection of sophistication in favor of strong feeling. Some even felt compelled to eat "soul food"—deep South and ghetto dishes like ham hocks and collard greens, pigs' feet, pigs' knuckles and chitterlings.

A fraternal term, "soul brother," has had recent ominous manifestations, as in the Watts riots when Negro businessmen chalked it on their stores so the antiwhite rioters would pass them by. It also operates as a commercial thing, as when New York's WWRL calls itself "soul brother radio" and gives its predominantly Negro audience a steady diet of rhythm-and-blues music, an elemental, emotional kind of popular music with a strong, pounding beat, right down to an R & B version of the Pepsi singing commercial.

Now, in the pop music field, "soul" has entered the vocabulary as a loose description of the kind of music made by invariably Negro performers, many of whom record for Motown—performers such as James Brown, Otis Redding, and the Supremes, who are Motown's star vocal group and probably the leading girls' vocal group in the world, based on their record sales and international appeal.

Inside the austerely appointed auditorium, the Soul Show opens with a white Southern comic named Dick Davey, . . . telling reverse Dick Gregory jokes slanted at the 90 per cent Negro audience. He tells of doing a show in Harlem ("They was real polite to me in Harlem. Kept calling me 'Mr. Charley' all the time.") and draws applause when he says he asked a colored dancer why she was enjoying herself so much and she replied: "Honey (infectious laugh), if you could be colored five minutes you'd never want to be white again."

Next come the Miracles, four cat-like young men attired in bright red shirts with flowing sleeves. Robinson does the solo, singing in a near-falsetto voice, and the other three back him while performing intricate, whirling figures of choreography. The choreography is a great crowd pleaser in its own right, bringing frequent cheers, and has something of the unintentional camp quality as though they had been choreographed by George Raft in the thirties and never changed since. At one point, a buttery Pearl Bailey voice wafts down from the balcony: "When you get done singing, Smoke, you come on up here."

"Moms" Mabley closes the show with some wry jokes about crime in the streets encountered while walking down "Saint Ann-Twine" (St. Antoine) street in Detroit, and tells of the poor beggar who came up to her and said in a pitiful voice: "Moms, Moms, I ain't got any money. I ain't got any friends. I ain't got any warm clothes. I ain't got nuthin' "—her voice shifts into menace—" 'cept this gun!" She closes with a pitch for brotherhood to the tune of "Together":

> If we do the right thing together
> We'll bring peace together
> No more black and whites
> Only wrong and right

—and so on. Such is the current state of soul, baby.

The offices of Motown (for Motor Town) Records are in a cluster of seven neat, middle-class brick bungalows with porches and green lawns, spaced among a funeral home, doctor's office and private residences on both sides of a wide tree-lined boulevard in a middle-class, integrated residential section of Detroit. On a fine autumn day knots of producers, song writers, performers stand around, shooting the breeze. A group of colored school kids arrives and casually circulates among the groups, collecting autographs from their favorites. Only one of the Motown buildings jars the tranquility of the scene. It is painted a glaring white and bears a big sign: HITSVILLE, USA.

Berry Gordy and his company have been a mecca for Detroit's rock and roll talent, the majority of whom are Negro youngsters who grew up in the Detroit slums, ever since he founded the company on a song ("Way Over There") which he wrote and which the Miracles recorded and which became Motown's first hit, plus $700 borrowed from his family's credit union. The Motown complex now houses four separate companies: Jubete, a highly successful musical publishing company; International Talent Management Incorporated; Hitsville, USA, which owns Motown's recording studios; and the Motown Record Corporation, which issues singles and L.P.'s under a variety of labels, including Gordy, Tama, Motown, VIP and Soul. In addition, the company has a burgeoning foreign business conducted by indigenous licensees and international distributors. The international flavor—symbolized by the globes on display in Motown offices—reflects the global scope of American teenage music today.

Though Motown is a predominantly Negro corporation, one sees a healthy sprinkling of white faces in every department and it is integrated at all levels of management. At the same time, it is still very much a family firm; there are presently 10 Gordys and in-laws now employed in Motown in a variety of positions. Gordy's sister, Esther, wife of a Michigan legislator and active in civic affairs, is vice president in charge of management and wields authority second only to Gordy in the company's affairs.

Motown began as one of a number of small R & B record companies which sprang up in Detroit during the fifties, partly in response to a demand for such music by Negro-oriented radio stations, which were also born at about the same time to serve Detroit's large (now over 500,000) Negro population. "On nearly every block in some neighborhoods," says Peter Gzowski of *The Toronto Daily Star,* a close observer of the Detroit musical scene, "there seems to be at least one small record firm, sign over door, Cadillac in driveway. Motown is the first of these firms to break into the big time."

The extent to which Motown has broken into the big time was, the week I was there, obvious for all to see: in the sales surveys that week, the company had three of its single records in the top five positions. Such a near-monopoly was unprecedented even for Motown, which has been, for the past two years, the leading vendor of single 45 r.p.m. records in the nation. When one asks Motown's controller, Edward Pollak, about the firm's income, he declines to answer on the grounds of the 16th (income tax) Amendment, but the company will probably gross about $15 million this year, according to other sources.

Such success is reflective of a growing demand for R & B music among teen-agers, who, of course, make up the bulk of single-record buyers. R & B music, once known as "race music," used to be considered music primarily for a Negro market (record-trade publications still maintain separate R & B charts, measuring air play by Negro-oriented radio stations and sales in predominantly Negro outlets). And since the strictly R & B market is limited, the name of the game is to score what the record industry calls a "pop break-out," i.e., a song played by pop "top 40" disc jockeys, and achieve ranking on the pop charts, which reflect sales in the broader mass market.

Motown's performers and composers, under the generalship of Berry Gordy, Jr., have come up with a style of music that embodies a consistent "breakout" formula, yet which still does well on the R

& B charts. Lately, other R & B artists in other cities—Memphis, Chicago, New York—are more frequently "breaking pop." As Dave Finkle, an editor of *Record World* magazine, explains, "This is due in great measure to the sound of Tamla-Motown, which created a wide market so that R & B broke across the racial barriers."

Much of the credit for the spreading of the Motown gospel belongs to three herald angels known collectively as the Supremes, and individually as Diana Ross, Mary Wilson and Florence Ballard. "The Supremes were our big breakthrough," says Motown record promotion man Larry Maxwell, whose job it is to stimulate air play and sales of Motown records. "A few years ago we couldn't make a WABC pick[that is, be selected for air play]," Maxwell recalls, "because they'd say, 'That's a blues sound.' Used to be you had 'good' music or popular music and you had 'race' music. Then you had rock and roll and you had rhythm and blues. Now Motown's bridged the gap between pop and R & B." Translated, that means that R & B was once not generally considered a pop sound, hence, no pop air play and no pop charts; now it is a pop sound, and the deejays will play it.

Of course, ever since Elvis Presley began twitching his hips, R & B has been a major influence on teen-age music. Elvis is supposed to have developed his singing style by imitating a Negro R & B performer named Arthur Crudup. The pop music that came to be known as rockabilly, a mixture of country music and R & B, has been called a "whitened" R & B. In other words, mass audiences would accept R & B only when filtered through white performers— including, recently, British performers, most of whom borrowed from Negro R & B performers.

In today's pop sound mix, the heavy reliance on electronic distortions has helped considerably to make the sources of pop music extremely eclectic. A long-time student of pop music, WMCA disc jockey Joe O'Brien, thinks R & B no longer has much meaning as either a term of classification or ethnic orientation. "These boundaries no longer mean a damn thing," he says. "You have whites out in Wasp areas buying just as much Negro music as they do white. Sometimes we play Motown records on WMCA before they do on WWRL. In today's pop music, any imaginative musician will use any style or sound. There is no longer even a straight 'white sound.' Everything is fair game—Latin, folk, country and Western, Viennese, schmaltz—you name it. Anything can be used because there's no longer a right way to make a record. Whatever works, works."

Today's pop record is a palimpsest of noninstrumental sounds; even an old hand such as O'Brien, who plays the stuff for four hours every morning, confesses that he can no longer identify the instruments used because of the use of such sound techniques as reverb, overdub and feedback. The biggest influences on contemporary pop music, O'Brien says, are Latin groups, the Motown sound, and folk music (not traditional folk, but contemporary folk by such groups as the Mamas and the Papas and the Lovin' Spoonful, who, of course, write their own folk songs). In such a climate the novelty and variety of R & B performers seem to be finding a hospitable teen-age ear.

Thanks to the Supremes and other Motown artists such as Stevie Wonder, Marvin Gaye, the Temptations, the Four Tops, and Martha and the Vandellas, as well as three of the hottest composers in the pop market, none of them over 25, named Brian Holland, Lamont Dozier and Eddie Holland (known in the record world as Holland-Dozier-Holland, or simply HDH—names with the solid ring of Merrill Lynch, Pierce, Fenner & Smith in the financial world), plus a number of other composers and producers of energy and talent. Motown has come to stand for a distinctive kind of R & B. It is so distinctive that it is known the world over as the Motown sound or the Detroit sound.

Roughly, that sound may be described as a sophisticated, slicked-up, unique R & B sound that is an amalgam of gospel harmonies, a blues beat, symphonic effects, electronic gimmickry, and a "sweet" kind of rock 'n' roll. The lyrics usually convey a sort of inspirational message or hymn the yearnings of adolescent love in a direct and energetic manner that avoids soppiness. The lyrics of "You Can't Hurry Love" may be taken as an example:

> I need love, love to ease my mind
> I need to find, find someone to call mine
> But mama said you can't hurry love
> No, you just have to wait
> She said love don't come easy
> It's a game of give and take. . . .

Gordy describes the music simply as, "a happy sound, a big happy beat with a good strong bass. Tambourines gave it a gospel flavor," he says, "but it doesn't have so much of that now."

Gordy—husky, taut, a Napoleonic head, shy engaging grin—is sitting at the desk in his paneled, darkened office. With a turntable at his side and big speakers concealed in the walls, he monitors records, deciding whether they should be released. Much of his time nowadays, he says not too happily, is spent in meetings and reading countless memos, or else traveling with his artists on tours (he had just returned from the Far East with the Supremes). But he still listens to all the company's records at one stage or another.

An assistant brings in the newest Supremes and Miracles records, and Gordy places the Supremes on the turntable, cocks his head, and turns up the volume to about 100 decibels. He sends back the Supremes, saying it needs more work, commenting: "It's O.K., but not really the one." Gordy calls my attention to the "Bach counterpoint" in the lead-in to the Miracles and suggests that the title be changed from "Come Around Here, You're the One I Need" to, simply, "You're the One I Need."

"Most people think all rock 'n' roll sounds the same," Gordy says, "but that's not true. You have to be a creative artist to decide what people will like." To prove his point, he sends for the three current Motown hits and plays a little of each, pointing out the differences and analyzing each record in a terse esthetic which is encompassed in a few words such as "strong," "good rhythm" and "that song has a philosophy."

The Supremes' "You Can't Hurry Love," No. 1 that week, has that "good rhythm," and it is obvious from the fondness with which he says it that this is the heart of the matter. Lyrics are important, he indicates, praising the "philosophy" in the Temptations' "Beauty Is Only Skin Deep":

> So in love, sad as I can be
> 'Cause a pretty face got the best of me
> Suddenly you came into my life and gave it meaning
>   and delight
> Now good looks I've learned to do without
> 'Cause I know now it's love that really counts
> 'Cause beauty's only skin deep. . . .

But most important is the sound and the successful merger of rhythm and melody. And, of course, each record must have a quality of novelty that will catch the listener's ear.

Without overpraising the musical values of the records (Motown's critics accuse its song writers of writing sounds rather than songs), one agrees with Gordy that each one is different and clever, distinctively styled and lathed to a shining chromium perfection. Perfection is another of Gordy's talisman words, and I am told that Motown will record a song 20 or 30 times and then "if it still isn't right, we'll record it 15 more times."

"A Supremes record will sell 500,000 almost automatically," Gordy says. "Kids buy their records without even listening to them.

We are putting something into their homes sight unseen so we want it to be good."

Watching Gordy in the mastering room, where the producers are editing a final tape of a Supremes record, you sense, as he helps them solve a cutting problem by clapping and stomping out the beat himself ("That's strong. Fine. Right there."), that he has that big, happy Motown beat throbbing inside him like a coiled, twanging string. He frequently hums a little bluesy tune under his breath—wooo-wooo-wooo-wooo. There's the Motown sound, on a little tape recorder playing inside Berry Gordy, Jr.'s head. Bimbimbimbimbim. Wooo-ooo-ooo-ooo. What more can one say?

But don't get the impression that Motown is a sort of hit-hazardous operation. Berry Gordy, Jr., the one-time auto worker, has built himself something of a pop assembly line. He has attracted a lot of young raw talent and created an organization capable of nurturing and polishing that talent until they become smooth, well-drilled performers who are capable of holding a night club audience, as well as catching a teen-ager's ear for a couple of minutes.

There is at Motown, for example, something called an artists' development department, whose function is to take rock and roll kids and convert them into a viable night club act. This "finishing school," as it is known among the Motown performers, employs a galaxy of veteran showmen to train the kids to make the break from the sound studio to a live performance on stage. As one faculty member says: "Rock 'n' roll shows us the plum. Our job is to bring it in here and can it."

Canning it involves teaching that intricate Motown choreography and blocking, as well as broadening the repertoire so the businessman at the Copa will hear something like "There's No Business Like Show Business" as well as "Baby, Baby I Need You" with his $7.50 steak. Portly, genial Maurice King, an experienced bandleader, either conducts the night club orchestra himself or else selects the conductor and musicians—who play Motown arrangements, of course. Gordy insists on keeping the Motown style, King says, even in the case of standards. There is also a charm school in which girl performers are taught how to sit, how to hold a fork, how to walk, how to speak. "They learn how to behave both on stage and off," says Mrs. Ardenia Johnston, the smiling, maternal lady who teaches them, with something of a school marm's glint in her eye. "I just can't tell you what Motown has meant to these kids," Mrs. Johnston says. "Some of them would have ended up juvenile delinquents if they hadn't had this opportunity."

One of Motown's most charming and accomplished finished

products is the group known as the Supremes. Since their first big-selling record, "Where Did Our Love Go?" in the summer of 1964, the three girls, still in their early 20's, have amassed a continuous string of top-10 hits (including six gold, or million-selling, records), won a worldwide popularity among teen-agers and appeared with great success on television and in night clubs.

Chic in their dazzling array of gowns (the girls call them "uniforms"), most of which are selected for them by Mrs. Harvey Fuqua of Motown's special projects department, the group is full of youthful exuberance and gives off a charming naivete. They were praised by reviewer Robert Shelton as "unusually vibrant, exultant vocalists who soar with seemingly endless energy."

Diana Ross, the lead singer, has been compared often to Eartha Kitt, but she has a flexible, sweeter style of her own that can shift gears from a gospel fervor into a romantic ballad. Florence Ballard and Mary Wilson are posted in the background, adding a vibrant, close harmony, delicately tapping their tambourines against their hips, or chiming in with jokes from time to time. The Supremes have a hard, driving quality, too, deriving both from sheer energy and an intense competitiveness; though they will boost other Motown performers with company-girl correctness, they also will give their all to outstrip them when playing on the same bill.

Such was the case at a Forest Hills Stadium concert last August. The Temptations' flashy and well-choreographed act had drawn three encores and the singing of Stevie Wonder, the blind blues singer, had drawn enthusiastic ovations. It was a simple matter of pride to the Supremes to close the bill with the greatest applause of all and, as witnesses present will attest, they went out and gave the performances of their lives. Or, as Diana put it, "We got out there and worked like hell. I wasn't really nervous until I heard that crowd screaming. It was a big shock. The audience was so far away, you couldn't see them, and I worried about that. I wanted to see everyone. I was soaking wet when we finished."

It is sometimes said about the Supremes that they have a "white sound." Diana rejects the description. "The white sound means the commercial sound," she explains a little hotly, as if to say, "This is our sound, baby, not theirs." She gives credit to British pop groups for making R & B more palatable to American audiences, but adds: "They copied a Negro sound and sang a popular version of R & B."

The girls, who grew up in Detroit's slum ghetto, have been singing together since they were about 14. They gravitated to Motown and Gordy after high school ("Everybody was talking about him," says Diana); he started them dubbing in background on records and christened them the Supremes. They began to record, while learning as much as they could from other groups. "The Temptations would teach them harmony to get them off their backs," Gordy recalls.

For a time, they were at the bottom of the Motown pecking order and were known as "the girls." (Now another, newer, group is known as "the girls.") Success began coming their way after they were placed in the hands of Holland-Dozier-Holland, who wrote their first hit, "Where Did Our Love Go?", and just about all their subsequent ones; the producing team of Brian Holland and Lamont Dozier gave their records a style and identity they had previously lacked, emphasizing Diana's voice in the solos, with Mary and Florence contributing in the harmony.

Offstage, the Supremes are friendly, rather ordinary girls with a bouncing sense of humor; their conversation is studded with little injokes about one another based on what someone had written about them. Diana seems a trifle more mature than the others, displaying an earnest, serious manner and a cool professionalism. She is almost achingly thin (size 5) with fine, large eyes set in a feline face and she speaks in a hoarse June Allyson voice. Mary is small and nicely proportioned, demure in a tan suit and frilly blouse. In conjunction with the others she tends to fade into the background, which is deceptive because she has a distinctively droll sense of humor; when she smiles, her eyes crinkle into two horizontal crescents. Florence is earthier. She is usually known as "the quiet one," but she can be outspoken in an abrupt, flaunting way if the spirit moves her.

Gordy speaks about them in a bemused, detached manner. "We had some trouble with them at first. You must be very strict with the young artists. That instills discipline. But once they have a No. 1 record they tend to get more independent. They start spending their money extravagantly." In the case of the Supremes, in their first flush of success they bought new homes with lots of expensive furniture and moved in their families.

"After a year, they saw their mistakes and came to appreciate our handling of their affairs," Gordy observes. The Supremes' money, as is the case with many Motown artists, is invested for them in a variety of business interests, stocks and bonds. Though their yearly income nowadays is in five figures—record royalties are divided equally—they have been put on an allowance of $50 a week. "If I'd been strict when they had their first hit, it would have been bad," Gordy says. "They were growing up, demanding to live their own lives, so I loosened up on them. Now they're more sensible, and they seek and appreciate advice." His brow furrows as he adds:

"I don't know what the next phase will be." Then, hopefully: "But now they're less mixed up, more relaxed about their love lives. They take more interest in learning about the world. It's amazing how they've educated themselves in their traveling."

I sense that keeping happy these volatile, ambitious girls who account for a sizable percentage of Motown's record sales is one of Gordy's important executive functions. Anyhow, he spends a lot of time with them on the road. "Every company has trouble with its artists," he says. "It's always the little things that blow up. If the little things can be cleared up before they get big, trouble can be prevented."

Next day, at Diana's home—a comfortable, two-story brick affair—we have coffee and doughnuts in a shiny kitchen that has an air of unopened newness and Diana muses that she has never cooked on the stove or even sat down in the kitchen, so rarely is she at home. Her mother, Mrs. Ernestine Ross, used to travel with the girls as chaperon, but now stays home to devote more time to Diana's youngest brother, Chico. When it is time to go, Florence and Mary are collected at Florence's home, which is diagonally across the street from Diana's (Mary lives down the same street). Then, with a minimum of fuss, the girls gather their luggage for an engagement in Las Vegas, pile into the station wagon, wave good-by and vanish.

Florence's oldest brother, Cornell, a husky good-natured chap who is an investigator with the Michigan Department of State's driver improvement program, takes me to meet Florence's mother. She is a stout impassive woman and Cornell kids her about becoming "more glamorous, more outgoing," now that her daughter is a singing star. "Why, you never used to leave the house—did you?" he asks.

"I'm going to the Rooster Tail Monday," Mrs. Ballard says, a calm, satisfied smile on her face. "I'm going to Puerto Rico in March with the girls. I want to go to New York, too. I've never been to New York."

Back at Motown, I say good-by to Gordy. We are standing on the sidewalk; the knots of producers, writers and performers are gathered as usual. Gordy answers a question about the white HITS-VILLE, USA building, and explains that he used to live there. The company's grown a lot since then and is planning to build a new office building in Detroit.

Gordy worries about things like a shortage of executive talents, and outgrowing the present staff. "Yes," he says, "we've expanded from that one building. Now, of course, we've got . . . we've got—"

He is stumped. "How many buildings do we have now?" So Berry Gordy, Jr., pokes out a finger and begins counting the number of buildings at present making up his Motown record corporation.

During the past half century Michigan voters have had the opportunity to express their opinions on a variety of political, social, and economic issues, particularly various types of taxes, the size of state legislative districts, and a new state constitution. In May, 1972, the state's citizens also had the chance to express their candidate preferences in a presidential primary. The result of the vote cast assured Michigan's voters, at least a majority of those who voted in the Democratic primary, a place in the nation's political history. For the first time the citizens of a northern state cast a majority of their primary ballots for Alabama's favorite son, Governor George C. Wallace. The reasons why a Michigan voter would cast a vote for Wallace are more than adequately spelled out in the following newspaper feature by *New York Times* writer Nan Robertson. The fears and frustrations of Redford Township's Dewey Burton, however, are hardly atypical; indeed, Burton's opinions are shared by millions of other middle-class Americans.

A Michigan Man Votes for George Wallace in the 1972 Presidential Primary

NAN ROBERTSON

DETROIT, May 13—Dewey Burton is going to vote for George C. Wallace for President in the Michigan primary on Tuesday.

He is 26 years old, short and thick, with a gravelly voice and a gap-toothed grin. He lives with a warm-hearted, pretty wife, a rollicking 5-year-old son, a scramble-footed Great Dane puppy in an immaculate bungalow he owns in Redford Township, a white working class suburb on Detroit's western edge.

He struggles out of bed at 4 a.m. five days a week. He drives 20 miles to the Ford Motor Company plant at Wixom. His job begins at 5:42 a.m. as the first car moves past him on the assembly line. It ends at 2:12 p.m. after he has wiped clean one side of 217 Thunderbirds, Mark IV's and Lincoln Continentals before their first coat of paint.

He then drives his beat-up 1960 Thunderbird back to the tiny house with the orchid colored front door and a plaster reproduction of Rodin's "The Kiss" near the living room sofa. After supper, he goes to his neighbor's garage to work long hours on the family heirloom—a shark-nosed 1963 Stingray he "customized" himself. The neighbor, thrown out of work 18 months ago, has posted a sign by his back entrance: "Our God Is Not Dead—Sorry About Yours."

A Man of Contrasts

Dewey Burton is a man of contrasts: independent, energetic and sensitive, yet seeming old and trapped.

He is in love with cars; he hates his job at the auto plant, which he finds boring, brutalizing and endlessly repetitive.

He is smart, driving, a compulsive worker, spilling over with ideas; he cannot be promoted.

He does not read newspapers; but he speaks his mind and his friends listen.

He resents welfare cheats; he was on welfare as a child after his parents deserted him.

He calls the black man who is president of his local union "the best president we've ever had." He has no qualms about his son David going to school with blacks. And if a black family moved on his block—and he would not object—he bets they would take better care of their home than the white folks on welfare down near the corner, whose conduct scandalizes him.

But he is violently opposed to busing, even one-way busing that would bring black children into his son's school three blocks away, saying:

"My child will never be bused into Detroit or anywhere for integral purposes. Busing—that's the only issue I'm interested in. It's the biggest issue in this campaign."

A Liberal Tradition

Like Dewey Burton, there are hundreds of thousands in the state of Michigan who will vote for George Wallace in Tuesday's primary—and they will make the Alabama Governor the most important political phenomenon in this traditionally liberal state.

Dewey Burton will count for not one vote but four. He is the undeniable head of an affectionate, trusting, but disheartened family that could include his wife, Ilona, a platinum blond with a 5,000 watt smile; his mother-in-law, Violet Kish, a lickety-split talker who makes Edith Bunker of "All in the Family" seem positively taciturn by comparison; and his father-in-law Stephen Kish, who works at Detroit Edison by day and is a gas station attendant at night.

As Mr. Burton votes, so will the three others.

He buys a Sunday newspaper mainly to pore over the classified ads for hotrods.

But there are about 150 books in his house, ranging from Jean-Francois Steiner's "Treblinka," through volumes on algebra and trigonometry, Erich Segal's "Love Story," Gordon Seagrave's "Burma Surgeon," and "Inside the Ku Klux Klan."

Mr. Burton rarely watches television. Saturday nights, however, he and his wife invariably sit down to watch "All in the Family."

We Call Him 'Archie'

"We all call him 'Archie' now," Mr. Burton said. "He's a fool. He's taken hate and bigotry and turned them into the most fun things I know. It's like Mark Twain's satire—it's hilarious."

It is one of his few diversions. He has not had a vacation since he and Ilona went to Niagara Falls on their honeymoon eight years ago—work has been his whole life.

He was born in Detroit of Southern parents who were on the verge of divorce. When he was 3 days old, his mother turned him over to his grandmother, who lived in Mount Vernon in southern Illinois.

It galls him to this day that, when he was 11, he and his grandmother spent Saturdays packing rice, beans and flour at the welfare outlet to get a pound of cheese in pay. "Then those guys setting on their cans all week at home came in to pick up their food. We didn't get no meat or cheese because I wasn't her legal child," he said.

Now there is the white welfare family on Mr. Burton's block in Redford—an unmarried mother with eight children and many male visitors. Mrs. Kish railed against them: "Filthy-mouthed, busted for drugs, kicking in the storm doors, boys turning into girls. There she is, having a ball in bed every day and we got to go out and work our tails off for them. They're giving America away free."

The young Burton was sent back to Detroit when he was 12, supported by an aunt. That year, he was putting roofs on houses for $1 a day. Other jobs followed: short-order cook, gas station attendant, playing drums and guitar in bars in a band that he formed at the age of 16.

He became a "line rat" at Ford's Wixom plant when he was 18 years old, full of hope for the future. His son David was born. Five years ago, he and his wife bought their bungalow for $14,800.

"There are two things you buy a home for—how close you are to a school and how close you are to a shopping center," Mr. Burton said. "What burns me to the bottom of my bones is that I paid an excessive amount of money so that my son could walk three blocks to school. I'm not going to pay big high school taxes and pay more for a home so that somebody can ship my son 30 miles away to get an inferior education."

But he also insists "if a black mom and daddy buy or rent a house here and send their kids to David's school and pay their taxes, that's fine."

"Busing black kids to white neighborhoods and white kids to black neighborhoods is never going to achieve integration. It's upsetting. It's baloney." He went on. "Who's going to pick up the tab for the buses? I'm going to wind up paying part of it anyway."

Only his family, and cars, give him solace now. Mr Burton spends almost all of his time outside the factory fashioning cars into wondrous shapes and painting them with exotic designs and colors: candy apple, diamond dust, metal flake, pearl. He can build a car from scratch.

For three years, while his wife took one job after another, including hiring out as a maid, Mr. Burton struggled toward an industrial management degree in a community college, going "half whipped" to his regular job. Often he would be able to snatch only two hours of sleep, parked in his car at the plant after the night shift before going to early morning classes. In late 1970, he quit six months short of "that piece of paper" and it almost broke his wife's heart.

Last year he spent six months trying to run a small bumper and paint shop—"Dewey's Custom Illusions"—on the side. It went bankrupt.

He passed tests for foreman and skilled trades apprentice, but he's never moved up. He's still at what Ilona bitterly calls "a dummy type job."

'I Hate My Job'

"I hate my job. I hate the people I work for. I hate having to drive so far to work," he said. "I'm doing the same job as the fellow working across from me and he quit in the eighth grade. It's kinda stupid to work that hard and achieve so little."

"Once you're there, there's no other way to make as much money and get the benefits. Ford's our security blanket. I'm a scaredy-cat. If I leave, I lose eight years seniority."

During those years at Wixom, Mr. Burton has been given every kind of work on the line except what he wants to do most—the difficult status job of painting cars with a spray gun.

What his wife calls his "mouthing off" at the plant has led to a bad record of disciplinary actions for what seem to be minor infractions of the rules. His foremen find him "pushy" and much too outspoken about his complaints.

At the age of 26, Mr. Burton feels exhausted and deeply frustrated. He has arthritic gout. His wife has an ulcer.

Backed Humphrey in '68

The Burtons think his wages—his gross pay was $189.90 last week and his take-home pay $134.68—are enough to carry them. But "I don't have no self-satisfaction in my job," the husband said.

In 1968, Mr. Burton voted for Hubert H. Humphrey, "as a union man coming from a long line of F.D.R. Democrats."

"People have been telling me since I was a child that when the Democrats were in office, everybody was put to work," he said.

He thinks President Nixon means unemployment but he would not vote for Humphrey now. The reason is that he is convinced that Mr. Humphrey "said right here in Detroit, in simple, plain English, 'I believe in forced integration through busing.' I will not send somebody to the White House who doesn't represent what I believe in."

"I used to think Muskie was one candidate for me. He seemed to be a guy who could stop and look sensibly at things. But all of a sudden I began to feel it was just his way of talking around issues and not taking a stand. He's not a decision maker. If you're President, whether you decide right or wrong, you've got to make decisions 24 hours a day."

"McGovern to me is like a dark shadow—like McCarthy—he strikes me as the kids' candidate."

Mr. Burton, never a soldier, does "not give a deadly damn about the war."

"It has never concerned me," he said. "People getting killed concerns me. When this war is over, there'll be another one. Maybe it's because it keeps big industry going, keeps people employed."

"The trouble with this war is that we're not fighting a Hitler or

Mussolini or little slant-eyed Japs who bombed Pearl Harbor," he said. "We're fighting a civil war. You see 30 Vietnamese running down a road in the newsreels and you don't know if they're friends or enemies."

Mr. Burton has never seen a Presidential candidate, or been to a political rally, or even put on a button or a bumper sticker.

But he'll vote Tuesday. He will vote against the dreariness of his dead-end job, the threat to take his child away, and the dollars he thinks he's forced to pay to support welfare drones.

Dewey Burton knows only one way to protest now:

"I'm for Wallace."

4: Reflections on Growing Up in Michigan

Long ago novelist Thomas Wolfe told us that we can't go home again, and in many respects Wolfe's admonition is probably quite accurate. Yet on another level, a level that might be called the autobiographical urge or tendency, many of us do go home again, at least in the realm of memory. Today Americans seem to be more than mildly obsessed with a desire to recall earlier, less complex times as witnessed by the box-office success of such films as "The Summer of '42" and "The Last Picture Show."

The first two of the final three selections are quite definitely of this genre in that for the authors, John Thompson and Willis Dunbar, the opportunity to reflect on growing up in Grand Rapids and Hartford respectively, gave each man an opportunity to recount with obvious enthusiasm some of the events of his youth.

Professor Thompson, who teaches English at the State University of New York, grew up in Grand Rapids during the 1940s. His chance to return home came at the request of *Harper's* editor Willie Morris, who was doing a series of articles based on a going back home theme. The Grand Rapids of Thompson's youth and the Grand Rapids of the late 1960s are obviously very different worlds, something that Thompson makes quite clear. But his beautifully written essay certainly captures a great deal of the flavor of growing up in the Furniture City.

The late Willis Dunbar, one of the state's foremost historians and for many years chairman of the department of history at Western Michigan University, was born in Hartford in 1902. During the twilight of his historical career Professor Dunbar published a book entitled *How It Was in Hartford*, an unabashedly nostalgic view of his youth in a rural Michigan community. In the summer of 1967, Dunbar also returned to his hometown and was struck not only by the many changes that had taken place but also by how much remained the same.

The final selection departs completely from our nostalgic model. For the late black leader Malcolm X, growing up in Lansing, East Lansing, and, finally, Owosso in the 1930s was, as he himself puts it in his autobiography, a "nightmare." Malcolm's boyhood memories are primarily those of fire, murder, parental disagreements, the teachings of Marcus Garvey, emotional religion, and a growing awareness that to be young and black was to be young and different in white society—in other words, to be a second-class citizen. As a matter of historical record Malcolm X spent the summer of '42 working in Small's Bar in Harlem

and preparing, as he notes, for such hustles as numbers, pimping, con
games of many kinds, peddling dope, and thievery of all sorts, including
armed robbery.

Yesterdays in Grand Rapids

JOHN THOMPSON

> *Reckoning from a tablet placed by engineers of the United States
> Government in the center of the Public Square, or Fulton Street Park,
> Grand Rapids is in latitude 42° 57' 49.02" north; and in longitude 85°
> 40' 1.65" west from Greenwich, England, and 8° 37' 13.65" west of
> Washington, D. C. Our time is therefore 34 minutes and 28.91 seconds
> slower than that of Washington. In latitude we are very nearly upon a
> line with Portsmouth on the Atlantic coast, with the interior cities of
> Buffalo, Milwaukee and Madison, and midway between San Francisco
> and Portland on the Pacific coast side. We are but very little north of the
> European cities of Madrid, Rome, and Constantinople.*
>
> Albert Baxter, A History of the City
> of Grand Rapids, *1891*

I

It used to be coming home, not going home. I would sneak in
like a thief in the night. I came on the train then, up from college in
Ohio through the flatlands and into Southern Michigan, a real milk
train. It stopped often and they loaded the domed forty-gallon milk
cans from the racks where the farmers left them by the roadbed.
There was an engine and sometimes a mail car and the milk car and
a passenger car that was like a caboose, with a coal stove in the
middle. I remember once the engineer or the fireman saying something to a man in a buffalo-check mackinaw by one of the milk
platforms and the man said, Oh, he had forgotten—with the engine
throttled down you could hear them easily. Their voices were like
lettering in the air. It was a clear cool day, probably Thanksgiving
vacation. After a while the man came back with two boxes of eggs
and handed them up to the cab. The Iron Horse snorted and we
rattled on to the next place. Retired railroaders used to deadhead
on that train just for something to do, and they were about the
only passengers. They wore vests and looked at their chained
watches a lot, as trainmen used to. It was thirty years ago.

Coming in to Grand Rapids we went through Cutlerville and past the new General Motors plant and Plaster Creek and past the sidings of the gaunt old brick furniture plants, then dead or dying, soon to be as otherworldly as Roman aqueducts, to the marshaling yards, past blown smoke and those junk-fenced backyards with dead hollyhocks and sunflowers that line all American railway tracks, and two-and-three-story wooden tenements with washings on the back railings where the outside stairs go up, and past the asphalted truckline parks where the herds of trailers rested, twice as big as boxcars and already carrying more goods than the rails did, and into Union Station.

It would not really be night and I would not really be sneaking in like a thief, because my father and my two sisters and my brother-in-law would be there to meet me. I was more like some uncaught criminal who had to go back again and again by daylight to the scene of the crime. I didn't know what the crime was. All I knew was that there was something I had to hide and that it was shameful to be that way. Now I think that what I had to hide, what I had to hide so hard it almost killed me, was that I loved them.

Union Station had a big humpbacked shed that could take six or eight trains under it. It was cold and full of the sweet smell of coke. They met me there. For that milk train, there would be no crowd, but years later after the War when I used to come in on the Pullman off the Wolverine with Dilly and maybe Robie Macauley and Joe Brewer, also going home from New York for Christmas, and the train full of college kids, all of them somebody's friends or relatives, there might be big crowds with many people one knew. There were suitcases, and eyes darting everywhere, hands waving, glad cries, hugs, jostlings, steam hissing from the airbrake couplings and every-body's breath white in the cold air of the shed, everybody talking at once, laughter, and my older sister Kathryn and my father standing there at the edge of a bottomless pit where I would fall. I could never get used to discovering again that I was taller than she, to say nothing of him. She would smile with that look on her round face that I believe now was, for that moment, simply an expression of the kind of love and pride that anyone, any woman at all, is entitled to feel for her brother who has grown up and gone away and who comes home. My father fidgeted beside her, eager but shy, grinning, ready to be told he was doing something wrong. There were, at that moment, no tears in my sister's eyes. Someplace deeper than Hell yawned at my feet and I walked straight across it on nothing but the rickety scaffold of my own loud laughter and blabber, looking around, sideways and back, counting them all, bumping suitcases, collecting and being collected, herding and being herded through the crowd. I was a steer in the slaughterhouse chute. The façade of the station was two or three blocks long, brick with tall sort of Italian Renaissance arched windows and for the main entrance a pediment with four enormous sooted Ionic pillars, and then up behind the pediment a dome with clocks in it. Union Station has been torn down now for the Expressway, which is no wonder because like so many American towns Grand Rapids by the middle 1950s had already become impossible to get to on the train.

II

All hometowns are like Troy, of course, and we all believe with the accurate faith of Heinrich Schliemann that the true Ilion, "seventh of nine settlements on the same spot," still lies there under the mere huge windy tumulus of the present. The Ilion of our childhood has little but its geographical location in common with what stands there now; and that great place established as if by the gods expressly for us to grow up in had little to do with what may have stood there before. Before? Except for Southerners and for some New Englanders, there is no Before for American children. Past, present, and future are all there in that seventh city of Ilion and not only can we excavate it easily and completely but, when we do, it all switches on like some toy city, the lights, trolleys, automobiles, people, all begin to jerk about, there are sounds, whistles, horns, songs; and all those poor little persons, switched back to life, loom once more into their Homeric order, lifting stones such as twenty men couldn't budge today. They rule our lives, rising before us shining or baleful with an intensity far beyond the weak abilities of any other time; they are as irreplaceable, they are as inimitable and yet as potent in stamping with their typed identities all mere mortals who follow them as were the ranked deities of Olympus.

> In the early days game of many kinds, and fish, were abundant; but of the native meats, except fish, the near-by supply is exhausted. Fish are yet taken from the river and adjacent waters in considerable quantities; but the bear, the deer and the wild geese, ducks and turkeys, partridges and quails, are no longer the ready victims of the huntsman for the morning meal. By the pioneers, wolves, bears, and wildcats were often encountered, and even so late as 1856 wild bear were sometimes seen perambulating the streets of the city. Deer and bears once had a "runway" crossing the river at the still water just above the rapids. But their day is long since passed.
>
> Baxter, Grand Rapids, 1891

III

—When I grew up here the Negro community was—

—Black. Let's say Black.

—I know. I'm old-fashioned I guess. Even my students have to remind me sometimes to say Black.

—Yeah. You know, as long ago as when I was a kid I never liked that word Negro. It sounded—well I guess even then it sounded like a euphemism.

—For Nigger. Or as they say down South, Nigra.

—Nigra. You can't mispronounce Black.

—With my friends, you know, in New York you're a Spade.

—Yeah, that's a little in-group word. It's getting kind of old now. You were to say that to the kids these days, it's bad news.

We talked about Small's Paradise and the Red Rooster in Harlem where, as I explained, I don't feel much at home anymore. Reggie Gatling, executive director of the Kentfields Group Rehabilitation Center in Grand Rapids, combed the splendid bush of his moustache and laughed, tilting back behind his desk. Clearly he was a very busy man and yet one so secure, even so comfortable in his total occupation—in charge not only of his Rehabilitation Center for youths, with, he says, the lowest recidivist rate in the country, but obviously involved far beyond that, a very busy executive and organizer—so comfortable that like good generals in books he knows how to live at ease in constant crisis. He can turn off his telephone and send his assistants away, if he feels like it, to chat for most of a morning with an inquiring stranger.

Reggie Gatling was amused by what I said about the old self-contained community with its ghetto and its churches and its own regulation of a complex social life under its own Captain Coe of the Grand Rapids Police Force, and amused by what I posited as the disruption of that system by the waves of immigration.

—That's not it at all. That's not what it's all about. You're all wrong. What's changed is just Black Power. We are not going to have our children destroyed anymore by white racism. We are for Black Power by any and all means whatsoever. By all and any means whatsoever. . . . Vietnam? Hell, I hope that war goes on forever. When our boys come back from there, they're trained. And they understand. They're for the Cong, all of them. . . . Sure, sure, I know. These liberals come around with their Planned Parenthood. And we run 'em out. It's genocide. We want Black babies. We told them to go to hell. You say we're ten per cent. I say we're more like forty-nine per cent and it won't be so long before we take over. . . .

Elect? Sure, we can elect a few niggers here and there. Can't elect a Black man, yet. . . . They can't find Black teachers with all the qualifications you can name, right down the line. . . . Look, I know my phone's tapped. I know what happened to Eldridge and Malcolm and LeRoi. . . .

He admires the young people today. He hadn't had that kind of nerve, to stand up to a cop and say Pig.

In music class at Sigsbee School we sang "Old Black Joe" and, *Down in the cornfield, hear that mournful sound, all the darkies are a-weepin, Massa's in de cold cold ground.* Charles Molson, small Black—not "black" of course any more than I am "white," I can see his face now, round smiling, the color of polished slate; he grins among us as we all tag along up Fuller Avenue one afternoon after school, walking Dorotha Riekse home, the belle of the sixth grade. We walk not exactly with her but in our eleven-year-old loutishness we skulk a few paces behind her where she strolls with two or three attendant maidens of her Court of Venus. Dorotha had come to us in the fifth grade from some unknown elsewhere, tall, sophisticated, in a fascinating way horse-faced, and bearing under her cashmere sweater the first pair of breasts we had ever seen on a contemporary of ours. We all fell head over heels in love with her. We sat behind her every Friday night at the movies and had a soda with her afterwards at Dutmer's, and sometimes, as we are doing on this afternoon, we walk her home: Ben Litscher, Ruben Frost, Guy Dygert, a couple of other fellows. Charles Molson is with us.

Someplace along the way, Charles drops off, and it is at this moment I look into his eyes. I too will drop off at my corner, so will each of the other boys, wishing probably each of us that we might be asked to continue on along but not expecting it. I was never in my life inside the door of Dorotha Riekse's house, never was invited to her birthday parties.

Yet when Charles dropped off there, attired in a hideous mustard-and-raw-sienna diamond-patterned sweater just like the rest of us, with corduroy or blue-serge knickers, sagging knee stockings and high tennis shoes, just like the rest of us, when he dropped off it made somehow a picture to remember always.

He is not saying anything. His round cheeks, color of polished slate, bulge in a slight and terribly complicated grin. There must have been a moment we looked at one another, a look that petrified the air along the line of sight between our two faces into an eternal rod like an iron crowbar, Dorotha and her entourage prattled on along the sidewalk under the maple leaves, and then he was gone, in this one moment that I recorded to last as long as I live. He drifts on across the street, westerly where the houses are one size smaller and less adorned with front porches and bay windows, over there where in the section of some forty or fifty city blocks the Dutchmen live and then past that the niggers.

Chuck Molson was recklessly brave in football. He wrote for our mimeographed Annual the account of the great Henry School game. *Bob Palmer got the ball and made a remarkable run which brought the ball to within five yards from their goal and Charles Cadey carried it over—Sigsbee 6—Henry 0.* Chuck Molson made the second, and, as it proved, the winning touchdown. He wore the same clothes we did and talked just like the rest of us, the way people in Michigan talk, a standard enough accent distinguished only by the peculiar slow sort of ironic intonation many of us have. In the "Jokes" section of our Annual he is immortalized thus.

Molson: "Yes, sah, I'm a great singah."
Boy: "Wheah you all learn to sing?"
Molson: "I graduated from correspondence school."
Boy: "Boy, you suah lost lots of your mail."

In high school, where we still sang "Old Black Joe" and "Massa's in de Cold Cold Ground," and where we put on a blackface minstrel show in which my girl's brother Ernie sang "Chloe," strutting in blackface with enormous painted red lips and a gold-headed walking stick, to our applause (even though stagefright pinched off most of his noisy bass voice), there, in Ottawa Hills High School, our best athlete was also Black. It was impossible for him to make any movement that was not totally a flowing forth of the most delicate grace and the most overwhelming power. My girl said she didn't care about basketball as a game but she just liked to see him move. I remember that very clearly, where, and when, and what it smelled like in the crowded balcony of the gym. He was our black panther.

And I remember as perfectly as we remember all those trivial things that somehow stir up our ignorance, that transfix and dismay the circuits of our memory like some unwelcome surge of voltage beyond their capacities, I remember that at one of those games some friend in judicious approval told me to note how carefully Bernard, when the water boy brought the one towel to the five gasping and sweating players at a time-out, how carefully but casually Bernard would flip the towel on along around the ring, and managed always to use it last. He went to college and flew a P-47 against the Germans and survived that and became a lawyer. I don't know where he is now, nor where you may be, Charles Molson, Chuck, who won the game against Henry School and whose eyes I met one afternoon on the east side of Fuller Avenue just south of Bemis Street when we were eleven years old.

Reggie Gatling recommends for the Hong Kong flu, which has me halfway down today and all the way down some other days, plenty of Scotch. We talk about this and that, and then, Well, maybe, he says, maybe he'll just go to Africa and die.

GRAND RAPIDS
Its Many Charms and Superior Advantages.

Busy, beautiful and prosperous—this describes Grand Rapids. Covering the hills and spreading over the valley of the river Grand, the metropolis of Western Michigan is a modern city. It has business houses of which any city might be proud. It has stately mansions, improved streets and twentieth century conveniences. Its public buildings are ample, its parks are spacious, its schools are up-to-date. The city is an industrial center containing many factories and is surrounded by rich farming country. . . . No city in the land offers greater advantages to the business man . . . or more attractions for the home seeker. No city in the land gives a more cordial welcome to the new comer.

Grand Rapids Illustrated, *1902.*

The only thing comparable to going home were those days of "depression" that used to dog me wherever I might be. How apt that term, for mental states and for the economic and political era in which I grew up. "A sunken place; dullness or inactivity, as of trade; dejection; sadness greater and more prolonged than that warranted by any objective reason. . . ." The simplest normal activities of everyday life slump to a halt. The wheels rust and all the pleasures of active getting and spending corrode in crusts of lethargy, introspection, memory, and the soul is left sunken as if at the bottom of a mine shaft. Even the rages that burn underneath are smothered and damped so nothing comes of them but coiling fumes too heavy to rise, too thick to disperse, great slowly-writhing hawsers of darkness, and you lie bound in them. There were days here in New York (well, now and then there still are) when I could see the flowers I love in the bowls and windowboxes withering, their leaves drying to paper, the basil pot in the kitchen visibly shriveling and turning gray, and I would not bring them water. —Now suddenly I think why it should be this particular and insignificant inability I recall. It is because when I was a boy I spent long hours spraying the lawn and watering the flower beds my father cultivated all around our lot: idle hours of daydreaming, below the level of dreams, mooning unaware over my losses and my hopeless wishes, holding in my hands the end of the long stiffly pliant hose and its unfailingly potent knurled brass nozzle.

On those days of depression, my dreams—and in depression I sleep long, long, and can be cured by dreaming enough—my dreams take me back to Grand Rapids, to the short street of small houses of wood or brick or stucco which are the allegorical mansions of my life, to the modest backyards and leafy curbsides which are its enchanted landscape.

Entire families I may never have seen since the age of ten appear charged with the grandeur of the ranked and anointed get of some belted duke or earl, and with all their patents of capability for being remarkable in each feature or gesture. Poor little Mrs. Wennemer shines so for me now. Still muddling about in the Wennemer house they left so many decades ago, next to the vacant lot where Jack O'Neill led us against the Norwood gang in snowball fights—Mrs. Wennemer's benign blank eyeglasses shine softly at me now over some platter of cookies or maybe toast spread with butter and brown sugar, in her shielded eyes some progenitive strain of the curse on the eyes of her son, Willy Wennemer, my playmate, some invisible guilt for the uptilted sidelong glare of his so wrenchingly crossed gaze.

Willy Wennemer moved away from my neighborhood before he was ten and I never thought of him again! Back, with the other drifting and voiceless shades. . . . Fluttering, twittering shades, leave me now. But look, I see them, the others, that host of nymphs and maidens, they unveil their dim transparent faces, unravished brides hovering for the blood: there is one who truly died, that tiny figure there, and is more surely buried than in the tomb of my memory alone, Geraldine Chaffee, sweet butter-cheeked girl, I used to walk past her house down on Carlton Avenue in hopes of seeing her on the porch swing, and we all went to her funeral when we were in the eighth grade. I will not speak; an old man like me might frighten such a child. Caroline Lachniet, I see you there. Eleanor Bowman and the McIntyre girls. I see Dorothy Jane Moshier, so petite, I see Jeanne Baribeau and Sara Jean Paul, Nefertete, the beautiful Sara Jean whom I did not treat well, and Barbara Dorman, Hod's girl from Central High who was such a good dancer, and Marcia Kirk-hoff, and there, dramatic even here among the shadows, Jeanne Ulrich, we thought she looked like Eustacia Vye. There is Dorotha, and Mary O'Brien, and Betty Crabbe, lovely and fresh as a pink peony, and Norma whose last name I can't remember and who kissed me when I was thirteen—she was a Catholic—and Jean Fales! Think of it, Jean Fales! Freckle-faced, long-stemmed, dashing, Faulkner might have written about her. She lived on my street for a few years, her father was an Army officer and had a Franklin touring car. She kissed me when I was fourteen. And Barbara East! We lay in one another's arms, unhappy, each of us in love with somebody else. Opulently beautiful Gwen Evans, to you I would speak, but you raise the veil and turn aside, refusing to remember. And always and forever my Bernice, who was and then was not mine, who here in the deep shadows is always seventeen. I see you now, Bernice, your sideways laughing glance, just as when you were in the bright air. So many losses cannot be good for a man. But how could I blame you? I was by no means any kind of Odysseus, and who at that age could be Penelope? Especially with no Odysseus. A man has to grow old and tough and wily to be him, or even to know much about women.

A few weeks ago, I went up Glenwood Avenue again for the first time in years (I don't know why going south was going up, on that flat street, and north was down, but it was)—when I went up and past our house, that whole world, all of it, both those two blocks, had shrunk to a fraction of its former scale, as anyone would expect. For a few years, of course, that street was not only Grand Rapids but the world. Any trip away from there carried me over distances as weird and empty as Space to land me somewhere as strange as the moon. . . .

The street itself had shrunk, the houses had diminished themselves, the yards where I used to roam as in vast pastures had all but disappeared; they had become nothing really. The little houses stand shoulder to shoulder, with space between them only for a narrow driveway to the garage at the rear of a backyard you can scarcely turn around in: big enough once for a baseball game.

If I want to know anything about these houses, even about our house, my house, my father's house, I cannot simply look at them from the window of my rented car and recall who lived here. Nobody ever lived in these dingy dollhouses! No, I have to call back from its buried depths that seventh level of Troy, and look at that lost city in my mind's eye, where it is restored to its full size and color and mystery and terror, and then how clear and simple it is. That is the O'Neills', on that side there the empty lot with the big apple tree that was Jack O'Neill's to climb in by right of seniority and to let others climb by his whim and favor (they built a double house there, goodbye apple tree, and Myron Kozman moved in upstairs), then there are the Bowmans', the Geisslers', McIntyres', Kendricks', Wolffs', and on the corner of Sherman Street the Schwanks' later to be the Logies'. So much for that side of the street.

Let me mention only one house on our side of the street. In

some summer before I was old enough to go to school they built two houses in the vacant lot next door to us. The second of these houses had a hipped roof and blue shutters. Don Webber moved in and he was my age. But one day I was walking past the house, when it was brand new, with my mother. She walked slowly and there was a nurse with us. We walked up to the corner where there flourished a magnificent fountain-top elm; an old forest giant some farmer had spared. On the way back from the corner, my mother said as we passed the new house, "That's a storybook house." I remember that because I didn't understand it, which is why we remember so many things. My mother was smiling and holding the nurse's elbow. I don't have many memories of my mother. She said, "That's a storybook house." It was a sunny day, maybe early in autumn, and I would just as soon I had died that day as any other.

In almost every house on the street there were children, nearly of an age. When Chuck and Don Webber and I invited Jack O'Neill to come along while we played Doctor with—I suppose even now it is not fair to give her name—with a little friend of ours, he declined because his was too big and might hurt her. It was Donald who instructed us in these things. He had come to the neighborhood from someplace else, into that new house the other side of Hake's, and he was full of strange lore, much of it about girls. He even claimed that Muriel across the street, who was as old as my older sister, had hair growing between her legs, but this I found unbelievable, and I still to this day think of him as some kind of crook. There is a certain sort of swindler, a glib, plausible, sexual, handsome variety of fellow you run into here and there, likely to be redolent of foreign places and of the couches of more than a few famous ladies: he is always Donald.

In a recent visit to Grand Rapids I took Susan for a drive up that street which was my world for five years, and then down around Wilcox Park where Ben Litscher lived before the Depression, and around the block at Sigsbee School, my world for seven more years. Then we drove around and looked at the houses where my friends had lived, past Johnny Nind's on Woodward Lane (another and later casualty of the Depression), and Ottawa Hills High School, up where Dave Evans lived, and we drove along all the streets I had walked all those years in high school, and back over to Sigsbee Street where my girl lived (in front of her house a Black man was shoveling his walk). I had set off with some idea that I was taking Susan on a great expedition. What happened was that even though I did a lot of doubling back it was all over before I knew it. If I hadn't managed to get the Hertz car stuck in the snow as I tried to show her the circle by Reeds Lake in Hodenpyl Woods where in the back seat of a Buick I first got layed, if I hadn't done that the whole trip would have been over in fifteen minutes. We saw everything there was to see in fifteen minutes. Such has it come to, the vast and monumented city of my youth.

IV

The real Grand Rapids is not mine. The real city is there, it actually exists, with 177,000 people in its central limits, the seventy-first city in the United States, just above Springfield, Massachusetts, and Nashville, and just below St. Petersburg and Gary. This real city has the problems of all American cities, people have moved out to the metropolitan areas, downtown is blighted, shoppers go to the great interplanetary shopping centers out on the Belt Line. It costs a fortune to get enough water, to get rid of the sewage, to build enough schools for the kids. The Black citizens want this and that. (The words "Grand Rapids" leap right out of any page of print for me, often enough in error when my glance has caught some other collocation of words with a capital G and a capital R. But now and then this flick of recognition is accurate. How strange to read, in the New York papers, about riots in Grand Rapids.)

It is often said that Grand Rapids has taken care of many of these things better than a lot of other cities. Of course there are stories about the money made off the first Lake Michigan pipeline, but the pipeline was built; and they built us a Civic Auditorium in the very depths of the Depression. There have always been capable people willing to pitch in and get these things done, and we must not take them for granted. These things get done in some parts of the world and do not get done in others. There are plenty of places on earth where they can't figure out how to bring clean water in or how to get rid of their own shit.

Rich people in Grand Rapids, unless they have some really enormous pile of inherited loot, so big it takes them two quarts of gin a day to stay on top of it, unless they are in these extremities they tend to go in for some sort of civic enterprise. And the factories are booming, printing, metals, furniture, and there is a big transport business, and the city does the banking for a large part of Michigan, and buys and sells. There are lots of jobs. You can spin along north, south, east, or west on the new expressways. Lower Monroe has been cleaned out, the old nineteenth-century buildings are gone, those odd old Germanic brick structures so pilastered and corniced and silled, replaced by parking lots and various city buildings, miniatures of the bronze Seagram Building or of some other cleancut cube on stylish stilts. . . . When I was a child, the Hearst papers on Sundays often had full-page pictures of the world of the future, with big highways zipping around through the sky like spilled ribbons and shiny buildings all over. And just such a vision our renewals all over America have confirmed. Only we never guessed how scruffy it could get down there under the expressways, how easily concrete gets shabby, how monstrous the long long ramps can be. They are nothing like those marvelous structures, real bridges over water, as we might have supposed they would be. Hearst's artists drew those aerial ribbons without underpinnings, and they didn't have to worry about litter. We never guessed that those big open spaces would have to be filled up with autos. And most of all, we never guessed at the disorientation these settings can induce. They're all just like going to New Haven. Whisk, you're off the New England expressway, and though your car slows down, your head is still going seventy miles an hour. The sign says "New Haven" all right, but what the hell is this? Is it supposed to be finished? Is this the city, or an airport, or what? What are those strange buildings standing isolated and at such peculiar angles to one another? Are there people in there? What is all this space, space, space? How do I get out of here? The urb has been Renewed by an Expert. But in Grand Rapids, maybe it will look nice. You can't say they didn't try.

D.A.R.

Each year Mrs. William Gay of the Daughters of the American Revolution donates a sum of money to be used to cover the expense of a trip to Lansing, by one representative from each Republic Club in our local schools.

This year, I was chosen to represent Sigsbee School, and on May 14th, we met at the Rowe Hotel at nine o'clock. We were all given arm bands of Red, White, and Blue ribbon. . . .

In Lansing, we went first to the State School for the Blind. There we saw blind boys and girls learning to read and write, and do various things by which they earn their living, such as typewriting, broom-making, wood-working, shoe-repairing, etc. I had not known that our state did so much for blind people.

Then we went to the State Armory, where we saw guns of all kinds. Among them was a large gun attached to an automobile. It shot bullets that weighed thirty-five pounds, and was designed to hit Airplanes.

On our way to dinner we drove through Blair Gardens, which were lovely. We had our dinner in the main dining room of Michigan State College. We had more than we could eat, so we saved our cookies to eat on the way home.

We spent most of the afternoon in the Capitol Building, where we saw
a great many interesting and historical things. . . .
*   At three o'clock, we all had the honor of shaking hands with our*
governor, Mr. Green. . . . We left for home about four-thirty, having had
a very wonderful day. —Margaret Thwaites

"His adolescence, each one's homeland," said Delmore Schwartz. Any of us could carry on forever about our high-school years, and yet those years have almost no literature worth mentioning. *The Catcher in the Rye* never seemed very real to me. Nor, I must admit, does what I observe of actual high schools seem very real. How impossible to believe that these kids we see now, fifteen or sixteen years old, our own children perhaps, are living as we lived then in a turmoil of pain and discovery and elation, living in a world of heroes and heroines, gods and goddesses really, and learning the language and customs of that country, acquiring the ways of feeling and acting which will never be lost no matter what passports we acquire and what other lands we may come to inhabit. There is never another girl like the first real girl, never such friends, never such necessary teachers.

It is a time like that period of our infancy when, so we are told, we acquire suddenly the capability of language, and toddling at our mother's apron strings we master the unbelievable intricacies of human speech, so complex in their structures and transformations that no grammarian has ever been able really to describe them. It is the greatest intellectual feat of our lives no matter who we are. If a child should miss that, if he should somehow be shut away from people when he is three and four years old, then that mysterious quickening of the lobes of his brain would be all for nothing: this is our one chance and it cannot come again.

So it may be for us in our adolescence. Yes, some people get through these years without goddesses and without gods, without much love or much dread. And I believe I recognize them, too. *Who moving others, are themselves as stone, Unmoved, could, and to temptation slow. . . .* Yes, they are the ones, *they are the Lords and owners of their faces.* And, I believe, it really is they who found adolescence to be an entire world, well, many of us were lost there and it can take years and years to get out.

There was my girl. There was my teacher, "the Chief," Mary Baloyan, fierce, generous, dark-eyed, noble, her profile that of her ancestors who wielded scimitars in Asia Minor. She taught me to read poetry and made me write things, and made me an actor in our school plays; she was so good to me, a savior of the order which can only be called that of absolute necessity. There is Dave Evans, who taught me to be a Socialist and to drink like a gentleman. I did once believe in both those noble attainments, and again it was necessary that this should have been. But I have no friends left from that age. They are still boys and girls in my archaeologist's Troy. I do not go back home to them and while I have not forgotten our clubs and our dances and our huddling in frozen automobiles it would not amuse me to recall it now. The scars of my accent still show where I came from, but that country no longer exists and I have denied it.

There was another Grand Rapids, too, this time almost the real one. Out of high school, I was still around for a while. The town was poor then. And like so many who grew up in the Depression, we never expected we would ever have real jobs. There was no place for us in the world. It was depressing. . . . Then the war came, and then after that Grand Rapids, like all of America, was flooded by the great overflowing and unreceding Nile of prosperity. My home-town was gone forever, gone for good.

The city I knew later, with Dilly and our children, when we came for so many years to wonderful homely old Gun Lake, this was no longer my hometown. It was someplace else. Oh, I could talk about it, but it was someplace else and not my hometown.

LONG-SMOLDERING FEUD IGNITES GVSC FRACAS

by Robert Alt

Grand Valley State College may be growing up.

Last week, a feud that had been brewing for months between Ottawa County officials and GVSC students erupted with the closing of the student newspaper, Lanthorn, and the arrest of its editor by the Ottawa County prosecutor's office. The prosecutor charged that the paper was obscene.

Friction between students in social organizations such as fraternities and those students who traditionally reject fraternity-sorority life increased.

While the Ottawa County police action may be unprecedented in Michigan, the feud between town and gown is traditional as is the friction between students associated with fraternities and those students highly critical of the fraternity life.

The Interpreter, *December 11, 1968*

Shall I now explain myself, shall I make clear what all my maundering in memories has been about, with scarcely so much as one real incident anywhere? It is very simple and it will not take long. There are three cities. First is the city of infancy, so tiny to everyone except to ourselves as infants; and to us then the whole world. There we learn to live among gods and goddesses, goblins and princesses, hairy giants and broad-shouldered heroes. How can we ever ourselves expect to grow so large, to learn such strange ways, to command such nourishment, such obeisances, such freedom, and such power? Sometimes it almost seems better that we should remain forever small, roly-poly, appealing, helpless, prized by them in their foolishness because, although they must never know this, we have cast a spell over them with those secret and evil energies that burn like a hidden blast furnace within our childish souls.

And also, and to the contrary, because in that world contraries don't exist, we want things to be just, to be honest and balanced and out in the open and fair! Helpless except for our secret black magic, we know as infants that we could not survive if our giants had no sense of justice. And how bitterly we know its lack. Blind goddess indeed, goddess of threats and punishments, your scales in balance were our only hope! Let justice be done though the heavens fall. Thus children will say of a table arrangement that is not symmetrical, of a picture not in balance, of a view of scenery even, "It's not fair!" (When Louise was three she said this.) When we are so very little we believe in that Ideal Justice, and then we seek it again and where do we find it, how do we make it?

And how are we ever to gain entrance into that magic land that they inhabit, that great castle where utterly transformed at nightfall they dance in their marvelous plumed masks after we have been packed off to bed? What will they do to us when we claim entrance, what will we do to them? On both sides we are murderously armed.

In our adolescence we live in another city, big, pristine, all stretched out for us. Here we search for Man, Woman, Table, Chair, and so on. How often we think we have found them, only to see that this one we have fastened on is not really Man, is not really immemorial Woman. That is not true chair nor this true table. But perhaps we do find them. . . . Perhaps we find the gods and goddesses and the wise one, the Sybil, as I found Dave Evans and my Bernice and found Mary Baloyan; and then, the next thing we know, from that city we are exiled, no sooner do we learn our way round in it than we are pushed out. Joe McGee! It took me two or three minutes to remember his name. He was a senior in high school when I was a sophomore. I think he hadn't much money, but he was desperately handsome, belonged to a classy club, and danced with all the most beautiful girls. One day, later on, by what chance I don't know, I was eavesdropping around the fringes of some talk he was having with his peers, in the drugstore or someplace. How well I knew what he meant when he said, "What am I doing? I'm savin' up my money to go back to high school." You see what had happened to Joe McGee.

Others, as I said earlier, do not conduct this search for avatars, or do not find them, or cannot remember the images of infancy so as to know how to look for them—and these, as I have said, are the lords and owners of their faces. They conduct the governments of our cities, they solve the very real and unquestionably fascinating problems of water supply, sewage disposal, fire protection, law enforcement: never doubt that these affairs demand anything less than a very alert intelligence and a determination to finish a job, never doubt that it is worth a man's time to do them. More loftily, they meet payrolls, they buy and sell, they gamble in the great game of American capitalism, they propose and they dispose. This is the real city; gods do not haunt it and no one would look there for Man, for Woman, for Chair or Table.

V

I have described three cities, three levels of our Troy. But what have I said about the third city, the real city, the actual Grand Rapids, Michigan, where every living man has to get up the rent and bring home the bacon, where there are payrolls to be met and children to be fed and housed and hauled in station wagons to the ski slopes, where fortunes and careers are to be made—where, for the citizens to contemplate if ever they go downtown, and for convention visitors to buy pictures of on colored postcards in the Pantlind lobby, there will be mounted an assemblage of sheet steel costing $100,000.

Neil Munro told me about this city. Of course I knew it was there but I didn't really know it until he told me. Neil is around thirty years old, very modern, editor and publisher of the new weekly, *The Interpreter,* and his Grand Rapids is not the Grand Rapids of the Depression, when there were no jobs, no money, no girls—when there was no Neil Munro either with whom to have a very long and very wet lunch. But then what? Neither of us can remember who it was that said America is the only country that went directly from barbarism to decadence without ever passing through the stage of civilization.

John O'Hara, Neil says, is the only writer this city makes him think of. Nobody else says anything about this kind of town. Neil is right. John O'Hara's people live all of them haunted by nothing more than the ghost of their first love affair. After that there is no place to go, and the work and the banks offer them nothing but a flat success and, rolling in money, they don't know what is wrong.

And yet we still think of the American Midwest as though it were Winesburg, Ohio. In my day, or perhaps it was really only in my own sunken place, my dullness or inactivity, my dejection, my depression—in my own city, yes, there were the lovelorn, the mute, the unequipped, the unsponsored, and the uninstructed, the frightened, a young man could hardly get layed, the girls were all married or crazy virgins who went to church. Now it's like everyplace else.

We interrupt ourselves, Neil and I, and we remark how the Grand River is about the size of the Arno, that the wealth of Florence under Lorenzo de Medici and of Grand Rapids under—but we no longer have our old city boss, Frank McKay—under whatever constellation rules it now, are not dissimilar. This is not a happy thought and we look around the dark restaurant, packed with steak eaters and bourbon drinkers and gin drinkers and think for a moment of Florence, of frescoes and bell towers and bronzes. Well, why not? Why not indeed. It is enough to make you want another martini. . . . But at least it is no longer Winesburg, Ohio.

When you go to a cocktail party now you would go not to one of those mansions I called bulgy packing crates, but to something designed by Alden Dow, elegant long tiers of brick and glass. Larry Rivers over the fireplace, both fireplace and Rivers big enough to walk into. And if not precisely there, then surely at the consecutive cocktail party you can't help it that there will be three or four girls each wanting to take you home to get screwed. And everyone is off to Paris or St. Tropez. To have your new suits made you go to New York. . . . Still, what is it for? Money flows down the troughs like swill to hogs, we can get layed, we say the old dirty words that used to be said only on the way to Baldwin on Opening Day now out loud in the presence of ladies, and the ladies say them back. . . .

This third of my cities, the real Grand Rapids, with its pavements and payrolls and sewers and school bills, its money and its jobs, its money, this city will never be real to anyone who has even the vestigial ghost of a memory of having once inhabited that first city of childhood. A city begins in dreams, or, in order that I should not sound too much like those brochures on the charms of Grand Rapids, it begins in nightmares, which are the same thing. Dreams, nightmares, they are built of the past but they are about the future. If the real city denies these, then it is not real.

Was it a good hometown? Was it? I would not have thought to say so before I began writing this, but yes, it was. I think it is a better town for Reggie Gatling's boys than it ever was for me, though. They will succeed, no doubt in ways they don't expect, but I never really tried. I thought it should be some kind of Florence, some kind of Athens, some kind of city connected with my mother's face and with Dave Evans' bitter sense of justice and with Mary Baloyan's passionate conviction that expression must be true, but I couldn't think of anything to do about it.

I don't care now, and I am surprised, really, that I can remember so much. Most of your people, Grand Rapids, are less frightened, from day to day, than most people in most places or most times have been. They are not threatened by starvation nor by whips nor by enemy swords, as most of mankind has always been threatened. If they have the supreme threat of hydrogen dissolution hanging over their heads day and night, hanging by a hair plucked from the head of Richard M. Nixon, well, we all live with this (how do we?) and who is to say that this is your fault, or who is to say that anyone knows better than you what to do about it. You are not deliberately cruel, except to yourself, as you say over and over again, "I must be ignorant, I must not aspire, I must not cast doubt, I must bring home the bacon." And yet you know as well as I do what was said in that little volume which has been one of my favorite books for as long as I have been able to read, the one from which I cribbed the title for this procession of dim reveries. In its narrow green cover it stood between the bookends under the tasseled lamp of our "library table" on Glenwood Avenue, *The Yesterdays of Grand Rapids.* Its author, Captain Charles E. Belknap, still poses in his bronze Boy Scout uniform with his bronze moustaches in the little park named for him at the fork of Fulton and Lake Drive. He was a wonderful writer gifted in natural comedy and thus he was unafraid to know tragedy when he saw it:

"Although Grand Rapids was a good-sized town when I came here, the islands were still in the river. . . . I was somewhat older before I really appreciated the great sycamores at the water's edge, the island plateau of giant water elms, the almost tropical mass of grape vine that festooned the trees, and in every depression the wild plum and crabapple that crowded the elder bushes and sumac. . . . But even then the three islands were almost without a blemish. Indians never built a fire at the foot of a tree and the high water that flooded the islands each year washed them free of all refuse of their camps. The heavy covering of grass and plants prevented washing of the soil. The prevailing west winds wafted the odors of trees and flowers over the village.

"May not an old man of today be forgiven for a longing that this beautiful playground of his boyhood might have been spared for his great-grand-children? Only men of deep thinking can tell you how long nature was in creating these islands, but any schoolboy with a piece of chalk can figure how long man was in obliterating the last trace of them."

Those islands in his dream city had actually existed, rooted in earth and watered by our river and flowering magnificently in the bright real air as well as in his dreams, but we know what he was talking about. He was talking about the city we have all destroyed, cowards, dirty cowards, our hometown of justice and truth where I was born in Grand Rapids.

A Native Returns

WILLIS F. DUNBAR

During the summer of 1967 I spent several days in Hartford just to see what the old town was like. Of course I noticed all the changes, and at first it seemed to me these had completely overwhelmed the character of the town as I had known it. None of the stores along Main Street is run by the people who operated them in my youth. Most of the names have changed, too. I found that Hartford at long last had secured several factories, which appeared to be in a flourishing state. There were supermarkets on the edge of the town, a big trailer camp, a large number of itinerant Mexican fruit-pickers on the street, a new water tower, and a large new school building, located on a different site from the old one.

But I discovered that some things had not changed. I went to see Jennette Manley, a maiden lady now in her seventies, who has devoted a lifetime to taking and collecting pictures of Hartford and Hartfordites and gathering historical information about the town. She lives in the same house where she was born, on Shepard Street. I also went to see Don Cochrane, who had been a good friend in my youth. He is the son of the man who edited the *Day Spring* when I lived in Hartford. I found him still a bachelor, living in the old Cochrane home, and as bright, stimulating, and alert as always. This set me to thinking about all the ways in which the town had *not* changed.

The layout of the streets has not been altered. There are more streets, especially north of the main stem, but chiefly they are

From *How It Was in Hartford*, pp. 218-220. Copyright © 1968 by Wm. B. Eerdmans Publishing Company. Reprinted by permission.

extensions of older streets. A good share of the homes as I knew them are still in use, with alterations, additions, and improvements. For a number of years, as traffic increased on US-12 through the town—a main highway between Detroit and Chicago—trucks roared through the village day and night, not to mention a steady stream of cars and buses. Then I-94 was built, bypassing the village on the south, taking all the through traffic off the old road, now called the Red Arrow Highway. This development restored to a considerable degree the peace and quiet I associated with the Hartford of my youth.

The *Day Spring* still comes out every week, but now it has its own building in the north end of town instead of being housed in the Olney Bank building. The old depot still stands, and the C&O even operates a couple of passenger trains each way daily. One pair operates in the nighttime, just as they did when I was a boy. There is one, which goes to Chicago, that leaves around nine in the morning, just about the hour I used to watch for it at the depot, and one headed for Grand Rapids around eight in the evening—the same time Will Saunders used to arrive in the old days. But some of these trains stop at Hartford nowadays only on signal. In my time, there always were people who wanted to take the train, and it stopped every trip. The Chesapeake and Ohio does a big freight business on the main line, and also runs quite a few freights over the branches that reach to Paw Paw on the east and South Haven to the west—the old Fruit Belt. There is a movie house on Main Street, exactly where it used to be. The election returns indicate that the town still votes almost as faithfully Republican as in the old days. Edson Harley, who used to be the night watch, is still around, only now he sits on the city council and, I am told, exercises a considerable influence in restraining the enthusiasm of those who want to change the town in one way or another.

Hartford is still heavily dependent on the rural community around it. But general farming has given way to specialized farming, especially in fruits and vegetables. Freezer plants have replaced the old canneries. To some extent, Hartford has become a bedroom for people who work in towns and cities like Benton Harbor located anywhere from five to thirty miles distant. A 4-H fair has replaced the old county fair, and the fair grounds are not kept spic and span as they once were. The old grandstand has disappeared. But the fair goes on. The town has new churches. Some of the lodges continue. In spite of repeated efforts, none of the noonday service organizations has succeeded in establishing a club at Hartford that lasted more than a brief time. Apparently the town still has more than its share of rank individualists.

Growing up in Hartford today would certainly be a different kind of experience than it was in the first and second decades of the century. But it would still not be the same kind of experience as growing up in a big city or in the open country. There still is space. The air is clear; the streets are not thronged with people. Youngsters can still go fishing and swimming in nearby lakes and streams. There is quiet, peace, and serenity in the town. Yet living there would not be the same as living on a farm. There is a neighborhood and communal life that is lacking in a strictly rural environment.

Hartford in 1968 is distinctly less a concentration of people in a rural community than it once was. It is as much a little city as it is a focus for a farming area. Like other little towns, it has its own character. Those who like to classify people as being either rural or urban fail to account for those who live in little towns like Hartford. Much more attention needs to be paid by historians and sociologists to the enduring impact of the small town on American life.

Growing Up in Michigan

MALCOLM X

Our family stayed only briefly in Milwaukee, for my father wanted to find a place where he could raise our own food and perhaps build a business. The teaching of Marcus Garvey stressed becoming independent of the white man. We went next, for some reason, to Lansing, Michigan. My father bought a house and soon, as had been his pattern, he was doing free-lance Christian preaching in local Negro Baptist churches, and during the week he was roaming about spreading word of Marcus Garvey.

He had begun to lay away savings for the store he had always wanted to own when, as always, some stupid local Uncle Tom Negroes began to funnel stories about his revolutionary beliefs to the local white people. This time, the get-out-of-town threats came from a local hate society called The Black Legion. They wore black robes instead of white. Soon, nearly everywhere my father went, Black Legionnaires were reviling him as an "uppity nigger" for wanting to own a store, for living outside the Lansing Negro district, for spreading unrest and dissension among "the good niggers."

As in Omaha, my mother was pregnant again, this time with my youngest sister. Shortly after Yvonne was born came the nightmare night in 1929, my earliest vivid memory. I remember being suddenly snatched awake into a frightening confusion of pistol shots and shouting and smoke and flames. My father had shouted and shot at the two white men who had set the fire and were running away. Our home was burning down around us. We were lunging and bumping and tumbling all over each other trying to escape. My mother, with the baby in her arms, just made it into the yard before the house crashed in, showering sparks. I remember we were outside in the night in our underwear, crying and yelling our heads off. The white police and firemen came and stood around watching as the house burned down to the ground.

My father prevailed on some friends to clothe and house us temporarily; then he moved us into another house on the outskirts of East Lansing. In those days Negroes weren't allowed after dark in East Lansing proper. There's where Michigan State University is located; I related all of this to an audience of students when I spoke there in January, 1963 (and had the first reunion in a long while with my younger brother, Robert, who was there doing postgraduate studies in psychology). I told them how East Lansing harassed us so much that we had to move again, this time two miles out of town, into the country. This was where my father built for us with his own hands a four-room house. This is where I really begin to remember things—this home where I started to grow up.

After the fire, I remember that my father was called in and questioned about a permit for the pistol with which he had shot at the white men who set the fire. I remember that the police were always dropping by our house, shoving things around, "just checking" or "looking for a gun." The pistol they were looking for— which they never found, and for which they wouldn't issue a permit—was sewed up inside a pillow. My father's .22 rifle and his shotgun, though, were right out in the open; everyone had them for hunting birds and rabbits and other game.

After that, my memories are of the friction between my father and mother. They seemed to be nearly always at odds. Sometimes my father would beat her. It might have had something to do with the fact that my mother had a pretty good education. Where she got it I don't know. But an educated woman, I suppose, can't resist the temptation to correct an uneducated man. Every now and then, when she put those smooth words on him, he would grab her.

My father was also belligerent toward all of the children, except me. The older ones he would beat almost savagely if they broke any of his rules—and he had so many rules it was hard to know them all. Nearly all my whippings came from my mother. I've thought a lot about why. I actually believe that as anti-white as my father was, he was subconsciously so afflicted with the white man's brainwashing of Negroes that he inclined to favor the light ones, and I was his lightest child. Most Negro parents in those days would almost instinctively treat any lighter children better than they did the darker ones. It came directly from the slavery tradition that the "mulatto," because he was visibly nearer to white, was therefore "better."

My two other images of my father are both outside the home. One was his role as a Baptist preacher. He never pastored in any regular church of his own; he was always a "visiting preacher." I remember especially his favorite sermon: "That little *black* train is a-comin' . . . an' you better get all your business right!" I guess this also fit his association with the back-to-Africa movement, with Marcus Garvey's "Black Train Homeward." My brother Philbert, the one just older than me, loved church, but it confused and amazed me. I would sit goggle-eyed at my father jumping and shouting as he preached, with the congregation jumping and shouting behind him, their souls and bodies devoted to singing and praying. Even at that young age, I just couldn't believe in the Christian concept of Jesus as someone divine. And no religious person, until I was a man in my twenties—and then in prison—could tell me anything. I had very little respect for most people who represented religion.

It was in his role as a preacher that my father had most contact with the Negroes of Lansing. Believe me when I tell you that those Negroes were in bad shape then. They are still in bad shape—though in a different way. By that I mean that I don't know a town with a higher percentage of complacent and misguided so-called "middle-class" Negroes—the typical status-symbol-oriented, integration-seeking type of Negroes. Just recently, I was standing in a lobby at the United Nations talking with an African ambassador and his wife, when a Negro came up to me and said, "You know me?" I was a little embarrassed because I thought he was someone I should remember. It turned out that he was one of those bragging, self-satisfied, "middle-class" Lansing Negroes. I wasn't ingratiated. He was the type who would never have been associated with Africa, until the fad of having African friends became a status-symbol for "middle-class" Negroes.

Back when I was growing up, the "successful" Lansing Negroes were such as waiters and bootblacks. To be a janitor at some downtown store was to be highly respected. The real "elite," the "big shots," the "voices of the race," were the waiters at the Lansing Country Club and the shoeshine boys at the state capitol. The only Negroes who really had any money were the ones in the numbers racket, or who ran the gambling houses, or who in some other way lived parasitically off the poorest ones, who were the masses. No Negroes were hired then by Lansing's big Oldsmobile plant, or the Reo plant. (Do you remember the Reo? It was manufactured in Lansing, and R. E. Olds, the man after whom it was named, also lived in Lansing. When the war came along, they hired some Negro janitors.) The bulk of the Negroes were either on Welfare, or W.P.A., or they starved.

The day was to come when our family was so poor that we would eat the hole out of a doughnut; but at that time we were much better off than most town Negroes. The reason was we raised much of our own food out there in the country where we were. We were much better off than the town Negroes who would shout, as my father preached, for the pie-in-the-sky and their heaven in the hereafter while the white man had his here on earth.

I knew that the collections my father got for his preaching were mainly what fed and clothed us, and he also did other odd jobs, but still the image of him that made me proudest was his crusading and militant campaigning with the words of Marcus Garvey. As young as I was then, I knew from what I overheard that my father was saying something that made him a "tough" man. I remember an old lady, grinning and saying to my father, "You're scaring these white folks to death!"

One of the reasons I've always felt that my father favored me was that to the best of my remembrance, it was only me that he sometimes took with him to the Garvey U.N.I.A. meetings which he held quietly in different people's homes. There were never more than a few people at any one time—twenty at most. But that was a lot, packed into someone's living room. I noticed how differently they all acted, although sometimes they were the same people who jumped and shouted in church. But in these meetings both they and my father were more intense, more intelligent and down to earth. It made me feel the same way.

I can remember hearing of "Adam driven out of the garden into the caves of Europe," "Africa for the Africans," "Ethiopians,

Awake!" And my father would talk about how it would not be much longer before Africa would be completely run by Negroes— "by black men," was the phrase he always used. "No one knows when the hour of Africa's redemption cometh. It is in the wind. It is coming. One day, like a storm, it will be here."

I remember seeing the big, shiny photographs of Marcus Garvey that were passed from hand to hand. My father had a big envelope of them that he always took to these meetings. The pictures showed what seemed to me millions of Negroes thronged in parade behind Garvey riding in a fine car, a big black man dressed in a dazzling uniform with gold braid on it, and he was wearing a thrilling hat with tall plumes. I remember hearing that he had black followers not only in the United States but all around the world, and I remember how the meetings always closed with my father saying, several times, and the people chanting after him, "Up, you mighty race, you can accomplish what you will!"

I have never understood why, after hearing as much as I did of these kinds of things, I somehow never thought, then, of the black people in Africa. My image of Africa, at that time, was of naked savages, cannibals, monkeys and tigers and steaming jungles.

My father would drive in his old black touring car, sometimes taking me, to meeting places all around the Lansing area. I remember one daytime meeting (most were at night) in the town of Owosso, forty miles from Lansing, which the Negroes called "White City." (Owosso's greatest claim to fame is that it is the home town of Thomas E. Dewey.) As in East Lansing, no Negroes were allowed on the streets there after dark—hence the daytime meeting. In point of fact, in those days lots of Michigan towns were like that. Every town had a few "home" Negroes who lived there. Sometimes it would be just one family, as in the nearby county seat, Mason, which had a single Negro family named Lyons. Mr. Lyons had been a famous football star at Mason High School, was highly thought of in Mason, and consequently he now worked around that town in menial jobs.

My mother at this time seemed to be always working—cooking, washing, ironing, cleaning, and fussing over us eight children. And she was usually either arguing with or not speaking to my father. One cause of friction was that she had strong ideas about what she wouldn't eat—and didn't want *us* to eat—including pork and rabbit, both of which my father loved dearly. He was a real Georgia Negro, and he believed in eating plenty of what we in Harlem today call "soul food."

I've said that my mother was the one who whipped me—at least she did whenever she wasn't ashamed to let the neighbors think she was killing me. For if she even acted as though she was about to raise her hand to me, I would open my mouth and let the world know about it. If anybody was passing by out on the road, she would either change her mind or just give me a few licks.

Thinking about it now, I feel definitely that just as my father favored me for being lighter than the other children, my mother gave me more hell for the same reason. She was very light herself but she favored the ones who were darker. Wilfred, I know, was particularly her angel. I remember that she would tell me to get out of the house and "Let the sun shine on you so you can get some color." She went out of her way never to let me become afflicted with a sense of color-superiority. I am sure that she treated me this way partly because of how she came to be light herself.

I learned early that crying out in protest could accomplish things. My older brothers and sisters had started to school when, sometimes, they would come in and ask for a buttered biscuit or something and my mother, impatiently, would tell them no. But I would cry out and make a fuss until I got what I wanted. I remember well how my mother asked me why I couldn't be a nice boy like Wilfred; but I would think to myself that Wilfred, for being so nice and quiet, often stayed hungry. So early in life, I had learned that if you want something, you had better make some noise.

Not only did we have our big garden, but we raised chickens. My father would buy some baby chicks and my mother would raise them. We all loved chicken. That was one dish there was no argument with my father about. One thing in particular that I remember made me feel grateful toward my mother was that one day I went and asked her for my own garden, and she did let me have my own little plot. I loved it and took care of it well. I loved especially to grow peas. I was proud when we had them on our table. I would pull out the grass in my garden by hand when the first little blades came up. I would patrol the rows on my hands and knees for any worms and bugs, and I would kill and bury them. And sometimes when I had everything straight and clean for my things to grow, I would lie down on my back between two rows, and I would gaze up in the blue sky at the clouds moving and think all kinds of things.

At five, I, too, began to go to school, leaving home in the morning along with Wilfred, Hilda, and Philbert. It was the Pleasant Grove School that went from kindergarten through the eighth grade. It was two miles outside the city limits, and I guess there was no problem about our attending because we were the only Negroes in the area. In those days white people in the North usually would "adopt" just a few Negroes; they didn't see them as any threat. The white kids didn't make any great thing about us, either. They called us "nigger" and "darkie" and "Rastus" so much that we thought those were our natural names. But they didn't think of it as an insult; it was just the way they thought about us.

One afternoon in 1931 when Wilfred, Hilda, Philbert, and I came home, my mother and father were having one of their arguments. There had lately been a lot of tension around the house because of Black Legion threats. Anyway, my father had taken one of the rabbits which we were raising, and ordered my mother to cook it. We raised rabbits, but sold them to whites. My father had taken a rabbit from the rabbit pen. He had pulled off the rabbit's head. He was so strong, he needed no knife to behead chickens or rabbits. With one twist of his big black hands he simply twisted off the head and threw the bleeding-necked thing back at my mother's feet.

My mother was crying. She started to skin the rabbit, preparatory to cooking it. But my father was so angry he slammed on out of the front door and started walking up the road toward town.

It was then that my mother had this vision. She had always been a strong woman in this sense, and had always had a strong intuition of things about to happen. And most of her children are the same way, I think. When something is about to happen, I can feel something, sense something. I never have known something to happen that has caught me completely off guard—except once. And that was when, years later, I discovered facts I couldn't believe about a man who, up until that discovery, I would gladly have given my life for.

My father was well up the road when my mother ran screaming out onto the porch. *"Early! Early!"* She screamed his name. She clutched up her apron in one hand, and ran down across the yard and into the road. My father turned around. He saw her. For some reason, considering how angry he had been when he left, he waved at her. But he kept on going.

She told me later, my mother did, that she had a vision of my father's end. All the rest of the afternoon, she was not herself, crying and nervous and upset. She finished cooking the rabbit and put the whole thing in the warmer part of the black stove. When my father was not back home by our bedtime, my mother hugged and clutched us, and we felt strange, not knowing what to do, because she had never acted like that.

I remember waking up to the sound of my mother's screaming again. When I scrambled out, I saw the police in the living room; they were trying to calm her down. She had snatched on her clothes to go with them. And all of us children who were staring knew without anyone having to say it that something terrible had happened to our father.

My mother was taken by the police to the hospital, and to a room where a sheet was over my father in a bed, and she wouldn't look, she was afraid to look. Probably it was wise that she didn't. My father's skull, on one side, was crushed in, I was told later. Negroes in Lansing have always whispered that he was attacked, and then laid across some tracks for a streetcar to run over him. His body was cut almost in half.

He lived two and a half hours in that condition. Negroes then were stronger than they are now, especially Georgia Negroes. Negroes born in Georgia had to be strong simply to survive.

It was morning when we children at home got the word that he was dead. I was six. I can remember a vague commotion, the house filled up with people crying, saying bitterly that the white Black Legion had finally gotten him. My mother was hysterical. In the bedroom, women were holding smelling salts under her nose. She was still hysterical at the funeral.

I don't have a very clear memory of the funeral, either. Oddly, the main thing I remember is that it wasn't in a church, and that surprised me, since my father was a preacher, and I had been where he preached people's funerals in churches. But his was in a funeral home.

And I remember that during the service a big black fly came down and landed on my father's face, and Wilfred sprang up from his chair and he shooed the fly away, and he came groping back to his chair—there were folding chairs for us to sit on—and the tears were streaming down his face. When we went by the casket, I remember that I thought that it looked as if my father's strong black face had been dusted with flour, and I wished they hadn't put on such a lot of it.

Back in the big four-room house, there were many visitors for another week or so. They were good friends of the family, such as the Lyons from Mason, twelve miles away, and the Walkers, McGuires, Liscoes, the Greens, Randolphs, and the Turners, and others from Lansing, and a lot of people from other towns, whom I had seen at the Garvey meetings.

We children adjusted more easily than our mother did. We couldn't see, as clearly as she did, the trials that lay ahead. As the visitors tapered off, she became very concerned about collecting the two insurance policies that my father had always been proud he carried. He had always said that families should be protected in case of death. One policy apparently paid off without any problem—the smaller one. I don't know the amount of it. I would imagine it was not more than a thousand dollars, and maybe half of that.

But after that money came, and my mother had paid out a lot of it for the funeral and expenses, she began going into town and returning very upset. The company that had issued the bigger policy was balking at paying off. They were claiming that my father had committed suicide. Visitors came again, and there was bitter talk about white people: how could my father bash himself in the head, then get down across the streetcar tracks to be run over?

So there we were. My mother was thirty-four years old now, with no husband, no provider or protector to take care of her eight children. But some kind of a family routine got going again. And for as long as the first insurance money lasted, we did all right.